HISTORICAL RECORDS

OF THE

32ND (CORNWALL) LIGHT INFANTRY.

Printed and bound by Antony Rowe Ltd, Eastbourne

Monument in Exeter Cathedral,

Erected to the Memory of the Officers, Non-commissioned Officers, and Men of the 32nd Regiment Killed and Died during Lucknow and Indian Mutiny, 1857.

HISTORICAL RECORDS

OF THE

32ND (CORNWALL) LIGHT INFANTRY,

NOW THE

1st BATTALION

DUKE OF CORNWALL'S L.I.,

FROM THE FORMATION OF THE REGIMENT

IN 1702 DOWN TO 1892.

Compiled and Edited by

COLONEL G. C. SWINEY,

From the Orderly Room Records and other sources.

London:
SIMPKIN, MARSHALL, HAMILTON, KENT, & Co., LIMITED,
32 PATERNOSTER ROW.

Devonport:
A. H. SWISS, 111 & 112 FORE STREET.

1893.

PREFACE.

DURING the time that I was connected with the 32nd Regiment I frequently heard it deplored that there were no printed *Historical Records* of the Regiment. As the generation of those who wore the old number, **32**, is rapidly passing away, I felt that it could not longer be delayed, and undertook to do what I could to supply the deficiency. I feel sure the kindly indulgence which I have experienced so often in the past from my old brother officers will be extended to me on the present occasion, and that they will overlook any shortcomings and help to supply the omissions in some future edition.

The idea has been to give an account of the regiment from the time it was raised in 1702 as Marines, and continue it year by year up to the time when it became the Duke of Cornwall's Light Infantry, and then, under its present title, up to the present time.

The fact of the Records having been lost on three occasions has added much to the difficulty. I tender my very best thanks to my friend, Captain F. M. Lowe, Royal Artillery, for his kindness in making numerous researches to fill up gaps in the Records. Captain Lowe has throughout taken a great interest in this history, from the fact of his grandfather, Major Ross-Lewin, having served for so many years in the regiment, during perhaps almost the most interesting period of its existence, viz., the Peninsular war.

To Mr. Milne, of Calverley House, near Leeds, I am also very much obliged for his interesting account of the various uniforms worn by the regiment, and for his kind assistance in the preparation of the different coloured plates, and for many useful hints which his long experience has suggested.

To Mrs. Martin-Atkins, daughter of General Johnson, I am much indebted for the loan of her father's portrait and his interesting diary. To Mr. T. Hyde-Drake I am specially grateful for his efforts on my behalf, and many others, who, I hope, will allow me here to thank them for their assistance rendered.

In conclusion, I need hardly say that the self-imposed task has been a labour of love. Twenty-one of the happiest years of my life were spent in the regiment, and although many of those who served with me are no longer here, yet it is pleasant to think that the sad duty of recording their names on the rolls of honour have fallen on an old comrade and friend.

G. C. SWINEY.

Bodmin,
 2nd January, 1893.

CONTENTS.

YEAR		PAGE
1701	Introduction—First period	1
1702	Raising of the regiment	4
——	First roll of officers 32nd Regiment	5
——	Expedition against Cadiz	8
1703	As Marines, under Sir Cloudesley Shovel	13
1704	Surprise of Gibraltar and its capture	15
——	Defence of Gibraltar	17
——	Death of Brigadier General Fox	18
1705	Attempt to storm the Round Tower	19
1706	Action near Balbastro	22
——	Operations against the West coast of France	22
1708	Siege of Denia	24
1710	Expedition against Isle of Cette	25
1713	32nd Regiment disbanded	25
1715	32nd Regiment reinstated	25
1716	32nd Regiment on the Irish Establishment	27
1734	Landed at Bristol	27
1738	Colonel T. Paget transferred to 22nd Foot	29
1743	Action near Dettingen	31
1744	Attempted invasion of England	32
1745	Campaign commenced—Fontenoy	33
1746	French repulsed on the Jaar	38
1747	Battle of Maestricht Plain	41
1756	War with France	45
1773	Death of General Francis Leighton	46
——	Extract from General Johnson's diary	49
1796	St. Domingo—Siege of Burgos	51
1807	Copenhagen—Danish Fleet	56
1808	Spanish revolution	60
——	Battle of Roleia	61
——	Battle of Vimiera	63
1809	Battle of Corunna	68
——	Extracts from Captain Evelegh's diary	70
1810	Walcheren Expedition	77

YEAR		PAGE
1811	Peninsula—effects on Regiment	78
1812	Siege of Rodrigo	79
——	Battle of Salamanca	81
——	Account of Thomas Palmer	88
1812	Siege of Burgos	90
1813	Death of General James Ogilvie	98
——	Battle of the Pyrenees	99
——	Battle of Nivelle	101
——	Battle of the Nive	102
1814	Battle of Orthes	103
1804	Formation of 2nd Battalion	107
——	Battle of Quatre Bras	108
1815	Battle of Waterloo	115
1816	Return of the Regiment	133
1819	The Citadel Barracks at Corfu	135
1820	Garrison orders	136
——	Extract from general order	139
——	Major Sir J. F. Dillon	140
1829	Regiment inspected	142
1831	Celebration of the King's birthday	143
1838	Regiment frozen in	146
1839	Regiment in New London	148
1847	Retirement of Major George Browne	149
1848	The Regiment in India	149
——	Siege of Mooltan	153
——	Battle of Goojerat	156
1852	Regiment at Peshawar	159
——	The Indian Mutiny	160
——	Horse Guards letters	174
——	General Edmondstoune	206
1858	The Regiment at Cawnpore	212
1877	The Regiment at the Cape of Good Hope	223
1881	Formation of Territorial Regiments	228
1882	Death of Major-General Bassano	229
1883	Brevet Major Cochrane at Hong-Kong	229
1885	Death of Lieutenant Homfray	230
——	Presentation of New Colours	230
——	Embarkation of battalion for Malta	233
1886	Colonel G. C. Swiney assumed command	234

YEAR		PAGE
1887	Death of Lieutenant J. T. Bowles	235
——	Death of Lieutenant A. E. Bassano	235
——	Embarkation of battalion for India	236
1890	Memorial windows in Bodmin church	237
1889	H.R.H. Prince Albert Victor, K.G. at Madras	240
1890	The Regiment ordered to Burmah	240
1891	The Wuncho expedition	241
——	The Manipur disaster	241
——	Major Disney-Roebuck gazetted as successor to Colonel J. G. B. Stopford	241
1892	Death of Lieutenants Vyvyan and Hill	242
——	Death of Lieutenant H. J. G. Lambe	242
1882	Services 2nd Battalion Duke of Cornwall's L.I.	244
——	Engagements of El Magfar, Tel-el-Mahuta, and Massameh	244
——	Actions at Kassassin	244

1702-1881.

Notes on the costume and equipments - 245

APPENDIX.

Battle of Chinhut	267
The Burmese bell at Bodmin	270
Roll of officers and men present at the engagement of Waterloo	276
Casualty return—battle of Salamanca	289
Notes on services of 32nd in defence of Lucknow	290
Expenses of a Marine regiment in 1702	295
Establishment and rates of pay, 32nd Regiment, in 1762	295
Rolls of officers from Army Lists, etc.	299
Regimental march and Cornish motto	314
Victoria Cross roll	314
Biographies of colonels	315
Memoirs of officers	337
Services of the officers	343
List of warrant officers, D.C.L.I.	386
List of original subscribers	

ILLUSTRATIONS.

The Photogravures are by the Typographic Etching Company.
The Coloured Plates of Costumes are all from reliable sources, and every care has been taken to copy faithfully the work of the original artists.

FULL-PAGE ILLUSTRATIONS.

	ARTIST.
Monument in Exeter Cathedral	*From a Photograph.*
Private, 1742	*From an Original in British Museum.*
Grenadier, 1751	*David Morier.*
Grenadier, 1768	*Copied from a MS. Work in the Prince Consort's Library at Aldershot.*
Earl Ross, 1781	*After an Oil Painting.*
Officer, 1792	*E. Dayes.*
Officer, 1808	*From Contemporary Evidences.*
Private, 1814	*From Contemporary Evidences.*
Captain Cassan, 1815. (Uniform fully described on page 254.)	*From an Oil Painting.*
Officer (Levée Dress), 1828	*From Contemporary Evidences.*

Private 1742.

Private - Grenadier Company 1751.

Private Grenadier Company - 1768.

Officer 1792.

Officer 1804.

Private-1814.

Officer Levee Dress 1828.

Officer 1840.

Private Light Company, 1851.

Colour Sergeant 1859

ILLUSTRATIONS.

	ARTIST.
Captain Thomas Impett	*From an Engraving.*
Officer, 1840	*From Contemporary Evidences.*
Private, 1851 (Light Company)	*From Contemporary Evidences.*
General Sir J. Inglis, K.C.B.	*From a Photograph by Mayall.*
Colour-Sergeant, 1859 (Light Infantry)	*From a Picture, drawn for Her Majesty, by Thomas.*
Memorial Windows in Bodmin Church	*From a Photograph.*

ILLUSTRATIONS IN TEXT.

Plan of Cadiz and Neighbourhood	page	9
General Johnson	,,	49
Major Henry Ross-Lewin	,,	56
Private Thomas Palmer	,,	88
Major Wallett	,,	115
Major Sir J. F. Dillon	,,	140
General Edmondstoune	,,	206
Private Soldier's Button, 1795	,,	250
Officer's Gilt Button, 1815	,,	253
Officer's Breastplate, 1815	,,	254
Officer's Shako-plate, 1816-24	,,	257
Officer's Breastplate, 1817-28	,,	257
Officer's Breastplate, 1824-54	,,	259
Officer's Shako-plate, 1830-45	,,	259
Officer's Shako-plate, 1845-55	,,	263

SUCCESSION OF COLONELS OF THE 32ND REGIMENT.

Name.	Date of Appointment.	For Biography, see page
Edward Fox	12th Feb., 1702	315
Jacob Borr	5th Dec., 1704	315
Charles Dubourgay	28th June, 1723	316
Thomas Paget	28th July, 1732	317
Simon Descury	15th Dec., 1738	318
John Huske	25th Dec., 1740	318
Henry Skelton	27th Aug., 1743	319
William Douglas	29th May, 1745	320
Francis Leighton	1st Dec., 1747	320
Robert Robinson	11th June, 1773	321
William Amherst	18th Oct., 1775	321
Lord Ross	17th May, 1781	322
James Ogilvie	4th Sept., 1802	322
Alexander Campbell	15th Feb., 1813	323
Sir S. V. Hinde, K.C.B.	28th Feb., 1832	324
Sir R. Macfarlane, K.C.B	26th Sept., 1837	325
Sir J. Buchan, K.C.B.	12th June, 1843	326
Sir R. Armstrong, K.C.B.	25th June, 1850	327
Sir W. Cotton, G.C.B., K.C.H.	17th April, 1854	328
Sir John Inglis, K.C.B.	5th May, 1860	329
Lord Melville, K.C.B.	17th Oct., 1862	330
Sir G. Brown, G.C.B.	1st April, 1863	331
William George Gold	28th Aug., 1865	332
Sir G. Bell, K.C.B.	2nd Feb., 1867	332
Lord F. Paulet, C.B.	3rd Aug., 1868	334
Sir W. Jones, K.C.B.	2nd Jan., 1871	335

THE DUKE OF CORNWALL'S LIGHT INFANTRY.

First Battalion.

John Thomas Hill	8th April, 1890	336

Second Battalion.

Charles Stuart	August, 1881	336
(Colonel 46th Foot, 20th June, 1870.)		

(xiii)

SUCCESSION LIST OF LIEUTENANT-COLONELS COMMANDING THE 32ND REGIMENT, 1842 TO 1880, AND SINCE ITS FORMATION INTO TWO BATTALIONS IN 1881.

1842-92.

Name. First Battalion.	Became Senior in Battalion.	
Frederick Markham	22nd July,	1842
Richard Tyrrell Robert Pattoun	5th Dec.,	1843
Henry Vaughan Brooke	13th Sept.,	1848
Sir John Eardley Wilmot Inglis	7th June,	1849
Charles Assheton Fitz-Hardinge Berkeley	13th Dec.,	1850
James Dodington Carmichael	26th Nov.,	1857
Edward W. D. Lowe	20th Sept.,	1858
Granville George Chetwynd Stapylton	25th Sept.,	1860
Patrick Johnston	1st April,	1866
Hon. Bernard M. Ward	12th June,	1869
Hon. Raymond Harvey de Montmorency	14th June,	1876

THE DUKE OF CORNWALL'S LIGHT INFANTRY.

First Battalion.

Henry Sparke Stabb	29th June,	1881
George Clayton Swiney	29th June,	1886
John G. B. Stopford	1st July,	1887
Francis H. A. Disney-Roebuck	1st July,	1891

Second Battalion.

William S. Richardson, C B.	1st July,	1881
Frank Grieve	26th July,	1885
William E. Roberts	31st July,	1889

SUCCESSION OF LIEUTENANT-COLONELS COMMANDING THIRD BATTALION SINCE THE FORMATION OF THE REGIMENT IN THREE BATTALIONS IN 1881.

Lord St. Levan	1st May,	1882
Edward St. Aubyn	16th Feb.,	1884
Hon. G. C. Eliot	29th June,	1889

HISTORICAL RECORDS

OF THE

32ND REGIMENT.

FIRST PERIOD.

From date of Raising to Peace of Utrecht.

INTRODUCTORY.

IT will be necessary before proceeding with the History of the THIRTY-SECOND REGIMENT, to give a short sketch of the state of Europe and the events which gradually led to the increase of our standing army; for, up to the period when this history commences, viz. :—1702, there was only a very small regular Army,* our standing force being the Navy, and all, or nearly all, the troops were raised as adjuncts of that service, and trained on board ship, to be landed as occasion demanded. Up to this period England can hardly be said to have had any position as a mercantile nation, and it was to push our trade that most of our wars from this period are to be traced. There was little sentiment, but shrewd common sense was the guiding star of the nation, and led to most important results.

The Continental wars† in which England was engaged after the deposition of James II. were rendered necessary to some extent by the tremendous power of France under Louis XIV. William III.

---

* It was not until **1689** that it became necessary to pass a measure for the regulation of the army, *i.e.*, the first Mutiny Act.

† Gibbon, *Industrial History of England.*

B

saw it was inevitable for the interests of England that Louis XIV. (1643-1715) should be checked, and the war of the Spanish succession, "fruitful in great actions and important results,"* 1702-13, was carried on with the object of preventing that king from joining the resources of Spain to those of his own kingdom. For, had he done so, two disastrous results would have happened : the Stuarts would by his help have been restored to the English throne, and the struggle against absolute monarchy and religious tyranny would have had to have been fought over again. Secondly, the growth of English commerce would have been checked, if not utterly annihilated.

On the death of William III., his policy was adopted by his successor, Queen Anne, who entered into treaties of alliance with the Emperor of Germany, the States General of the United Provinces, and other princes and potentates, for preserving the liberty and balance of power in Europe, and for defeating the ambitious views of France.

The naval and military forces of the country were not sufficiently strong to stand the strain of a prolonged campaign, or indeed any campaign at all ; it therefore became necessary to raise men to meet any danger that might threaten the country.

A regiment which had been originally raised for sea service during the reign of Charles II., under the title of the Admiral's Regiment, had been incorporated in the 2nd Foot Guards (now Coldstream) by William III. Two Marine regiments which had 1 een raised for sea service about the same time, and had been disbanded in 1698, were again raised in 1702.

On the commencement of hostilities in 1702 with France and Spain, both of which nations possessed powerful fleets, as well as numerous armies, the British parliament felt the expediency of enabling the Queen to increase the efficiency of her navy by forming corps of Marines, which could act at sea as well as on land.† Six regiments were accordingly added in the year 1702 to the regular army as marine corps, and six other of the regular regiments of

---

* Cannon, *Historical Records of 31st Regiment.*
† Cannon, *Historical Records of Marine Corp*s.

infantry were appointed for sea service. The six regiments of marines were* :—

Colonel Thomas Saunderson's	afterwards	30th.
,, George Villiers'	,,	31st.
,, Edward Fox's	,,	32nd.
,, Harry Mordaunt's	disbanded	1713.
,, Henry Holt's	,,	1713.
,, Viscount Shannon's	,,	1713.

The six regiments of foot for sea service were :—

Colonel Ventris Columbine's	afterwards	6th Foot.
,, Thomas Erle's	,,	19th ,,
,, Gustavus Hamilton's	,,	29th ,,
,, Lord Lucas'	,,	34th ,,
,, Earl of Donegal's	,,	35th ,,
,, Lord Charlemont's	,,	36th ,,

Her Majesty's order for levying this body of men was contained in the following Royal Warrant, dated 1st June, 1702 :—

"Our pleasure is, that this establishment of six regiments of "marines, and six other regiments for sea service, do commence and "take place from the respective times of raising.

"And our further pleasure is, that the order given by our dearest "brother the late king, deceased, and such orders as are, or shall be, "given by us, touching the pay† or entertainment of our said forces, "or any of them, or any charges thereunto belonging, shall be duly "complied with, and that no new charge be added to this establish-"ment without being communicated to our High Treasurer, or "Commissioners of our Treasury for the time being.

"Given at our court at S. James's, on the first day of June, in the "first year of our reign.

"By Her Majesty's command.

"GODOLPHIN."

---

* At this period regiments were called after the names of their respective colonels. On the 1st July, 1751, a Royal Warrant was issued, on the recommendation of Boards of General Officers, numbering the infantry regiments of the British army in order of seniority, as it was found that calling them by the names of their colonels led to confusion. It will, however, make it clearer if the number to which each regiment mentioned succeeded is placed after the colonel's name.

† For rate of pay see Appendix.

Rules and instructions for the better government of the Marine regiments were issued by authority of Her Majesty Queen Anne on 1st July, 1702, in which it was directed—"that when on shore, "they were to be quartered in the vicinity of the dock-yards, in order "to guard them from embezzlement, or from any attempt that might "be made on them by an enemy."

Full instructions were also given as to their pay, subsistence, and clothing, which directed that the same deductions should be made for clothing as was usual in the land forces. Also that one day's pay in every year be deducted from officers and soldiers for the hospital.

When on board ship they were to have an equal proportion of provisions with the seamen, without any deductions from their pay, the soldiers receiving short allowance money like seamen.

The Marine forces having been placed under the control of the Lord High Admiral by Her Majesty Queen Anne, His Royal Highness was pleased, in 1702, to nominate Colonel William Seymour, of the 4th Foot, to superintend the whole, with the rank of brigadier-general, whose peculiar duties were to observe that the men were comfortably quartered, that the officers were attentive in their respective departments, and that the marine soldiers—when embarked on board of ship, were supplied with proper sea-clothes etc. When actually afloat, the marines were under the command of the naval officers of the ship.

1702.

Raising of the Regiment.

On 13th March, 1702, a Royal Warrant was issued, authorising Colonel Edward Fox to raise a regiment of Marines, to consist of twelve companies, with two sergeants, three corporals, two drummers, and fifty-nine privates each; one sergeant extra for grenadier company, besides officers.

I venture to think that I am justified in recording the names as they appear in the official list, although they appear again in the Appendix, from the fact that they are the founders of the regiment which has added so much to the lustre of the British army.

LIST OF THE OFFICERS IN COLONEL EDWARD FOX'S REGIMENT OF MARINES,*

dated 10th March, 1702 ; except the field officers' commissions that were signed by the late King the 12th of February before.

Captains:	1st Lieutenants:	2nd Lieutenants:
COL. EDWD. FOX	CAPT.-LT. WM. LEE	THO. SKINNER
LT.-COL. P. HOWARD	JAS. STEWART	HEN. BROOKS
MAJOR JACOB BORR	CHA. BOURGH	PETER COLBOURNE
HUMPH. COREY	DANIEL SINAULT	THO. PRETTY
FRA. FOULK	HEN. HARRIS	ISAAC DUPLEX
ROBT. KEMPE	THO. BROWNE	ISAAC DROUART
CHA. MONGER	JNO. BOURGH	R. COLLINGWOOD
JNO. WILDBORE	RICHD. MULLINS	EDWD. ATKINSON
RICHD. OXENDEN	RICHD. ALLISON	FRA. GINCKS
JNO. GIGNOUX	BARNABY BOWTELL	JNO. DOWIER
RICHD. COBHAM	ADRIAN VAN ALPHEN	JAS. COLLYAR
WM. HELMSLEY	RIXTON DARBY	THO. PORTER.
(Grenadiers)		

Staff Officers:

HEN. HARRIS, Adjutant.   RICHD. MULLINS, Quarter-Master.
THO. HESKITH, Chaplain.

Their arms were the same as those of other foot regiments.†

Colonel Fox appears to have obtained his recruits in Sussex and the adjacent counties ; the *War Office Marching Books* of 1702 direct the Corps to assemble at their respective quarters, preparatory to moving to Portsmouth, not later than the 11th April, 1702.

From the same source, it appears that Fox's marines were at Arundel, Midhurst, Liphook, Halleck, Steyning, Terring, Godalming, and Guildford.

---

* From the Home Office Series *Military Entry Book*, vol. iv., p. 385, at the Public Record Office.

† Cannon, *Historical Records of Marine Corps*, see 31st Foot.

On 13th May, 1702, the following order was addressed to Colonel Edward Fox:

"ANNE R.

"Our will and pleasure is that, so soon as you shall have "received tents out of the stores of our ordnance, you shall cause our "said regiment to march from its present quarters, according to the "route hereunto annexed, to Portsmouth, whence they will pass over "to the Isle of Wight, and there encamp at such places as shall be "appointed by our trusty and well-beloved Anthony Morgan, Esq., "Lieutenant-Governor of our said Island. And that you follow all "such orders, in respect of your embarkation with the said regiment, "as you shall receive from our Right trusty and Right entirely well "beloved Cousin and Counsellor, James, Duke of Ormond. And that "the officers take care that the soldiers behave civilly, and pay their "Landlords. And all Magestrates, Justices of the Peace, Head-"boroughs, constables, and others—our officers—to be assisting to "this same by imprissing carriages, or in other ways as there may be "occasion.

"Given under our hand, etc., etc.,

"By her Majesty's Command."

The movement was preparatory to the despatch of the expedition against Cadiz, war having been declared against France and Spain on 4th May, 1702, (old style) and had been originally planned by the late King William. The command had been entrusted to the Duke of Ormond, "a man of high character and considerable attainments, "but nature had by no means marked him out for a statesman or a "soldier."*

Extract from BOYER'S *Annals of Queen Anne*, vol. i., p. 49.

"1702.—On the 2nd June, at night, Prince George of Denmark arriv'd "at Portsmouth, where he was receiv'd both by the Magestrates and the "Governour of that Place, with all the Honour and Respect due to his "Royal Birth, his Station, and the dear Consort of her Majesty. The

---

* Lord Stanhope.

"next day his Royal Highness went to the Isle of Wight, review'd the "Forces encamp'd there, which he found in very good order, particularly "the new rais'd Regiments of the Lord Shannon and Colonel Fox, who "perform'd their exercises uncomparably well."

The armament consisted of a powerful fleet of English and Dutch men-of war under Sir Admiral George Rooke, with seventeen thousand troops on board under Sir H. Bellasis and the Dutch General Sparre, and was composed as follows :—

	MEN.
Lloyd's Dragoons (now 3rd Hussars)	275
Detachments 1st and 2nd Foot Guards	755
Bellasis' Foot (afterwards 2nd Queen's)	834
Churchill's Foot (afterwards 3rd Buffs)	834
Seymour's Foot (afterwards 4th King's)	834
Columbine's Sea Service Foot (afterwards 6th Royal Regt.)	724
O'Hara's Foot (afterwards 7th Fusiliers) three companies	313
Erle's Sea Service Foot (afterwards 19th Foot)	724
G. Hamilton's Sea Service Foot (afterwards 20th Foot)	724
Villier's Marines (afterwards 31st Foot) five companies	520
Fox's Marines (afterwards 32nd Foot)	834
Lord Donegal's Sea Service Foot (afterwards 35th Foot)	724
Lord Charleville's Sea Service Foot (afterwards 36th Foot)	724
Lord Shannon's Marines	834
Total	9653
Dutch Troops	3924
Grand Total	13577

The expeditionary fleet consisted of fifty sail of the line (thirty English, twenty Dutch) under Sir George Rooke. English fleet : Vice-Admiral Thomas Hopson and Rear-Admirals Fairborne and Graydon. Dutch fleet : Lieutenant-Admiral Van Allemond ; Vice-Admirals Callenburg, Vandergos, and Pieterson, and Rear-Admiral Wassenaer.

English land forces, about ten thousand men, commanded by the Duke of Ormond. Under him were Lieutenant-General Sir Henry Bellasis ; Major Generals Sir Charles O'Hara and Lord Portmore; and Brigadier-Generals Seymour (commanding marines), Matthews (commanding the guards), and Gustavus Hamilton. Staff Officers : Adjutant-General, Major Joslin ; Quarter-Master, Colonel Sir Thomas

Smith ; Chief Engineer and Commandant of Train, Colonel Carles.

Dutch: about four thousand men, under Major-General Baron Sparre and Brigadier-General Pallant.

The fleet and transports, numbering one hundred and sixty ships, sailed from Spithead 12th July, 1702, (new style). From an extract of the orders given to Sir G. Rooke and the Duke of Ormond, they were told " to reduce and take the town and island of Cadiz, or if " this appeared for any reason impossible, Vigo, Ponte Vedra, " Corunna, or any place belonging to Spain or France, as shall be " judged proper."

The garrison of Cadiz at this time consisted of nine regiments of infantry, with about one thousand cavalry, besides militia for coast defence.

The fortifications were fairly strong, and between the puntals was a chain boom, behind which were drawn up seven French men-of-war and eight galleys. On the Matagorda puntal was a fort of twelve guns, and on the opposite point a castle with thrice that armament. Along the shores were several batteries. The fortress was in good order and well supplied. The Governor of Cadiz was the Duc de Brancacio ; the Viceroy of Andalusia and " General of the Coasts " was the Marquis de Villadarias.

On 23rd July, 1702, (new style) the fleet anchored in the Bay of Bulls. Ormond strongly advocated an immediate landing in one of these bays, but he was resolutely opposed by Rooke, who was alarmed for the safety of his ships, and feared that if it came on to blow he would have had to leave the army without supplies.

By some the delay was thought to be on account of the generals not agreeing as to the best place for landing ; every hour was of consequence, as it gave time to the Spaniards to strengthen their works, which they were not unwilling to avail themselves of. A decision was arrived at, however, by the 26th, and the troops commenced to disembark between the promontory of Rota and Fort Santa Catalina. Two days' rations of bread, cheese, and beer were issued to every man. In rear of each regiment was an officer of artillery with twenty "*chevaux-de-frise.*" No drum was to be beaten and no colour uncased, save in the boat of the general commanding.

When a drum beat, then the lines of boats were to row; when it ceased the men were to lie upon their oars. No soldier was to fire, " under pain of death while in the boat, or to unshoulder his musket " when landed."*

26th July, 1702 (new style). Little resistance was offered to the troops landing, although some twenty men were drowned in the surf.

The marines landed with the first troops, and on 27th July Rota surrendered without resistance, and the disembarkation continued.

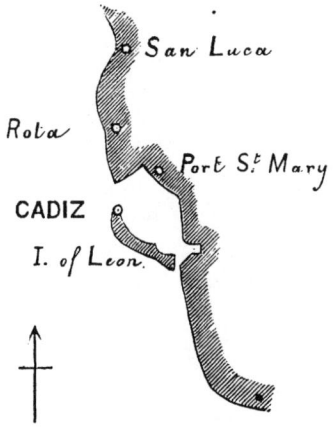

31st July (new style). The whole army had landed by this date and advanced on the town of Port St. Mary. It was found deserted by its inhabitants and was looted by the army and navy, in which plunder General Sir Henry Bellasis and other officers were not above participating.†

The eventual failure of this expedition may be traced to this act, which gave great offence to the Spaniards of influence and brought ruin on Bellasis himself. Fort Santa Catalina surrendered on being summoned to do so on 2nd August. On the following day the troops encamped at Santa Vittoria on their march to Matagorda

---

* Smyth, *Historical Records of 20th Regiment.*

† Special instructions against marauding had been issued by Ormond previous to the setting out of this expedition.—Parnell, *Spanish War of Succession.*

Fort, before which trenches were opened. The enemy sunk three merchant ships in the entrance of the harbour on 8th August. On the 13th the newly-constructed batteries and fleet opened fire on the Matargorda Fort, but after four days the siege had to be abandoned, owing, it is said, to the marshy nature of the soil, and the troops returned to camp at Santa Vittoria, having lost sixty-five men killed or wounded.

At a council of generals it was proposed to bombard Cadiz or accept a ransom of one hundred thousand pistoles, against which Prince George of Hesse-Darmstadt strongly protested. Although at first in favour of the bombardment, Rooke, with his admirals, now considered "in regard, the swell of the sea continues so as to render "the bombardment of Cadiz ineffectual," they therefore abandoned the idea, and instead made preparations to re-embark the troops, and on the 23rd Ormond commenced the retreat to Rota, pursued by Villadarias. Colonel Fox commanded the rear guard and succeeded in repulsing the Spanish attack;* next day Fort Santa Catalina was blown up, and the small army reached Rota in safety. From the 25th to 28th August was taken up in re-embarking the force; Colonel Fox again, with his rear guard, protecting the embarkation, and eventually gained the boats with little or no loss. The following day the fleet sailed for England.†

After having been some days at sea, a change was accidentally brought about, with fortunate results. Some of the ships having put into Lagos for water, learned by chance that Chateau-Renaud, the

---

* The *London Gazette*, 2nd November, 1702, after describing the rear guard action in the retreat from Rota, goes on to say: "By the extraordinary good "conduct of Colonel Fox (32nd), who had the management of the whole disposition "made by His Grace, a better could never have been, considering the "advantage the Spaniards had over him."

† On October 5th, 1702, in accordance with previous instructions, a squadron, under Commodore Walker, with four regiments on board, was despatched to the West Indies, and it appears from a warrant to the Ordnance to issue stores, that each of the Marine regiments sent a company with this squadron.

The warrant was dated 2nd January, 170$\frac{2}{3}$, and, as far as Fox's regiment (32nd) was concerned, directed the issue of fifty stand of arms to replace those sent to the West Indies, and one hundred and forty tents, lost either at the Bay of Bulls or at Vigo.

French admiral, with fifteen sail of the line and seventeen galleons loaded with treasure from the West Indies had reached Vigo. Captain Wishart, who was the senior officer present, immediately sailed, in the hopes of overtaking Rooke and his fleet, and on 17th October came up with them, with the result that the course of the fleet was at once changed, and steered for Vigo, and on 22nd October came to an anchor off the bay. Arrangements were made at once for landing a force under Ormond, with a view of taking the land batteries in flank; the fleet was to advance up the harbour. The French admiral had defended it with a strong boom formed of chains, ships' yards, and topmasts bound together. On Ormond signalling that he had captured the battery, the leading ship, the *Torbay*, Captain Andrew Leake, bearing Vice-Admiral Hopson's flag, steered straight for the boom and broke it, and cast anchor on the other side between the French vessels, followed by the remaining ships. After a short struggle, most of the galleons and booty to the value of one million pounds sterling fell into our hands. Ormond was desirous of attacking Vigo itself, but Admiral Rooke again put a veto on it, as "he could only spare five or six frigates and six weeks' or "two months' provisions, and that the frigates would scarcely be safe "except whilst cruising at sea." Ormond was therefore obliged to relinquish the idea and to re-embark.

The news was received in England with extravagant joy, and Queen Anne, attended by the lords and commons, went in state to S. Paul's Cathedral, to return thanks for this success, and each of the regiments of infantry received the sum of £561 10s. prize money out of the two millions sterling, the reputed value of the booty.*

Fox's marines, we have seen, took an important part during the late expedition, and from *The Diary of an Officer of the Navy*, in the Radstock collection, United Service Institute, the following interesting extract occurs :—" On the 17th July, in the morning, a court-martial "was held on board us, on the account of one Lieutenant Harris—of " Collonel Fox's regiment—for mutiny, &c., of which he was " found guilty, and received sentence accordingly." What the offence

---

* Cannon, *Historical Records of 31st Regiment.*

was we are not told, but the trial apparently took place before the arrival of the expedition at Cadiz. We read further on that the Duke was magnanimous, as on "Thursday, 13th August, 1702, His Grace's "pardon was sent for Lieutenant Harris, who lay under sentence of "death."

From the same authority, under date 16th September, 1702, orders were given overnight that the boats from the fleet should rendezvous at Rota by break of day to take on board the remainder of the army, and that the youngest regiment should march first, and the rear guard should be commanded by Colonel Fox (32nd.) The retreat was effected with a loss of only five soldiers killed and as many wounded, and by the good conduct of Colonel Fox, who had the whole management of the dispositions made by His Grace the Duke of Ormond.

Colonel Fox's regiment (32nd) was, on starting on the expedition, six hundred and fifty-eight strong, in the attack upon Vigo,* (?) 12th October, 1702, and attached to first brigade.

The troops under the Duke of Ormond subsequently returned to England, and on their arrival, in November, 1702, Fox's marines (32nd) were landed at Portsmouth, to march to Arundel, Horsham, Crickfield, &c., to remain, under a War Office order, dated 2nd November, 1702.

A letter, some days later date, addressed to the Commissioners for the Sick and Wounded states that the detachments of Fox's marines at Midhurst and Chichester have been ordered to "be present and "assist in the removal and exchange of prisoners of war." The following subsequent orders, addressed to Colonel Fox, also appear under the dates specified :—

"3rd January, 1703. Her Majesty having ordered Colonel Holt's "and Sanderson's regiments, now at Portsmouth, to embark on board "the fleet bound for Portugal, Colonel Gibson has thereupon been "directed to send for the regiment under your command to march "into Portsmouth to do duty there.

"26th January, 1703. The companies of the regiment under your

---

* It is presumed that this refers to the battery which flanked the harbour, as Vigo itself was not attacked.

" orders at Chichester to march to Shoreham and Brighthelmstone.

" 30th January, 1703. His Royal Highness finding occasion to
" send six companies of the regiment under your command, to be
" put on board the fleet for Her Majesty's service at sea, which are
" to march and embark at Portsmouth, according to such orders as
" you will receive on such behalf. The officers to provide proper
" bedding for their men to take on board."

The number of companies was increased to seven. The remainder of the regiment removed, under command of Colonel Fox, from Horsham and the neighbourhood to Winchester. These were subsequently embarked on board the fleet.

The regiment served on board the fleet in the Mediterranean, under Admiral Sir Cloudesley Shovel, who was instructed to make every possible arrangement, by conciliation or conquest, among the dependencies of the French and Spanish monarchies, in order to ensure a cordial reception of the Archduke Charles of Austria, in opposition to Philip, Duke of Anjou,* of France, to the throne of Spain.

1704.

Nothing very decisive having taken place up to the end of 1703, it was determined to attack Spain at home, with the aid of the Portuguese, and an expedition was despatched from the Tagus, consisting of five thousand men, under Prince George,† with thirty-one English and nineteen Dutch men-of-war, besides numerous frigates and smaller vessels. Admiral Rooke was the naval chief, under him were Vice-Admiral Sir John Leake and Rear-Admirals Dilkes and Wishart, whilst Lieutenant-Admiral Callenberg, with two vice-admirals, commanded the Dutch fleet. The land force actually embarked only comprised one thousand nine hundred

---

* Second son of Leopold I. of Germany, who claimed the throne of Spain in the right of his mother, Margaret Theresa, daughter of Philip IV. of Spain.

† Prince George of Hesse Darmstadt was born at Darmstadt on 25th April, 1662. Second son of the seventeen children of Ludwig VI., Landgrave of Hesse Darmstadt, and of Elizabeth Dorothea, his wife, daughter of Ernest, Duke of Saxe-Gotha.

English and four hundred Dutch marines, with seventy Spanish foot soldiers. Brigadier-General Edward Fox, who had been in charge of the rear-guard during Ormond's retreat from the Mortagorda commanded the marines.

The English marines were drafted from the seven Marine regiments of the army, viz. :—Seymour's, or the Queen's (afterwards the 4th Foot), Sanderson's (afterwards the 30th), Luttrell's (late Villier's, and afterwards the 31st), Fox's (afterwards the 32nd), Shannon's, Holt's, and Henry Mordaunt's. The three last corps were disbanded on the conclusion of the war.*

On 21st May the fleet put into Alten Bay, on the coast of Valencia. Prince Henry of Hesse Darmstadt (a younger brother of Prince George) proposed that an attempt should be made on Barcelona, and on the 29th the fleet arrived there. One thousand six hundred marines were landed on the 30th, in the forenoon, without opposition, to the east of the fortress, and encamped. The commander, Velasio, was summoned to surrender; he, however, rejected the summons, having learned from a deserter that the visit of the fleet was no more than an incidental episode of its voyage to Nizza.†

A few shells were thrown into the town, and early on the morning of 1st June, Rooke being anxious to sail, Darmstadt re-embarked the troops without being molested in any way by Velasio, and continued his course to Nizza.

Information was brought to the fleet when at Hières, that the French fleet, from Brest, was endeavouring to make Toulon, but Rooke deemed it wiser to await reinforcements from England, which were expected shortly, under Sir Cloudesley Shovel, and in spite of instructions having been sent from home, urging him to attack Cadiz, in the absence of most of the Spanish soldiers who were fighting the Portuguese, he refused " unless a large force were despatched from " Lisbon to co-operate with him "—and in spite of other despatches urging him to take action, he persistently refused, and let the French fleet slip.

---

* Parnell, *Spanish War of Succession*, p. 46.
† Parnell, *Spanish War of Succession*.

The Surprise of Gibraltar.

Rooke received a fourth despatch, 28th July, urging him to attack Cadiz, but he was unmovable. Prince George then suggested that in place of Cadiz, Gibraltar should be attacked; and, knowing that sooner or later he (Rooke) would be called to account for his want of enterprise, agreed to cannonade the sea-front of that fortress. On 31st July the Allies, numbering fifty-nine sail of the line, anchored before Gibraltar.

Five thousand men were landed* before the north front of the Rock for the purpose of cutting off supplies to the garrison. The garrison was completely surprised; it is said to have only consisted of one hundred and fifty regulars, and citizen soldiers and militia, numbering in all, according to the Spanish authorities, not more than five hundred men; the arms were one hundred pieces of cannon, of heavy make for that day.

The Old Mole and the New Mole were garrisoned by citizens and militia; the Landport Gate was guarded by a weak force of sixty invalids; in the Castle, sixty-two soldiers of divers arms.†

The first offensive step was taken by the Captain of the *Dorsetshire*, of eighty guns, Captain Whittaker, who (says Sayer) was sent with boats to burn a French privateer of twelve guns which lay at the Old Mole. More serious demonstrations followed on the morning of 3rd August; the fleet, after throwing a few shots into the fortress and receiving prompt replies, poured out its missiles with unflagging fierceness, and maintained the fire until long after noon. Six Dutch ships and sixteen English vessels fronted the line wall between the heads of the moles, three other ships took up positions on the rest of the others and the New Mole. The efforts of this great force soon told on the walls; the guns on the New Mole were rapidly silenced, and its garrison fled. Sir George Rooke's despatches state

---

* The marines had no artillery, but took with them crowbars and hatchets to assault the Landport Gate, should the attack from the sea fail.

† Ayala: Monte, *Hist. de Gibraltar*.

that he ordered Captain Whittaker to make an attack on this mole in boats, but Captain Hicks intercepted the signal, and anticipated the orders it conveyed; with Captain Jumper of the *Lennox*, seventy guns, he pushed to the shore, losing forty men and two officers, owing to a mine having been sprung under them as they landed. Captain Whittaker was more fortunate, and succeeded in taking the New Mole, repulsed the enemy, and assailed Jumper's bastion. The effect of this attack was extended to the Line Wall; this part, the fort on the point of the Old Mole and that defence itself, was successively captured by Whittaker's party and the marines (32nd), who had landed soon after the arrival of the fleet.

It was difficult to say who fought the harder, but the odds were against the brave defenders, and after a struggle of three days they capitulated,* and finally surrendered with the honours of war.

Thus this famous fortress once more underwent a change of masters; the Prince of Hesse-Darmstadt took possession in the name of Charles III.

A garrison of eighteen hundred English seamen and marines, amongst which was Fox's regiment (32nd), was placed in the fortress.

The total loss of the Allies was three officers and fifty-eight men killed, eight officers and two hundred and fifty-two men wounded.

There is not the slightest foundation for the story given out by nineteenth century writers—Lord Stanhope, Captain Sayer, &c.—of Rooke taking down the Spanish colours and hoisting the English standard.†

On 21st August half the marines were taken on board the fleet—the French fleet having been sighted—and took part in the undecisive battle of Malaga on the 23rd; total loss of Allies, killed or wounded, two thousand seven hundred and eighteen. On 30th August Rooke landed all his available marines at Gibraltar, sixty heavy guns, and three months' provisions for two thousand men and sailed for England.

---

* 2nd August, 1704.
† Parnell, *Spanish War of Succession*.

Prince George now commenced to repair the fortifications and erect fresh batteries. His garrison consisted of:—

English Marines	1900
Dutch	400
English Seamen	72
Catalans	70
Total	2442

The governor was Colonel Henry Nugent. The marines were commanded by Brigadier-General Fox (32nd); second in command, Lieutenant-Colonel Jacob Borr, of Fox's marines; Catalans and Volunteers under Prince Henry.

"Gibraltar was taken from the Spaniards on 24th July, 1704, "(old style). Sir G. Rooke was returning from an untoward cruise "in the Mediterranean when it accidentally occurred to him to attack "the town, which, with the usual improvidence of Spaniards, was "only garrisoned by one hundred and fifty men. George I. was pre-"vented from restoring it at the Peace of Utrecht, by the expression "of public feeling in England." So says Captain C. R. Scott, in his *Sketches of the inhabitants of the South of Spain.*

The old fortress was not long in the hands of its captors before a supreme attempt was made by the Spaniards to retake their beloved Rock. Eight thousand men, under the Marquis de Villadarias, were immediately detached from the Spanish army to retake the fortress. On 4th October the French admiral received orders to engage the British and Dutch fleets, and to co-operate in the operations.

Sir John Leake and Admiral Vanderdussen were left at Lisbon to protect the coast of Portugal and relieve Gibraltar if it should be besieged, as was anticipated.

The Marquis de Villadarias commenced the siege of Gibraltar on 22nd October, 1704, and the garrison—composed of marines— under the command of the Prince of Hesse, sustained a siege by twelve thousand men.

The purpose of the enemy was to have stormed from the South Mole, united with the desperate attempt of a Spanish forlorn hope climbing the rock, and a general attack from the mainland. The fortress was maintained against very superior numbers, and the fire of the enemy's batteries having damaged the works, a body of men were landed from the fleet to assist in the defence.

Fire opened 27th October, and on 9th November, Colonel Nugent, the governor, was mortally wounded, and Brigadier-General Fox (32nd) was killed by a round shot.*

On the 10th, Villadarias had intended to have delivered a grand night assault from different quarters and to scale the Rock on the precipitous side, where it was expected that the garrison would be more off their guard. Admiral Leake's arrival, however, prevented the boat and beach assaults, but the plan of scaling the eastern side was nevertheless undertaken, and in the night an advance party of five hundred Spaniards, under Colonel de Figueroa, started for their destination.

Led by a Gibraltar goat-herd, they proceeded along the dangerous eastern side of the Rock by an almost unknown track, and, gradually ascending its steep and rugged slope, reached the summit at a place called the Silleta.

A little below the Silleta, on the western side, is a cave known as St. Michael's, and here—concealed from the view of the guard, Figueroa waited to be joined by the main body of the assaulters. But, through some misunderstanding, these never arrived, and at daybreak the adventurous party were discovered by the garrison. The Prince at once sent a detachment of five hundred marines, under Borr (32nd) to dislodge them. The grenadiers were led by Prince Henry, who, whilst bravely ascending the hill under the fire of the Spaniards, was wounded in the shoulder. Borr (32nd) charged them briskly, killed two hundred and took one hundred and ninety prisoners, amongst whom was Figueroa and thirty-three other officers, the remainder escaping by the way they came.

The garrison had only one thousand men fit for duty on 2nd December, and a great deal of discontent prevailed among them. Fortunately, reinforcements arrived on the 14th, just in time to prevent the outbreak of a mutiny, for everyone was getting disheartened at the

---

* *London Gazette*, 4th to 7th December, 1704.

heavy losses, and many of the officers had actually formed a mutinous conspiracy against the Prince, to oblige him to yield the fortress.

The relieving troops numbered about one thousand nine hundred and seventy men. On the death of Nugent and Fox, Borr (32nd) succeeded to the command of the English troops.

On 23rd December the Prince made a sortie on the enemy's advanced works, and destroyed them, and again on 1st January, 1705, he made a second sally, and managed to keep down the fire of the enemy.

1705.

On 2nd February, 1705, the Spanish commander attempted to storm the Round Tower, but was unsuccessful; nothing daunted, he again made the attempt. The Round Tower was defended by Colonel Borr* (32nd), who had succeeded to the command of Fox's marines, with his battalion. The assailants, by throwing from above great stones and grenades on his men, at last obliged him to retire into that part of the works where the foot guards were posted. Flushed with success, they advanced too far, and were met by Colonel Moncall† and his battalion, who soon reinstated the former holders, and, uniting with the remainder of the garrison, drove the enemy out of the works. They made a precipitate retreat, losing seventy killed and over two hundred wounded; one captain, four lieutenants, and forty men taken. The garrison casualties were twenty-seven killed and one hundred and twenty wounded.

In a work entitled *The Triumphs of Her Majesty's Army*, published in 1707, appears the following remark, anent the defence of Gibraltar: "Encouraged by the example of the Prince of Hesse, the garrison

---

* With regard to Colonel Borr (32nd), it may be interesting to add an extract from *Boyer*, vol. III., p. 163 :—" Neither must we pass over in silence the extra-" ordinary zeal of Colonel Borr, who on all occasions shewed himself ready to " ease the Prince as much as possible, and to execute his orders with the utmost " activity and distinguished courage, to reward which Her Majesty bestowed on " him the regiment vacant by the death of Colonel Fox, of which Mr. Borr was " before but Lieutenant-Colonel of Barrymore's, afterwards 13th Foot.."

† *Hamilton's*, vol. I., p. 377, vol. II., p. 2.

"did more than could humanly be expected, and the English marines "gained an immortal glory."

Hard as was the existence of the English, that of the enemy was even worse, and their sufferings must have been intense through the trenches filling with water, the cutting off of supplies by inland floods, and the progress of disease in their camp. Marshal de Tessé, a famous commander, was appointed to conduct further operations, and the hopes of the besiegers revived with the reinforcements which, on a great scale, he conducted to them.

A violent assault was made upon a breach, which was hardly large enough to warrant success, and ended in the useless sacrifice of more than two hundred lives. Another attack, this time by the combined armies and navies, was frustrated, so far as the latter were concerned, by the wind shifting to the south, converting that part of the Rock that had been appointed for the naval assault into a lee shore.

Meanwhile Sir John Leake surprised the French fleet under Baron de Pointi, and captured three of their ships. Two were driven ashore and burnt by the defenders.

The French commander-in-chief raised the siege on 18th April, six months after the task was begun, under hopeful declarations, having lost ten thousand men.

On 12th July a grand conference was held at Lisbon, King Charles and most of the leaders—who had been summoned to attend from Gibraltar—were present, when it was decided, on the recommendation of Darmstadt, that the conference should formally concur in the proposed expedition to Catalonia. The Earls of Galway* and Peterborough† concurred, and it was formally agreed that the fleet should proceed to Barcelona.

Although denuding his own force, Galway now strengthened the expedition with his two regiments of Dragoons, and, in exchange for the recruit corps of Elliott and John Caulfield, he authorised the fleet to take on board at Gibraltar the whole of the seasoned English

---

* Chosen by Marlborough to succeed the Duke of Schomberg, to command the Portuguese troops.

† Selected, through political influence, to command the Catalonian expedition.

battalions at that garrison. Owing, however, to unavoidable delays, six weeks elapsed before the troops could leave Lisbon.

On 24th July, King Charles and his court embarked on board the fleet—having joined the remainder of the fleet, under Sir Cloudesley Shovel—and arrived at Gibraltar on 3rd August. Next day King Charles landed in state, and was received by the inhabitants as their lawful sovereign. The recruits disembarked, whilst the guards, Barrymore's, Donegal's, Mountjoy's, and the English marines—eight battalions in all, numbering about three thousand two hundred men—joined the allied troops.

The marines were commanded by Colonel Jacob Borr (32nd), who, it will be remembered, had been awarded the full colonelcy of Fox's regiment (32nd.)

The expedition embarked again, and sailed on 5th August, arriving on the 22nd off Barcelona. Two hundred grenadiers were landed at once, and the remainder followed; there was no opposition made to their disembarkation. To assist the expeditionary force, Sir Cloudesley sent ashore from his ships' complements a force of one thousand one hundred and fifty marines, and next day the dragoons landed.

Peterborough, who appears to have been very half-hearted on the advisability of attacking Barcelona, seems to have thrown every obstacle in the way of its being carried out; but King Charles, who had accompanied the expedition at the express invitation of John Methuen,* (instructed by Godolphin) was determined that he would remain and aid his friends, the Catalans, who had risked so much for his sake. At a council of war it was eventually agreed that the attack should be made, and on 5th September Sir Cloudesley Shovel engaged to send ashore four thousand one hundred seamen, six hundred gunners, and fifty carpenters, in addition to one thousand one hundred and fifty marines already landed. But Peterborough again objected, and not until the 9th or 10th did he agree, and it was arranged that one of the outlying fortresses should be attacked first. Montjuic was agreed upon, and some severe fighting took place

---

* British Minister in Spain.

when, on the 13th, the Allies were driven back, losing their gallant leader Darmstadt, who met his death as he was endeavouring to rally the troops. It was not until the 17th, after having made a breach in the wall, that Fort Montjuic capitulated, which enabled the attack on Barcelona to be proceeded with; and, partly owing to an insurrection within the fortress itself and a breach having been made of sufficient dimensions to justify an assault, on 4th October, Valasio agreed to negotiate, and it was arranged that on the 14th the garrison should march out with the honours of war.

Although Colonel Borr's regiment (32nd) took part in the above siege operations, he had, through some misunderstanding with a brother officer, with whom he had fought a duel, not himself been present.

1706-7.

In the following December, some of Borr's marines (32nd) were sent to garrison the fortress of Lerida, and they were present at the decisive action near Balbastro, January, 1706, in which, after seven hours' hard fighting, D'Asfeld, the French commander, was forced to retire. This action is remarkable as being the only one of the campaign in which no Spaniards were engaged on either side. The Allies lost some one hundred and fifty killed and wounded; the French, four hundred.

About May, the marines returned to Barcelona. In June, Santa Cruz submitted to Admiral Leake, and was garrisoned by six hundred marines under Major Hedges.* On 28th September, Majorca surrendered, and Captain Lander, with one hundred marines, occupied the castle.

During 1706, Marlborough and the English ministers had directed their attention to the idea of operating, by joint expedition, against the West Coast of France. A scheme in which the French Huguenots took part was approved, and an expedition was fitted out, the fleet under Sir Cloudesley Shovel, and the army commanded by Earl Rivers. The adjutant-general was Colonel Kempenfeldt, and the quartermaster-general Colonel Jacob Borr, of the marines

---

* Of Villier's Marines.

(32nd.) Colonel Richards, chief engineer. The land force consisted of eleven squadrons of dragoons, sixteen battalions of foot, with a train of thirty-four heavy guns, six mortars, sixty cohorns, and six field-pieces. In all, eight thousand two hundred troops, besides artillery.

The following was the composition of the troops :—

Dragoons—Two squadrons of Carpenter's, afterwards 3rd Hussars.
          Two   „   Essex,   „   4th Hussars.
          Four   „   Guiscard's Huguenots.
          Three „   Slippenback's Dutch.
Foot—Hill's (late Stanhope's.)
      Mordaunt's, afterwards 28th Foot.
      Farringdon's   „   29th Foot.
      Watkins'.
      Hotham's.
      Mark Kerr's.
      Macartney's.
      Two battalions Marines.*
      Nassau's German.
      Six Huguenot regiments.

The expedition left England 12th October, 1706, and, after encountering severe weather, finally reached Lisbon, remaining there two months, and then went on to Alicante, where it landed 8th February, 1707. From this time until 24th April the force was marching and counter-marching without having gained any very decisive victory, but on 24th April the Allies advanced from Villeria, encamping at Candete. At daybreak on the morning of the 25th, Galway began his march, in four columns, towards Almanza, eight miles off. Berwick had his powerful army awaiting the attack, and after fighting for two hours, owing to the Portuguese commander falling back at a critical moment, what might have been a great victory was turned into a crushing defeat. The regiments which principally suffered were the guards, the marines (32nd), Mordaunt's, Bowles', Nassau's Germans, Huguenot and Dutch.

In this battle the Allies lost four thousand, killed or wounded ; the

---

* Borr's (32nd) believed to be one ; another, name not known.

English, however, lost none of their guns, and Berwick was unable to move for five days, owing to his losses. It is impossible to ascertain the losses in Borr's marines (32nd), but they must have been very heavy, if they in any way corresponded with those of other corps.

The English officers slain comprised one brigadier-general, five colonels, seven lieutenant-colonels, two majors, thirty captains, forty-three subalterns; or, eighty-eight in all. Two hundred and eighty-six officers were taken prisoners, of whom ninety-two were wounded There is a monument in Westminster Abbey to the memory of the officers. The victory, though a great one for the Bourbons, was by no means fatal to the Austrian cause, for, broadly speaking, its chief effect was merely to retreive the defeat received by Tessé before Barcelona.*

Major Humphrey Corey, of Borr's (32nd) marines, was taken prisoner at Almanza.

In less than five months after the defeat of Almanza, with wonderful energy, and without assistance either from home or from Charles, Galway had raised another army of fourteen thousand six hundred fighting men, who were well equipped, supported by a good train, provided with transport and ready to take the field; and by the 29th October were ready to move, to endeavour to relieve Lerida, which was situated on the right bank of the Segre, and was a fortress of considerable importance. The governor was Prince Henry, the garrison only consisting of one thousand eight hundred regulars and eight hundred miguelets. There were three English regiments, consisting of the Royal Fusiliers, Well's regiment, and one battalion of marines, Borr's (32nd). The Earl was too late, and the fortress, after making a brave defence, was compelled to capitulate, as all the provisions were expended, excepting bread and water.

In November, 1708, the French Commander, D'Esfeld, determined to raise the siege of Denia. The garrison was composed of two hundred and twenty seven officers and men, fifteen gunners under a lieutenant, and two hundred marines from Borr's (32nd) and other battalions, commanded by three captains and six subalterns.

---

* Parnell, *Spanish War of Succession.*

After a good defence of seventeen days, the place was taken and the garrison made prisoners of war.

About this period two of the marine regiments were drafted, and the officers and men were incorporated into the other four now employed in Spain. This measure had become necessary in order to supply the casualties which had occurred, and to render these corps effective. For this purpose all the marines capable of duty were drawn from the fleet about to return home, in order to assist in the reduction of Minorca, which it was expected would make a spirited and tedious defence. The island, however, fell after a few days, and capitulated to a force consisting of only two thousand four hundred men.

1709-14.

In the following year, 1709, the fleet having failed to relieve Alicante, it fell into the hands of the Bourbons. There were no marines there at the time, and the next year, 1710, an expedition was planned against the Isle of Cette, in the province of Languedoc. The troops and marines were landed on 13th July. The fort surrendered and the town was delivered up without resistance.

From this time until the close of the war and the signing of the Treaty of Peace of Utrecht, little is known of the marine corps. Among the reductions, 1713, they were included in the list of regiments to be disbanded, and there is little doubt that Colonel Borr's (32nd) regiment was disbanded in that year.* It was, however, reinstated, in recognition of its good services, with two others (30th and 31st), on 25th March, 1715, the New Year's Day of the old style, and became the 32nd Regiment, incorporated with the regiments of infantry of the line, and authorized to take rank according to the date of their original formation in 1702. Under these

---

* On the 9th November, 1713, instructions were issued for the disbanding of the Marine Regiments, and commissioners were appointed for making up their accounts and paying off the men.

The instructions are lengthy, and will be found in vol. viii., p. 327, *Military Entry Book*, Home Office Series, Public Record Office. However, from them it appears that each soldier was allowed to carry away his clothes, belt, and knapsack, and passes were granted to each man's home; but men were warned "not to "proceed thither in greater numbers than three together."

circumstances, it may be thought the regiment is entitled to Gibraltar on their colours, as they took such an important part in the taking of it, and also in the first defence.

There were additional reasons why the marines who had been disbanded should be again re-formed, and probably the real cause of their being re-formed so soon.

The decease of Queen Anne took place on 1st August, 1714, and King George I., who was then at Hanover, was immediately proclaimed as the Sovereign of Great Britain and Ireland.

The partizans of the Pretender, James Edward Stuart, son of the late king James II., renewed their exertions on his behalf, and Jacobite principles had become so prevalent in certain parts of the kingdom, that it was necessary that the army, which had been considerably reduced after the Peace of Utrecht, should be again augmented, and naturally the marines, who had so distinguished themselves in the last war, were the first to be called up.

The 32nd was sent to Ireland, where it remained for some years, and did not take any part in the next war. The period was by no means an idle one for the services, more especially for the navy. There was another war with Spain, lasting four years, in the course of which Gibraltar underwent another siege, being gallantly defended by a small English garrison, and the Spanish fleet experienced a crushing defeat off the coast of Sicily by a British fleet under Admiral Matthews.

There were troubles in Scotland and Ireland, which gave employment to the troops on shore.

This closes the first period of the Records. We have followed them now from the date of raising until the Peace of Utrecht.

SECOND PERIOD.
From Peace of Utrecht to Irish Rebellion.

1716-95.

IN 1716 Borr's regiment (32nd) was on the Irish establishment. The regiment was employed on board ship, according to the original idea for which it was raised, but little seems to be known of its career. A weekly journal in 1723 briefly alludes to the death of Brigadier Burr (Borr) "colonel of a regiment on the Irish "establishment," and—later—"Brigadier Dubourgey,* colonel of a late "regiment broke in Ireland some years since, as the regiment of the "Brigadier Borr." Brigadier Dubourgey appears to have been made colonel of a regiment as a reward for his services in Spain, where he commanded the regiment, succeeding Borr; and afterwards on special service at the Court of Berlin, and in Hanover. Having died in 1732, he was succeeded by Colonel Thomas Paget, one of Marlborough's soldiers. This officer was great-grandfather of the late Field Marshal the Marquis of Anglesey.

In 1734, the regiment was brought over from Ireland. Landing at Bristol, it marched to Hertford, Hatfield, Ware, and Hoddesden. A War Office order of 30th April, 1734, for the regiment to march to the above-mentioned places, concludes as follows :—" But as writs " are issued for the electing of members of a new parliament, it is " His Majesty's further pleasure that you direct the adjutant and " quartermaster of your regiment to march along two days before " the first division thereof, to the end that if he finds that by the " route assigned they are to pass through a city or borough where " such an election for a member of parliament may happen, he may " in such cases return at once to the first division and halt the same " until two days after the election is over, and give notice to the 2nd " division not to join the 1st division, lest they be too crowded in their

---

* Brigadier Dubourgey is described by Carlyle, in his *History of Frederick the Great*, as an old military gentleman of diplomatic merit, who spells rather ill ; was minister to the court of Frederick the Great in 1727-30. He conducted several delicate treaties, and nipped in the bud the marriage of Frederic, Duke of Edinburgh, with Wilhelmina, daughter of Queen Sophie.

" quarters, and so be inconvenient to the inhabitants where they halt." This was evidently done to avoid giving offence in parliament. Many of the members of that body viewed the standing army, then in its comparative infancy, with great jealousy, and as a sort of menace to the liberties of the people.

The regimental head-quarters was at Hertford, and afterwards at St Albans, during the summer of 1734; detachments at Ware and Barnet, moving afterwards to Chelmsford, with detachments at Dunmow, Brentwood and Grays. In 1735, the regiment moved to Canterbury, with detachments at Ashford, Faversham, Maidstone, Rochester, and Sittingbourne. In June of this year the company at Sittingbourne was sent, *via* London, to Hadleigh, Suffolk, " there to " be aiding and assisting the civil magistrates and officers of the " revenue in apprehending the offenders concerned in the murder of " William Cam, a dragoon, who was murdered by smugglers." This company subsequently returned to Sittingbourne.

In 1733, a secret treaty between France and Spain was made, the object of which was to prevent England trading with their American colonies, and, as far as possible, ruin her power on the sea. It had also another object, which was to recover, if possible, the whole of the old Spanish monarchy in Europe, especially in Italy, for the house of Bourbon. By the treaty of Utrecht the English had the right of sending one ship a year with a cargo of negroes to the Spanish colonies. This gave an opening for a vast system of smuggling, which was carried on by the English merchant ships. After the secret treaty, Philip V. vainly tried to restrict the English to their one vessel a year, which led to constant collisions, a great deal of ill-feeling, and, it is said, much cruelty shown by the Spaniards to the English sailors. This treaty was partly suspended during the seven years' war, and again renewed in 1761.

The state of irritation of the English merchants, and the illusage of their sailors by the Spaniards before mentioned, on account of the efforts of the Spanish authorities to put an end to the smuggling trade with their American colonies, were, however, the chief causes of the Spanish war in 1739. The war of the Austrian succession, which England was eventually drawn into, had arisen on the death of

Charles VI. The surrounding countries, wishing to divide his dominions, refused to acknowledge his daughter, Maria Theresa, as Archduchess of Austria and Queen of Hungary. England was bound by treaty to protect her rights, which she did, at first by advice and money, but being already at war with Spain, was by degrees drawn into the general conflict. The final cause of our joining in the latter war was our Hanoverian interests.

In January, 1735-36, the regiment was ordered to Ireland, and placed on the Irish establishment, marching from Canterbury to Bristol, the port of embarkation. Orders about the same date direct that certain non-commissioned officers and men of the regiment be sent to Chelsea and quartered there until passed by the Lords and other Commissioners of the Hospital. It has been suggested that these men were probable survivors of Fox's marines, who had claims on Chelsea through subsequent services in the land forces. In 1738 Colonel Thomas Paget was transferred to the 22nd Foot, and was succeeded by Colonel Simon Descury, and on his death by Colonel Huske, afterwards General Sir John Huske, K.B. He had distinguished himself in the command of a brigade at the battle of Dettingen, afterwards in Scotland, where he covered the retreat of the royal forces with his brigade, after the defeat of Falkirk. He died 18th January, 1761.

The following occurs among the Irish Records :—*

" Hugh Armagh Wyndham, (Chancellor.)

" In pursuance of His Majesty's commands, signified unto us by His " Grace the Duke of Devonshire, Lord Lieutenant of this Kingdom, in " his letter bearing date the 7th day of June instant. These are to direct " and require you to cause the regiment of foot under your command " forthwith to hold themselves in a readiness to embark, under the " directions of Lieutenant-General Napier, on board such ships as shall " be provided to receive and transport them Dublin to Greenock or " Glasgow, on the river Clyde.

" To Colonel Descurry, or the officer-in-chief commanding his regiment " of foot.

" Given &c., the 13th day of June, 1739.
                                              " Thos. Tickell."

---

* Sent to editor by Colonel Talbot-Coke.

These instructions were given to ten other regiments:—

"The eleven battalions ordered from Ireland to Great Britain are to "be augmented by the addition of one sergeant, one corporal, one "drummer, and thirty-six private men to each company.

"We hereby pray and require you forthwith to order the commanding "officers of the said regiments to send over proper officers into Great "Britain to raise the said additional men and to return with them to "Dublin or Cork ; and His Majesty being informed that notwithstanding "(orders) against Inlisting Irishmen into his foot regiments, many are still "received, it is his royal pleasure that you cause it to be notified to the "officers who are to raise the additional men that His Majesty will "shew his utmost displeasure at any disobedience to or neglect of these "orders.*

"Given on the 2nd day of July, 1739.

"THOS. TICKELL."

Further on, "13th August, 1739, His Majesty orders a general "officer should be ordered to Cork for the reviewing the recruits to be "brought from Great Britain for augmenting His Majesty's regiments "of foot."

And, again, "26th November, 1739. The adjutant-general to "review the recruits which shall be brought from Great Britain for "augmenting His Majesty's regiments of foot, on arriving at Dublin."

The regiment was at Fort Augustus, North Britain, in 1741 and 1761.†

A contingent of British troops was despatched to the continent in the summer of 1742 to co-operate with the Austrians and Dutch, but war was not formally declared between Great Britain and France until the spring of 1744.‡ This force was commanded by the Earl of Stair, and composed of some troops of horse and horse grenadiers, eight other regiments of horse and dragoons, three battalions of foot guards, and thirteen other foot regiments, viz. :—

---

* With regard to the order in 1739 prohibiting the enlistment of Irishmen, it is well known that the charge of the Irish Brigade gained the battle of Fontenoy. "Accursed," exclaimed King George, on hearing of this battle, "be the laws "that deprive me of such soldiers !"—AUBREY DE VERE.

† Some idea of soldiering in Scotland in the middle of the eighteenth century can be obtained from Boswell's *Life of Johnson*, chap. xxxv., date 1773.

‡ A war with France was the favourite measure of the king at this time, on account of his German dominions.—*Anecdotes and Speeches of the Earl of Chatham.*

3rd, 11th, 12th, 13th, 20th, 21st, 23rd, 28th, 31st, 32nd, 33rd, 37th, and 39th, with a train of artillery; altogether about sixteen thousand men.*

The British were quartered for the winter at Ghent, Bruges, and Courtray; the head-quarters, with the guards, being at Ghent, and most of the foot regiments at Bruges.

1743.

In the spring of 1743, Stair, tired of Dutch inaction, began to move his troops towards the Rhine, and after rendezvousing at Aix-la-Chapelle, reached the Rhine by toilsome marches in the middle of May; the snow falling nearly the whole time. Ascending the left bank, the British crossed that river a few miles below Coblentz, and pursuing their march by Ehrenbreitstein and Ems, and up the right bank until opposite Mayence, turned up the course of the Maine and reached Hoetch about the middle of June, where a junction was effected with the Austrians and a corps of Hanoverians. From Hoetch, the army proceeded through Frankfort-on-the-Maine up the right bank of that stream to Hanan and Aschaffenburg, where it took up a position watching the French, who had crossed the Rhine at Worms and Spires. Here King George II.† joined, and assumed command of the army in person. Finding the army was in a perilous position, he commenced its withdrawal at once. The French had sixty thousand men, under the Duke de Noailles, encamped on the opposite side of the river, who watched every movement of the Allies, and cut off all their supplies. The king, who appears to have grasped the situation at once, not only saved the army from a defeat, but by retreating drew the French from their strong position. When approaching the village of Dettingen, on 27th June, it was observed that the enemy had crossed the river with part of their army, and were prepared to oppose the further advance of the English on their line of retreat. The army was confined in a

---

* Notes on "History and Services of the 32nd Regiment."—*United Service Magazine, September, 1879.*

† The king was accompanied by the Duke of Cumberland, his son.

narrow plain, bounded on the right by hills and woods and on the left by the river, on the opposite bank of which the French had erected batteries. It would have been as hazardous to retreat as to advance; fortunately there lay a narrow pass, with a morass in the middle, between the English and French armies, and the latter, rushing impetuously down this defile, were repulsed with so much firmness that, after a short but fierce conflict, they were obliged to recross the river with the loss of five thousand men. The victors lost two thousand men in this action, and the Duke of Cumberland was wounded in the leg. The 32nd (Huske's) was in reserve on this occasion. Colonel Huske, who commanded the brigade, was severely wounded in the heel; three rank and file wounded. Want of supplies prevented the Allies from following up their victory, and by the end of August they had recrossed the Rhine. In November they returned to their winter quarters in Flanders, leaving three thousand sick men behind them in Germany. On 27th August, Major-General Huske was transferred to the Royal Welsh Fusiliers, and Brigadier Henry Skelton was appointed colonel in his stead.

1744-45.

Preparations for the next campaign were commenced in the spring of 1744. The English troops, now commanded by Field Marshal Wade, concentrated at Aschel in May, but nothing was done, and in October the troops went back again to winter quarters at Ghent, Bruges, and Ostend.

In the beginning of 1744 an invasion of England was attempted by a French force of fifteen thousand men, under a convoy of twenty ships of the line, but was unsuccessful. It had been represented to the French that England was ripe for revolt, and it only required the Pretender to raise his flag to have a large following; it was therefore thought to be a favourable opportunity; moreover, King George was away in Hanover and the Duke of Cumberland, with the most serviceable part of the army, in Flanders. It was not, however, until the following year, 1745, that James deputed Prince Charles Edward, his son, to make another attempt, which is only referred to here as showing a concurrent event, and one in which the 32nd took a minor part. In the meantime the campaign of 1745 commenced. The circumstances which led to it were as follows : on the death of the Elector of Bavaria, the Grand Duke of Louraine, husband of Maria Theresa, was, in the imperial diet, chosen emperor. As the French king could not prevent the succession of the grand duke to the imperial throne he resolved to humble the house of Austria by making a conquest of the Austrian Flemish provinces. For that purpose an army, consisting of eighty thousand men, was assembled under Marshal Saxe, in Flanders, who suddenly invested Tournay in the beginning of May, 1745. To resist the design of the French the Duke of Cumberland, who had been appointed to the chief command of the allied army, assembled at Soignies, marched to the relief of Tournay, and, on 28th April, took post at Maulbre, in sight of the French army, which was encamped on the heights that rise from the right bank of the Scheldt, with that river and the village of Antoine on the right, the village of Fontenoy in their front, and the wood Vezon on their left.

Battle of Fontenoy.

Fontenoy and Antoine were strongly fortified and garrisoned, and redoubts were thrown up between these two villages. On 30th April the Duke of Cumberland, having made the requisite dispositions, began his march against the enemy's position about 4 o'clock in the morning. A brisk cannonade was opened on both sides, which soon developed into a general action, and by 9 o'clock both armies were closely engaged. Little advantage seemed up to this period to have been gained by either side. A supreme effort was now made by Cumberland against the left of the French line, and for this purpose the British and Hanoverian infantry were hurled at them, supported by the Dutch on their left. The contest became a hand-to-hand struggle, and assumed terrific proportions; the turning movement was successful, and the French were driven back beyond their own lines, and that part of the position carried. But when the conquerors looked to their left for the Dutch, who were to have attacked simultaneously the right of the French position, it was found they had retired in place of advancing, as they got disheartened at the galling effects of the French batteries; one regiment of cavalry—the regiment of Hesse-Homburg, seized with panic, galloped without drawing rein as far as Alby, from which town its colonel wrote a letter to the Dutch government informing them that the allied army had been cut to pieces.

Undiscouraged, however, by the cowardice of their Allies, the heroic British and Hanoverian infantry advanced to the charge of the enemy on the right with redoubled ardour; but, alas, the odds were against them. Being exposed on both flanks to a destructive fire, the Duke of Cumberland judged it most judicious to retreat, which was effected in tolerable order about 3 o'clock in the afternoon. The British cavalry coming up prevented further pursuit, and the infantry again presented a formidable front to the enemy.

A military writer says: "There is no other example on record of a " body of unsupported infantry penetrating a position in the face of a " force five times more numerous than itself, under the cross-fire of " redoubts full of heavy artillery, and overthrowing successive charges " of cavalry and infantry. Though, by the contraction of the ground, " it was compressed into a dense and elongated mass of narrow front, " it still preserved its stern, undaunted aspect; and pursuing its " daring and deliberate advance, the bravest efforts of the chivalric " nobility of the French household troops, as well as those of the " Irish brigades, in succession, were in vain employed to arrest its " progress; and it was only when it had reached the heart of the " enemy's position, and its ranks were mowed down by artillery, and " overwhelmed in front and on both flanks by a simultaneous onset " of all the cavalry and infantry whom it had repeatedly repelled, that " the gallant band was at last cut down and swept off the field, " without a symptom of dismay or an effort to disperse."

In this battle the loss of the English in killed and wounded was about four thousand men; and that of the Hanoverians, two thousand. The French acknowledged to the loss of seven thousand. The Allies left behind them but few pieces of artillery, and lost no standards or prisoners.

The 32nd lost two sergeants and fourteen rank and file, killed; Lieutenants Lindsay, Meslin, Banks, 2nd Lieutenant How, Ensign

Prescot, five sergeants, and ninety-five rank and file, wounded; and Captain Farquhar and seventeen rank and file missing.

The following is an extract from the Duke of Cumberland's General Orders, issued shortly before what was in them termed the expected " day of action " :—

"Date 29th April, 1745.

"Genl and Staff Officers to attend the British Forces in Flanders :—
"His Royal Highness the Duke.
"Brig^r Churchill to the Brigade of Royals* (1st).
"Brig^r Skelton to the Brigade of Howard's (3rd)."

Orders for the march towards the French position :

"Hall Camp, 1st May,
"Parole St. Marie et Cassel.

"The Q$^{r.}$·Masters and Camp Collourmen, & the new grand guard shall "assemble to-morrow morning at 2 o'Clock at the head of the Dutch "guard Drag^s on y^e left of y^e army. The Highland Regim^t to march "along w^h the Q$^{r.}$·Masters, and to detach 1 Captn, 2 officers, and 60 men "to secure the Genl· Officers' Qua^{rs,} till y^e Genl· Officers' guards come up.

"The Genl· beats at 5, the Assembly at 6, & march be half an hour "after. The 1st Line by the right of the Causeway & y^e 2nd on the left.

"English and Dutch Train of Artillery are to march abreast on the "Causeway, the English on the right, and the Dutch on the left.

"The Baggage to follow their respective Artillerys, as they are incamp'd. "The Hanoverian Artillery and Baggage to follow the English.

"For the future Sr John Ligonier to march at the head of the Foot "Guards, & Maj$^{r.}$·Genl· Ponsonby at the head of the Infantry of y^e 1st "Line.

"The Com^{ding} officers of the Roy^{ls} (1st Royal Scots), Lord Rothes' "(25th), & Skelton's (32nd), to attend Sr John Ligonier to-morrow upon "the march."

The retreat of the beaten army was covered by General Ligonier and Lord Crawford with bravery and coolness, and Marshall Saxe was blamed for not turning the defeat into a rout. He defended himself

---

* Brigades were not numbered at this time ; the senior regiment gave its name as a distinction to the brigade to which it belonged.

on the grounds that "We had enough of it; I thought only of "restoring order amongst the troops."*

"Everybody knows," says a writer of the day, "that, after the "battle of Fontenoy, our army lay encamped at Lessines. Our "situation there was such as must have either kept the French behind "the Scheld, or have obliged them to fight us on ground of our own "choosing, and in a plain where our cavalry could have acted. This "was evident to the meanest soldier in the English troops; and our "generals to a man were sensible of what importance, for the pre- "serving Flanders, their preserving that situation was. But, to the "amazement of all Europe, an ignominous precipitate retreat was "resolved on, and urged in such manner by the generals of our "allies, as demonstrated it to be agreeable to the inclinations, if not "in consequence of the orders, of their masters. The French could "scarcely believe their own good fortune; and even the people of ' Brussels hooted and hissed at our troops as they passed along."

The head-quarters remained at Vilvorden from 3rd August to 19th October. This is a small town situated about the centre of the canal between Brussels and Antwerp, the whole length of which was entrenched and fortified.

The following extracts from General Orders are of interest:

"Camp of Ath, May 13th,
"Parole St. Jean et Prague.

"400 Foot, 100 Horses, and 50 Hussars, w^h a Lieut.-Col. and Major of "the Right Wing, must be ready to march, and take their tents along w^h "them. They are to be commanded by Brig^r Skelton, and to parade at "the head of M : G : How^{drs} (19th Foot). Lt.-Col. Earl Panmure and " Maj^r Cornwallis for this Com$^{d.}$"

"Augt 8^h.

"Maj^r Genl Zastrow & Brig^r Duglass to have the direction of the "Intrench^{ts} which are making on y^e canal."

On 19th July, 1745, little more than two months after Fontenoy had been fought, the young Chevalier landed in the Highlands, and the Scottish clans began to rally round him. It was not until the

---

* *Hayward's Essays.*

beginning of September that the king and his ministers began to realize the importance of the crisis ; nay, had become fully aware that the young Chevalier was actually at that moment upon British soil. A message was then despatched to the Duke of Cumberland with directions that a part of the Flanders army should at once return home. The first general order which intimated such a movement occurs under date of September 24th, when as after orders "all "the posts of Sowles' (11th), Pultney's (13th), M. G. Howard's "(19th), Bragg's (28th), Douglas' (32nd), Johnson's (33rd), and "Cholmondeley's (34th) regiments to be relieved immediately. "These seven regiments to be ready to march at an hour's warning."*

These regiments, with the exception of the 19th, and with the addition of the brigade of Guards and the Buffs, embarked at Wilhelmstadt in October, under the command of Sir John Ligonier, and ten days later arrived off Gravesend. The steadiness and good order of these troops on embarkation elicited the highest praise from Ligonier.

After its arrival in England, the 32nd Regiment (now commanded by Colonel William Douglas,) in the army of the Duke of Cumberland, moved northwards. On 4th December the duke's head-quarters were at Stafford, the young Pretender and the Highland army being at Derby and in its neighbourhood. The Duke of Cumberland's army was brigaded as the following extract from General Orders shows :—

          EXTRACT FROM GENERAL ORDERS.

" L : G : Anstruther & Brig^r Bligh—Sempill's (25th), Scotch Fuzileers, "(21st), Johnson's (33rd), Douglas' (32nd).

" M : G : Skelton & Brig^r Price—How^{ds} (3rd Buffs), Skelton's (12th).

" Brig^r Douglas—Sowle's (11th), Handyside's (31st), The Train."

The regiment subsequently did good service in Lancashire,† but does not appear to have taken part in the battles of Falkirk Moor or Culloden.

---

* William Augustus, Duke of Cumberland, by Campbell Maclachlan.

† In Henderson's *History of the Rebellion*, Douglas' regiment (32nd) is mentioned with others " who had served so well under the eye of His Royal Highness " in Lancashire and Cheshire."

1746.

The regiment proceeded to Scotland on the dispersal of the clans, remaining there but a short time, as they could ill be spared from Flanders, where their services were urgently needed. In the autumn of 1746 they were back again in that country, under their old chief, Sir John Ligonier.

On 7th October a sharp affair occurred on the Jaar, in which the French were repulsed; but Saxe, reinforced by Clermont, re-crossed that stream a few days later, and the Allies—instead of opposing the passage—sent off their heavy baggage to Maestricht and chose a new position in rear of the villages of Endist, Slinge, and Fixhé, where they awaited the French attack. Between Fixhé and Liers was a plain, in front of the Hanoverians; the British and Hessians were posted in rear of Liers; the Hanoverian general, Zastrow, and Brigadier Douglas, 32nd regiment, held Warem and Roucoux, and the Prince of Waldeck occupied the suburbs of Liege. In this position the Allies were vigorously assailed by the French, who advanced in three columns, covered by a powerful artillery, and, though at first repulsed on the left, gradually extended their attacks along the whole front, driving Zastrow out of the villages of Warem and Roucoux and compelling the Allies to fall back upon the Meuse, leaving five thousand of their dead, chiefly Hessians, on the field. The French, too, had been roughly handled, and the retreat was effected without interruption.

This affair ended the year's operations, and on 26th October the British and Hessians marched to Venloo, whence they proceeded to their winter quarters in the duchies of Limburg and Luxembourg.

1747-55.

The Allies were in the field again in April, 1747, the Duke of Cumberland having made great preparations during the winter; but ill luck seemed to hover around them, and they were outnumbered and outmanœuvred by the French.

Extract from the diary of an officer of the Artillery with the army in Flanders, 1747-48:

32ND REGIMENT.

"On 22nd May a review of part of our Artillery, with 8 pieces of our "short 6-pounders, and 4 regiments of Foot—Conway's (48th), Duglesses' "(32nd), Crawford's (25th), and Degon's (37th). The Duke came about 10 "o'clock to review us. Fired about 60 rounds from our guns, and was Done "about 1 o'clock. Further, on May ye 24th news came to the Duke that "Admir'l Anson had taken six men of war from the French, on y^t account "our train was ordered to fire, which we performed after sunset. The "Austrians Fir'd 30 pieces of cannon at the right of ye camp, the Hano-"verians 30, and ye English 21, and a running fire with small arms by the "whole allied army—the running fire between every round of cannon three "times."

This was probably the action off Cape Finistere, 3rd May, 1747. It must be remembered that the dates in this diary are old style, and therefore ample time would have elapsed for the news of this victory to have reached Flanders. It will be observed that the Orders were dated new style, following the Continental usage, which did not become general in England until September, 1752. The day following the 2nd of that month was styled the 14th.—(See Lord Stanhope's *History of England*, vol. iv., ch. 31.) The Order runs thus :

"Camp of Bauwell, Sunday, June 4th,
"Parole St. Joseph & Berlin.

"The Army to fire a *feu de joye* this evening for the Victory gained by Admir'l Anson over the French fleet which he took off Cape Finister."

On April 20th the British Army was brigaded.

EXTRACT FROM GENERAL ORDERS.

"Parole St. Paul & Cassell.

"Duglas, Bri^r—N : B : Fuzil^{rs} (21st), Johnson's (33rd), L : G : How$^{d's}$ "(3rd Buffs).
"Mordaunt,* Bri^r—Duglas (32nd), Conway (48th), M : G : How^d "(19th), Wolfe,† B.M."

---

* John Mordaunt, nephew of the celebrated Earl of Peterborough.
† Afterwards the hero of Quebec.

In the meantime the Duke of Cumberland posted his whole army between the two Nethes, to cover Bergen-op-Zoom and Maestricht; Marshall Saxe called in his detachments, with a view to hazard a general engagement. On 2nd July the Allies were posted with their right on Bilsen and their left on Wirle, within a mile of Maestricht and the village of Laffeldt, which lay on their left front, and was held by several British regiments. The French occupied the heights of Herdeeven, and proceeded to attack on the following morning the village of Laffeldt and met with a stubborn resistance, and, although repeatedly driven back, their places were taken by fresh troops with astonishing perseverance; and—after the village had been three times lost and carried—they maintained their position in it. On this the Duke of Cumberland made a supreme effort and advanced with the whole of his left wing. When victory seemed within his grasp, the Dutch cavalry in the centre gave way, and in their flight upset a brigade of infantry, who also began to retire, whereupon the French cavalry charged and completed the victory for the French. The Allies were only saved from the defeat becoming a disaster by the brave Sir John Ligonier charging at the head of his cavalry, resolving to sacrifice himself and a part of his troops to the safety of the army—enabling the Duke of Cumberland to effect an orderly retreat to Maestricht. He himself was taken prisoner, having had his horse killed under him. The 32nd lost Major Roper and four rank and file, killed; Lieutenants Stephens and Gore, and sixty-four rank and file, wounded; and twenty-six rank and file missing.

Extracts.

"June the 20, 1747.

" March'd by 3 o'clock in the morning and Left Mastrick 1 mile to y^e
" Left about 12 o'clock ye French Hussars attack'd our Hussars on a Hill
" whereof Proceeded a Smart Engage^t In a Little time made y^m Retreat
" into a village where they had a Battery of 5 or 6 Guns, but the English
" Immediately brought up to the top of the Hill six six pounders a great
" Many Shots fir'd on both Sides. we blew up one of their Batterys with
" a shell and kill'd a Great Many of them tho' there was scarce any such
" thing as Seeing of them by reason the Village was so thick of Trees, they
" Killed but two of our men that evening 1 Bombardier and 1 Mattross, it

"rain'd so prodigious hard that at Last both Parties Left of Fireing, in the "mean time we Detach'd two Pieces of Cannon to every Reg^t as far as "they would allow of Number they was Short Sixes and Long three "Pounders. Draw'd the rest of the heavy Cannon into the Park and in "the night Erected Batterys for our 12 and 9 Pounders faceing the Village "and Prepar'd ourselves in readiness for an Engagement the Next Day. "Lay on our Arms all that night in the Open Field Continued Rayning all "night nothing to be Got to Eat."

"Battle of Mas^{tk} Plain.
"Sunday June ye 21 1747.

"The English begun Cannonading from our Battery, that was erected "in the night we begun about 5 o'clock morning the French begun about "6 o'clock and Continued Cannonading until half an hour after 8 o'clock, "then the French Advanc'd Accordingly the English, Hanoverians, and "Hersoins advanc'd with two pieces of Cannon with every Reg^t. advanc'd "and Fir'd at one another for three hours and a half as fast as we could "load. at half an hour after 11 o'clock they at last retreated we following "with Loud Huzzas. the Dutch Horse gave way and the Austerians "never comeing to Back us, and a large boddy of both horse and Foot "Comeing from the right to the Assistance of the French and as they say "the French King Comeing up Inspir'd them with new Life and Courage "which Caused them Immediately to turn and Advance on us, most "Furiously and they really behav'd Very Well. Tho' we Cut them Down wth "Grape Shot from our Batterys of 12 Pounders y^{ey} Did not Seem to mind "it, but fil'd up their Intervals that we made as they Advanc'd.

"Being over Power'd we was at Last Oblig'd to retreat Something "faster than we Advanc'd, and In our retreat we left 9 three Pounders "6 Short Six pounders 1 Long Six pounder with three Colours and a "Kittle Drum the Hanoverians Lost Six pieces of Cannon as to the Loss "of Men on both Sides I Cannot tell as yet. Sr Jo^n Ligonier was Taken "Prisoner and several officers of Distinction we Lost More of the Artillery "People that Day than Ever was known at any Battle before. but if the "Dutch had done their Duty and Austerians had come to back us we "should have woon the Day, but was Oblig'd to Retreat as far as Mastrick, "and Lay on our Arms that night, and if it had not been for the Town "that Cover'd our retreat we should certainly been all taken prisoners. "This battle was on the plains of Mastrick Near Elke was call'd ye Battle "of Val or Laffelt."

The Duke of Cumberland, in his despatch, acquitted the Austrians of the charge of bad behaviour on this occasion.

Saxe next determined to attack Bergen-op-Zoom, the strongest fortification of Dutch Brabent, the famous work of the engineer Coehorn, and looked upon as invincible. No attempt appears to have been made to relieve it by the Allies after the siege had actually commenced, probably on account of the obstinacy of the governor, Baron Cronstrom, who considered that the fortress was impregnable. After great loss of life and innumerable unsuccessful attempts, Count Lowendahl determined to storm the place and was successful—not, however, without meeting with great resistance, after he had obtained possession of the ramparts from some Scotch regiments, who disputed every inch of ground as the French troops penetrated into the town. On the conclusion of this siege an armistice followed; the British moving to cover Maestricht and Breda.

13th September, 1747. To quote from the before-mentioned diary:

"We have an Epidemical Disorder Throughout all our allied army "which is the Bloody Flux* carries several off in a Day, they say the " French has the same distemper but more violent. At the end of October "the Army went into winter Quarters, many officers proceeded on leave to " England."

It appears from the same source (although not absolutely stated) that Douglas' regiment (32nd) occupied winter quarters in Breda, 1747-48. Early in March, 1748, troops were moved towards Maestricht "for it is thought that the French are going to lay siege to it." There marched to defend that town, fifteen regiments of foot and five of horse, two guns being sent to every foot regiment, following the unaccountable fashion of the time; Douglas' (32nd) was apparently not with this force.

Whilst at Breda a curious oath was administered to the army which is best described by the writer of the before-mentioned diary—

---

* Dysentery.

"1747, Breda Town, November ye 7th.

"At 11 o'clock all the English Soldiers Likewise the Artillery People
"was under arms on the parade and took an oath, at the same time held
"up the two first fingers of their Right hand while the oath was reading, which
"was, that we was to aid and to assist the inhabitants and not to wrong or
"Defraud them, the oath was taken before my Lord Albemarle and y^e
"Governor of ye Town.

"On April 29, 1748, a cessation of arms was wrote in orders, the Duke
"at the same gave orders that the Troops should render the same discipline
"as usual notwithstanding the cessation.

Under date May 11th the diary continues :

"Encamped on an open moor 10 miles from the Bush of Brabent where
"we joined all the English army and four more Reg^ts. that Lay at Breda
"with 3 more that came from England—Nesselroy Camp.

"June 11th all ye Regiments was under arms by 4 evening for a *Feu-de-*
"*Joy* it being the King's Succession to the Crown, there was 22 Regts. of
"English Infantry and 5 Reg^ts. of Cavalry and the Heavy Train which was
"6 Twelve pounders 6 Nine pounders and 14 Long Sixes ye Hanoverians
"y^t was under arms was 21 Reg^ts. of Infantry and 10 of Horse they was
"drawn up in two lines. The English and Hanoverians Horse at y^e
"First and second line and ye Hanoverians Infantry at ye left of ye first
"and second, the front line reached about 3 miles and half as Likewise
"Did ye second. The English Train was drawn up in the center of y^e
"rear Line. Y^e Duke took his post between the Hanoverians and y^e
"English, at Sun Set ye train Fir'd 50 and then they begun at ye Right of
"ye front line with a running fire and came down to ye Left and so went
"back in the Rear to ye Right, then the Artillery Fir'd 50 Rounds more
"and the foot took it up as before with a Running Fire which was per-
"formed three times with 3 Huzzas up and Down the Lines in ye manner
"of ye running Fire, and then ordered to march to our Camp where we
"arrived by 9 o'clock."

At the end of June, 1748, the camp was broken up and the troops went into Cantonments, Colonel Leighton's (32nd) regiment being at Boxtel together with Colonel Woolf's.

"August ye 4th 1748.

"General Sickness thro' all ye English Regiments, Taken with a Pain in
"the head, Fever & Eague, above three fourths of ye Regiments had it
"and a Great Number Died, Especially those which Lay on ye Low
"Ground, the only remedy was Setons in ye neck and drinking ye water
"after it was boil'd."

In the closing months of 1748 a general peace was negotiated, bringing to a conclusion a war which was prosecuted on the side of the Allies without conduct, spirit, or unanimity. In the Netherlands they were outnumbered and outwitted by the enemy. They never hazarded a battle without sustaining a defeat. Their vast armies, paid by Great Britain, lay inactive and beheld one fortress reduced after another, until the whole country was subdued; and as their generals fought, their plenipotentiaries negotiated. What, then, were the fruits which Britain reaped from this long and desperate war? A dreadful expense of blood and treasure, disgrace upon disgrace, an additional load of grievous impositions, and the National Debt accumulated to the enormous sum of eighty millions sterling.*

Such is the historian Smollett's opinion, but had he lived in our time, he would probably have considerably modified his opinions. It must be remembered that his criticisms were written at a time when many believed that England had been worsted, had given up the important isle of Cape Breton for a *petty factory in the East Indies belonging to a private Company*,† and relinquished her conquests in North America.

Brigadier Douglas having died the year previous, viz., 1st December, 1747, was succeeded by Colonel Francis Leighton, as colonel of the regiment.

On the conclusion of peace, before narrated, the whole of the British troops were withdrawn from the Low Countries. In December, 1748, the 32nd Regiment was at Chelmsford, and was reduced by two companies. In 1749 it was sent to Gibraltar, the scene of its earliest experiences.

The original idea for which the regiment was raised appears to have been carried out from this station, and detachments were sent from time to time to serve on board the ships of war as occasion required. The regiment remained in Gibraltar from 1749 to 1753, when they were relieved by the 6th regiment, sent to England, and stationed in North Britain for ten years. In 1755 it was in Edinburgh: Francis Leighton, colonel; Richmond Webb, lieutenant-colonel; William Taylor, major.

---

* Smollett, *History of England*, vol. iii., p. 232. † Afterwards East India Company.

1756-72.

War was again declared with France 10th February, 1756, in consequence of the French menaces against the Island of Minorca, when Admiral Byng's fleet failed to relieve it; but the 32nd took no part in it, and therefore only indirectly concerns us here.

The army had been considerably reduced on the conclusion of the Peace of 1753, so now it had to be suddenly augmented at a vast expense, and fifteen new second battalions were raised; the 2nd battalion 32nd being raised in Scotland, where a considerable addition to the Government bounty was made by the several counties. The following officers of the 1st battalion 32nd Regiment were appointed to the 2nd battalion:

Captain William McDowall	Major.
Captain-Lieutenant Robert Rogers	Captain.
Lieutenant Patrick Blake	Captain.
Lieutenant James Stuart	Captain.

In less than two years the 2nd battalion was formed into a separate regiment, became the 71st, and was disbanded in 1763, having only existed for seven years. It does not appear to have been employed abroad during its short career as 2nd battalion 32nd Regiment.

In 1762, the 32nd was at Glasgow, the strength of the regiment being forty-two officers, fifty-six non-commissioned officers, and eight hundred and fifty-six privates; total, nine hundred and fifty-four. The establishment was at that time one thousand and thirty-four of all ranks. After the peace the following reductions were made, viz., one surgeon's mate; one lieutenant, one sergeant, and fifty-three privates per company.

In February, 1763, a General Peace was signed at Fontainebleau, and the usual reliefs and reductions followed. The 32nd was sent abroad to the Island of St. Vincent, Christmas, 1764, and, from an old manuscript which was sent to the compiler of this history by Colonel O. H. A. Nicholls, R.A. (now major-general), it appears the regiment suffered considerably from sickness in that island.

The mortality was excessive,* the *Official Army List* shows the regiment during this period as in "the Charibbee Islands," viz., from 1764 to 1774.

1773—75.

In 1773 the colonel of the regiment (General Francis Leighton) died, and was succeeded by Lieutenant-General Robert Robinson, who resigned it for the governorship of Pendennis Castle, and was in turn succeeded by Lieutenant-General William Amherst, 18th October, 1775, adjutant-general at head-quarters.

The regiment returned home in 1773, and was stationed at Wells; from thence they proceeded to Bath,† and in 1774 we find them in Salisbury, probably having been moved about in the hopes of raising more men after their losses in the Carribbee Islands. In October of that year they took part in a grand review at Richmond. On December 17th, 1775,‡ they were moved to Ireland; the head-quarters and three companies, together with women and children, and all the records of the regiment, embarked in the *Rockingham Castle*, transport, which was wrecked outside the Cove of Cork.§ An interesting account of the sad event appeared in the *Gentleman's Magazine*, vol. xlvi., p. 43, December 23rd:—" The *Rockingham*, transport, was "unfortunately lost by mistaking Robert's Cove for Cork Harbour "in the night. She had three companies of the 32nd Regiment of "Foot on board; Lieutenant Marsh and his wife, Ensign Sandiman, "Lieutenant Barker's wife, and upwards of ninety soldiers, with "the captain and crew, perished. The officers saved were Captain

---

* According to the report of the Secretary at War, of the troops sent to the West Indies from 1764 to 1774 only nine hundred and thirty-five had died out of over four thousand. Southey, *History of the West Indies*.

† On the 24th May, the 32nd Regiment of Foot, which had been stationed at St. Vincent upwards of eight years, marched into Bath from Wells. The private soldiers were only eighty-five in number—*Gentleman's Magazine*, 1773.

‡ This year the 32nd, while at Chatham, was augmented by one sergeant, one corporal, and eighteen privates per company.

§ The day previous to the loss of the *Rockingham Castle*, Lieutenant-Colonel Campbell and Captain Parker went on board a pilot boat, and thus escaped the fate of the others.

"Glover, Lieutenants Booth and Cator, and the doctor's mate. "'It is impossible,' says the writer of the account, 'to paint the "distress of the officers and soldiers who were saved; the greater "part of whom, being cast on the rocks, had their flesh torn in a "most shocking manner, and, instead of receiving the least assistance "from the inhabitants, were attacked by some thousands of the "Common people, who carried away every article that could be "saved from the wreck.'"

Captain Glover, probably John Flower, Captain, 15th July, 1768.
Lieut. Marsh   ,,   Robert March, Lieutenant, 13th April, 1774.
,, Barker   ,,   Edward Parker, Lieutenant, 25th December, 1770.
,, Booth   ,,   Leeds Booth, Lieutenant, 7th June, 1773.
,, Cator   ,,   J. Chilton L. Carter, Lieutenant, 8th June, 1774.

Ensign Sandiman does not appear in the *Annual Army Lists* of this time, probably he had lately joined.

Another account from the *Annual Register*, vol. xviii., p. 187, states that "five officers and twenty soldiers saved themselves in the flat-"bottomed boat."

1774—82.

The remainder of the regiment reached its destination safely and were quartered in Ireland during the next few years—years of trouble and anxiety. The rupture with the American colonies took place about this time, and was followed by a declaration of war against France and Spain. The 32nd Regiment, as before stated, took no part in these wars beyond furnishing volunteers for different regiments as occasion required. Its first station was Cork, where it remained until February, 1776; and during its stay there some men were drafted into the 15th and 16th regiments, about to embark for America.

The regiment then went to Clonmel and Waterford, furnishing a draft of one hundred men to the 9th Regiment. In June, 1777, it was ordered to Dublin, having been completed to six hundred rank and file; and, as far as can be ascertained, remained there until

October, 1783. It was during this time that an unfortunate affair took place, in which one officer lost his life, but as it appears to have been only a personal matter, and—more or less—the result of an accident, it has not been thought necessary to place it on record here.

At this period of the existence of the regiment, county titles were assigned to the regiments of infantry of the line, and a letter, dated 31st August, 1782, conveyed to the regiment His Majesty's pleasure that county titles should be given to regiments of infantry, and the 32nd was directed to assume the name of the "Cornwall Regiment," in order that a connexion between the corps and that county should be cultivated which might be useful in furthering the success of the recruiting service.

1783—94.

The preliminaries of the treaties between England, France and Spain, were signed at Versailles on 20th January, 1783. St. Lucia was returned to France, also the settlements on the river Senegal and the city of Pondicherry, in the East Indies. France relinquished all her West India conquests, with the exception of Tobago; Spain retained Minorca (which she had captured in the previous year) and West Florida; East Florida was ceded in exchange for the restitution of the Bahamas to Great Britain. The preliminaries of peace with the Dutch were not signed until 2nd September, 1783.*

In October, 1783, the regiment was ordered to embark, under the command of Major Strachan, for Gibraltar,† where it was stationed until the winter of 1792, when it proceeded to the West Indies, under the command of Major Edwards. It reached Barbadoes, and, with the exception of the companies detached to Tobago, remained there until 1793, when those men who were deemed fit for service were drafted to other regiments.

---

* Cannon, *Historical Records of 31st Regiment*.

† It is recorded of a distinguished soldier, General Lord Blayney, who joined the 32nd Regiment at Gibraltar, in 1789, as an ensign, that he had the opportunity of forming his principles and future conduct from the regiment being at that period remarkable for its excellent order, and most perfect state of exemplary good discipline.—*R. M. Calendar*, iii., 3.

GENERAL JOHNSON.

The officers, non-commissioned officers, and remaining privates returned to England, and were subsequently stationed in the island of Jersey, where, in the year 1794, the regiment was rendered fit for service by drafts from Duncannon Fort, and again ordered to the West Indies, proceeding—for the purpose of embarking for that station—to Plymouth, where transports were in readiness. A delay in the sailing of those vessels occurred, and the men became sickly. The following interesting extract is from the journal of a very young officer, Captain (afterwards General) Johnson,* who was transferred to the 32nd from the 2nd Queen's when little more than sixteen years of age. He relates how the 32nd were very nearly wrecked a second time, and what a narrow escape they had :

"However, we was not long with out orders to sail imediatly. I then
"went on Board our Transport (which was called the *Thomas*), where I
"wated some time for a wind, and one day the wind came a little fare the
"Signal was made & our anchor was up, when the wind came about again,
"so we was obliged to wate some time longer. Dureing this time our
"men, from being so much crowded, got very sickly. This at first was
"not Paid much attention to. We was still waiting for a wind, & lying in
"the Sound, when one day it blew reather fresh, and at Night a very great
"storm. About eight o'clock our cable Broak, & as we was one of the
"nearest to the Shore, our Ship drifted till we was dashed against the Rocks,
"the sailors then got up & Backed the main & misen Top Sails & by great
"good luck we did not stick fast (but we got three or four thumps, that I
"thought would have nocked the ships bottom out) so went sturnmost into
"Catwater, where we put out our other ancor and there Road in safety till
"morning, when our ship was ordered to be looked at and we found some
"of the Peaces of rock sticking to the bottom, which had prevented the

---

* For services of this distinguished officer, see *Appendix E*.

"ship from sinking. Everybody on board, even the Master of the Ship, "said he never heard of such an escape in his life. Our Transport was so "much disabled that we was ordred on Board the *Autumn* Transport, "soon after this there came an order down that all the Regts. should be "disembarked that was not five hundred strong and fit for service. We at "that time had more than two hundred men sick, & by that means we had "not more than three hundred men fit for service, so our Regt., with 17th, "31st, 48th, & 67th, was ordered to disembark and go in Temporare "barracks. Our Regt. was at Mill Prison, the others in the New Barracks "in Plymouth. The Officers had lodgings in the Town of Plymouth."

1795.

After waiting some time, expecting fresh transports, the regiment was ordered to Cork, and thence to Spike Island into camp—as the writer of the foregoing extract says, "a nasty, boggy place"—and was there when the 105th and 113th regiments mutinied,* "which was "near being a very serious business, but by Genl. Massey's exertion "they all laid down there armes. There were near 2,000 men that "mutinied."

---

* Both these regiments were afterwards disbanded.

Richard Earl Ross.

THIRD PERIOD.

1796-1812.

St. Domingo.—Siege of Burgos.

AN extensive rising of slaves on the French plantations in St. Domingo (Hayti) having occurred in 1791—in a few days the insurgents mustered one hundred thousand men, and it would be impossible to depict the horrors which had been perpetrated by these desperate men, who had been driven into revolt by the barbarous cruelties practised by their former masters—the most fertile portions of the island became a desolate waste; the French settlers managed to hold out in a few isolated positions, and it was at this time that the British government resolved to interfere. Jeremie was taken by Commodore Ford, September 1793; Cape St. Nicholas Mole followed; then, in 1794, Cape Tiburon and Port au Prince. Although some of these places were retaken by the French republic, others remained in the hands of the British; amongst them St. Nicholas Mole and another place were retained and occupied by small British garrisons. It was at this juncture of affairs, in 1795, that the British government despatched a relieving force to succour their own garrisons, and, at the same time, to endeavour to bring to an end the state of anarchy which was becoming chronic in St. Domingo.

1796-1806.

Sir Ralph Abercromby was appointed to command the expedition, Major-General White going out with him in command of one of the divisions. The 32nd was one of the regiments ordered out with the expedition, and formed part of the force under the latter general. This portion of the force reached St. Nicholas Mole in May, 1796. A curious incident occurred as the transport, with the 32nd Regiment on board, was entering the harbour: a fine horse was observed swimming across the bows of the ship; the animal was secured, and was afterwards used by Colonel Mason, as his charger, up to the time of his death.

One of the transports bringing the force had been captured by a French cruiser. Amongst the troops there were some 32nd men, and an assistant-surgeon of the same regiment; they were taken into Guadeloupe; Victor Hugues was the governor at the time. He released the assistant-surgeon at once, with the laconic remark that, " wherever he went he would do far more harm than good with his " medicines and flannel shirts." Another very interesting incident may be related here, as it occurred about the same time, and refers to the captured transport before mentioned. Lieutenant-General Wetherall* was also a passenger on board, having been sent out with despatches for Sir Ralph Abercromby. He was kept a prisoner for upwards of nine months, closely confined in a dungeon, in irons, without any other clothing than a shirt and a pair of trousers, and on a daily allowance of three biscuits and a quart of water. The detachment of 32nd that were taken prisoners at the same time, but who had been given their liberty to roam about the town, hearing of the inhuman treatment of General Wetherall, raised a subscription of eleven guineas amongst them, which they forwarded to him, concealed in a small loaf of bread, through the medium of a negro employed in the delivery of provisions to the English prisoners, with a note from the sergeant, requesting—in the name of the men—his acceptance of the money as a small token of their esteem, and in the hope of its affording some relief and comfort to him under his sufferings. For this noble act a commission was subsequently conferred on the sergeant.† One more incident, which reflects great credit on the discipline of the regiment, may here be narrated, as told by Major Ross-Lewin, who, during the stay of the regiment at St. Nicholas Mole, was a youthful subaltern of the grenadier company, and, during the latter part of the time, one of the two effective officers present

---

* For services of General Wetherall, see *R.M. Calendar*, vol. ii., p. 351.

† Sergeant Henry Boone, promoted Ensign in 2nd West India Regiment, 24th October, 1798.

with the regiment. "When I fell sick," he says, "I had payment of
"the grenadier company, and during my illness the money for that
"purpose was kept in a trunk in the hospital, as my pay-sergeant, like
"myself, was confined to his bed. The soldiers paid themselves,
"taking what dollars they required when they pleased, yet, when I
"was afterwards called upon to make up my accounts, these men
"came forward, much to their honour, and acknowledged every
"dollar they had taken."

To return to the disembarkation: the troops were landed as early
as possible. Brigadier-General Forbes, with part of the 13th Light
Dragoons, and the 32nd, 56th, 67th, and 81st regiments, proceeded
to attack the fort of Bomparde, sixteen miles off. The column
paraded very early in the morning, receiving their rations, biscuits,
salt pork, and grog. They were kept under arms until 9 a.m., by
which time most of the men had emptied their canteens.

Two paths led to the fort, one of which it was said was intercepted,
and the other ran through a deep close ravine, the sand from which
rose in fine dust as the troops advanced. The route was devoid of water,
and, apparently, none was taken; the consequence being that many of
the men fell out, and fourteen died of heat apoplexy before having
advanced two miles; and those who had imprudently drunk up their
grog were to be seen sucking the perspiration out of their shirt sleeves,
the tongues of many of them hanging out of their mouths dry and
swollen and black with flies; some even had recourse to the last
extremity to quench their thirst. After frightful sufferings and
considerable loss of life, Bomparde was reached: a strong quadrangular fort, with cannon mounted at the angles, and a formidable ditch,
with a sort of town beyond. Water was here obtained, and the
survivors refreshed. Opening a fire on the fort, which was quickly
responded to, Lieutenant Nesbitt and Adjutant Ross, of the 32nd,
were wounded. The enemy, however, evacuated the fort before very
long, and the brigade marched in and took possession.

The duties were heavy and arduous, and the losses considerable,
not only from the enemy, but on account of the deadliness of the
climate. Major Ross-Lewin relates as follows, "one of the worst
"checks we received was owing to being surprised by the enemy one

"morning before daybreak at the advanced post of Palissée, about
"two miles distant from the fort and on the road to the mole. A
"captain, with three subalterns and fifty men of the regiment, were on
"outpost duty: they were surprised and cut to pieces, only the
"captain and one soldier escaped into a wood adjoining. Lieutenants
"Williams, White, and Power, together with forty-nine non-
"commissioned officers and men, were overpowered. The post was
"retaken during the following day by the 32nd and 81st regiments and
"a few men of the 13th Light Dragoons. Fort Bomparde was eventually
"evacuated. Lieutenant R———t, of the regiment, died very
"suddenly, and the force suffered much from the swampy nature of the
"soil."

Defences had been erected at the mole, close to the place of embarkation; and the force having been ordered to withdraw, owing to the difficulty of keeping up communication with St. Nicholas, the 32nd embarked with nothing but the mere skeleton of the regiment, after a twelve months stay in St. Domingo, where it lost thirty-two officers. It was then sent to Nassau, where it remained some time, having been filled up with convalescents from other corps.

The following incident in connexion with this movement is related by the same officer:—

"At the nearest part of the seashore, about seven miles from us, a
"platform for guns was laid, in order to cover the embarkation of the
"guns and sick, and a ship of war and some transports were sent
"round to receive them. As there was only one pathway leading from
"Bomparde to this point, the transport of the sick was very tedious.
"They were conveyed on hospital stretchers fitted with long poles,
"and borne on men's shoulders; but all hopeless cases, not expected
"to last many hours, were ordered to be left behind. Among the sick
"so condemned was a brother officer of mine, and him I was deter-
"mined not to abandon before every effort in my power had been
"made for his removal; but it was with regret that I saw the last
"fatigue party move off after having applied in vain to the
"commanding officer—an officer who declared that no man could be
"spared. My only resource then was to go to a few black prisoners,

"who were digging graves near to the hospital huts, and I brought
"two of them, without orders, to the sick man's room. He was lying
"on a stretcher, quite insensible, and swollen to an enormous size,
"being naturally very tall and robust, and I am very confident that
"four of our men would have found it a severe task to carry him to
"the shore. The blacks could not lift the stretcher, but gave me to
"understand that they could carry it if once placed on their heads. I
"had this done, and they moved off apparently with ease. They had no
"escort, not even a single person to watch them, and might easily have
"got rid of their burden and made off into the woods. Nevertheless,
"they conveyed it faithfully to the platform. He was then taken on
"board on a stretcher, and shortly afterwards his honest heart, poor
"fellow, had ceased to beat for ever."

The regiment was sent to New Providence, and, remaining there only a short time, returned to Portsmouth in a very weak state, probably owing to having given drafts to other regiments; it was then sent on to Guildford to be completed by Irish drafts from Chatham. From Guildford it was ordered to the West of England, and stationed at Tavistock and Launceston.

From Launceston the regiment removed to Bridgewater, where there had been serious riots, owing to the high price of bread. The officers took the initiative in getting up a subscription for the relief of the starving people.

While at Bridgewater, the whole of the Irish lads in the regiment were drafted to corps in India, and the regiment removed to Bristol, *en route* to Waterford, leaving recruiting parties at Launceston, Bodmin, Truro, Exeter, Tiverton, Barnstaple, and Minehead.

From Waterford the regiment moved to Dundalk, and, after a sojourn there, to Kilkenny, and thence to Dublin, where it was employed with the force in quelling the rising of July 23rd and 24th, 1803.

The insurrection broke out with the murders of Colonel Browne, 21st Fusiliers, and Lord Kilwarden, whose nephew met a similar fate. Lord Kilwarden was dragged out of his carriage and mortally wounded by the mob, and died in the arms of Assistant-Surgeon Emery of the regiment.

MAJOR HENRY ROSS-LEWIN.

A second battalion was added to each regiment of the line, and officers were sent into Cornwall to recruit.

1807.

The 1st battalion 32nd was ordered to Kinsale, Charlesfort, and Bandon until July, 1807, when they embarked for Portsmouth to join the expeditionary force proceeding to Copenhagen, which was kept a profound secret at the time. Captain Ross-Lewin says:— " My corps (32nd) was at " this time a beautiful one, " mustering one thousand strong, and did not leave a man behind, " a very unusual circumstance with regiments."

Copenhagen.

Portsmouth was reached on the 16th July, after an eight days' passage, and on the 17th all the transports, with troops on board, having arrived, the whole fleet weighed, and sailed for the Downs. The 32nd was disembarked at Ramsgate and marched to Deal, remaining there three or four days, and then returned to Ramsgate, where it was again embarked, and sailed with the rest of the fleet which had rendezvoused in the Downs.* Here the destination of the fleet was first learned—namely, to Copenhagen—there to seize the Danish fleet, though this act of hostility had not been preceded by a formal declaration of war. " Five days after, we landed and proceeded " to invest the town. Our first work was the erection of batteries.

---

* The 32nd Regiment embarked July 26th and 27th, 1807, at Ramsgate, on board the *Peggy*, *Success*, *Princess of Wales*, and *Retreat*, with the Expedition to Copenhagen.—Extract from MSS. at Royal United Service Institution.

"The troops bivouacked in the fields, building wigwams of branches of "trees and thatching them with sheaf corn. The Danish gunboats and "praams threw heavy shot amongst us occasionally, but they did little "damage. The Royal Family retired into Holstein ; and the greater "part of the country people in the vicinity fled into Copenhagen at "our approach.

"About the 25th, mortar batteries were erected within a quarter of "a mile of the city. The weather became very sultry and the dews at "night heavy. The Danes did not seem to be inclined to venture out, "and the few that showed themselves were picked off by our riflemen. "At length they made two sorties ; the first along the lower road near "the beach, on the extreme left of our line, where a heavy battery had "been lately erected and two field-pieces placed behind a traverse by "the British. Sir George Smith,* a zealous and indefatigable soldier, "had been stationed since the investment at this post, and soon re-"pelled the attack. It was a point of much importance, as the battery "covered the landing of our stores. The second sortie was made not "quite so much to the left as the former one. The Danish force con-"sisted of detachments of the Danish guards, Norwegian life regiment, "and Volunteer rifle corps. The advanced picquets of the left wing "of our army alone were engaged with them, and succeeded in re-"pulsing them. The front of the picquets was protected by a sunk "fence, which was calculated to afford them tolerable cover.

"Sir Arthur Wellesley proceeded with the light brigade into the "interior of the island to prevent the militia from assembling. On "29th July, 1807, he defeated the Danes near Kioge, and took about "eleven hundred prisoners.

"On 1st September the City was summoned in vain, and the following "night we commenced shelling it, and not until eleven hundred of the "inhabitants were killed and one-third of the town in ashes was there "any sign of surrender. On 6th September a flag of truce was sent "out, and on the following day it was stipulated that all vessels and

---

* Lieutenant-Colonel Smith, with the 82nd Regiment under his command, held the post at the windmill on the left, which for the greater part of the time was the most exposed to the gunboats and sorties of the enemy.—Extract from Lord Cathcart's despatch.

"naval stores belonging to the King of Denmark should be yielded
"and immediate possession of the citadel and arsenal given to the
" British, on condition that the island of Zealand be evacuated by them
"within the space of six weeks. After the fall of Copenhagen the 1st
"battalion 32nd Regiment did duty in the dockyard, and whilst there
"received a draft of two hundred and forty-one men, under Captain
"Gibson, from the 2nd battalion."

It was also agreed that a mutual restitution of prisoners should take place, and that all public and private property, with the exception of the royal shipping and naval stores, should be respected.

Thanks to the exertions of the seamen and soldiers, the prizes were ready for sea before the stipulated time, and on 21st October the Expedition, with prizes in company, sailed out of the Sound on the way home. The value of the ships thus brought away, each ship equipped with stores for three years, was estimated at four and a half millions sterling; but, as no formal declaration of war had been made, it was held that the captors were ineligible for prize money. A grant of £900,000 was, however, given by way of compensation.

The regiment returned to England in His Majesty's ship *Ganges* and her prize, the *Princess Sophia Frederica*,* and landed at Deal, remaining a few days at Margate and Ramsgate, and then were ordered to Gosport, where a draft of ninety-nine men, under Captain Crowe, joined from the 2nd battalion.

The commanding officer, Lieutenant-Colonel Hinde, received the following communication from Lieutenant-General Lord Cathcart:

" Gloucester Place,
" 1st February, 1808.
" Sir,
" I take the earliest opportunity of transmitting to you a copy of the
" resolutions of the House of Lords, and of those of the House of

---

* The *Prince Sophia Frederica* was built in 1775; length on gun deck, 175 feet; extreme breadth, 48 feet; depth in hold, 19 feet 8 inches; number of gun ports, 56.—*Naval papers respecting Copenhagen, &c.*, presented to Parliament in 1808.

She was not in commission at the time, so the discomfort for those on board can be imagined.

" Commons, dated 28th January, 1808, which contains the thanks of both
" Houses of Parliament to the army employed in Zealand. In communi-
" cating to you this most signal mark of the approbation of Parliament
" of the United Kingdom of Great Britain and Ireland, allow me to add
" my warmest congratulations upon a distinction which the battalion under
" your command had so great a share in obtaining for His Majesty's
" service, together with the assurances of the regard with which Lt.-Colonel
" Hinde, Commanding 1st Batt. 32nd Regt., upon the expedition to the
" Baltic, was held.

" I have, &c.,
" (Signed) CATHCART, Lt.-General."

In November, 1807, the 2nd battalion of the regiment proceeded from Weely Barracks, near Colchester, to Guernsey.

Extract from the sixth report of the Patriotic Fund :

" 8th March, 1808.
" Read :
" An application, certified by Colonel Burnet, of the Royal College of
" Chelsea, from John Lees, private in the 32nd Regiment of Foot, having
" lost his left leg, and who was otherwise severely burnt in action with the
" enemy at the Siege of Copenhagen.
" Resolved :
" ' That the sum of £25 be given to John Lees.' "

1808.

In December, 1807, the 32nd, under Lieutenant-Colonel Hinde, embarked, with other troops, upon a secret expedition under Major-General Spencer, and, after having experienced a succession of gales for seventeen days, put back to Portsmouth, where the regiment remained a few days, and then proceeded to Falmouth to join some of the other ships of the fleet that had been caught in the same storm. Adverse winds kept the regiment at Falmouth until 1st March, 1808, when another start was made, and Gibraltar was reached 9th June. Major Johnson, commanding a part of the regiment which had sailed in another transport, had arrived before the head-quarters, and been sent on to Sicily. An officer writes : " We were informed that, on our "departure from England it was settled that General Spencer should "attack Ceuta ; but that Sir Hew Dalrymple, Lieutenant-Governor "of Gibraltar, having received intelligence of the growing disaffection "in Spain, which threatened to manifest itself in a general rising, had "sent the troops to Sicily as fast as they arrived, with the view of "protecting that island from an invasion by the French, who had "assembled a strong force in Calabria, and that a portion of these "troops had since received counter-orders and were to return to "Gibraltar, being replaced by the Germans, under General "McFarlane."

On 15th May that part of the regiment which had not proceeded to Sicily embarked with Major-General Spencer and steered for Cadiz. On arriving there, they found Lord Collingwood's fleet at anchor in the harbour, from whence they had been watching the French Admiral Rossilly's squadron of five sail of the line and one frigate which lay in the inner harbour.

On 12th June the fleet of transports got under weigh, and sailed for the mouth of the river Guadiana, which divides Spain from Portugal. In the meantime the remainder of the regiment rejoined head-quarters. The 32nd Regiment was present at the opening of the Spanish batteries on the French ships of war, in the harbour of Cadiz, on the day the Spanish Revolution broke out, in 1808, and immediately after disembarked at Fort St. Mary, and was stationed there about six weeks. It was subsequently ordered to Mondego Bay, in Portugal, there forming part of Sir Brent Spencer's division of the army, with orders to co-operate with the troops under the command of Major-General Sir Arthur Wellesley, which were daily expected from Cork.

On their arrival the army disembarked, in the beginning of August, and advanced towards Lisbon.

The disembarkation of the small army took some time, owing to the heavy surf.

The following appeared in General Orders, dated 7th August, 1808 : Major-General Spencer having joined the army, the regiments were brigaded as follows :—

1st Brigade	{ 5th Regiment 9th " 38th " }	Major-General Rowland Hill
2nd Brigade	{ 2nd Regiment 29th " 82nd " }	Major-General Nightingale
3rd Brigade	{ 36th Regiment 40th " 71st " }	Major-General Ferguson
4th Brigade	{ 6th Regiment 32nd " }	Major-General Bowes
5th Brigade	{ 45th Regiment 50th " 91st " }	Colonel Catlin Craufurd
6th Brigade	{ 2/95th Regiment 5/60th " }	Brigadier General Fane

The Battle of Roleia.

The battalion, having landed, marched to Leira on 11th August, and on the 15th a skirmish with the enemy took place at Obidos, with trifling loss. The battle of Roleia was fought on 17th August; Captain Ross-Lewin relates :—" The villages of Celdos "and Roleia are built opposite to each other at the extremities of "a large valley, and nearly equidistant from the small town of "Obidos, which is remarkable for its fine aqueduct and ancient "castle.

"The French were posted on an elevated but level space in front "of Roleia; this rear was covered with low trees and close underwood, "and several paths led from it to the neighbouring mountains, of which "a remarkably strong ridge offered an excellent second position at an "easy distance. The advantages presented by the nature of the "ground in a great measure compensated for the disparity of numbers, "and, circumstanced as Junot and Lorrion were, it was of consider- "able importance to the French that Laborde should resist our "progress.

"On the morning of the 17th, at daybreak, we broke up from "our bivouac. Flank movements were made to threaten the enemy's "rear with a portion of the British and Portuguese; but it ap- "peared to some officers that sufficient time was not allowed to give "these movements the desired effect, a circumstance tending to

"occasion a great and unnecessary loss of lives. We continued to
" advance in three columns; as we approached the enemy the
" utmost order was preserved, and the columns were increased and
" diminished with as much regularity as if we were at a review. The
" enemy appeared at the foot of the position outside the wood, but
" retired under cover as we advanced.

"The columns pushed on and drove the enemy before them to the
" second position; here the mountain passes were defended with
" great pertinacity. The 29th Regiment, who had to advance up a
" steep grass path in the centre of the position, suffered severely, and,
" after losing their colonel, the gallant Lake, and all but fifteen of
" their grenadier company, succeeded in obtaining a lodgment on the
" summit and dislodging their opponents. The French General,
" Laborde, was wounded and about six hundred of his division killed
" and wounded, while the British loss in killed, wounded, and prisoners
" was five hundred; two hundred and twenty* of whom belonged
" to the 29th Regiment.

"The fighting was over by 4 p.m. Sir A. Wellesley followed as far
" as Villa Verde, but hearing that General Anstruther was off the coast
" with reinforcements, he altered his route. The heat during this day
" was excessive. A white precipitate was found in some of the
" French soldiers' packs, and a report got about that the wells were
" poisoned; the precipitate was afterwards discovered to be used
" to destroy vermin.

"The army rested for the night some distance beyond the field of
" battle. The next day we marched to Lourinha; on the morning
" of the 19th Sir Arthur Wellesley took up his position at Vimiera, a
" pleasant village in a fine valley, watered by a small river called the
" Maceira, which empties itself into the sea about three miles away.
" Here Major-General Anstruther's reinforcements were landed,
" which brought up the strength of the army to sixteen thousand
" men.

---

* Losses of the Army, 17th August, 1808 :—4th Brigade, Brigadier-General Bowes, 32nd Foot :—One rank and file killed, and three rank and file wounded.— *London Gazette*, 3rd September, 1808.

"The short queues worn by both officers and men were cropped
"on the field this day, in obedience to orders that had arrived from
"England, much to everyone's delight.

"On the 20th, Sir Harry Burrard arrived in the offing, and before
"night he came into the Maceira roads.

"Marshal Junot now made all preparations to advance towards
"Vimiera.

"The greater part of our infantry were posted on the highland on
"the left of the river. The village of Vimiera was occupied by
"cavalry, artillery, and commissariat. Major-General Bowes' brigade
"—6th and 32nd regiments—were posted in the rear of the village,
"on a sugar-loaf hill. The riflemen and the 50th Regiment, under
"General Fane, occupied the right of a table-land before Vimiera;
"General Anstruther's brigade the left, on the extremity of which
"there was a church."

Battle of Vimiera.

On the morning of 21st August, about 8 o'clock, Junot's army was first observed advancing along the road from Torres Vedras to Lourinha. The action commenced shortly afterwards. The French had fourteen thousand men and twenty-three field pieces; the British were stronger in infantry, but had fewer guns. The French made simultaneous attacks on several points, but were held in check and then driven back at all points. Junot, however, managed to draw off the remnant of his force in fair order, owing to the British being very weak in cavalry. General Breunier was among the prisoners; thirteen guns and twenty ammunition waggons were taken. Sir Harry Burrard, who had landed, was in the field, but honourably refused to take the command. Upon the final defeat of the French, Sir Arthur Wellesley urged the necessity of following up the advantage and moving with the utmost celerity on Torres Vedras; but in vain.

The officer quoted before also relates that "during the attack
"on our left, the 71st were ordered to oppose the enemy with the
"point of the bayonet. The pipers of the regiment in the advance to
"the charge struck up a national Scottish air, as is generally their
"custom, and in the middle of it one of them, a highlander, named

"George Clerk, received a severe wound in the groin, which brought
"him to the ground; but he supported himself in a sitting posture,
"exclaiming with apparent indifference, 'The deil take ye, if ye hae
"'disabled me frae following, ye winna keep me frae blawing for 'em,'
"and he continued to play and encourage his comrades untill the
"enemy fled. This gallant soldier recovered from his wound, and
"was promoted to the rank of sergeant and pipe-major by Colonel
"Pack."

Sir Harry Burrard, who opposed Wellesley's suggestion of following the French up, then retired unmolested, and the army waited at Vimiera. On the 22nd, Sir Hew Dalrymple arrived from Gibraltar, and took command of the army, making the third change within a few days. On the evening of this day, General Kellerman was sent in by Junot with a flag of truce, which ended in the British general agreeing to an armistice, as Junot was disposed to evacuate the kingdom of Portugal on honourable conditions; and now, to use the expression of Sir Arthur Wellesley, it seemed that "all we had to do was to prepare "to shoot red-legged partridges." The Convention of Cintra, as it was called, received scant consideration in England, and the generals who were concerned in it were ordered home. In the meantime the French at Lisbon embarked in three divisions, mutually protecting one another; the British protecting the rear one. Considerable difficulty was experienced, as any stragglers were immediately stilettoed by the enraged mob, and English officers were compelled to take any Frenchmen who were alone under their protection, and so saved the lives of several.

An officer states as follows: "The inhabitants of Devonshire were
"so incensed by the Convention of Cintra that they seem to have
"forgotten Roleia and Vimiera, and consequently received Sir Arthur
"Wellesley with every mark of disapprobation; indeed, hissings and
"hootings greeted him at every town and village of that county; but
"the people of England should have considered that, had he been
"left to follow up his victories, there would have been no necessity,
"in the opinion of any person, for such a convention, nor for any-
"thing more, very probably, than the fixing of the hour on which the
"troops of Junot should lay down their arms."

On being appointed to the supreme command of the British army in Spain, Sir John Moore set to work to make preparations for a general advance on Madrid, but, finding that there were no magazines or stores ready, he had to considerably modify his plans and send the army up by different routes, with orders to concentrate near Salamanca. He himself left Lisbon soon afterwards, and joined them in November, 1808. A considerable reinforcement had arrived from England, consisting of ten thousand men, under Sir David Baird, and these, together with the army distributed about in the North of Spain, brought his forces up to nearly thirty thousand. In the meantime Mr. Stuart, the British *chargé d'affaires* at Madrid, had been superseded, as he was not sufficiently pliable in the hands of the Home Government, and Mr. Frere was appointed his successor. He was given the superior rank of Minister Plenipotentiary. To his want of judgment and blindness to the character of the Spanish ministers may be traced most of the disasters which followed in quick succession. Fortunately, Sir John Moore was not a man to be influenced by those who were not qualified to give advice, and by a man who had unwittingly become the tool of the Spanish Juntor, who were prepared to sell their country to the highest bidder. In spite of all their promises and oaths, expressed both verbally and in public documents, backed up by the assurances of Mr. Frere, Sir John found, after he had pushed one division of his army, under Hope, with the object of drawing off the French from the Spanish armies as far as Madrid, that the feeling was far more in favour of the French, to whom these patriots were prepared to open the gates of Madrid and welcome them with open arms ; and moreover that there was very strong evidence of a compact having been made with the French whereby the English army was to have been sacrificed. Buonaparte's one object was to humiliate the British force, and with an eagle swoop he entered Spain at the head of fifty thousand trained soldiers, with the object of catching the British army in a *cul-de-sac* and cutting off their retreat, either back into Portugal or to the north coast of Spain. Fortunately, Sir John had penetrated the designs of the French Emperor, and, in spite of further assurances from the Spanish, again backed up by the British Minister, who ignored the fact that Madrid had fallen

F

into the hands of the French, he made a retrograde movement towards his base. Unfortunately, in the retreat discipline got slack, and many scenes of disorder occurred, which called forth the bitterest censure from the gallant old chief, and not until he had determined to make a stand and drive back his relentless enemies was he able to recall men to their sense of duty, But the effect was magical; discipline was restored at once, and the army made a gallant fight, covering the embarkation and preventing their enemies from disturbing them, except with cannon at long range. But we must not anticipate.

Sir John Moore having assumed command of the troops, preparations were commenced for an advance into Spain. The troops were divided into the following divisions and brigades by a General Order, dated Lisbon, 8th October, 1808:

Lieutenant - General Mackenzie Fraser's division	Major-General Lord W. Bentick—4th, 28th, 42nd, and 60th (five companies) regiments.
	Major-General W. C. Beresford—9th, 2nd battalion 43rd, and 52nd regiments.
Lieutenant-General Sir J. Hope's division	Brigadier-General Catlin Crauford—36th, 71st, 92nd, and 2nd battalion 60th (five companies) regiments.
	Brigadier-General W. P. Acland—2nd and 6th regiments.
	Major-General R. Hill—5th, 32nd, and 91st regiments.
	Brigadier-General H. Fraser—38th, 79th, and 2nd battalion 95th (four companies) regiments.
Major-General the Hon. Edward Paget's division	Brigadier-General Anstruther—20th, 1st battalion 52nd, and 1st battalion 95th regiments.
	Major-General C. Baron Alten—1st and 2nd Light Infantry (King's German Legion).

CAVALRY.

Major-General the Hon. C. Steward's division.	3rd and 18th Hussars (King's German Legion).

Sir John Moore commenced his march from Lisbon towards the Spanish frontier on 26th October. Passing through Portugal by rapid marches, the troops accomplished a distance of two hundred English miles in a very short time, and were speedily engaged in operations in Spain.

On 1st December, 1808, a redistribution was made, and Major-General Rowland Hill's brigade consisted of the 2nd Queen's, and the 5th and 32nd regiments.

The Spaniards, under Cuesta, Blake, and Palafox, had been routed at all points, and as the French, in overwhelming numbers, were moving on Madrid, Sir John Moore made preparations for a retreat into Portugal, by way of Ciudad Rodrigo.

It was reported to him, however, that Madrid was disposed to hold out, and he therefore determined to effect a junction with Sir David Baird, who had landed at Vigo with reinforcements, so as to make a diversion in favour of Madrid by attacking Soult on the Carrion. This junction was effected at Mayorga on 20th December. A redistribution of brigades then took place, in which the 32nd, with the 1st, 2nd, 5th, and 14th regiments were brigaded under Major-General Rowland Hill, in Lieutenant-General Hope's division.

On 21st December the British forces—twenty-nine thousand strong—had their head-quarters at Toro ; and on the 23rd, Moore advanced with his whole army. The cavalry had already met that of the enemy, and the infantry were within two hours' march of their opponents when an intercepted letter communicated the intelligence that Napoleon had entered Madrid—in person—three weeks before, and was then in full march towards Salamanca and Benevente. This rendered a retreat through Portugal impracticable, and it was decided to retire through Galicia to Vigo or Corunna. The several divisions were accordingly put in motion towards the Esla, the greater portion crossing by the bridge of Benevente on 26th December. Here the British cavalry, under Lord Paget (afterwards Marquis of Anglesey), after a brief halt, had an affair with some of the imperial guard which had forded the Esla under General Le Fevre, who was taken prisoner with several of his men. In the depth of winter, in the heart of a bare and desolate country, buried in snow or deluged with heavy rains, without shelter, uncertain of their supplies and destitute of fuel, the troops hurried on, by long and toilsome marches; baggage, ammunition, stores, and even money (£25,000 was thrown over the side of a mountain) being destroyed to prevent it falling into the enemy's hands.

1809.
Battle of Corunna.

On 5th January, 1809, the army reached Lugo, and bivouacked in order of battle, resuming its march on the night of the 9th, and reached Corunna—*via* Bentanzos*—on the 11th, after having traversed a distance of two hundred and fifty miles under difficulties and privations rarely exceeded. At Corunna a delay ensued, owing to the transports not being ready, but by the 16th the sick and what remained of the baggage had already been embarked, when the French began to move down from the heights, about 2 p.m., and a sanguinary battle ensued, the brunt of which fell on Lord W. Bentick's brigade. In the end the French were repulsed, and the British were allowed to commence embarking next day without molestation, although, later, some guns on the heights of St. Lucia— in the words of an eye-witness—" began to knock the dust out of the " sides of the old transports, so that they were glad to cut and run;" and the business ended in hurry and some confusion.

The 32nd, with General Hill's brigade, were this day on the British left, and lost two hundred and fifty non-commissioned officers and men.†

Sir John Hope, who succeeded to the command on the death of the gallant Sir John Moore, writes, in his despatch announcing the victory :‡

" The enemy not having rendered the attack on the left a serious " one, did not afford the troops stationed in that quarter an opportu-

---

* In the march from Lugo to Bentanzos the loss of the army was greater than in the whole of the previous part of the expedition.—Clinton, *The War in the Peninsula*, p. 70.

† Strange to say, the returns of killed and wounded were never, I believe, published.

‡ *London Gazette.*

" nity of displaying that gallantry which must have made him repent " the attempt.

" The principal and advanced parts of the line, under Major-" Generals Hill, Leith, and Catlin Crauford, conducted themselves " with great resolution, and were ably supported by the officers " commanding these brigades and by the troops of which they were " composed.

" It is particularly incumbent on the lieutenant-general to notice " the vigorous attack made by the 2nd battalion of the 14th Regiment, " under Colonel Nicolls, which drove the enemy out of the village on " the left, of which he had possessed himself."

The 32nd Regiment was principally employed during the retreat in the arduous duty of escorting the ammunition and stores of the army, suffering great loss and misery by the unavoidable circumstances attending that retreat.

After the final action at Corunna, the 32nd embarked, and in a very sickly state returned to England with the rest of the army, where it arrived about the 24th June, 1809.

Corunna is a weakly fortified town on the south-east of an irregularly shaped peninsula. The town is commanded by heights, which approach close to the walls on the south, extending from Mero, at El Burgo, and would have been the best position to occupy: but such an extended line was more than Moore would attempt with his diminished army. The position was occupied by the French, under Soult, and commanded the whole front. Some of Moore's generals advocated negotiations, to admit of the troops embarking, but Moore would not hear of it, as no defeat had been sustained. Moore hoped to be able to embark his army without molestation, but on the afternoon of the 16th January the French were observed to be in motion, and the British infantry—fourteen thousand five hundred strong, with forty of the 15th Hussars—proceeded to take up their allotted positions. Moore's line extended along the range between the villages of Elvina and Airis. Nine six-pounders—the only guns which had not been embarked—were posted on advantageous points, under Colonel Hardinge. The centre of attack was the village of Elvina, and it was during the advance of the 42nd to take it, that Sir John Moore received his death wound from a cannon ball.

The following extracts from the diary of Captain Evelegh, Royal Horse Artillery, quoted at length in "*Corunna to Sevastopol*," by Colonel Whinyates, will be read with interest:—

"Wednesday, 4th Jan., 1809.—At 7 marched for Nogales. This was a "march over an immense snow mountain, with ruts cut into the snow ice "two feet deep, and large holes so that the horses could scarce move. The "road strewed and blocked up with ordnance carriages and others of every "description; numbers of dead horses, men, women, and children frozen "to death.

"Monday, 16th Jan.—Began to embark. About 3 p.m. the enemy being "reinforced made an attack upon our outposts which soon became general "with all the troops on shore. The fire from the Artillery on both sides "and musketry was very heavy and incessant until dark, when the enemy "retired to his original position. The 4th, 5th, 14th, 32nd, 43rd, 50th, "51st, and 95th Regts were engaged (together) with Truscott's and Wall's "Brigades R.A. The picket was commanded by Colonel Napier, who was "killed. Sir David Baird wounded. Sir John Moore shot in the shoulder, "and died on the road to Corunna.

"Tuesday, 17th January.—A strong picket was left out during the night, "and all the remaining troops retired into the town after dark, and about "12 o'clock began embarking, which continued going on through the "night, with some confusion, as it was very dark, and the boats were "running foul, and very few found the intended ships. .... This morning, "at day-break, the picket came in, and were soon followed very near to "the town by the French, who were popping at them great part of the way. "About half-past 12 they opened several guns upon us, and kept up a "smart fire of shot and shell, to the great annoyance of the inner part of "the Fleet, about eighty or ninety sail crowded together as thick as "possibly and full of troops. Every ship now went to work getting up "anchor, or cutting cable and setting sail, to make an attempt at least to "get away. Numbers of boats were away from their ships fetching more "of the army off, and rowing about between the ships. The shot and shell "now fell very thick among them, the ships all in motion and the confusion "great. Many ran foul, and many upon rocks. The wind, however, "became more moderate, and Providence made it change two points in "our favour, which enabled us and many others to weather Castle Point, "and we were happy in getting soon out of their reach, with only our "rigging damaged and the loss of two anchors.

"Wednesday, 18th Jan.—Off and on all the morning waiting to collect "the Fleet.... many of the transport got out during the night, and the "Men-of-War got hold of the rest of the Army..... About 4 o'clock the "whole fleet made sail for Old England, going right before the wind.

"Monday, 23rd January.—At 12 a frigate signalled us into Plymouth. "Anchored about 5 o'clock p.m."

The thanks of both Houses of Parliament were voted to the Army "for its distinguished discipline, firmness, and valour in the battle "of Corunna."

For the services of the regiment in this campaign, Lieutenant-Colonel Hinde received two gold medals—one for Roleia and Vimiera, and one for Corunna.

The regiment was assembled at Horsham, where it was, by the exertion of Lieutenant-Colonel Hinde, soon re-equipped—having received no supply of equipment since 1807—and rendered fit for service, its strength being six hundred and eighty rank and file.*

Extract from MSS. in the Royal United Service Institution:—

Establishment 1st April, 1809, previous to militia volunteering	616
Volunteered from English militia	26
Volunteered from Irish militia	1
In Portugal	90
Total, 10th May, 1809 ...	734
Left in Spain	132
Grand Total ...	866

Captain Ross-Lewin relates:—"In July, 1809, a most extensive "armament was collected in the Downs. The army consisted of

---

* In the returns of troops under orders for active service in the Walcheren Expedition, rendered to Parliament by the adjutant-general, the strength of the 1st battalion 32nd Regiment is given at five hundred and seventy-nine officers and men.—Walter Grey, *Walcheren Expedition.*

"upwards of forty thousand men, and the fleet of thirty-nine sail of
"the line and thirty-six frigates, besides numerous gunboats, bomb
"vessels, and other small craft. The latter was commanded by Lord
"Gardner, and the former by the Earl of Chatham, but no more like
"his father than I to Hercules. My regiment (32nd) formed a
"portion of the land force. The destination of the expedition was at
"first kept a profound secret, and an embargo was laid on the
"shipping in all the ports of Great Britain and Ireland, to continue
"until we should sail. The troops were embarked on board the
"ships of war as well as the transports. . . . each seventy-four took
"a regiment. The object of this expedition was two-fold; it was only
"at the moment of sailing that it was said that a diversion in favour of
"our Allies and an attack on the French fleet, near Antwerp, was
"meditated. We sailed from the Downs on the 28th July, and were
"off the Dutch coast in the morning, nearing the island of Walcheren.
"The fleet soon came to anchor, and immediately preparations were
"made for our landing, which was effected without opposition at a
"point about ten miles distant from Flushing. That place was
"strongly fortified and garrisoned by French troops.

"A battery which had commenced firing on the shipping quickly
"fell into our hands, followed the next day by the town of Ter Veere,
"which lies on the north-eastern part of the island. All the enemy's
"posts outside Flushing were also driven in, and we entered Middle-
"bury—the capital of Walcheren, and an open town—without opposi-
"sition, having first promised to respect property.

"A strong division of sailors was landed when we appeared before
"Flushing, to assist in the erection of batteries. Their station was
"on the extreme right. They threw up a considerable work, armed
"with twenty-four pounders, and their fire from it soon became so
"incessant as to excite general astonishment. . . .

"'The picquets continued to skirmish with little intermission. The
"32nd Regiment was much engaged, and behaved with distinguished
"spirit. Sir Eyre Coote expressed his high approbation of the con-
"duct of the corps, and said that '*when the 32nd was on the advanced
"posts, he could sleep sound.*' At this time the French understood
"irregular firing much better than our men; the file did not separate;

" one fired at random, knowing that a British soldier would pop up
" his head to see from what point the shot proceeded, and the other,
" being at the ' present,' was ready to fire on the first person that
" should show himself. We lost several men by this stratagem. On
" one occasion I dined with Major Johnson, 32nd regiment, and one
" or two other officers, behind some hurdles on the advanced posts.
" His servant, who had prepared the dinner, said he would take a
" peep at the French, who were within a few yards, and have a crack
" at them. He must have exposed himself, for in a few minutes we
" discovered he had been shot through the heart; and, as so many
" shots came about our heads when we tried to bury the poor fellow
" near where he had been slain, we brought him behind our shelter
" and there buried him. One morning, before a part of the line of
" advanced posts had been relieved, the old picquets belonging to it,
" by some mistake, moved off, and our vigilant and active enemy had
" nearly profited by this occurrence, to our annoyance. The 32nd
" Regiment was to take the outpost duty there on that day, under
" the command of Major Johnson. This officer was proceeding to
" the place of his destination by the usual, but circuitous, route,
" when he observed that the picquets had quitted their ground and
" that the enemy might make a sudden attempt to occupy it. Accord-
" ingly, seeing that there was no time to be lost, he procured some
" planks in an adjoining house, passed his men by means of them
" over a deep ditch, and thus was enabled to take a shorter way and
" reach the important point before the French. They were, however,
" in motion and creeping on, when they were checked by a sharp
" fire, which they returned, though finally compelled to fall back to
" their original station.

" On 7th August the garrison made a sortie. The greater part of
" them were drunk, and they were easily driven back. A laughable
" occurrence took place, in which our fat brevet major was concerned.
" He happened to be posted in an advanced position, and, having a
" quiet moment, took advantage of it to perform the operation of
" shaving behind a haystack. His wig was off, and only half his task
" accomplished, when a party of French sallied out and attacked his
" post. The alarm was given, and he rushed instantaneously from

" his toilet, just as he was, and razor in hand, to head his men. He
" soon repulsed his assailants, but, had the fortune of the fight gone
" against him and he been taken prisoner, his extraordinary figure,
" without coat, hat, or wig, his face half-covered with soap, and his
" hand armed with a razor instead of a sword, would, no doubt, have
" excited much merriment at his expense among his lively and
" sarcastic captors.

" On 10th August, General Monnet, who commanded in Flushing,
" ordered the banks to be cut and the sluices opened, inundating the
" surrounding country. A violent thunderstorm broke out at the same
" time, causing great damage. On the 13th the bombardment com-
" menced, and the town was set on fire in several places. Lord
" Gardner, in the *Blake,* sailed up the river, followed by the other line-
" of-battle ships. Each as they passed, in succession, fired a broad-
" side. The facing of the parapet being of cut stone, the splinters
" flew about to such a degree that the French artillerymen deserted
" their guns. The place eventually capitulated. The garrison defiled
" out before Lord Chatham the following day, the unfortunate French
" troops being kept seven hours under arms in very hot weather. They
" were five thousand strong, and a large proportion of Irishmen among
" them."

After the fall of Flushing, part of the army proceeded to South Beveland, and some regiments embarked and sailed up the Scheldt towards Antwerp, the 32nd Regiment being amongst the number. They anchored within ten miles of Antwerp, in sight of the French fleet. The French had in the meanwhile thrown forty thousand men of the National Guard into the Netherlands, under Bernadotte, and put Antwerp in a state of defence, Fort Lillo providing them with a strong garrison.

Heavy chains were thrown across the river, and the French ships of war were so moored that they could concentrate their fire on certain points and sweep the entire channel. Strong batteries were erected on the banks of the river, and the surrounding country was laid under water.

Under these circumstances, Lords Chatham and Gardner thought that any attempt on Antwerp would be unsuccessful, and retired; at the same time, it was a bitter pill for the fleet and army to be within reach of such a noble prize and to have lost it through what was believed at the time, the supineness and incapacity of the commanders.

During the whole of the operations against Flushing, the regiment was actively employed, and on the surrender of that fortress was transferred to Brigadier-General Ackland's brigade, and proceeded up Scheldt, where it remained on board the transports, opposite Fort Batz, in South Beveland, until further operations were discontinued.

The losses the regiment sustained during the Walcheren expedition, from the landing, 30th July to 1st August, were: one sergeant and one rank and file killed, and two sergeants and five rank and file wounded; and from the 2nd to 6th August, two rank and file killed and fifteen rank and file wounded.

It was decided by the authorities to leave a force of twenty-one regiments in Walcheren, under command of General Don. The 32nd was one of the regiments, and formed part of the garrison of Middleburg until the final evacuation on 9th December following.

The excessive mortality made the expedition a by-word. A military writer says: "The mortality was truly dreadful. The 23rd, 81st, and "91st Regiments were struck off duty on the 1st October, not having "a single man on that day out of hospital. An order to bury the dead "at night was given, with a view of concealing the frightful extent of "the daily ravages of the fever in our ranks. All the carpenters in "Middleburg were busily employed in making coffins for the British "troops. In a few weeks there were barely three thousand fit for "duty in the entire force. The Dutch physicians did not approve of "the treatment employed by our own medical men, and offered to "take charge of a hundred soldiers in hospital, and to allow any of "our medical men to select an equal number, in order to see which "treatment was the most successful, but the offer was rejected."

It now became evident that unless reinforcements were received the remnant of the force would be shut up in Flushing, as the French continued to move troops into Beveland. Orders were accordingly given for their return, which was effected—after blowing up the defences—by 20th December, 1809.

The disastrous consequences of this ill-conducted expedition created considerable discontent at home, and certainly with perfect justice; for, in addition to our failure before Antwerp, the mortality that thinned our ranks could not have been equalled in the most sanguinary campaign, and the services of nearly half the men of whom the army in Walcheren consisted were lost for ever to the country. Lord Castlereagh and Mr. Canning themselves quarrelled on this unpleasant subject, and finally fought a duel, in which the latter was wounded.

The Depôt which had been formed at home was augmented considerably, with a view of supplying the great losses the regiment had sustained in Walcheren. The following is from a newspaper account of the period :

"1809.

" The Jubilee of George III. was kept on the 25th October, 1809, and "at Horsham was celebrated 'in the most joyous, loyal, and benevolent "manner.' The day was ushered in by the ringing of bells, which con-"tinued till noon, when the garrison, consisting of the 51st Regiment, with "part of the 23rd and 32nd, fired a *feu de joie* on Den hill, which was "returned by the Volunteers in the town ; after which the regiments of the "garrison marched to the Market-square, and gave three hearty cheers, in "which they were joined by the inhabitants with the greatest enthusiasm. "(Jubilee Year of George III., 1809)."

Return of corps at Walcheren, 7th September, 1809 (32nd Regiment) :

Field Officers	3	
Captains	7	
Subalterns	21	
Staff	4	
	—	35
Sergeants—Present fit for duty	34	
,, Sick	6	
	—	40
Drummers—Present fit for duty	11	
,, Sick	9	
	—	20
Rank and File—Present fit for duty	366	
,, Sick	192	
	—	558

The 32nd Regiment was brigaded with the 2nd Queen's and 76th, under Brigadier-General Ackland.

1810.

The 32nd Regiment mustered little more than two hundred men on embarking. The fact of its having landed one of the weakest and returned one of the strongest is, perhaps, worthy of remark.

The regiment landed at Portsmouth and marched to Hailsham, where it arrived in the middle of January, 1810, and received a draft from the 2nd battalion at Cork.

The effects of the unhealthy climate of Walcheren, however, rendered a change of air necessary for the re-establishment of the health of the regiment, and it was ordered, in July, to Bexhill, and on the 12th August took part in a grand review of thirteen thousand men on Brighton Down, before the Prince of Wales, all the royal dukes, and a brilliant staff. There appears to have been some misunderstanding, in consequence of the numerous nobles present who wore stars, and foreign officers in uniform at this review; and several officers in marching past saluted different persons before they had come near the prince. The staff galloped about, exclaiming to the blunderers—
" Gentlemen, you are saluting the wrong person, the prince is farther
" on, dressed in the uniform of the 10th Dragoons."

The 32nd Regiment was moved to Bexhill, into Nut barracks, brigaded with the 1st and 2nd light battalions King's German Legion, from whom most valuable instruction was obtained in outpost duties, in which the English troops were then proverbially deficient. Lieutenant-Colonel Hinde, who commanded the first battalion at this time, paid much attention to light infantry duties—and had commanded the Provisional Light Infantry battalion in Dublin in 1803. The air of Bexhill not producing the desired effect, the regiment was ordered to Guernsey, arriving there 3rd September, and remaining in that island until June the following year, (1811) during which period the health of the men was re-established, the equipment completed, and discipline improved. Recruiting parties were sent out, and some volunteers from the Militia joined, raising the strength up to six hundred men, notwithstanding the number invalided from the effects of the Walcheren fever.

1811.

The regiment had been for some time under orders to proceed to the Peninsula a second time, and at length embarked on 24th June. On its arrival it disembarked, and occupied quarters in the castle of Lisbon; while there a draft from the 2nd battalion, consisting of three hundred men, joined under the command of Captain Portley.

" On 19th July the regiment, being provided with field equipment,
" embarked on board boats in the Tagus, and proceeded to Villada,
" about two leagues from Santarem; landed, and marched to join
" Brigadier-General Burns' brigade, in the 6th division, at Nave-d'-Aver
" in the August following.

" Lord Wellington's head-quarters were at Fuente Guinaldo on 10th
" August. On 17th August we reached the miserable village of
" Barquilla, in Spain, distant four leagues from Ciudad Rodrigo, and
" thence moved to Villa de Porco.

" The British and Portuguese army, with the exception of Sir
" Rowland Hill's corps of fourteen thousand men, then in the Alentejo,
" went into cantonments on the line of the Agueda. The infantry
" were about thirty-eight thousand strong, and cavalry only four
" thousand.

" The food served out here was of the coarsest, consisting of
" over-driven beasts and ship's biscuit. One officer died from absolute
" want of nourishment, and many others suffered terribly, more
" especially as the want of money began to be felt.

" The next move of the 6th division was to Gallegos and its vicinity,
" moving subsequently more to the right.

" While we were thinking of laying siege to Ciudad Rodrigo, the
"force in Spain was considerably augmented by the arrival of
" reinforcements from France, a great part of which consisted of
" troops long inured to war."*

An action took place near Guinaldo on 24th September, but the

---

* Ross-Lewin, *Life of a Soldier.*

regiment, with the 6th division, were not engaged. On 29th August the 3rd division crossed the Coa and went into cantonments, leaving three divisions to watch Ciudad Rodrigo; the 32nd Regiment occupied Chiras. On 24th October the army advanced; the 32nd Regiment marched to Galligos, but when it reached Fuentes d'Onor Captain Ross-Lewin was sent back to Almeida with a working party, who remained there five days, returning to Chiras.

The 5th and 6th divisions moved towards the Douro and Mondego, leaving Chiras on 2nd December.

The transport of the army was considerably improved here by Lord Wellington, who had ordered six hundred waggons to be made. After three long marches the regiment reached Musquetilla, a very small village, which scarcely afforded room for it.

1812.

The army was now paid up to 24th October, 1811, and the messing considerably improved throughout. The sick list rapidly decreased in consequence; all the troops, including the 32nd Regiment, were employed in making fascines and gabions, with a view to the siege of Rodrigo, which commenced on 14th January, 1812; different detached points having been seized during the night of the 8th; and on the 19th, Ciudad Rodrigo fell. Marmont, who was advancing with a force of sixty thousand men for the relief of Rodrigo, believing he had ample time, was incredible, and had to remain inactive in the neighbourhood of Salamanca. The 6th division remained in their cantonments until 1st February, when they fell back; the 32nd Regiment marched to Nave d'Aver, reaching Marialva, which stands on the summit of a high craggy mountain, on 21st January; marched to Alentigo, Guarda, and Alpedrinja, and, on the 29th, to Castello Branco, thence to Villa Velha, crossing the Tagus, ascending the river on the right bank, and, after a fourteen days' march in a lovely country, entered Estremos, a large and handsome town, and remained there a week to recruit their strength, as men and horses were very jaded by the length of the march.

On 15th March the 32nd Regiment camped at Elvas, where every preparation for the siege of Badajoz had been made. On the morning of 16th March, General Graham,* with the 1st, 6th, and 7th divisions and the cavalry brigade, crossed the bridge of pontoons two miles below Badajoz, and reached Santa Martha under incessant rain, the men having to pass the inclement night without cover. Next day the divisions passed through Albuera and the position occupied by the allied armies two years previously (16th May, 1810); the bones of men and horses testifying to the struggle which took place there.

The day that the troops marched from Elvas, Marshal Beresford also crossed the Guadiana, with the light, 3rd and 4th divisions, about twelve thousand men, and immediately invested Badajoz. The 32nd Regiment moved with the 6th and 7th divisions to cover this force and to watch Soult's army.

On 25th March the 6th division marched to Llerena, distant some forty-two miles, with the object of surprising about two thousand of the enemy; but after a long and tedious march found the enemy had gone. Pursuing for two days as far as Usagre, but not overtaking them, the division fell back on Almandralejo, which was reached 4th April.

In the meantime Badajoz had fallen amid much bloodshed. On 16th April the 6th division went to Portalegre, thence to Castello Branco, returning to Escaldos de Cima, two leagues to the northwards.

The 32nd Regiment was very sickly here and did not muster half its number on parade. From Escaldos de Cima the regiment recrossed the Tagus to Alentejo, occupying Castello de Vido for a week, thence to Azume, where the regiment was inspected by General Clinton, and received a draft of one hundred and forty men from the 2nd battalion. On 12th May marched to Aronches, halting for a week, and then to La Palla, Castel de Vido, and Povo, reaching Castello Branco on 3rd June.

---

* Afterwards Lord Lyndock.

Battle of Salamanca.

The neighbourhood of Salamanca was reached on 17th June, 1812. At 8 o'clock that evening the 32nd Regiment sent the first working party, under Captain Ross-Lewin, to break ground before the convent of San Vincente, and they managed to obtain cover without much loss although the French had destroyed several fine Spanish buildings to give a more extensive range to their fire.

It was soon found that the newly-constructed earthworks were ill-placed, the ground being too low and the men insufficiently covered. Several valuable lives were lost in consequence. On the 23rd a battery on higher ground was completed and armed, but the fire from it appears to have been ineffective. Lord Wellington visited this work, and while viewing the enemy's position from it was warned of the danger of remaining where he was, as several four-pounder round shot had previously dropped there. He had only moved off a few minutes when a shot fell which would, but for this timely warning, have certainly deprived the army of its able commander.

On the evening of that day a flag of truce was sent out by the besieged, but the proposals made were rejected, and at 8 o'clock the firing recommenced. It was then determined to storm the enemy's works. The storming parties consisted of the light companies of the 2nd, 32nd, and 36th regiments, under the command of Lieutenant-Colonel Hinde,* and those of the other brigade under Lieutenant-Colonel Bingham, 53rd regiment. Preceded by twenty men carrying ladders, the assaulting party, led on by Major-General Bowes, who had the chief command, commenced their advance. The instant they showed themselves they were received with a withering fire. In a few minutes more than half of the assailants were placed *hors de combat*, and the remainder had to retire. Major-General Bowes was also killed. "At the siege of the forts of St. Vincente, "St. Cajetano, and La Mercet, from 18th to 24th June, 1812, the "32nd lost ten rank and file killed, and two sergeants and twenty-six

---

* 32nd Regiment.

"rank and file wounded. For their conduct on these occasions the "6th division received the thanks of the commander of the forces, in "General Orders, dated Salamanca, 28th June, 1812."

An attempt to set fire to one of the fortified convents was successfully carried out on the 26th. At the same time the fire from the recently completed battery on the right broke down some of the enemy's palisades. Ensign Fitzgerald, of the 32nd, was killed by a fragment of a shell.

On the morning of the 27th, the fire from our batteries having proved very destructive, the French commandant requested a cessation of firing for three hours, in order to make terms, but his request was refused, and directions given for storming. Ensign Newton (32nd) led the forlorn hope. The assault was completely successful. The fort, in which a breach had been made, was quickly carried, and the whole French garrison surrendered at discretion, after having kept an entire division at bay for ten days. The forts were now blown up by victorious troops; all the guns and a considerable supply of clothing fell into the hands of the English. The 6th division, which had lost nearly five hundred, killed and wounded, then marched to join the remainder of the army.

On the 29th, Lord Wellington moved from Salamanca towards the Douro, which is about eleven leagues distant. The enemy fell back as Wellington advanced. On 15th July the allied army moved to the left. The main body moved to Villa Pena, six leagues from Salamanca. On the 17th the whole French army crossed the Douro, and by a forced march nearly succeeded in cutting off the 4th and light divisions.

There was a good deal of skirmishing in the front of Villa Pena, which was much to our advantage. On the 20th, Marshal Marmont fell back, after having failed to relieve Salamanca, behind the Douro, while the Allies took up a position on the opposite bank and enjoyed a fortnight's rest. A series of manœuvres followed, which ended by the contending armies finding themselves face to face on the Tormes, on 23rd July, when the 6th division crossed and bivouacked on its banks.

"When night came on a terrific thunderstorm, accompanied with

"heavy rain, broke over us," writes an officer;* "peal upon peal
"succeeded in increasing vehemence; the electric fluid literally
"hissed through the air, and such was the vividness of the lightning
"that I was deprived of sight for some moments. The horses of the
"5th Dragoon Guards became dreadfully frightened, broke from their
"picquets, and ran over the men who were stretched on the ground,
"inflicting severe injuries on several of them. It was, indeed, as wild
"and fearful a night as ever preceded a memorable day of strife
"and slaughter; no sound was heard but the heavy splash of the
"incessant rain, the trampling of the terrified horses, and the shouts
"and groans of the men, save when they were all confounded in the
"stunning reverberations of the aërial artillery, which at brief intervals
"poured forth an awful note of warning for the bloody work of the
"morrow.

"At daybreak on Wednesday, 22nd July, the troops began to
"move into their positions, the British left resting on the Tormes,
"their right on the lesser of two rocky eminences known as the
"Arapiles. Marmont occupied a mountainous ridge in front, his right
"resting on the greater Arapiles. The chief part of the day was
"spent in manœuvring; Marmont, whose chief object seemed to be
"to turn our position and cut off our retreat, endeavouring to deceive
"the British commander; but he did not know his man. In this
"manœuvre the French general incautiously weakened his own line,
"and his antagonist was too much on the alert not to profit by the
"blunder. The enemy began what was destined to be the serious
"business of the day by a heavy cannonade. At this time the 6th.
"division was halted in columns of companies. A light battalion of
"the King's German Legion marched by, and as the last section of
"this corps was passing an opening in the heights on their flank, the
"first shot that I saw take effect came through and killed five of
"them. The enemy next threw out a thick swarm of tirailleurs along
"his front and flank, and simultaneously extended his left, apparently
"with the view of cutting off our communication with Rodrigo. Our
"1st and light divisions were then on the extreme left, the 4th and

---

* Major Ross-Lewin.

"5th in rear of the Arapiles, and the 6th and 7th in reserve; the "3rd division and cavalry occupied the right. The enemy began an "attack upon the village of Arapiles, but they could not dislodge the "Guards, who held it. It was now that Lord Wellington saw that the "favourable moment had arrived, and he rapidly made dispositions "for the onset. General Pakenham was directed to turn the "enemy's left with the 3rd division, supported by artillery and "Portuguese horse.

"Upon their ascending the heights a large body of cavalry came "on to charge them, but the 5th Foot being thrown into a good "position, poured in such a well-directed volley that the dragoons "retired in confusion. The division then pressed on, and everywhere "outflanking the enemy drove them from point to point, making a "great number of prisoners. Sir Stapleton Cotton advanced with our "heavy cavalry, and in a brilliant charge cut to pieces a brigade of "infantry, but the arm to which he belonged suffered a severe loss "here by the death of General Le Marchant, who was killed by a "musket ball. The 4th and 5th divisions, supported by the 6th and "7th, moved against the enemy in front nearly at the same time, and "General Pack, with a Portuguese brigade, against the greater "Arapiles. The latter officer failed in all his attempts to dislodge his "opponents from this steep and rugged hill, and his men suffered "severely. On the retreat of this brigade, the enemy pushed forward "a large body of infantry—attacking the 4th division, who then were "gaining ground, with great spirit—and caused some confusion. "General Cole was wounded in the conflict. But the 5th division came "up, and, by a judicious movement under the direction of Marshal "Beresford, retrieved the fortune of the fight at this point, and the "enemy, taken in flank, were compelled to retreat. Our success on "the left and centre of the French was completed by the 6th division, "who succeeded in carrying the greater Arapiles. As we advanced, "we marched over a brigade that was lying on the ground.*

---

* Lieutenant Smith, of the 11th Regiment which, with the 53rd and 61st, formed the other leading brigade of the 6th division, records: "The advance was "so rapid, that very many of a body of riflemen, more numerous than the British,

"By this time the loss sustained by the enemy was considerable. One of their colonels lay immediately in front of the colours of the 32nd Regiment; he was badly wounded, and begged hard to be removed from the field, and Colonel Wood humanely directed the drummers to take care of him.

"Our work was not finished yet. Notwithstanding his discomfort at all other points the enemy's right was still unbroken, and was quickly reinforced by the beaten battalions. Marmont was wounded and obliged to quit the field, but the command devolved upon General Clausel, who with equal firmness and ability rallied the fugitives, and, with the approach of evening in his favour, exerted himself to prevent our further success. His new position was well selected; both his flanks were protected by a numerous cavalry, and the face of the heights offered an unobstructed range for the formidable artillery that he had disposed along his front. Wellington was not long in preparing for the attack, but the hour, unfortunately for him, was very late. It was half past seven when the 6th division, under General Clinton, was ordered to advance a second time and attack the enemy's line in front, supported by the 3rd and 5th divisions.

"The ground over which we had to pass was a remarkably clear slope, like the glacis of a fortification, most favourable for the defensive fire of the enemy and disadvantageous to the assailants, but the division advanced towards the position with perfect steadiness and confidence. A craggy ridge, on which the French infantry was drawn up, rose so abruptly that they could fire four or five deep, but we had approached within two hundred yards of them before the fire of musketry began, which was by far the heaviest that I have ever witnessed, and was accompanied by constant dis-

---

"covering the retreat of the main body of the defeated army, not having time to get out of the way, threw themselves on the ground--as if dead--and were run over. It was not generally known that many of them fired at the backs of the advancing line; one, it is certain, drove his bayonet into the back of a grenadier of the 11th, and before he could withdraw it, was cut down by Brigade-Major Cotton, who was following the brigade on foot, his horse having been killed."—Cannon, *Records of the 11th, North Devon Regiment.*

"charges of grape. An uninterrupted blaze was then maintained, so that the crest of the hill seemed to be one long streak of flame. Our men came down to the charging position and commenced firing from that level, at the same time keeping their touch to the right, so that the gaps opened by the enemy's fire were instantly filled up. At the very first volley that we received, about eighty men of the right wing of the 32nd fell to the rear in one group; the colonel immediately rode up to know the cause, and found they were all wounded. Previously to the advance of the 6th division, the light companies of the right brigade were formed on the right of the line, and as we moved on one of the enemy's Howitzers was captured by the light company of the 32nd Regiment. It had been discharged once, but, before the gunners could reload it, it was taken by a rush. The success of the attack was complete, for as soon as the 6th division got near enough they dashed forward with the bayonet, and, another portion of our troops acting on Clausel's right flank, his army was quickly driven from the position into the wood in their rear; but before this, night had come on, and to the convenient cover and darkness alone were the French, who fled in great disorder, indebted for the safety of their whole force.

"They retreated next morning through Alba de Tormes, followed by our cavalry, who came up with the rear guard and threw it into confusion. Three battalions of their infantry, being deserted by their cavalry, threw themselves into square near the village of La Serna. They were at once charged with great spirit and promptitude by the 1st and 2nd Regiments of heavy German horse, led on by Baron Bock, and broken. Many of their men were cut down, and about nine hundred prisoners taken. Three French generals were killed in the battle, and three more wounded, besides Marmont, who had to undergo amputation of one arm. Eleven pieces of cannon were taken, and brought into Salamanca the following day. It was a curious circumstance that the 32nd in this engagement recovered their big drum, which had been lost in the retreat to Corunna."

Extract from Lord Wellington's despatch to the Earl of Liverpool, dated 30th June, 1812:

" Major-General Clinton mentions, in strong terms of commendation,
"the conduct of the General officers, officers, and troops . . . particularly
"Colonel Hinde, of the 32nd Regiment . . . and Ensign Newton, of the
"32nd Regiment, who distinguished himself in the attack on the night of
"the 23rd instant, and volunteered to lead the advanced party in the attack
"of the 27th." *Wellington Despatches*, vol. ix., p. 260.

Heavy losses among the British were the price of the victory, of which the historian, Napier, has said that, " Remarkable as it was "in many points of view, it was not least so in this, that it was the " first decided Victory gained by the Allies in the Peninsula. In " former actions the French had been repulsed; here they were " driven headlong, as it were, before a mighty wind, without help " or stay, and the results were fearful."

The official returns show the loss in the 32nd Regiment to have been :—one lieutenant (Seymour), one ensign (Newton), one sergeant, and fourteen men, killed ; and two captains, five lieutenants, two ensigns, eight sergeants, and one hundred and three men, wounded.

It may be interesting here to give an extract from a contemporary newspaper :

" Ensign Newton, of the 32nd Regiment of Foot, who so eminently
" distinguished himself on the night of the 23rd June, 1812, in the attack
" of the forts of Salamanca, and who so gallantly volunteered his services
"to lead on the storming party on the 27th of the same month, is a
" Canadian by birth, son of an Irish gentleman, originally from the county
"of Wexford, who for many years held an important situation under the
" British Government in North America. Ensign Newton has from his
"youth been bred to arms. At the age of fifteen he obtained a commission
" in the Nova Scotia Fencibles, in which he served for upwards of eight
" years, and was a captain in said regiment some time before its reduction,
"which took place during the last short peace. About three years ago
" Mr. Newton came over to England, and, feeling an ardent desire again
" to enter the British Service, was, at the particular request of his Royal
" Highness the Duke of Kent, appointed to an ensigncy in the 32nd
" Regiment."

An extract from the bulletin contained in the *London Gazette Extraordinary*, of 16th August, 1812, gives the following interesting particulars :

"Despatch, dated 21st July, 1812.
"Names of officers killed, wounded, and missing, of the Allied Army, "under the command of His Excellency General the Earl of Wellington, "in the battle near Salamanca on the 22nd July, 1812.—32nd Regiment :
"Killed—Lieut. Seymour, Ensign Newton, 1 sergeant, 14 rank and file.
"Wounded—Captains Ross-Lewin, Toole (slightly); Lieuts. Greaves, "Eason (severely); Lieut. R. Robinson (slightly); Lieuts. Bowes, "Butterworth ; Ensign Newton (2nd) (severely) ; Ensign (Volun-
"teer) Blood* (slightly) ; 8 sergeants, and 103 rank and file.
"Missing—None."

NOTE.—It will be seen on comparison that the spelling of names differs in one or two cases in the *Gazette* and *Army List* (1812), and it is curious to note that there were two ensigns in the regiment of the same Christian and surname.

THOMAS PALMER.

An old veteran of the 32nd Regiment, Thomas Palmer, was born on the 30th November, 1789. In January, 1807, he enlisted into the 32nd Regiment, and in September of that year was present with his corps at the attack on Copenhagen. In 1808 and 1809 he served in Sir John Moore's army, and was present at Corunna. Then he served in the Walcheren expedition, and in August, 1809, was severely wounded at the siege of Flushing. He served again in the Peninsula during the years 1811 to 1814, inclusive ; was present at the siege and storming of Badajos, the battle of Salamanca, and the capture of Madrid. He was discharged from the army in 1814, at Kilmainham Hospital, Dublin, when he was twenty-

---

* Officers of militia were permitted to volunteer for service in line regiments, provided they would bring a certain number of militiamen with them.

five years old, on a pension of nine-pence a day, and his papers show that throughout his service he was "*a steady, good soldier.*" After leaving the army he learnt the trades of shoemaking and farming, and he practised these callings for many years, but on reaching the age of seventy he was obliged to give up all work. Although his service with the colours was less than eight years, he (in common with his comrades) experienced at times the most dreadful hardships and suffering, and had very many narrow escapes and some marvellous personal adventures. It has been calculated that since his enlistment in 1807, Palmer must have received in pay, pensions, grants, &c., the sum of £1,400 of public money; besides which, during the last three years Major Shanks, R.M.L.I., (who has taken the deepest interest in the old man's welfare, and through whose generous efforts the funeral was made a military one) has most kindly raised no less than £100 for his benefit, of which upwards of £14 was contributed by Palmer's old regiment and the depôt. He died at Weston-super-Mare, on 10th April, 1889. One officer (Lieutenant Chapman), one warrant officer, and two colour-sergeants, from Bodmin, attended his funeral.

A portion of the troops—including the 6th division—was left on the Douro, and Wellington, with the main body, then proceeded to Madrid.

Major Ross Lewin says: "Our wounded officers and men re-"covered very slowly, a circumstance attributable either to the "influence of the climate or the state of the blood, impoverished by "bad living."

The result of Wellington's advance to Madrid was not so advantageous as he had reason to expect, and nothing seemed to rouse the Spaniards to action. On 1st September he quitted Madrid with four divisions, and marched through Valladolid, in the direction of Burgos, a fortress of great strength and well garrisoned, and was joined by the Spanish Gallician army. Although unprovided with heavy artillery, Wellington determined to lay siege to that place. It was invested on the 20th by the 1st and 6th divisions and two Portuguese brigades, the rest of the army taking up an advanced position to cover the beseiged force.

FOURTH PERIOD.

Siege of Burgos—India, 1851.

1812-51.

AFTER the battle of Salamanca the British followed the broken fragments of the French army. The 6th division was however left on the Douro with some other troops, and Wellington, with the main body, proceeded to Madrid, making a triumphal entry into that city on 12th August, 1812. Returning from Madrid, he drove the French out of Valladolid, which had been evacuated by the British and occupied by the enemy, down the fertile valleys of the Pisuerga and Ailanjen, taking up a position covering Burgos, which was still held by a French garrison.

The Castle of Burgos, with its formidable outworks, enclosed a rugged hill commanding the city, which lay between that defence and the river, and contained a garrison of fourteen hundred French, with a numerous artillery, under General Dubretor, a bold and skilful soldier. The place was invested by the 1st and 6th British divisions, with two brigades of Portuguese, on 19th September, and Lord Wellington found it to be, in his own words, "the toughest job yet undertaken." A detached work, in a commanding situation, was carried by assault. Here batteries were erected, but Wellington had only three eighteen-pounders and five Howitzers. On the night of 22nd September an attempt to scale the outer wall failed, and two of the three eighteen-pounders were dismounted by the superior fire from the castle. The besiegers next tried the sap and the mine, but with a considerable loss of life on their part, and when a breach was effected in the first wall on the 29th, by the explosion of a mine, the troops directed to storm lost their way, and the garrison, in the space of a few hours, repaired the damage done.

On 4th October another breach was made, and a lodgment was effected by the assailants; but a sortie of the garrison on the following day caused considerable mischief, though they obtained only temporary possession of the post. A parallel was then commenced toward the second line of defences. Throughout the siege the workmen had to contend with many difficulties and great dangers; it was nearly impossible for them to cover themselves, as they had to work on rock, barely concealed by the surface clay, and so hard that it required extraordinary labour to make the slightest impression on it. When our troops had established themselves within the outer wall, the enemy placed shells in long scoops, and, lighting the fuses, rolled them over the glacis, where they exploded, carrying death and destruction amongst the working parties. This, combined with a galling musketry fire, rendered the works almost untenable. On the night of the 8th another desperate sortie on the part of the garrison was attended with much loss on the part of the besiegers; and ten days later another unsuccessful assault was made on the works.

The city of Burgos, once the capital of Castile, lies close under the castle; and, although in our possession, it was commanded by the castle. The 32nd Regiment was quartered in an old convent in the town. Owing to the absence of heavy artillery, the siege made little progress, and the delay became a serious matter, as Soult had formed a junction with King Joseph, and together mustered nearly sixty thousand men. Strong reinforcements had been pushed into the castle by the French, who succeeded in driving in the outposts, but eventually occupied their old position.* On the 21st Wellington decided to fall back and relinquish the siege.

"Our retreat commenced after nightfall. We passed over the
"bridge of Burgos, which was commanded by the Castle, on a still,
"dark night, with the utmost caution. Not a word was spoken, and
"not a sound was heard, save the tread of the numerous troops
"marching past, while the garrison threw blue lights at short intervals
"over the ramparts, that no enemy might approach unobserved.
"There was something peculiarly awful in this night march of so
"great a body of men—the cautious silence, the dead hour, and the
"consideration that in an instant the guns of the Castle might send

---

* During the operations before Burgos the 32nd lost one man, killed; Ensign Quick, two sergeants, and one man, wounded.

"death amongst us. Some of the last troops had a few shots fired at
" them, but, altogether, this clever movement was so well conducted
" that the garrison was ignorant of it until it was too late for them to
" cause us any serious annoyance.

"The army was much reduced by sickness; the 32nd did not
" muster more than one hundred and fifty men, although there were
" seven hundred and fifty in the country.

" The French army followed us, and on the 23rd some skirmishing
" took place between the enemy's van and our rear-guard ; the French
" were superior to us in cavalry. We marched for the Douro under
" circumstances of severe privation; only one pound of biscuit was
" served out to each man for his six days' provisions. All the bridges
" were blown up as soon as the last of our men had passed over,
" which checked the pursuit ; but we were generally overtaken in the
" evenings, when a show of resistance would be made on our part.
" In the mornings we continued our retreat some hours before day-
" break. We had to ford a number of small rivers, which, having
" become much swollen by the late heavy rains, contributed to render
" our march still more uncomfortable. . . . Having crossed the
" Carrion, we took up a very strong position at Duenas, on rising
" ground, with the stream in our front. Some of our troops occupied
" a large convent before the town, with some guns masked there.
" Unfortunately, they fired on the first few dragoons that came within
" range, thus uselessly exposing their position with no adequate result.
" A village in front of our left was seized by the French ; some
" Spaniards and Brunswickers were sent to re-take it, but did not suc-
" ceed until after a rather long and hot contest. . . . After halting
" here for one day, the retrogade movement was continued. Upon
" our crossing the Douro, the bridges were blown up, and, as the river
" was not fordable, and the French were endeavouring to repair the
" bridge of Tordesillas, we rested for two days in front of this place.
" Here we ascertained that several men had deserted, and that some
" sick, who were unable to keep up, had been made prisoners.

" The retreat was still conducted under very disastrous circum-
" stances. Our light cavalry were done up, and the artillery horses
" nearly so. Men, spent with fatigue, fell into the enemy's hands,

" and desertions continued. The roads were in dreadful condition;
" the streams to be forded, many and swollen ; the bivouacs wet, and
" almost without fires ; and food was as scarce as fuel. Many of the
" troops had neither bread nor biscuit, and only rations of carrion-like
" beef. The excessive dread that seemed to be felt, lest any part of
" our commissariat should fall into the enemy's hands, proved very
" injurious to our troops, whose physical strength was exhausted
" through want of the necessary supplies. We reached our old
" position in front of Salamanca on 8th November, halting there for
" four days. Sir Rowland Hill effected his junction with Wellington
" three days before. Ballasteros, the commander of the Spanish
" army, was subsequently banished to Ceuta for his disgraceful in-
" activity and obstinacy in not entering into the views of the British
" leader. The light division had been a good deal engaged during
" the retreat. The loss occasioned to us by fatigue and desertion
" was considerable, and some baggage fell into the hands of the
" enemy.

" Soult at this time assumed command of the united French army,
" mustering ninety thousand men and a formidable artillery. The
" British only mustered fifty-two thousand strong, of all nations. The
" French, as usual, were strong in cavalry—nearly three to one as
" compared to the British, whose generals were always crippled by
" weakness in this arm. We could make no stand in our position at
" San Christoval against the pursuing armies. We crossed the Tormes
" by the bridge of Salamanca, marching through the town ; but how
" different were our sensations at this time from those that we ex-
" perienced on our first entry ! We passed one night on the ground
" where the battle was fought. The enemy did not seem to be
" desirous to force us into action, but, by threatening our communi-
" cations with Ciudad Rodrigo, Wellington was compelled to set his
" army in motion without loss of time and take the roads leading to
" Portugal.

" So much rain had fallen latterly that the roads were in a most
" wretched condition, and in many places knee-deep, and we had, as
" usual, various deep streams to ford. All this was dreadfully dis-
" tressing to men who were already nearly worn out by long marches,

" want of rest, bad living, and the weight of their arms and accoutre-
" ments; and several, sinking through weakness, were smothered in
" the mud.

" Such tents as we had began now to be left standing on the ground
" that we had occupied for the night, as we no longer possessed the
" means for carrying them.

" On the 17th November Sir Edward Paget was taken prisoner.
" The French pursuit was somewhat relaxed as the Allies neared
" Ciudad Rodrigo, but, had it not been for that active partizan, Don
" Julian Sanchez, who mounted about eight hundred helpless men of
" ours behind his guerillas, and conveyed them in that manner to the
" before-mentioned fortress, we must have lost them, in addition to
" the many others who perished in this disastrous retreat.

" The 32nd lost fifty men; the 82nd, two hundred men; and every
" corps in the army had their casualties to a greater or less extent.
" On the thirty-first day from the date of our departure from the
" position in front of Burgos we arrived under the walls of Ciudad
" Rodrigo.

" From Ciudad Rodrigo we marched to Barquilla, where we made
" a halt of three days before crossing the border. We entered
" Portugal drenched with rain, and took up our ground in a ploughed
" field. The green wood was so wet that it would not burn, and
" those who had provisions could not cook them; consequently it
" was hardly possible to conceive anything much more wretched in
" its way than our situation. Much amusement was, however, caused
" by the General sending his aide-de-camp to us to say ' he had no
" objection to our making ourselves as comfortable as circumstances
" would permit!' "

The army, with the exception of Sir Rowland Hill's corps, which
returned to Estremadura, now went into cantonments in the province
of Beira. We took up our winter quarters on 3rd December, at
St. Jago. The battalion here received their new equipment. During
this year a draft from the 2nd battalion, consisting of six sergeants
and one hundred and fifty rank and file, under the command of
Captain Purcell, joined the regiment.

The regiment was brigaded with the 36th, 1st battalion 11th, and 61st regiments, under the command of Colonel Hinde, 32nd regiment, as the 2nd brigade of the 6th, or Lieutenant-General Sir H. Clinton's, division.

The following extract from a MSS. journal, lent to the editor by Colonel Bingham, R.A., of Shoeburyness, will be read with interest, as it serves to throw fresh light on this memorable retreat, which has received but scant notice by the historians:

" October 31, 1812,
"Camp in front of Tordesillas.

" General Souham having taken the command of the French army and "great reinforcements having arrived from France, particularly cavalry, it " was necessary to give up the ill-fated siege of the Castle of Burgos, and "retire; which determination was carried into effect on the night of the "21st; our battery guns, three in number, that were in fact not worth "bringing away, were destroy'd, and part of the covering army, passing "through the city of Burgos over the bridges, which were previously " prepared with dung to prevent the noise of the guns and horses being "heard in the Castle, which commanded them within musquet shot. " Favor'd by the darkness of the night the whole of the baggage, artillery, " cavalry, and a part of the infantry made the passage without being " discovered, having only a random shot from a sentry now and then; the "remainder (our division forming a part) left the town on our left, and "being much detained by dreadful roads we arrived at Celada del " Caminha by noon of the 22nd. I should have told you, that we had "been moved up to the covering army on the night of the 20th, through "the town; so that the 21st, the first night of the retreat, was the second " we have been on the march. We moved again at 7 o'clock, on the "morning of the 23rd, and arrived after dark at our ground near " Torquemada, marching, as we computed it, a distance of nearly 60 miles " in the two days, fortunately, fine weather; and after we had got into the "great Madrid line, the road was broad and good; the retreat was "unmolested on the 22nd. On the 23rd, the enemy's cavalry followed " very closely; the brigade of heavy German cavalry having failed in a " chaige, the enemy's cavalry broke in on ours, and there was a complete " race and mellée for three or four miles. Lord Wellington and his staff " were in the crowd, and it was who could get off the fastest; the enemy's "cavalry were brought up by two squares of Light Infantry who stood

"very steadily, and behind them our cavalry rallied and formed. After all,
" the loss was not great. Colonel Paly of the 16th Dragoons was taken ;
" the French who came up in no state to make an impression on our
" squares of infantry suffered from their fire. On the morning of the 24th
" our brigade was moved at daylight into the town of Torquemada ; a
" masqued battery of 18 guns was established opposite the bridges (the
" great road crosses the Pinaga, which—though not a very wide—is always
" a deep river) and we were placed in the houses, which we loopholed to
" protect the battery, the remainder of the army who moved off at the
" time we went into the town was in a sad state. On the outside of
" Torquemada, on the side where the army bivouac'd, there was a small
" hill, which had been hollowed into wine vaults, and where the inhabitants
" kept their wine. As the troops took up their ground after dark this was
" not known and no safeguards were posted ; these vaults were soon
" discovered, and as soon as discovered entered. The consequence was,
" the whole army was drunk ; the brigade I commanded was fortunately
" farthest from the scene of disorder, and it was not until the morning
" that our people made the discovery. I heard a noise, and got up, and
" found some men of the 61st drinking wine out of a camp kettle, which I
" immediately overset. I immediately awakened all the officers, and as we
" had the officers of three regiments to somewhat about 1000 men, we
" contrived to keep the people sober, and so were able to undertake the
" post of rear guard. About 11 the advanced guard of cavalry made
" their appearance, and were allowed nearly to pass over the bridge when
" the masked battery opened on them—this rendered them cautious
" throughout the day ; and we retired 12 miles, to the position of Duñnas,
" without molestation or interruption, and fortunate that it was so ; the
" army, from drunkenness, being in a complete state of disorganization.
" On the 25th we remained in position ; the enemy made a smart attack
" on the left, where the 5th Division was posted, and heavy columns were
" directed toward Pulintin ; at first they appeared to carry all before them,
" but, in the afternoon they were driven out of Villa Muriel, which they
" had possessed, and across the river, with the loss of about 100 Prisoners.

"At another point on our right they were successful ; their cavalry
" charged at the Bridge of Teriego, which was preparing for explosion,
" and dispersed a party of the 1st Division ; our cavalry retired and left
" the point in their hands, as well as a party of about 60 infantry, the
" immediate guard at the Bridge, who were made Prisoners. On this day
" the 1st Guards joined. . . . . . . We were moved in a hurry to
" Uriana, to cover a ford and support the cavalry ; here we remained the

" whole of the 27th. On the 28th (the enemy having extended themselves
" along the right bank both of the Premerja and Duero, and pushed on as
" far as opposite this place) we retired also, having blown up the Bridges
" of Cabezon, Valladolid, and the Puente de Duero, after the army had
" passed; we halted for the night on the banks of the Duero, and
" yesterday morning we came to this place, a report having been sent that
" the enemy had repaired the Bridge and crossed; and our baggage
" having been sent away, we prepared to give Battle. On our arrival we
" found the report not correct, a small picquet only having crossed. Our
" baggage did not join us until 9 o'clock at night, and our situation in the
" middle of a dreary plain, raining hard, with nothing to eat and nothing
" to make a fire with except thistles, was not very pleasant. The enemy
" have moved again in the direction of Toro; what Ld Wellington's plans
" are, no one can tell; for we seem inclined to make a corresponding
" movement. It is said, our army is to be reinforced by two Divisions
" from the centre army, in which case, General Souham may find himself
" in the wrong box in having pushed so far down the Duero as Toro; he
" will have to fight with the river in his rear, and we could always be at
" Valladolid before him, and then his line of operations being cut off, he
" would be obliged to escape in some manner very difficult if not
" impossible; in the meantime Soult may and will advance, and occupy
" Madrid, but will not be able to penetrate the passes of the Guadarama;
" so that if we could gain a decisive advantage over Souham, he might
" find his retreat difficult to accomplish. . . . . We lost
" 9 men on the night of the 22nd. I dont exactly know where, but I
" believe that as we were passing a camp where brandy was destroyed for
" want of means to carry it off, they rendered themselves incapable of
" marching. I am afraid the losses of the army in that manner amounts
" to something considerable; our men are so greedy of drink, and so
" utterly careless of consequences, that a night march, a retreat, or
" enforced march of any kind, costs us as many men as a smart skirmish.
" The army is not a little out of humour with his Lordship (Wellington) at
" present, who—in a circular letter he has addressed to the Generals
" commanding Divisions—has laid the blame of the losses in the last
" retreat to the want of energy and activity of the officers comm^g
" Brigades, Regiments, and companies; he affirms the army suffered no
" privations except such as they were exposed to from the severity of the
" weather; but the wearied, famished wretches who perished by hundreds
" on the roads, and were left unburied and half devoured by dogs and
" wolves, as an encouragement I suppose to others, is a refutation of this

"accusation. The army were (for the greatest part) twice, three days
" without bread, and the whole were six months in arrear of pay ! having
" no money to buy salt or vegetables after marching all day ; the time the
" men ought to have rested was employed in working ; in fact the men
" were worn out with constant marching, having travelled over 2,000 miles
" of country in the last 11 months, each man loaded with 60 rounds of
" ammunition, a great coat, and a blanket. Are these no privations?"

1813.

General James Ogilvie, who had been colonel of the regiment for nine years, died on the 12th February, 1813, and was succeeded by General Alexander Campbell,* of Monrie, North Britain, from the 13th Foot.

In May, 1813, Wellington entered Spain once more, driving the French out of Salamanca, quickly turning their positions on the Douro, and forcing them back upon Burgos, whence they retreated to the Ebro, after blowing up the castle.

The 6th division crossed the Douro on 19th May, halted on the 20th at Toro de Monte Corvo, reached Malados on the 26th, and— after resting for one day—resumed its march and entered Spain on the 29th by crossing the river Corsa at Murza, where Hinde's brigade halted till the 31st.

On 1st June the division crossed the Esla, by a pontoon bridge, and continued its march until the 19th, when a halt was made near Vittoria to observe the movements of a corps of French, under General Clausel, who was advancing from Bilboa.

---

* This gallant veteran entered the Black Watch, then stationed in Ireland, in 1769. He subsequently joined the 1st Royals in Minorca, and was afterwards promoted in the 50th, with which regiment and the 62nd he served in the earlier campaigns of the American war, including the battle of Saratoga. During the later campaigns he was employed as major in one of the Light Infantry battalions. He served with the 3rd Guards, under the Duke of York, on the Continent ; and as a major-general on the staff with Sir Ralph Abercromby in the West Indies, and afterwards in Ireland and Scotland. He raised the 116th Perthshire Highlanders, a corps which had a brief existence in 1794-96, and was subsequently colonel in succession of the 7th West India Regiment, the 13th Foot, and the 32nd Foot, which latter appointment he held for twenty years, up to the time of his death, in 1832.

Meanwhile, Wellington had turned the French on the Ebro by a flank march, and driven them back to Vittoria, where, in a general engagement, on 21st June, they were put to utter rout. Hinde's brigade did not reach Vittoria until the following day, when it was successful in intercepting a movement of Clausel's corps to recapture the town and booty, when the main body of the Allies had advanced in pursuit. From Vittoria the 6th and 7th divisions were despatched to blockade Pamplona, and subsequently, when relieved in this duty by a Spanish corps, proceeded to join Wellington, who—having marched six hundred miles, gained one great battle and invested two positions, San Sebastian and Pamplona, within the space of seven weeks—now stood triumphant on the Pyrenees, behind which Soult had withdrawn.

Battle of the Pyrenees.

Soult once more made a desperate effort in advance; forced the passes of Maya and Ronsesvalles, and marched upon Pamplona, in front of which Wellington concentrated most of the British troops. The 6th division was moving up from St. Estevan on 27th July to support the troops attacked in front, but were halted—by Wellington's order—for the night. On the following morning it marched to join the army which was formed up for battle among the mountains, forming across a valley on the left rear of the 4th division. Immediately after the advance of the French columns of attack commenced the conflict since known as the battle of the Pyrenees.

A body of French moving along the valley of Lanz towards the mountain at its extremity, Hinde's brigade was ordered forward at a run to seize the mountain. The British mounted one side of the hill as the French climbed the other, but the British gained the summit first, and opened fire with deadly effect. Taken in either flank as well as in front, the French were driven back, with terrible carnage, beyond the village of Sauroren, whither they were followed by Hinde's brigade. The firing was maintained on both sides until after dark. During the day the 6th division, commanded by General Pakenham, bore a most distinguished part. The 32nd was warmly engaged, and the loss of the battalion was very severe. Lieutenant-Colonel Wood fell in front of the colours. Lieutenant-Colonel

Hicks then assumed the command, and during the succeeding operations of the day led the left wing to the charge against the 32nd French regiment, which it dispersed, and carried off ten brass drums marked with the number of the regiment.

On the 29th the armies remained quiet in their respective positions; but, on the 30th, the light companies of the 6th division and 32nd Regiment were ordered to dislodge a portion of the enemy posted between Sauroren and Ostiz, which service they most gallantly performed under the command of Lieutenant-Colonel Hinde. The regiment was actively employed during the remainder of the operations in the Pyrenees.

During the operations, between the 28th and 30th July, the 32nd lost one lieutenant-colonel (Lieutenant-Colonel Wood), killed; Captain Toole and one volunteer—Lloyd—severely wounded; one sergeant and fifty rank and file, killed and wounded.*

Lieutenant-Colonels Hinde and Hicks, and the representatives of Lieutenant-Colonel Wood, received gold medals.

On 2nd August the 6th division was within sight of the fair fields of France. Moving down the French slope of the Pyrenees, it advanced a short distance into France, and, subsequently falling back, relieved the 2nd division in position on the Heights of Maya, watching the pass of that name. Major-General (afterwards Sir John) Lambert here succeeded to the command of the brigade, Colonel Hinde reverting to the command of his regiment, the 32nd.

On 1st September, 1813, the 32nd, with the rest of the division, was employed in driving the enemy from the heights in its front, and again, on 7th October, in creating a diversion in favour of the troops engaged in the passage of Bidassoa. During the operations Colonel Hinde received a severe wound in the leg, which necessitated his return home; this unfortunate occurrence deprived the regiment of the services of that officer, and the command again devolved upon Lieutenant-Colonel Hicks. Major-General Sir A. Colville was pleased to express himself in the following manner, in Division Orders, on this occasion:

---

* *London Gazette Extraordinary*, August 16th, 1813.

"Major-General Colville cannot conclude these observations, "occasioned by the demonstrations ordered to be made by the "Division on the 7th inst., without expressing the sense of the loss it "must feel in the valuable services of Colonel Hinde, from the "unlucky wound he received that day."

From 7th October until 9th November the regiment continued in the Pyrenees, and suffered considerably from the extreme inclemency of the weather, which retarded any forward movement of the army until 10th November, when the whole advanced to dislodge the enemy from a formidable line of works on the Nivelle, which they had been preparing with great labour since the failure of their efforts on the Pyrenees.

Battle of Nivelle.

"At daybreak on 10th November ninety thousand troops, British, "Portuguese, and Spanish, with ninety-five pieces of artillery, made "a concerted attack upon the French position, in columns of "division, each division led by its own general and forming its own "reserves. The French were driven from their advanced post, back "upon their main position in rear of the village of Nivelle, which was "ultimately carried, fifty-one guns and fifteen hundred prisoners "falling into the captors' hands." In his description of the progress of the attack, Wellington has left on record, "that he had the "pleasure of seeing the 6th division, under Lieutenant-General Sir "Henry Clinton—after having crossed the Nivelle, and having "driven in the enemy's picquets on both flanks, and having covered "the passage of the Portuguese division, under Lieutenant-General "Sir James Hamilton, on its right—make a most handsome attack on "the right of the enemy's position behind d'Arrhune, and on the "right of the Nivelle, carrying all the entrenchments and redoubts on "that flank." *

In this action the left brigade of the 6th division, composed of the 11th, 32nd, 36th, and 61st regiments, under the command of Major-General Lambert, particularly distinguished itself in carrying the

---

* *Wellington's Despatches*, vol. vii.

heights of d'Arrhune. The 32nd lost on this occasion Ensign O. B. Butler, one sergeant, six rank and file, killed; Lieutenant Boaz, four sergeants, one drummer, and forty-nine rank and file, wounded.

The army was thanked in General Orders, and the word "NIVELLE" was permitted to be worn on the colours and appointments of the regiment. The commanding officer, Lieutenant-Colonel Hicks, received a gold medal.

After the battle of Nivelle the 6th division went into cantonments, the 32nd Regiment occupying Ustaritz, a small town on the river, about ten miles above Bayonne.

On 8th December the regiment moved from its cantonments, crossing the Nive by a bridge of boats, and during that and the following day was warmly engaged with the enemy; recrossed the Nive on the evening of 9th December, and returned into old quarters at Ustaritz. The returns show a loss in the 32nd of two men, killed; five wounded; and one missing.

In the memorial porch, erected to the English church, at Biarritz, in 1885, are marble tablets in Gothic frame work, bearing inscriptions in lead lettering, to the memory of the British officers and men killed in the actions which took place between October 7th, 1813, and April 14th, 1814. Amongst them is the following, under 32nd:

"THIRTY-SECOND FOOT.
" Ens. J. O. Bryon Butler, Nivelle, Nov. 10th.
" N.C.O., i., Nov. 10th.
" R.F., iv., Nov. 10th; ii., Dec. 9th."

Battle of the Nive.

On 12th December the 6th division was ordered to cross the Nive in support of a series of operations in course of execution on that river by the corps under the command of Lieutenant-General Sir Rowland Hill. In these operations the 32nd Regiment shared the duties of the left brigade, and only sustained a trifling loss. For its services on this occasion the regiment was permitted to bear on its colours and appointments the word "NIVE," and Lieutenant-Colonel Hicks received a gold medal.*

The enemy now retired beyond the Adour, and the 6th division went into cantonments near Villefrancha, on the Nive, above Bayonne, where the 32nd remained until 21st February, 1814.

During the year 1813 the 32nd Regiment received the following reinforcements from the 2nd battalion, viz.: Captain Jones, with five sergeants and one hundred and one rank and file; Ensign Sayer, with one sergeant and fifty rank and file; and Ensign Small, with three sergeants and forty-two rank and file.

1814.

On 21st January, the 6th division removed from its cantonments near Villefrancha, and marched in the direction of Orthes. In the middle of February, Wellington made a general advance, in order to drive Soult out of his line of defence on the Adour. Sir Rowland Hill had forced the enemy back behind the Gave de Pau; the centre of the allied army was put in motion, and Bayonne was invested. On the 26th, the 3rd division and the cavalry forded the Gave de Pau below Orthes, and the 4th and 7th divisions at a point still further down the river. It was intended that Sir Rowland Hill's corps and the 6th and light divisions should force the bridge of Orthes, but it was afterwards thought advisable not to make the attempt.

Battle of Orthes.

On the morning of the 27th, the 6th and light divisions had already moved down to the point where the 3rd division had forded the day before, and crossed by a pontoon bridge that had been laid down for the guns. Soult occupied a range of hills, his left resting on the village of Orthes and his right on a steep declivity behind the village of St. Boes, with a strong reserve behind. The 4th and 6th divisions, under Marshal Beresford, attacked the position, but failed; on this the 7th division, with one brigade of the light division, were led

---

* Probably a bar to the original medal.

against the enemy's right; the 3rd and 6th divisions, with the 32nd Regiment, advanced at the same time, under Sir T. Picton and Sir Henry Clinton respectively. In the meantime Sir Rowland Hill, with his division, endeavoured to cut off the French line of retreat. The French were believed to have lost six thousand—killed, wounded, and taken prisoners. The 32nd Regiment did not advance beyond Orthes with the 6th division. The next day the 32nd crossed the Adour, which was nearly five feet deep, and very great difficulty was experienced, as the wooden bridge had been broken down the day before. For the services here the commanding officer—Lieutenant-Colonel Hicks—received a gold clasp to his medal.

The regiment having been a long time in the field without receiving any supplies, it was found necessary to send it back to St. Jean-de-Luz —about eight days' march—where it arrived on 14th March; and, having received clothing for the men, proceeded to join the army, but was halted at Tarbes, by order of Wellington, in consequence, it was believed, of the enemy being in possession of the Castle of Lourdes. During the halt at Tarbes the regiment was joined by a detachment of sergeants and one hundred and nine rank and file, under the command of Captain Whitty, from the 2nd battalion.

"On 10th April we were directed to proceed from Tarbes to "Toulouse with the battering train, pontoons, and boats. After a "march of ten days we joined the 6th division about six leagues "beyond Toulouse. The battle had been fought. After the "battle of Toulouse, hostilities having ceased, the 6th division "occupied Auch as its head-quarters, and the 32nd Regiment, "having joined, was cantoned at Pavie, a small village in its "vicinity." *

Lieutenant-General Sir Henry Clinton, being called on another service, relinquished the command of the 6th division, which he had held during the most brilliant services of the army in the Peninsula. He was succeeded by Major-General Lambert; Colonel Douglas, 79th regiment, being appointed to command the right, and Lieutenant-Colonel Hicks, 32nd regiment, the left, brigades.

* Ross-Lewin, *Life of a Soldier*.

On taking leave of the division, Lieutenant-General Clinton published the following Divisional Order:

"Auch,
"19th May, 1814.

" Being called on another service, Lt.-Genl. Sir H. Clinton takes leave
" of the 6th Division. He does not without regret give up the Command
" of Troops, who, in ever meeting with the enemy, have not failed
"honourably to distinguish themselves, while the orderly and generally
" soldierlike conduct has often attracted the notice and approbation of the
" great Commander of the Army.

" The Lieut.-General is desirous of acknowledging how highly he feels
" indebted to the brave 6th Division. He cannot better mark the interest
" he feels for the future reputation of those Regts., than by reminding the
" Commanding Officers how entirely their good order depended upon a
" prompt obedience to orders and a steady and continued observance of
" the Regulations named for the government of the army—that no
" Regiment can continue essentially in order unless the qualifications of
" its officers for the performance of its several duties be provided for and
" regularly required, and that for the instruction of the Soldiers ranks
" foremost in the qualifications of the Regimental Officers.

"*(Sd.)* J. GURWOOD, A.A.G."

In the beginning of June, the 6th division received orders to march to Bordeaux, and arrived at Blaye fort on the 14th. Here the greater part of the British army had been previously assembled and encamped, awaiting orders for embarkation. They were received on the 13th by His Grace the Duke of Wellington, who was pleased to publish the following in General Orders, dated Bordeaux, 14th June, 1814 :

" Adjutant General's Office,
" Bordeaux, 14th June, 1814.

" The Commander of the Forces being on the point of returning to
" England, again takes the opportunity of congratulating the Army upon
" the recent events which have restored peace to their Country and to the
" World. The share which the British Army had in producing those
" Events, and the high character with which the Army will quit this
" Country must be equally satisfactory to every individual belonging to it
" as they are to the Commander of the Forces, and he trusts that the
" Troops will maintain the same good character to the last.

" The Commander of the Forces once more requests the Army to
" accept his thanks. Although circumstances may alter the relations to
" which he has stood towards them for some years so much to his satisfac-

" tion, he assures them he will never cease to feel the warmest interest in
" their welfare and honour, and that he will be at all times happy to be of
" any service to those to whose conduct, discipline, and gallantry the
" country is so much indebted.

"*(Sd.)*   E. M. PAKENHAM, A. General."

On the morning of 21st June the 6th division marched for Pauillac, on the Garonne, where it arrived and embarked the same evening. It sailed on the 26th, and proceeded to its several destinations in England and Ireland; and the 32nd Regiment arrived and disembarked at the Cove of Cork on 12th July, and marched the same day to Middleton.

For the services of the 32nd Regiment during the Peninsular War, His Royal Highness the Prince Regent was graciously pleased to authorise its bearing the following distinguished badges on its colours and appointments: " ROLEIA," " VIMIERA," " SALAMANCA," " PYRENEES," " NIVELLE," " NIVE," " ORTHES," " PENINSULA ;" and the following officers of the regiment were also honoured with the undermentioned individual marks of distinction: Colonel Hinde, for his services at the battle of Roleia, Vimiera, Corunna, Salamanca, and the Pyrenees, the gold cross* established by His Royal Highness the Prince Regent as a mark of distinction to officers who had commanded in four general actions; to the representatives of the late Lieutenant-Colonel Wood, for his services in the battles of Salamanca and Pyrenees, a gold medal and one clasp; and to Lieutenant-Colonel Hicks, for his services in the Pyrenees, Nivelle, Nive, and Orthes, the gold cross, he also having commanded in four general actions.

Shortly after the arrival of the regiment at Middleton, it received orders to proceed to Cloncorry barracks, where it was stationed for one month, and then marched for Fermoy, at which place one hundred men, who had enlisted for limited service, were discharged. A reinforcement, however, from the 2nd battalion, of seven sergeants and one hundred and thirty-one rank and file, made up for this diminution of its number, and it still mustered eight hundred rank and file.

---

* Now in the Murray collection.

RECORD OF THE SECOND BATTALION OF THE 32ND REGIMENT OF FOOT.

The SECOND BATTALION of the 32nd (or Cornwall) Regiment of Foot was, with a number of other second battalions, ordered to be formed on 1st August, 1804.

The head-quarters of the regiment was at Launceston, in Cornwall. The field officers, with the exception of Major Pye from the 3rd battalion reserve, were appointed from the 1st battalion, with a proportion of non-commissioned officers. The quarter part of the company officers were selected from other corps.

On 4th June, 1807, the battalion—consisting of twenty-eight sergeants, twenty-two drummers, and four hundred and eighty-three rank and file—received its colours; on which occasion Lieutenant-Colonel M. Power (who commanded) made an animated speech to the officers and men.

On 4th August the battalion marched from Harwich for Weely barracks, where it arrived on the same day. On 9th May, 1808, the battalion marched from Weely barracks, on its route to Guernsey, and arrived at Tilbury Fort. It embarked on the 12th, sailed on the 19th, and arrived at Tilbury, in Guernsey, on 31st December. On 1st June, 1808, it marched to Delaney barracks.

1809-15.

On 5th March, 1809, the battalion embarked for Ireland, and arrived in the Cove of Cork on the 13th, disembarked at Monkstown on the 15th, and marched for Fermoy, where it arrived on the 16th.

On 25th May, 1809, a second assistant surgeon was added to the battalion. It was quartered in many parts of Ireland from the date of its arrival to the time of its reduction, and nothing very important occurred, with the exception of its sending drafts to the 1st battalion on the following dates:

On 28th June, 1811, a draft, consisting of three hundred and nine privates, under the command of Captain G. W. Patley, was sent from Cork to Portugal; on 9th March, 1812, a draft of six sergeants, six corporals, and one hundred and fifty-one privates, under the command of Captain G. Purceel, from Omagh to Portugal; on 6th October, a draft of five sergeants, four corporals, and ninety-seven privates, under the command of Captain J. Jones, from Omagh to Spain; on 6th January, 1813, a draft of one sergeant, two corporals, and forty-eight privates, under the command of Ensign Sayer, from the depôt at Winchester to Spain; on 17th February, 1814, a draft of five sergeants, five corporals, and one hundred and four privates, under the command of Captain E. Whitty, from Cavan to France; and on 17th August, 1814, a draft of seven sergeants, four corporals, and one hundred and twenty-seven privates, under the command of Captain R. Dillon, from Omagh to Fermoy; the 2nd battalion being disbanded on 23rd October, 1814, the whole of the serviceable non-commissioned officers and men, consisting of eighteen sergeants, thirteen corporals, and one hundred and forty-two privates, marched from Omagh and joined the 1st battalion in Cork.

The regiment marched to Cork early in December, 1814, and in January, 1815, received orders to hold itself in readiness to proceed to America; but its departure being delayed till March, and Buonaparte having escaped from Elba, the destination of the regiment was changed, and on 28th April, 1815, it embarked from Monkstown for the Netherlands. It arrived at Ostend on 10th May, and was conveyed in boats up the canal to Ghent, where it halted for a few days for the purpose of being equipped for the field, after which it marched to Brussels and was attached to Major-General Sir James Kempt's brigade, 5th division, which was shortly after reviewed by the Duke of Wellington, who was pleased to express his approbation.

Battle of Quatre Bras.

The whole force at the disposal of the Duke was about sixty-eight-thousand, and was composed largely of foreigners, a great number of whom were militiamen. The native British troops, among whom there were also many young and untried soldiers, consisted of about twenty-four thousand, while of the remainder a large proportion were Hanoverians, recently raised and imperfectly trained; while others, like the Belgians, were troops of very inferior quality and hardly to be trusted at a pinch.

The British artillery consisted of thirty brigades,* with six guns to each brigade ; they were in admirable order. This army was divided into two corps ; the first commanded by the Prince of Orange, the second by Lord Hill. The cavalry were placed under the orders of the Earl of Uxbridge.

The army in Belgian territory was kept for strategical purposes, and also with an object of furnishing supplies, which were scattered over different parts of the country. The 32nd Regiment, with the 5th division, was in Brussels.

Ross-Lewin, in his *Life of a Soldier*, says : " During our stay, " Brussels was the scene of much gaiety ; war seemed to be totally " forgotten. The Duke of Wellington gave a grand *rout* on the 8th " June, at which the Prince of Orange, the Duke of Brunswick, and " all the British and foreign nobility then resident in Brussels " attended. Four cards of invitation were received by each regiment, " and one of those sent to mine fell to my lot. The company passed " through an illuminated garden to the reception rooms ; the Duke " of Wellington stood, distinct from all present, near the entrance to " receive his guests, and looked very well. Dancing was kept up to " a late hour. The Prince of Orange led the Duchess of Richmond " to the supper rooms, which were in the apartments of the middle " story. The rooms were excessively crowded, considering the time ' of the year, and not one half of the guests could find places at the " supper tables.

" The Duchess of Richmond gave a grand ball on the 15th. That " day I dined with Sir James Kempt. Coffee and a young aide-de- " camp from the Duke of Wellington came in together. This officer " was the bearer of a note from the Duke, and while Sir James was " reading it said : ' Old Blucher has been hard at it—a Prussian " officer has just come to the Beau, all covered with sweat and dirt, " and says they have had much fighting.' Our host then rose, and,

---

* Extracts from General Order : " Brussels, 21st May, 1815.—The 1st " Batt. 28th, 1st Batt. 32nd, 1st Batt. 79th, and 1st Batt. 95th are to form the " 8th British Brigade under M.G. Sir James Kempt. The 8th and 9th British " Brigades and 5th Hanoverians are to form the 5th Division of Infantry."

"addressing the regimental officers at the table, said: 'Gentlemen, you will proceed without delay to your respective regiments; and let them get under arms immediately.'

"On my way, I found several of our officers sitting at a coffee-house door, and told them Sir James Kempt's orders. They seemed at first to think that I was jesting, being hardly able to credit the tidings of so near and so unexpected an approach of the French; but they soon perceived that I spoke seriously, and dispersed each to his own quarters. In a few minutes, however, the most incredulous would have been thoroughly undeceived; for the drums began to beat, bugles to sound, and Highland pipes to squeal, in all quarters of the city. The scene that ensued was of the most animated kind—such was the excitement of the inhabitants, the buzz of tongues, the repeated words of command, the hurrying of the soldiers through the streets, the clattering of horses' hoofs, the clash of arms, the rattling of the wheels of waggons and gun carriages, and the sounds of warlike music. The different regiments of infantry closed up in Place Royale; and at daylight the whole were in motion towards Waterloo, the Duke and the generals riding on before us.

"We—the 32nd Regiment and 5th division—halted for some time near the village in the forest of Soigines, which some suppose to be a part of the immense one of Ardennes, so celebrated for its extent, and the deeds and adventures of which it was the scene, as well in the classical as in the middle ages. It now answers the useful purpose of supplying Brussels with firewood. When the bugle sounded to fall in again, one of our captains exclaimed, 'That is my death warrant!' The poor fellow's prediction was soon verified, for he was killed a few hours afterwards.

"From Waterloo we marched to Genappe, a league and a half further on. Genappe is nearly five leagues from Brussels; it has only one street, but the houses are large and comfortable. The country about it is quite open, and continues so for the whole distance between it and Quatre Bras, a small inn so called because the road from Brussels to Charleroi, by which we advanced, is there intersected by that from Nivelles to Namur, passing by St. Arnaud.

"The Prussian right rested on the latter place, and it was an essential "object with the Allies to keep open both these communications; "we therefore halted at Quatre Bras, a little after two p.m., there to "dispute this important point with the advancing enemy.

"Between the 10th and 14th of June, Napoleon had assembled "the first, second, third, fourth, and sixth corps of his army, close to "the frontier between the rivers Sambre and Maese On the 15th, "at daybreak, he attacked the Prussian posts at Thvin and Lobez, on "the Sambre. His attacks were successful; and General Ziethen, "whose corps had been at Charleroi, retired to Fleurus. Upon this "Blucher concentrated his forces upon Sombief, occupying also the "villages of St. Arnaud and Ligny in front of his position.

"On the evening of this day the enemy, advancing from Charleroi "along the high road to Brussels, drove a brigade of Netherlanders, "under the Prince of Wiemar, from Frasne, and compelled it to "retire to Quatre Bras. The Prince of Orange immediately sent to "its aid another brigade of the same division; and early in the morning "of the 16th some of the lost ground was recovered, so as to secure "the command of the communications with the Prussian position.

"The 32nd Regiment and 5th division was followed by the Duke "of Brunswick's corps, and these again by the contingent of Nassau. "The whole force in the field, after the arrival of the last-mentioned "troops, did not exceed nineteen thousand men; we were without "artillery;* not a single British dragoon appeared, and the Duke of "Brunswick's cavalry, though very fine men, were badly mounted. "Our position was of no strength; and all that, under Providence, "we had to depend upon in the endeavour to maintain it against a "very superior force, well provided with cavalry and artillery, was the "skill and presence of mind of our generals, and the courage and "discipline of the troops, and the God of Battles ordained that none "of these should fail us.

---

* This no doubt means that there were no artillery up at the commencement of the engagement. There were in all five brigades of artillery at Quatre Bras, of which Major Lloyd's and Major Rogers' were warmly engaged. Two guns belonging to the former were lost, but were afterwards recovered. *Vide* Duncan, vol. ii., p. 422.

"The ground we occupied for the most part swelled into gentle "slopes, and extended from the Namur road on the left to a thick "wood on the right, called the Bois de Bossu. The Charleroi road "ran through the position, and in front there were some fields of "amazingly tall rye.

"When we came up the firing had almost ceased, but it soon "increased again ; and shortly after we were hotly engaged with the "second corps of the French army, led by Marshal Ney.

"A heavy column advanced against the fifth division, the officers "marching in front, flourishing their swords and encouraging their "men ; but they were quickly driven back, and forced through the "hedge at the bottom of the slope on which we had been drawn "up. They had to cross a long narrow field and a second hedge "before they could get under cover from our fire, and an admirable "opportunity of taking a number of prisoners was lost here, while "they were making their way through a small opening. Indeed, "numbers of them had ordered their arms in the expectation of being "pursued and taken, but they escaped with inconsiderable loss, as "our troops were halted at the first hedge. The French, when they "had all passed to the other side of the fence, lined it, instead of "retiring, and commenced from behind it a most destructive fire on "our division, which was so much exposed on the side of the hill ; "in consequence, the regiments were ordered to fall back, and lie "down on the reverse slope. The 32nd, while retiring thither, "suffered severely from the fire of the troops that lined the fence. "Such attacks were continued with little intermission, but we main- "tained our ground, invariably repulsing all the enemy's efforts to "regain it.*

---

* Kempt's Brigade, in consequence of the greater proximity of its original position to that of the enemy, was the first to overthrow the French infantry. The 79th, on the left of the line, made a gallant· charge down the hill, dashed through the first fence, and pursued their opponents, who had advanced in two battalion-columns, not only across the valley, but through the second fence ; and, carried on by their ardour, even ventured to ascend the enemy's position. By this time, however, their ranks were much broken ; they were speedily recalled, and as they retraced their steps across the valley they derived considerable support from the adjoining battalion in the line, the 32nd Regiment

"As we had no British cavalry up, owing to the shortness of the "notice that the Duke of Wellington had received when Napoleon "advanced, and as the Brunswick dragoons were unable to make "head alone against those of the enemy, it, of course, became "necessary to throw two regiments on the left into square to resist "the charges of the French lancers and cuirassiers, and to re-form "line to meet the attacks of the infantry. When the hostile cavalry "were seen moving up to Quatre Bras, the 32nd formed a square "on the Namur road, as did the 28th, who were on our right and "a little in advance; and the 42nd, who were still more on our "right, were forming square when they were suddenly charged by "lancers, whose approach was concealed by a fence and some tall "rye, before they could complete their formation. Two companies "were nearly cut to pieces. Colonel Macara was killed, and Colonel "Dicks, who succeeded him in the command, was badly wounded. "About the same time the enemy's cuirassiers galloped up the high "road to Brussels; the Brunswick hussars attempted to check their "advance, but were overwhelmed by superior numbers and weight "of men and horses, and retired in confusion, pursued by the enemy, "toward Quatre Bras. The cuirassiers had gained the crest of the "slope, on which the house stands, when the 92nd, who had been "placed there in reserve behind a ditch, rose, and threw in a volley, "so sudden, so well-directed, and so deadly in its effect, that the "cavalry wheeled round and fled with precipitation, leaving many of "their number, killed or wounded, on the spot; and, as they returned, "suffering from the fire of one or two British regiments that they had "passed in the charge, the 28th distinguished themselves highly by "the intrepid and successful manner in which they resisted repeated "charges of cavalry.

"During the action the Duke of Wellington was reinforced by the "3rd division, under General Alter, and the Guards, under General "Cook. The 69th Regiment had hardly taken up its ground, when

---

(commanded by Lieutenant-Colonel Maitland), which was keeping up from the first hedge a vigorous fire against the French, who now lined the second fence.--Siborne, vol. i., p. 113.

"the French cavalry got in among them, and caused considerable
"loss in killed and wounded, but made no prisoners.

"The Belgians held the wood for some time, but at length gave
"way, and the French were in possession of it when the Guards
"arrived. General Maitland's brigade was immediately directed to
"dislodge them. The possession of the wood was of much conse-
"quence to the French, as they could debouch from it on the
"Brussels road, part of which it skirted, and if they had a chance
"of beating our troops anywhere, it ought to have been when General
"Maitland endeavoured to recover the wood. The Guards, on their
"advance, were exposed to a deadly fire from an enemy that was hid
"behind trees, bushes, and banks, and knew well how to take advan-
"tage of such means of defence; still they dashed on boldly, and
"finally remained undisputed masters of this important point, after
"three hours' hard fighting.

"Marshal Ney, alarmed by the failure of all his efforts to overcome
"the obstinacy of our troops, sent off in haste for the first corps,
"and found that Napoleon had employed it to support the attack on
"the Prussians at Sombref. He had then only to bring the reserve
"of the second corps into action, which he did with continued ill
"success. The first corps, having been despatched to Frasne by
"Napoleon, arrived too late to be of any use to Ney.

"The firing ceased as the evening closed, and at that time the
"British occupied a more advanced position than that which they
"had taken up in the morning. We slept on the ground that night.
"In the course of it the cavalry came up from Niouve.

"The loss of the Allies in killed, wounded, and prisoners was esti-
"mated at four thousand. A captain of my regiment (32nd), towards
"the close of the day, was remarking what a number of escapes he
"had had, and shewing how his clothes had been shot through in
"several places, when a musket ball entered his mouth, and killed
"him on the spot. Two more of our captains died of their wounds
"the next morning. It was thought rather singular that the only
"officers of my regiment who lost their lives at Quatre Bras—viz.:
"Jacques Boyse, Thomas Cassan, and Edward Whitty—should
"have been three captains successive in seniority, a leash of

"Irishmen, and the greatest of friends, generally messing together."

The losses the 32nd Regiment sustained on the 15th June were very severe in killed and wounded. Captain Edward Whitty and twenty rank and file, viz., Corporal John Sommers, John Annear, Thomas Caulfield, Thomas Chappell, Charles Cootes, Patrick Delaney, Phillip Darnven, Joseph Higgins, William Jenkins, William Lobb, James Lewis, John McCool, Hugh McGuire, Luke McKiernan, Thomas Moore, Thomas Potters, Patrick Quigley, John Rafter, W. Shackleton, and John Simmonds, killed; and Captains Thomas Cassan, Jacques Boyse, John Crowe, and Charles Wallett; Lieutenants H. W. Brooks, George Barr, M. W. Meighan, S. H. Lawrence, J. Boaz, James Robinson, James Fitzgerald, Edward Stephens and Henry Quill; Ensigns Alexander Stewart and Charles Dallas;

MAJOR WALLETT.

with six sergeants, one drummer, and two hundred and eighteen rank and file, wounded. Of the four captains wounded, Thomas Cassan and Jacques Boyse died of their wounds, and were interred the following day.*

Extract of a letter from an officer of the 32nd Regiment, dated Antwerp, June 25th, 1815:

"On the 15th an account of the French having attacked the Prussians "was brought to Lord Wellington. It was kept a profound secret from "the troops till night, when, just as I was stepping into bed, I heard the

---

* The very interesting roll of Waterloo officers and men, for which the Author is indebted to Mr. W. C. Murphy—whose grandfather was a colour-sergeant in the regiment—will be found in the Appendix.

"bugle sounding in every quarter of the town (Brussels). I put on my
"clothes and found it was an order for the army to advance. We marched
"about 2 o'clock, and at 3 in the day we came up with the enemy. There
"was only the 5th division, a brigade of Brunswick cavalry and some
"Belgic and Hanoverian troops, opposed to Buonaparte with 70,000 men.
"As the British troops were first up, the left brigade of the 5th division,
"under Sir James Kempt, was sent out; our regiment now in the centre,
"supported on either side by the Royals and 79th. Buonaparte took up
"his position on a large plain, rather rising ground, in front of a wood;
"we took up ours about 500 yards in front of him, in a large field of corn;
"between us was a little valley or hollow, through which ran a deep ditch.

"A little before four the action commenced, on the side of the French.
"We lay down in the cornfield till they came within forty yards of us,
"when a shout from our right caused us to rise. We fired a volley and
"charged them down to the ditch, in getting over which they lost
"numbers. When we got down the bugle sounded for us to return and
"form in line upon the colours, which we did, and were pursued by them
"again; we charged them a second time, and actually the ground was
"covered with dead and wounded bodies. As our company was next on
"the left of the colours, we were in the very thick of the fire all the time
"that the enemy were manœuvring, exchanging, and retreating—the
"heavy guns from either side continually playing. In the second charge,
"a shell burst right on the colours, took away the silk of the regimental
"colour and the whole of the right section of the fifth company, amongst
"whom was my lamented friend, Captain W——*; his head was literally
"blown to atoms. Mc——†, who held the colour that suffered, was only
"slightly wounded. This was not a moment for grief or much reflection,
"as the command of the company devolved on me. We fought from 4
"o'clock until half past 6, when we were relieved by the right brigade,
"consisting of the 28th, 42nd, and 92nd. We retired to the road in the
"rear, and our regiment, which mustered 600 men going into the field,
"came away with only 160; we had between 50 and 60 killed, and the
"remainder wounded, also 1 officer killed and 17 wounded. At 9 o'clock
"we were again called up to assist the 28th in taking a village on the edge
"of the wood. We were advancing in open column of division (as out of
"the ten companies we had in the morning we could only then count four
"divisions), when I was hit by a musket ball in the cap of the knee; in

---

* Whitty.   † McConchy.

"falling to the ground I had a very narrow escape that I did not lose my
"eye, as a poor fellow who was standing by me received a mortal wound,
"and in falling back—we both fell together—the point of his bayonet
"stuck under my right eye ; it was very bad for some days, but from the
"quantity of blood that I lost, and the blood which was taken from above
"the eye, I began to feel better, but I fear that it will injure my sight very
"much. After being hit, I was brought off the field, and taken to the
"hospital ; the next morning I was brought into Brussels, when my leg
"was so swelled for want of proper dressing that they could not tell
"whether the ball was in or not, although they probed it several times. I
"was just settled in bed after taking 30 drops of laudanum, when a report
"was spread of our army having been beaten, and were retreating fast, and
"we expected the French would be in Brussels the next day.

"I was so stupid from laudanum I knew not what I was doing, till next
"morning I found myself, with my servant and some wounded men, in a
"boat, proceeding for this place. The great road from Brussels to
"Antwerp is by the canal, and never did I witness so much confusion as
"was to be seen among the people on that day—the road covered with
"carriages, principally English, and the baggage of the army. You will
"see by the papers that on Saturday evening, when Lord Wellington
"despaired of victory, he tried to bring the French out of the wood, as the
"British Cavalry were then coming up ; to effect this the better, he
"retreated to a wood in his rear, but finding that did not succeed, he
"advanced again, and threw some Congreve Rockets into Buonaparte's
"wood, which soon set fire to it, upon which they were obliged to quit.

"On the next day (Sunday) they had another dreadful battle, and at 6
"o'clock in the evening Wellington was in doubt, when the Prussian
"General (Blucher) appeared, with an immense force, and enabled Lord
"Wellington to decide the fate of the day.

"I am going back to Brussels to-morrow, the Count de Cambray (son of
"the lady with whom I was billeted before the battle) has come down, and
"brought his carriage for me. Nothing can equal the attention of the
"people ; ladies of the first distinction attend the hospitals, and assist in
"giving comfort to the wounded. Wellington had several 'hair-breadth
"'scapes' ; he exposed himself too much ; I saw him different times on
"foot, along the lines, dressed in his Field-Marshall's uniform. The young
"Prince of Orange was taken by the French, and retaken by the National
"Guard of Brussels, chiefly composed of young men of rank and fortune,
"who formed themselves into his guard ; when they had retaken him, he
"tore the Star from his breast, and said, 'My Brave Belgians, take it, you

"have won it fairly.' He is adored by the people. I have just heard
"that Captains B—— and C——* are dead of their wounds."

During the time the action had been going on at Quatre Bras the Prussians had been hotly engaged and worsted, Napoleon detaching the 3rd corps, under Grouchy, to follow them on their supposed line of retreat, towards Liege and Namur. The gallant old Blucher had, by a masterly stroke, ignored his own line of retreat, and fell back on the British line, which enabled him to unite his forces. Wellington, who was expecting assistance from the Prussians enabling him to hold the position at Quatre Bras, on hearing of their defeat, fell back leisurably towards Waterloo at 10 a.m. on 17th June.

"We were followed by a large body of cavalry, and not until they
" had been dispersed by a gallant charge of the 1st Life Guards did
" they desist from annoying us. All that we suffered from was the
" weather, as the rain fell in torrents; we halted near Genappe and
" Waterloo, it being the Duke's intention to make a stand about half
" a league in front of the latter place. Each regiment took up its
" ground without the least confusion; and the fifth division, with 32nd,
" passed rather an uncomfortable night lying among high grass and
" corn, in thunder, lightning, and in rain.

"As morning dawned, on Sunday, 18th June, the men procured
"some wood and made large fires; biscuits and spirits were served
" out, and our clothes were nearly dry, when the enemy appeared on
" the heights opposite to us, standing to their arms. Our men
" immediately began to rub and dry their firelocks, put in new flints,
" and make all necessary preparations for the day's work."

Battle of Waterloo.

Wellington's army, mustering about sixty-eight thousand of mixed nationalities, with only twenty-three thousand British, was drawn up in position and occupied about one and a half miles. The right, under Lord Hill, was thrown back on a deep ravine toward Merke

---

* Captain Jacques Boyse died of wounds on the 17th June, and Captain Cassan on the 16th.—Extract from Casualty Return.

Captain Thomas Cassan,
32nd Regt.

Braine; and the village of Braine la Lende, beyond this hamlet, was also occupied.

The centre was composed of the corps of the Prince of Orange. In front of the right centre, and near the Nivelles road, was the chateau of Hougoument, which was surrounded by a grove of tall trees, an orchard, and walled gardens; this post, which was at the angle where the right wing was thrown back *en potence*, was of the greatest importance, and held by three companies of the Guards, the remainder of General Cooke's division being drawn up on the slope behind it.

The left wing consisted of the 5th division and 32nd Regiment, commanded by Sir Thomas Picton. Its right was on the main road from Charleroi to Brussels, and its left on a height above the hamlet of Ser-la-Haye, where the ground became woody and broken. On the right side of the road, and at the bottom of the hill, stood the farmhouse of La Haye Sainte; the ground from above this farm, nearly to the extreme right of the position, sloped gently down, and was quite clear of all impediments. A long lane, with a quickset hedge on either side, ran by the entire front of the left wing, and here also the ground lay in an easy slope.

" Our front formed an irregular curve, convex towards the enemy.
" The extensive wood of Soignies was in our rear, and would have
" been of great importance to us, had we failed to maintain our
" position at Waterloo."

A few minutes past eleven in the morning of the 18th the enemy sent forward a swarm of Tirailleurs to the attack of Hougoument; they spread over all the ground in front of the house and its plantations, and advanced firing without any seeming system, but were unable to dislodge its brave defenders, chiefly guardsmen, who resisted all attempts to capture it; and, though the building itself was set on fire by the French shells, and the surrounding orchards and enclosures carried at first by the vehemence of their onset, the assailants were soon driven out again, and the post was successfully held up to the close of the day.

While this attack was going on a heavy cannonade was kept up by the enemy upon the whole line, to cover the advance of cavalry and infantry.* The 5th division and 32nd Regiment were then in columns of regiments, and a body of Belgians, with some of their field pieces, occupied part of the lane, while the 95th and light companies were extended more in advance, with their right on a sand-pit that lay opposite the gate of La Haye Sainte. The French, who had brought several batteries of artillery into position down the slopes of the hills fronting the left wing, now commenced to open a galling fire on them, and under cover of this the enemy made a general advance, driving in the light troops and pressing their cavalry against the British infantry; the 32nd Regiment here formed square, and resisted the onset with the utmost intrepidity.

The enemy had advanced its artillery on the right side of the Brussels road to within one hundred and twenty paces of the crest of the hill, and every discharge made sad gaps in the infantry squares.

After making the most desperate efforts in other parts of the field, and especially at Hougoumont, the enemy turned their attention principally to the left and left centre. A strong body of French infantry advanced against the left wing, and pressed on to the lane. Sir Thomas Picton instantly placed himself at the head of his division to meet the attack, crossed the lane, and charged the French, who—firing a volley--retired. "The attack cost us a gallant leader. " Sir Thomas Picton received a ball through his right temple and fell " dead from his horse. His body was borne off the ground by two " grenadiers of the 32nd regiment, and not--as painters incorrectly " have it in their representations of this sad scene—by Highlanders.†
" During the charge a French officer seized a stand of colours " belonging to the 32nd Regiment; but he was instantly run through " the body by a sergeant's pike (Sergeant Switzer), as well as by the " sword of Ensign John Birtwhistle, who carried the regimental colour " until severely wounded."

" After the attack was repulsed, two French women were found " dead on the field—one with a bullet wound through her head. Our

---

* Nearly all the regiments in Kempt's and Pack's brigades had lost half their numbers in the battle of the 16th—" Les Quatre Bras."—Siborne, vol. ii., p. 7.
† Ross-Lewin, vol. ii.; Siborne, vol. ii., p. 11

" troops pursued the retiring column down the slope, and would have
" closed with them had they not rallied and opened fire. Ponsonby's
" cavalry brigade, however, appeared just in time, and swooped down
" upon them, capturing two thousand prisoners and two eagles. The
" prisoners were immediately sent off to Brussels, and it was their
" arrival which convinced the timid that the British were not
" getting the worst of it, as had been reported by the runaway
" Belgians.

" After the repulse of our assailants we resumed our former
" position, and Sir James Kempt* took the command of the
" division.

" About this time (6 p.m.) the captain who commanded at La Haye
" Sainte ran across the road to the 32nd, and requested that we would
" direct him where to procure ammunition, as his was nearly all
" expended, and he feared that he should not be able to defend his
" post much longer. He was, however, unsuccessful, and the French
" were enabled to carry the position. A dangerous gap was thus made
" in the British centre, and the result undoubtedly might have been
" serious if the attack had been at once promptly supported."

After the enemy's success at La Haye Sainte their fire from it was very annoying, and the 32nd Regiment suffered a good deal. At length the 28th Regiment, which had not been previously engaged, was led up by General Lambert and occupied the ground on which the 32nd Regiment had hitherto stood. The 32nd retired a few yards, formed square, and lay down; but even in this position some of the officers were wounded and many lives lost. Wellington, who at once perceived the danger, immediately sent up two of Lord Hill's brigades, and after an hour's time all danger was over. Napoleon now tried to make a general advance, as the Prussian columns had been already observed making their way on the Wavre road, and on the right flank of them, and must have seen now that a complete victory was no longer within his grasp, and that all he could hope for was such a success as might enable him to avert the calamity of a total defeat. With this object he placed himself at the head of his

---

* Kempt's brigade consisted of the 28th, 32nd, and 79th Regiments.

army and directed the attack, supported by cavalry and artillery, against the centre of the British army; but he himself did not proceed beyond a pit at the foot of the slope, where he took his station, sheltered from the fire by a small mound. The enemy advanced with great gallantry, and were held in check by the 52nd, 7th, and 2nd battalion 95th Regiments, together with Sir Colin Halkett's brigade. The French now attempted to deploy, but fell into inextricable confusion, which ended in their retiring precipitately in broken masses, followed by the British infantry and cavalry.

During this part of the day, Sir James Kempt was on the right of the division, watching with perfect coolness the progress of the attack, and soon, taking off his hat, he cheered the troops on towards the enemy.

"The British commander, now seeing that Bulow was again "engaged on the enemy's right flank, and that Ziethen's corps was "issuing from the woods on the left, ordered his whole line to "advance. This inspiriting order was received with a general shout, "and the movement was made with all the alacrity of which troops "so long and so harassingly engaged were capable. The Duke then "crossed the main road, with his glass in his hand, and galloped "down the slope in front of our left, to the spot where the remnant of "the 28th Regiment had halted. This handful of brave men gave "him three hearty cheers, and I am confident that there was not a "man in the army who did not feel elated at the sight of their "victorious chief, safe and unhurt after this perilous and bloody "day." The French army, after their last reserves had been repulsed, abandoned all their ground, and a total rout ensued. Wellington found the English too exhausted to take part in it, but the Prussians took it up with such indefatigable energy that by daylight next morning (19th June), some of their cavalry had reached Gosselies, twenty miles from the scene of the fight. The 5th division remained on the ground where the battle had been fought during the night. "When the excitement of the fight was over, our people felt much "oppressed by fatigue and want of refreshment; still, we contrived "to make large fires, and to sleep soundly for the remainder of the "night round the hot embers."

"The 32nd was reduced to one hundred and thirty, and my "company to eleven men."*

The regiment had not a single absentee. The following interesting statistics are taken from the *United Service Magazine*, March, 1880 :—

"Of eighty corporals who went into action, eight reckoned fourteen "years' service or over; eighteen had from seven to fourteen years' "service; and fifteen were under seven years' service. The oldest "corporal, Davey, had enlisted originally in the Devon and Corn- "wall Fencible Infantry in 1799. Of five hundred and sixty-eight "privates who went into action (*for Roll of Names see Appendix*) "eighty-one had fourteen years' service or over; one hundred and "eighty had from seven to fourteen years' service, and the rest—one "boy included—had under seven years' service. The old soldiers, "*i.e.*, the corporals and privates of fourteen years' service and over, "therefore constituted about fifteen per cent. of the strength. Of "these two had enlisted in 1793, one in the 4th Dragoons and one "as a boy in the 32nd; one had originally enlisted in the Devon "Fencible Infantry in the West Indies; thirty-three more enlisted on "its return home in 1799. The young soldiers, *i.e.*, the men with "less than seven years' service, formed about fifty-two per cent., "and most of them had only two or three years' service, being "transfers from the disbanded 2nd battalion."

The following account, which was written by a young officer to his friend a few days after the battle, is full of interest :

"Camp of Clichy.

"All the sharers of my tent having gone to Paris, and my servant "having manufactured a window-shutter into a table, and a pack-saddle "into a seat, I will no longer delay answering your two affectionate letters, "and endeavour to comply with your demand of an account of the battle, "such as it offered to my own eyes.

"On the 15th of June, everything appeared so perfectly quiet, that the "Duchess of Richmond gave a ball and supper, to which all the world "was invited, and it was not till ten o'clock at night that rumours of an

---

* Captain Ross-Lewin.

"action having taken place between the French and Prussians were
"circulated through the room in whispers; no credit was given to them,
"however, for some time; but when the general officers, whose corps
"were in advance, began to move, and when orders were given for persons
"to repair to their regiments, matters then began to be considered in a
"different light. At eleven o'clock the drums beat to arms, and the 5th
"division, which garrisoned Brussels, after having bivouacked in the Park
"until daylight, set forward towards the frontiers. On the road we met
"baggage and sick coming to the rear, but could only learn that the
"French and Prussians had been fighting the day before, and that another
"battle was expected when they left the advanced posts. At two o'clock
"we arrived at Genappe, from whence we heard firing very distinctly.
"Half-an-hour afterwards we saw the French columns advancing, and we
"had scarcely taken our position when they attacked us. Our front con-
"sisted of the 3rd and 5th divisions, with some Nassau people, and a
"brigade of cavalry, in all about thirteen thousand men; while the
"French forces, according to Ney's account, must have been immense, as
"his reserve alone consisted of thirty thousand, which, however, he says,
"Buonaparte disposed of without having advertised him. The business
"was begun by the 1st battalion of the 95th, which was sent to drive the
"enemy out of some cornfields and a thick wood, of which they had
"possession. After sustaining some loss we succeeded completely, and
"three companies of Brunswickers were left to keep it, while we acted on
"another part of the line. They, however, were driven out immediately,
"and the French also got possession of a village which turned our flanks.
"We were then obliged to return, and it took us the whole day to retake
"what had been lost. While we were employed here, the remainder of
"the army were in a much more disagreeable situation, for, in consequence
"of our inferiority of cavalry, each regiment was obliged to form a square,
"in which manner the most desperate attacks of infantry and charges of
"cavalry were resisted and repelled; and when night put an end to the
"slaughter, the French not only gave up every attempt on our position,
"but retired from their own, on which we bivouacked. I will not attempt
"to describe the sort of night we passed—I will leave you to conceive it.
"The groans of the wounded and dying, to whom no relief could be
"afforded, must not be spoken of here, because on the 18th it was fifty
"thousand times worse. But a handful of men lying in the face of such
"superior numbers, and being obliged to sleep in squares for fear of
"the enemy's dragoons—knowing that we were weak in that arm—might
"make a dash into the camp, was no very pleasant reverie to soothe one

"to rest. Exclusive of this, I was annoyed by a wound I had received in
"the thigh, and which was becoming excessively painful. I had no great-
"coat, and small rain continued falling until late the next day, when it
"was succeeded by torrents. Boney, however, was determined not to give
"us much respite, for he attacked our picquets at two in the morning.
"Some companies of the 95th were sent to their support, and we con-
"tinued skirmishing until eleven o'clock, when the Duke commenced
"his retreat, which was covered by Lord Uxbridge. The Blues and Life
"Guards behaved extremely well.

"The whole of the 17th—and, indeed, until late the next morning—the
"weather continued dreadful ; and we were starving with hunger, no
"provisions having been served out since the march from Brussels.
"While five officers, who composed our mess, were looking at each other
"with the most deplorable faces imaginable, one of the men brought us
"a fowl he had plundered, and a handful of biscuits, which, though but
"little, added to some tea we boiled in a camp kettle, made us rather more
"comfortable ; and we huddled up together, covered ourselves with
"straw, and were soon as soundly asleep as though reposing on beds of
"down. I awoke long before daylight, and found myself in a very bad
"state altogether, being completely wet through in addition to all other
"ills. Fortunately I soon after this found my way to a shed, of which
"Sir Andrew Barnard (our commandant) had taken possession, where
"there was a fire, and in which, with three or four others, I remained till
"the rain abated. About ten o'clock the sun made his appearance to view
"the mighty struggle which was to determine the fate of Europe, and
"about an hour afterwards the French made their dispositions for the
"attack, which commenced on the right. The Duke's despatch will give
"you a more accurate idea of the ground, and of the grand scale of
"operations, than I can do ; and I shall therefore confine myself to details
"of less importance which he has passed over.

"After having tried the right, and found it strong, Buonaparte man-
"œuvred until he got forty pieces of artillery to play on the left, where
"the 5th division, a brigade of heavy dragoons, and two companies of
"artillery were posted. Our lines were formed behind a hedge, with two
"companies of the 95th extended in front, to annoy the enemy's approach.
"For some time we saw that Buonaparte intended to attack us ; yet, as
"nothing but cavalry were visible, no one could imagine what were his
"plans. It was generally supposed that he would endeavour to turn our
"flank. But, all on a sudden, his cavalry turned to the right and left,
"and showed large masses of infantry, who advanced up in the most

" gallant style, to the cries of ' *Vive l'Empereur !* ' while a most tremen-
" dous cannonade was opened to cover their approach. They had arrived
" at the very hedge behind which we were, the muskets were almost
" muzzle to muzzle, and a French mounted officer had seized the colors of
" the 32nd Regiment, when poor Picton ordered the charge of our brigade,
" commanded by Sir James Kempt. When the French saw us rushing
" through the hedge, and heard the tremendous huzza which we gave,
" they turned ; but, instead of running, they walked off in close columns
" with the greatest steadiness, and allowed themselves to be butchered
" without any material resistance. At this moment, part of General
" Ponsonby's brigade of heavy cavalry took them in flank, and, besides
" killed and wounded, nearly two thousand were made prisoners. Now
" Buonaparte again changed his plan of attack. He sent a great force
" both on the right and left ; but his chief aim was the centre, through
" which lay the road to Brussels, and to gain this he appeared determined.
" What we had hitherto seen was mere ' boys' play ' in comparison with
" the ' tug of war ' which took place from this time (three o'clock) until
" the day was decided. All our army was formed in solid squares. The
" French cuirassiers advanced to the mouth of our cannon ; rushed on
" our bayonets ; sometimes walked their horses on all sides of a square to
" look for an opening through which they might penetrate ; or dashed
" madly on, thinking to carry everything by desperation. But not a British
" soldier moved ; all personal feeling was forgotten in the enthusiasm of
" such a moment. Each person seemed to think the day depended on his
" individual exertions," and both sides vied with each other in acts of
" gallantry. Buonaparte charged with his Imperial Guards. The Duke
" of Wellington led on a brigade consisting of the 52nd and 95th Regi-
" ments. Lord Uxbridge was with every squadron of cavalry which was
" ordered forward. Poor Picton was killed at the head of our division
" while advancing. But, in short, look through the list engaged on that
" day, and it would be difficult to point out one who had not distinguished
" himself as much as another. Until eight o'clock the contest raged
" without intermission, and a feather seemed only wanting in either scale
" to turn the balance. At this hour our situation on the left centre was
" desperate. The 5th division, having borne the brunt of the battle, was
" reduced from six thousand to eighteen hundred. The 6th division—at
" least the British part of it, consisting of four regiments—formed in our
" rear as a reserve was almost destroyed, without having fired a shot, by
" the terrible play of artillery and the fire of the light troops. The 27th
" had four hundred men and every officer but one subaltern knocked

" down in square, without moving an inch or discharging one musket,
" and at that time I mention both divisions could not oppose a sufficient
" front to the enemy, who was rapidly advancing with crowds of fresh
" troops. We had not a single company for support, and the men were so
" completely worn out that it required the greatest exertion on the part of
" the officers to keep up their spirits. Not a soldier thought of giving
" ground ; but victory seemed hopeless, and they gave themselves up to
" death with perfect indifference. A last effort was our only chance. The
" remains of the regiments were formed as well as the circumstances
" allowed, and when the French came within about forty paces, we set up
" a death-howl and rushed at them. They fled immediately, not in a
" regular manner as before, but in the greatest confusion.

" Their animal spirits were exhausted, the panic spread, and in five
" minutes the army was in complete disorder. At this critical moment firing
" was heard on our left. The Prussians were now coming down on the right
" flank of the French, which increased their flight to such a degree that no
" mob was ever a greater scene of confusion ; the road was blocked up by
" artillery ; the dragoons rode over the infantry ; arms, knapsacks, every-
" thing, was thrown away ; and *sauve qui peur* seemed indeed to be the
" universal feeling. At eleven o'clock, when we halted, and gave the
" pursuit to Blucher's fresh troops, one hundred and fifty pieces of cannon
" and numbers of prisoners had fallen into our hands. I will not attempt
" to describe the scene of slaughter which the fields presented, or what
" any person possessed of the least spark of humanity must have felt,
" while we viewed the dreadful situation of some thousands of wounded
" who remained, without assistance, through a bitter cold night, succeeded
" by a day of scorching heat ; English and French were dying by the side
" of each other ; and I have no doubt, hundreds who were not discovered
" when the dead were buried, and who were unable to crawl to any
" habitation, must have perished by famine. For my own part, when we
" halted for the night, I sank down almost insensible from fatigue ; my
" spirits and strength were completely exhausted. I was so weak, and
" the wound in my thigh so painful, from want of attention and in
" consequence of severe exercise, that after I got to Nivelles, and
" secured quarters, I did not awake regularly for 36 hours."

The loss of the regiment on this day was very severe, viz., twenty-eight rank and file killed ; Captain Harrison, Lieutenants Colthurst, Horan, and Jago, Ensigns McCouchy, Birtwhistle, Bennett, and Lieutenant and Adjutant Davis, twenty sergeants, one drummer, and three hundred and sixty-six rank and file wounded. Several of the latter died of their wounds. Lieutenant-General Sir Thomas Picton fell mortally wounded in the rear of the 32nd Regiment, while giving his orders to advance to the first charge. Major-General Kempt then took command of the division, and Lieutenant-Colonel Sir Charles Benson that of the brigade, which was vacated.

In consequence of Major-General Sir Manley Power's appointment to the command of a British brigade, the 32nd Regiment, of which he had been lieutenant-colonel, was removed from the 5th to the 6th division, and into his brigade. On this change the following order from Major-General Sir James Kempt was issued :

"EXTRACT FROM DIVISION ORDERS."

"Arneville, 5th July, 1815.

" The 32nd Regiment will join the 6th Division this day according to " General Order of 3rd instant.

" Major-General Sir James Kempt feels he cannot part with this Regi-" ment without again expressing the very high sense he entertains of its " very distinguished conduct in the Battles of the 16th and 18th June. It " was quite impossible for Troops to behave more nobly or better than the " 32nd Regiment did on these occasions, and he begs Lieutenant-Colonel " Hicks, the Officers and men will accept of his best thanks for their " distinguished Services while under his Command.

"(Sd.) JAMES KEMPT, Major-General."

" War Office, 25th July, 1815,
" H.R.H. the Prince Regent has been pleased in the name and on "behalf of His Majesty to approve of all the British Regiments of Cavalry " and Infantry which were engaged in the Battle of Waterloo being " permitted to bear on their Colours and Appointments in addition to any " other Badges or devices that may have heretofore been granted to those " Regiments the word "Waterloo" in commemoration of their distinguish-" ed services on the 18th June 1815."

On the march from Waterloo to Paris, a considerable number of men who had been slightly wounded, and others who had been employed in conducting the wounded to the rear, rejoined, so that on encamping at Neuilly, near Paris, the regiment mustered three hundred rank and file. Shortly after their arrival at Neuilly, Lieutenant-Colonel Hicks was appointed one of the commandants of Paris, and Major Calvert, who was promoted to lieutenant-colonel by brevet, took command of the regiment. They remained here until 28th October, when the camp was broken up and the troops got into winter quarters. The 32nd Regiment went into a small village called Carrieres, on the banks of the Seine, near Poisoy, which was the head-quarters of the brigade; St. Germains being that of the division. On 16th October, 1815, Lieutenant-Colonel James Maitland took command of the regiment, previous to its leaving Neuilly, and Major Calvert went to England on leave of absence.

"War Office, July 26th, 1816.

"The Prince Regent has been pleased to approve the regiments under-"mentioned, in consideration of their services, wearing the words as under "specified against their names. . . 32nd Foot—'Salamanca;' 'Nivelle.'"

"3rd July, Gonesse (head-quarters from 2nd July, 1815).
"The Fuziliers, 29th, and 32nd are to be the 11th Brigade, and in the "6th Division."

"Paris, 31st August.

"The undermentioned officers to be Commandants of the several "Arrondissements : . . 4th Arrondissement—Lt-Col. Hicks, 32nd Regt."

"Paris, 30th November, 1815.

"The British Troops to return to England are to be brigaded as follows "for their March: 3rd B., 27th, 32nd; Staff Corps, under Col. Sir J. "McLean; 27th Regt."

"Upon breaking up the Army which the Field Marshall has had "the honour to command, he begs leave again to return thanks to the "General Officers and the Officers and Troops for their uniform good "conduct in the late short but memorable campaign; they have given "proofs to the World that they possess in an eminent degree all the "good qualities of Soldiers, and the Field Marshall is happy to be "able to applaud their regular good conduct in their Camps and "Cantonments, not less than when engaged with the Enemy in the "Field.

K

" Whatever may be the future destination of those brave troops of
" which the Field Marshall now takes his leave, he trusts that every
" individual will believe that he will ever feel the deepest interest in
" their honour and welfare, and will always be happy to promote
" either."

It may not be out of place to append the following, which will be read with interest :—

When the celebrated model of the field of Waterloo—now in the museum of the United Service Institution—was being constructed, Captain Siborne addressed a circular letter to the then surviving officers who were present in the campaign of June 1815. Of this letter the most important queries were :

" 1.—What was the particular formation of your regiment at about
" 7 p.m., when the French Imperial Guards reached the crest of
" our position ?

" 2.—What was the formation of that part of the enemy's forces
" immediately to your front ? "

The replies received from officers of the 32nd Regiment are extracted from *Waterloo Letters*, by Major-General Siborne.

From Lieutenant-Colonel F. Calvert :

" Hemsdon House, Ware,
" April 19th, 1835.

" I must proceed as well as I can in answering your Queries, which I
" have numbered in the order they appear in your letter.

" 1st.—The 32nd Regiment was in line on the crest of the hill behind the
" hedge which was at right angles from the road leading from Brussels to
" Charleroi, nearly opposite to the farm-house of La Haye Sainte.

" 2nd.—The enemy descended from their position in columns along the
" aforesaid road, and on each side of it.

" The 32nd Regiment was in Sir James Kempt's brigade, and in the
" division of Sir Thomas Picton. It suffered severely in the action of the
" 16th at Les Quatre Bras, and on the morning of Waterloo was posted
" with its right on the road from Brussels to Charleroi, extending along the
" hedge mentioned in my reply to the first query. The remainder of the

"brigade was to its left, with the exception of the Rifle Corps, which, with
"a Belgian battalion, covered the front as skirmishers.

"From about half-past twelve p.m., the brigade had to sustain repeated
"attacks (in one of which Sir T. Picton was killed) from, I believe, the
"entire First Corps of the French army. At about three o'clock Sir John
"Lambert's brigade (27th, 4th, and 40th) arrived. The 32nd then formed
"in support, still keeping the ridge, from which it never was allowed to
"move.

"Shortly afterwards in was formed in square, though not menaced by
"cavalry, following the example of the rest of the army to the right and
"left of the road. At about five o'clock the Duke of Wellington rode up
"and ordered the regiment to deploy. Later in the evening (the 27th
'having nearly lost all its men) it advanced again towards the hedge until
"it joined the rest of the army in its final charge.

"I have, &c.,
"F. CALVERT, Lieut.-Col., H.P."

From the same :

"United Service Club, March 11th, 1837.

"The regiment marched from Brussels early on the morning of the 16th
"of June, and halted for a couple of hours near the village of Waterloo.
"It then resumed its march, and arrived at Quatre Bras about two o'clock.

"It was moved immediately along the Namur Chaussée until it came to
"the point which I have marked on the map, where it formed line, awaiting
"the approach of the enemy, who were descending in column from the
"opposite hill.

"When this attacking force had crossed both hedges lining the meadow
"in the bottom, and had commenced ascending our position, the 32nd
"Regiment poured upon it a heavy fire, succeeded by a charge. This the
"enemy did not wait to receive, but retired with precipitation, and, getting
"entangled in the hedges on returning to their position, must have suffered
"considerable loss. We halted and re-formed at the first hedge, when
"Sir Thomas Picton desired the regiment to retire to its original
"position.

"The 79th Regiment on our left, carried on by its ardour, went on much
"further, crossed the meadow, and even ventured to assail the enemy's
"position. They were, however, soon recalled.

"Attacks similar to the above were renewed several times during the
"evening, and always with similar results. After the action was concluded
"our ground was occupied by some German troops, when we moved to

"our right and took up our ground for the night near the high road between "Quatre Bras and Charleroi.

"On the following day we were the last infantry that left the ground, "and retired about eleven o'clock a.m., followed by the cavalry, which had "arrived during the night.

"I have, &c.,
"F. CALVERT, Colonel Unattached,
"Late of 32nd Regiment."

"From Captain R. T. Belcher, half-pay, Lieutenant, 32nd Regiment.

"Bandon, February 27th, 1843.
"Memorandum:

"The 32nd Regiment formed the right of Sir James Kempt's Brigade, "the 95th, which on the line of march usually formed the right, being "detached skirmishing. The Regiment was formed into six divisions in "consequence of its reduced numbers, having suffered severely at Quatre "Bras. I commanded the left centre division.

"In the second attack of the French Infantry on the left centre of the "line, the Brigade advanced in line to charge. Immediately on passing "the narrow road which ran along our front, the Ensign carrying the "Regimental Colour was severely wounded (Ensign Birtwhistle). I took "the Colour from him until another Ensign could be called.

"Almost instantly after, the Brigade still advancing and the French "Infantry getting into disorder and beginning to retreat, a mounted "(French) officer had his horse shot under him. When he extricated "himself we were close on him. I had the Colour on my left arm and was "slightly in advance of the division.

"He suddenly fronted me, and seized the staff, I still retaining a grasp "of the silk (the Colours were nearly new).

"At the same moment he attempted to draw his sabre, but had not "accomplished it when the Covering Colour-Sergeant, named Switzer, "thrust his pike into his breast, and the right rank and file of the division, "named Lacy, fired into him. He fell dead at my feet.

"Brevet-Major Toole, commanding the right centre division at the "moment, called out, 'Save the brave fellow;' but it was too late.

"ROBERT T. BELCHER."

Extract from letter of Lieutenant Colonel Leach, C.B., captain and brevet major, 95th Rifles;

"The fierce onset of the French, with overwhelming numbers, forced
"back my two companies on the main body of the 95th Regiment, which
" . . . was also instantly assailed in such a manner as to render it
"impossible for one weak battalion, consisting of only six companies, to
"stem the torrent for any length of time. We were consequently con-
"strained to fall back on the 32nd Regiment, which was in line near the
"thorn hedge which runs from the Genappe road to the left, and along the
"front of Picton's division.

"We were closely pressed and hotly engaged during the retrograde
"movement, and very soon after reaching the spot where the 32nd was in
"position, a volley and a charge of bayonets caused the French to recoil
"in disorder and with a heavy loss ; and it was at this moment of fire,
"smoke, and excitement that the heavy cavalry appeared among us, and
"instantly charged that infantry which the fire and charge of bayonets
"from Picton's division had previously shattered and broken."

1816-17.

Arrangements having been made for the formation of the army of occupation, all the weak regiments were sent to England, and the 32nd embarked at Calais, landing at Dover, and marched to Sheerness, where it was quartered. Some time after the regiment marched to Colchester, where it halted for twelve days, and then proceeded to Portsmouth and embarked for Guernsey and Alderney, remaining there until December 1816, and returned to Portsmouth, being quartered in Hilsea barracks until June, 1817.

Apropos of the returning of the regiments after the Waterloo campaign, a very interesting account is given in the Earl of Albemarle's *Fifty years of my life,* his battalion—3rd battalion 14th Regiment—having landed at Dover within a few days of the 32nd Regiment:

" Public feeling had undergone a great revulsion in regard to us
" soldiers. The country was saturated with glory, and was brooding
" over the bill that it had to pay for the article. Waterloo, and Waterloo
" men, were at a discount. We were made painfully sensible of the
" change. If we had been convicts disembarking from a hulk, we
" could not have been met with less consideration. ' It's us pays they
" chaps,' was the remark of a country bumpkin, as we came on shore.

"It was a bitter cold day when we landed; no cheers, like those "which greeted the Crimean army, welcomed us home. The only "persons who took any notice of us were the custom-house officers, "and they kept us under arms for hours, in the cold, while they "subjected us to a rigid search. These functionaries were unusually "on the alert, because a day or two before a brigade of artillery, with "guns loaded to the muzzles with French lace, had slipped through "their fingers. Our treatment was all of a piece. Towards dark we "were ordered to Dover Castle, part of which building served as a "prison. Our barracks were strictly in keeping with such a locality, "cold, dark, gloomy, and dungeon-like. No food was to be got but "our rations, no furniture but what the barrack stores afforded."

1818-19.

The regiment continued the whole of the year 1818 in the Citadel barracks, and did duty with the 10th and 28th regiments in the course of the year. The commanding officer, Lieutenant-Colonel James Maitland, exchanged with Lieutenant-Colonel the Honble. John Maitland, inspecting field officer, Ionian Militia, who joined and took command on the 24th July, 1818. The regiment remained the greater part of the year 1819 in the Citadel barracks at Corfu. In the month of February the regiment was reduced to the peace establishment.

In March the grenadier company embarked on board H.M.S. *Glasgow*, Captain the Honble. Anthony Maitland, for the purpose of cruising for six weeks off the fortress of Parga, on the coast of Albania, to throw this force into that garrison, then occupied by four companies of the 75th Regiment, in case of its being attacked by the Turks, which at this time was apprehended. Again, in the month of October, in this year, two captains, one lieutenant, three ensigns, and two hundred privates, with non-commissioned officers in proportion, were sent to the island of Santa Maria. Some fifteen hundred well-armed peasants made an attack upon the town, which was held by a party of the 28th Regiment and some Royal Artillery, under command of Colonel, (afterwards Sir Frederick) Stovin. A request for reinforcements was sent to Corfu, and on the arrival thence of the light companies of the 28th and 32nd regiments, the insurgents, who had got possession of the town, were driven out, and took up a position in the village of Spakiotes.* This position was subsequently stormed, and the insurgents dispersed, in which service a few men of the 32nd Regiment were wounded. Several of the Greek priests, who had acted as ringleaders, were hanged.

At the end of June, 1817, the regiment was ordered to embark for the Mediterranean, touching at Gibraltar and Malta on its way to Corfu.

It landed there on 30th August and was quartered in the Citadel Barracks, continuing to do duty in that garrison for the remainder of the year.

The Ionian islands, then governed by Sir Thomas Maitland, appears to have been by no means the agreeable quarters they became in after times. Their sanitary repute was indifferent, the political situation critical. Ali Pacha still held sway in Janina, and the Greek struggle for independence was just commencing. Maitland, whom Sir C. Napier pithily described as " a rough old despot, " surrounded by sycophants, who worshipped him because he had a "little more brains than they," was very high handed in his dealings ; the duties of the garrison were very severe, and—unless strangely misrepresented—discipline was occasionally enforced in a fashion which travested justice and common sense alike.

Order having been restored in the island, the detachment rejoined the head-quarters at Corfu on 3rd November.

1820-21.

The 32nd Regiment remained the greater part of the year 1820 in the Citadel barracks at Corfu, doing duty with the 8th and 28th regiments. On 9th and 10th June, Major-General Sir Frederick Adam made a minute inspection of the regiment, both in its field movements and interior economy, and expressed himself in a Brigade Order as follows :

---

* Subsequently destroyed by an earthquake, on which occasion the smaller detachment there stationed escaped through being absent on fatigue duty.

"GARRISON ORDERS.

"Brigade Major's Office,
"Corfu, 21st June, 1820.

"The Major-General has completed his inspection of the 32nd "Regiment, and has great pleasure in expressing his approbation of the "improvement which has taken place in that Corps, of the good order in "which he has found it in all respects, both of its interior economy and "discipline. There is a marked improvement too in the accuracy of its "movements in the Field since the Major-General had last an opportunity "of observing them previous to his going to England. The Major-General "does not form his opinion of the condition of a Corps merely from what "comes under his notice at a single Inspection, but it is the result of his "general and continued observation, and he is not inclined to express any "opinion on casual or temporary acquaintance with the Regiment.

"In a word, the improvement of the 32nd Regiment is 'Great,' and its "present state highly creditable to the exertions of Lieutenant-Colonel The "Honble. John Maitland and the Officers who have seconded him in "bringing it about.

"The great attention of the Non-commissioned Officers and the "improved behaviour of the men is best evinced by the state of the "Regiment and by the fact of the diminution in the 'Severe Punishment' "since Lieutenant-Colonel Maitland took the Command.

"(Sd.) J. RUDSDAIL, Major Brigade."

In answer to the Half-Yearly Report, the following letters were received by the commanding officer:

"Horse Guards, 10th Febry., 1821.
"Sir,
"I have not failed to lay before the Commander-in-Chief your "Despatch of the 16th December last with its enclosure, and am directed "to acquaint you that His Royal Highness has received, with great "satisfaction, the favourable report of the 8th and 32nd Regiments so "creditable to their Commanding Officers (Lieutenant-Colonel Duffy and "Honble. John Maitland) and he will not fail to recommend to His "Majesty that the suspension of all promotion in the former Corps shall "now in consequence of this Report be taken off.

"I have, etc.,
"(Sd.) H. TAYLOR.
"Lieutenant-General
"Rt. Hon. Sir Thos. Maitland, G.C.B."

"Corfu, 8th April, 1821.
"Sir,
"I have the honor, by direction of the Major-General Commanding, "to transmit for your information the enclosed copy of Letter from Major-"General Sir Herbert Taylor, together with an extract from one from the "Adjutant General of the Forces, conveying His Royal Highness The "General Commanding-in-Chief's pleasure on the Half-Yearly Report "made of the 32nd Regiment for the second period of the last year.

"I have, etc., etc.,
"*(Sd.)*   J. RUDSDAIL,
"Actg. Milty. Secretary.
"The Honble.
"J. Maitland,
"Commdg. 32nd Regt."

In the latter end of July a detachment of the regiment, under Major Dillon, proceeded to the island of Zante, for the purpose of quelling an insurrection of the inhabitants. They remained there until the end of the year.

In January, 1821, the head-quarters of the regiment were removed from Corfu to Caphalonia, for the purpose of relieving the 75th Regiment. That part of the regiment which had remained at Zante till the end of 1820 proceeded to Santa Maura and Ithaca. In the month of July the head-quarters were removed from Caphalonia to Corfu, having been relieved by the 36th Regiment, from Malta. In August, a company was sent from Corfu to the island of Cerigo, leaving only the two flank companies at head-quarters, under the command of Lieutenant-Colonel Maitland. The regiment now garrisoned the islands of Santa Maura, Ithaca, Paxo, and Cerigo, having its head-quarters at Corfu. In October of this year, the regiment was again reduced from ten to eight companies.

1822-25.

In the month of May, 1822, the regimental detachments were relieved by the 51st (or King's Own) Light Infantry, and the regiment being assembled at Corfu was quartered at Fort Neuf and the Citadel barracks.

The regiment continued doing duty in the Ionian islands for the next three years.

On 30th June, 1825, the commanding officer received the following notification relative to the return of the 32nd Regiment to England.

"London, 20th May, 1825.
"Sir,
"I have the honour to annex for your information, a copy of a Letter "from the Horse Guards relative to the return of the 32nd Regiment to "this country.
"We have, etc., etc.,
"(Sd.)   C. & E. HOPKINSON.
"Lieut.-Colonel The Honble. J. Maitland,
    Com. 32nd Regiment."

"Horse Guards,
    "14th May, 1825.
"Sir,
"I have the honor to notify to you, by the Commander-in Chief's "Command, that His Majesty is pleased to direct that the 32nd Regiment "shall return to this country from the Mediterranean on being replaced by "a Regiment which will be sent out for that purpose.
"(Sd.)   H. TORRENS.
"To Gen. Campbell,
    "Col., 32nd Regiment."

On 22nd and 23rd July the *Princess Royal* and *Diadem*, transports, arrived at Corfu, having on board the head-quarters and part of the 7th Royal Fusiliers for the purpose of relieving the 32nd Regiment. On the 28th the head-quarters and three companies embarked on board the *Princess Royal*, under the command of Lieutenant-Colonel the Honble. John Maitland, and three companies were embarked in the *Diadem*, under the command of Major Dillon. Having received orders to proceed to Portsmouth, they sailed the following morning.

The 32nd Regiment having been paraded for embarkation, the following General Order, from Lieutenant-General Sir Frederic Adam, commanding the forces in the Ionian islands, was read at the head of the regiment by Lieutenant-Colonel Knitt, deputy-adjutant-general, previous to marching off; and it was peculiarly gratifying to the corps to witness the feeling of regret evinced by the garrison and inhabitants in general, and the 28th Regiment in particular, at their departure.

EXTRACT.

"GENERAL ORDER, No. 1.
"Adjutant-General's Office,
"Ionian Islands, Head-Qrs.,
"Corfu, 28th July, 1825.

"The Lieutenant-General cannot allow the 32nd Regiment to quit "the Station in which it has been for eight years, under his immediate "Command and observation, without expressing to the Honble. Lieutenant- "Colonel Maitland, to the Officers, Non-commissioned Officers and "soldiers of this excellent Corps, the strong sense he entertains of their "exemplary and Military Conduct, and his entire approbation founded on "a thorough knowledge of the Regiment in all its parts and all its "details.

"If some instances of individual crime occurred in the Regiment during "the earlier part of its station, and if these from their nature have been "subject to Public investigation and Public punishment, still there is "nothing in them that could in any way reflect on the character and "reputation of the Corps, but they have been of a description which it "were absurd not to expect should occasionally occur in any large collected "body of men.

"Approving as the Lieutenant-General does of the whole deportment "and conduct of the Regiment, he must yet select one particular by which "it has been particularly distinguished. The orderly, tranquil, and "creditable conduct of the Officers and men in their quarters, and their "kind and friendly behaviour towards all the inhabitants in all the Islands "in which they have been stationed, a deportment this, which he wishes "to hold out as an example, because nothing can tend to raise the British "name or to conciliate the affections and respect of a population who are "protected by the British Crown.

"The Deportment of the Officers in general in all its bearings, whether "Military or social, reflects upon them the highest credit. It is due to the "Honble. Lieutenant-Colonel Maitland to state that the Regiment, since "he assumed the Command of it, has greatly improved in every particular, "and the Lieutenant-General has only to express his deep regret that he "has no longer the satisfaction of retaining under his Command a Corps "which has such strong claims on his approbation, and which he shall feel "a pride in seeing again under his command under any circumstances "either in Peace or War.

"*(Sd.)* D. KNITT, Dy.-Adjt. General."

The two remaining companies of the 32nd Regiment waited at Corfu until the arrival of the *Borodino*, transport, with the remainder of the 7th Royal Fusiliers, and they embarked in that transport on 24th August, and sailed the following morning.

MAJOR SIR J. F. DILLON.

The head-quarters, on board the *Princess Royal*, arrived in Plymouth Sound on 19th September and remained in quarantine until the 28th, when they disembarked and relieved the 24th Regiment, in barracks, at Devonport, which then embarked for Ireland The *Diadem*, transport, arrived with the detachment under the command of Major Dillon,* who had previously occupied the barracks, and the *Borodino*, transport, also arrived, with the two companies under Captain Reid, and disembarked on 17th November following.

That part of the regiment which had arrived in England was inspected by Major-General Sir John Cameron, K.C.B., on 22nd October, 1825, and the following is the extract from a letter from the adjutant-general to Lieutenant-Colonel the Honble. John Maitland, alluding to Sir Frederick Adam's order and Sir J. Cameron's report.

---

* Afterwards Sir J. Dillon, Bart.

"Horse Guards,
"16th November, 1825.
"Sir,
"According to your desire I return you a copy of the General "Order given out by Sir Frederick Adam on the departure of the 32nd "Regiment from the Ionian Islands.

"I have laid it before the Commander-in-Chief, and have to assure you "that His Royal Highness has expressed the greatest satisfaction at the "perusal of a Document so highly creditable to the old Corps you "Commanded and so very honourable to yourself.

"I have also brought to His Royal Highness' notice the very handsome "report of the Regiment transmitted from Plymouth by Major-General "Sir J. Cameron.

"*(Sd.)* HENRY TORRENS."

1826-28.

On 16th March, 1826, the regiment removed from Devonport and occupied the Citadel barracks at Plymouth, relieving the 8th Regiment, which embarked for Scotland, and on 26th May, Major-General Sir John Cameron made his half-yearly inspection of the regiment, and he again expressed himself in the highest possible terms on every part of its equipment and discipline.

On 19th June the route was received for the march of the regiment to the northern district. The 1st division marched the following day. The head-quarters left Plymouth on 8th July and arrived at Halifax, in Yorkshire, on 4th August. The 32nd Regiment was now detached to Bradford, Stockport, Bury, Rochdale, Wakefield, and Oldham.

The head-quarters and different detachments were inspected by Major-General the Honble. W. G. Harris, in October, 1826. In December of the same year the head-quarters was removed to Manchester, and on 10th January, 1827, the whole of the regiment was assembled at Liverpool for the purpose of embarking for Ireland, which it did on the 12th of the same month, and landed the following day in Dublin; three days afterwards it marched in four divisions for Parsonstown barracks, in Kings county, where it arrived on the 18th, 19th, 20th, and 22nd of that month.

On 28th April the regiment received orders to proceed to Limerick, and marched on 30th April and 1st and 7th May. The head-quarters was stationed in the Castle barracks. The 37th Regiment, which had lately returned from America, also occupied the Castle barracks and relieved the different detachments.

The regiment continued the whole of 1827 and the greater part of 1828 in Limerick, relieving the different detachments every three months, and sending out at these times between four hundred and five hundred men. On 17th May and 28th September, 1827, and 14th May, 1828, the regiment was inspected by Major-General Sir Charles Boyle, K.C.B., commanding the south western district, who, on all these occasions, was pleased to express his approbation in every respect.

On 28th September, 1828, the regiment received a route to march from Limerick to Kilkenny; two companies from the head-quarters on the 29th and the head-quarters on the 30th, and arrived at its destination on 3rd and 4th October. The different detachments in the counties of Clare and Limerick joined the head-quarters at different periods; the last outpost arrived on 23rd October. On 11th October routes were received to detach three companies, viz.: Carlow, Athy, and Maryborough.

1829.

On Sunday, 10th May, routes were received for the head-quarters and four companies to march from Kilkenny to Dublin. They marched on Monday, the 11th, and on the 18th the whole of the regiment was quartered in Richmond barracks. A few days after its arrival the regiment was inspected by Lieutenant-General the Rt. Honble. Sir John Byng, K.C.B., commander of the forces in Ireland.

1830.

On 11th May, 1830, the regiment received an order to hold itself in readiness to embark for Canada, and on the 15th a notification of the establishment of the service and reserve companies was also received. On the 29th, the 1st division, under the command of Captain Reoch, (consisting of one captain, four subalterns, one assistant surgeon, six sergeants, four corporals, two drummers, and one hundred and thirteen privates,) marched from Richmond barracks, Dublin, and embarked at Kingstown on board the *Britomart*, transport, and sailed from thence on 2nd June.

The 2nd division, under the command of Major Palk, (consisting of one major, two captains, three lieutenants, one ensign, one paymaster, eight sergeants, nine corporals, two drummers, and one hundred and fifty-seven privates) embarked on board the *Perseus*, freight ship, on 4th of June, and sailed on the 7th of the same month.

On 7th June the reserve companies, (consisting of one field officer, four captains, eight subalterns, twelve sergeants, twelve corporals, four drummers, and one hundred and thirty-three privates) marched to Boyle, under the command of Major Wingfield.

The head-quarters, under the command of Lieutenant-Colonel the Honble. John Maitland (consisting of one lieutenant-colonel, two captains, three ensigns, one adjutant, one quarter-master, one surgeon, fifteen sergeants, nine corporals, five drummers, and one hundred and eighty-eight privates), vacated Richmond barracks, being replaced by the 76th Regiment, and embarked at Kingston on board the *Hebe*, freight ship, on 8th June, and sailed on the 16th.

The *Britomart* arrived in Quebec harbour on 24th July, the *Hebe* on 6th August, and the *Perseus* on the 8th.

The 32nd Regiment now composed part of the garrison of Quebec, consisting of the 15th, 24th, and 32nd regiments. Shortly after the arrival of the regiment it was reviewed by Lieutenant-General Sir James Kempt, G.C.B., who, previous to his departure for England, in October, made his half-yearly inspection of the regiment.

1831-37.

From an account of the celebration of the king's birthday, on 28th May, 1831, it appears that the 24th, 32nd, and 71st Light Infantry then formed the garrison of Quebec. There is not much to be learned of the regiment during this period, but an interesting account of a boat race—which appeared in the *Quebec Mercury* of 26th May, 1832—in which Captains Markham and Hodges, with

Lieutenants Brooke and Baines, of the 32nd regiment, formed one of the crews, recalls incidentally the good services which have been done by British officers in all parts of the world in promoting a taste for manly sports and pastimes.

This year General Alexander Campbell, of Munrie, N.B., died, and the colonelcy of the regiment was conferred on Lieutenant-General Sir Samuel Venables Hinde,* K.C.B., who had commanded the 1st battalion 32nd Regiment throughout the Peninsular war.

The Regimental Records are absolutely silent as to the next five years, and one can only infer from this that the ordinary routine work, with little variation, took place. However, there were some hard days before the regiment, for in 1837 it had been removed to Montreal, where the Canadian rebellion—styled "the Papinean rebellion," by a body called " *Fils de la Liberté* "—broke out. The chief cause of this outbreak—which, however, seems to have been smouldering for some time—was brought about by the Canadian House of Assembly refusing to vote supplies. The 32nd Regiment was employed against the rebels in Lower Canada, who, under the influence of certain party leaders, had broken out into acts of open rebellion.

In the following November the rebel leaders were supposed to have taken up their quarters in the villages of St. Charles and St. Denis, on the right bank of the Richel, and their immediate capture being considered desirable, Colonel Gore, deputy quarter-master-general, was sent with a party of troops from Sorel, the advance of which was formed by the light company 32nd Regiment, under Captain F. Markham, to St. Denis, while Colonel Weatherall, of the Royals, with another party, proceeded to St. Charles.

After a toilsome night march of twelve hours through heavy rain, St. Denis, which was but eighteen miles from Sorel, was reached at 10 a.m., and a party of fifteen hundred rebels was found posted in a fortified stone house, with a well flanked barricade blocking the road. Some sharp fighting ensued, but as the field piece which had accompanied the party could make no impression on the defences,

---

*For services see *Appendix*.

Captain Thos. Impett.
1828.

and the men were much exhausted, their wet clothes frozen stiff upon their backs, Colonel Gore, after spending nearly all his ammunition, was compelled to retire, with a loss of six killed and ten wounded; of this number, the 32nd light company had two men killed, five men wounded, and four missing, including one wounded man. Captain Markham himself was severely wounded, having had two bullets through his neck, and whilst being carried away—on Colonel Gore retiring—by Sergeant Allcock and a private, was wounded by a third bullet through the calf of his leg, and several bullets grazed his knee.

Lieutenant Weir, 32nd regiment, in trying to overtake the detachment which left Sorel on the night of the 22nd (he having been despatched from Montreal that morning by land, to order the detachment at Sorel to be in readiness to join Colonel Gore's party) on landing that evening at Sorel, and arriving after the detachment had marched, (viz., 10 p.m., 22nd November) he having taken the front road, and the detachment marching by the back road, fell into the hands of the rebels at St. Ours, and was murdered by them. His body was found on 2nd December in the river Richelieu, at St. Denis, in about two feet of water, covered with large stones.

Colonel Wetherall, with better fortune, reached St. Charles after some delay, and drove the rebels out at the point of the bayonet.

On 30th November, Colonel Gore, with four companies 32nd, two companies 66th, one company 24th, and one company 83rd, with a twelve-pounder Howitzer, marched from Sorel, and on the following day attempted to break through the ice of the Richelieu with a steamboat, but, failing in this, crossed the ice and proceeded to St. Ours, and thence to St. Denis, which—having been abandoned the night before—was occupied without opposition.

Three companies of the 32nd Regiment and a field gun, under Major Reed, 32nd regiment, were left at St. Denis, and the rest moved on to St. Charles and afterwards to St. Hyacinthe. The rebel leaders had, meanwhile, escaped to the United States, and the four companies 32nd, with the rest of Colonel Gore's force, returned to Sorel.

The rebels under arms between the Yanaska and the Richelieu being dispersed, arrangements were made for sending a body of troops into the country of the lake of two mountains, their stronghold at Grand Brulé and Riviére de Chêne. The force consisted of the 32nd and 83rd regiments, brigaded under Colonel Maitland, and the Royals and some other troops, brigaded under Colonel Wetherall. The principal post, St. Eustache, was captured by Maitland's brigade, with a loss of one killed and eight wounded ; the 32nd had one man wounded only. Afterwards the villages of St. Scholastique, St. Therèse, &c., were occupied by the 32nd, the arms and ammunition of the inhabitants being given up without opposition. In his report, Colonel Maitland speaks highly of the steadiness and good conduct of the troops, and the forbearance shown by them towards the rebels.*

The foregoing movements were under the direction of General Sir J. Colbourne.

1838.

Early in January, 1838, the head-quarters of the regiment proceeded by water to the Upper Province, and while *en route* were frozen in among the Thousand Isles. After remaining some days in this position, they crossed on the ice, it being sufficiently strong to bear them, to the mainland, and thence proceeded to Kingston, Toronto, and New London. The remainder of the regiment had been previously stationed for some time in the latter place.

The greater part of the regiment was now sent on to Amherstburg, where the 34th regiment was also quartered, and Colonel Maitland took command of the District. A large number of American sympathisers having taken possession of the island of Point-au-Rils, an English force, consisting of two guns, a detachment of the 32nd Regiment, and a party of Volunteer cavalry, was organised against them. They proceeded up the lake to Chichester, about eighteen miles, arriving there on the evening of 2nd March, 1838.

Early the following morning the party crossed in sleighs from the mainland, a distance of about sixteen miles, arriving at the island about sunrise.

---

* *London Gazette*, 1838.

NOTE.—The late Dr. Henry, who was serving there (Canada) at the time as surgeon to the 66th Regiment, gives the following account of this affair in his *Events of a Military Life*, vol. iii. :

"A more serious attempt than any of these predatory irruptions was "made at a large British island, near the head of Lake Erie, called Point "Peleé island, which is inhabited, and about twenty miles distant from the "Canadian shore. Here a body of American brigands, armed to the teeth "with rifles, pistols, bayonets, and large carvers as sharp as razors, called "bowie knives, landed on 28th February, 1838, seized the inhabitants and "plundered them, and made preparations for crossing to the vicinity of "Amherstberg. But there was a vigilant officer there who anticipated "their attack.

"Colonel the Honble. John Maitland, commanding 32nd Regiment, "having previously sent Captain Glasgow, R.A. (an active officer through- "out this winter) to see if the ice was still passable, moved with a strong "detachment from Amherstberg, and after travelling all night in sleighs a "distance of forty miles, at a temperature below zero, arrived at the island "about daybreak. Here the Colonel detached Captain Browne, 32nd "Regiment, with two weak companies to the south shore, with the intention "of cutting off the retreat of the invaders to the American side ; whilst he "himself, with the main body, slowly penetrated through the deep snow, "at the northern end, in quest of them. The band of marauders, suddenly "finding themselves surrounded, boldly determined to concentrate their "force and attack Browne's detachment, not one hundred strong, thus "opening their way back to Sandusky. They accordingly advanced in "regular military order, throwing out skirmishers, who covered themselves "by large blocks of ice along the shore, and opened a hot fire on the "32nd. Browne was not slow in returning their fire ; but, finding himself "outflanked and his men falling fast, he formed his small force in line at "extended order, and so charged his assailants with the bayonet, who, "although four to one in number, immediately broke and took to the wood. "Soon after they escaped in their sleighs to the American shore, with the "loss of four of their chiefs killed and over seventy killed and wounded. "Now this was a very brilliant little affair, and did honour to the steadiness "of the 32nd and their intrepid leader, Browne, who proved himself the "man of resources, his power of mind and firmness giving promise of "future fame, and demonstrating that the lesson he received in early life at "Waterloo had not been forgotten."

The cavalry and two companies of the 32nd Regiment, under the command of Captain Browne, of the latter corps, were sent round to the end of the island to intercept the retreat of the enemy.

The main body, under Captain Birtwhistle, 32nd regiment, with two guns, advanced through the island and compelled the enemy to retire.

The Americans, while retiring, came upon a party sent to intercept them, when a smart action ensued, in which more than thirty of the small number of the 32nd regiment engaged were wounded, two of whom subsequently died of their wounds. Captain Browne, perceiving the loss he was sustaining, extended his small line by opening the files, and in this order charged down on the rebels, putting them to flight and making several of them prisoners. For his gallant conduct on this occasion he received a brevet majority.

1839-43.

In April, 1839, the regiment returned to New London, where Colonel Maitland died the following winter.

The regiment was subsequently stationed for twelve months at Toronto, and proceeded to Montreal, and thence to St. Helens, where it was quartered about two months.

The regiment continued in Upper Canada, under command of Lieutenant-Colonel Wingfield, until July, 1841, when it was brought down from Toronto to Quebec, and embarked for home in the *Apollo*, transport, which had brought the 68th Light Infantry from Jamaica to Canada.

The service companies landed at Portsmouth on 17th September, 1841, and marched into quarters at Fort Cumberland, where the four-company depôt which had been brought round from Plymouth awaited them.

Shortly after the arrival of the regiment at Portsmouth, Lieutenant Rashbrook, a very young officer, was drowned in the Dockyard while going visiting rounds at night. He was interred with military honours, " the grenadier company, to which he belonged, wearing " white favours in their bearskins."

From Portsmouth the regiment moved to Leeds, owing to disturbances having occurred there, where it was stationed in 1843.

General Sir Robert McFarlane, who had succeeded to the regiment on the death of Sir S. V. Hinde in 1837, died this year, and was succeeded by Lieutenant-General Sir John Buchan, K.C.B., K.C.T.S.

1844-47.

In 1844, the regiment moved from Leeds to Manchester, and in 1845 was transferred to Dublin, subsequently moving to Mullingar and Athlone.

On 19th March, 1846, the regiment moved to Fermoy, orders being received for it to proceed to India.

On 29th May, 1846, the regiment, in five detachments, under the command of Lieutenant-Colonel Fred Markham, embarked on board the transports *British Sovereign, Duchess of Northumberland, Edinburgh, General Palmer,* and *Abourkir,* for its first tour of duty in India. The transports reached Calcutta within a short time of one another—the first fortnight in September; and the troops proceeded by water to Chinsurat, *en route* to Agra. The destination of the regiment was changed to Meerut. It encamped at Benares on 1st January, 1847, while still *en route* to Meerut.

The regiment arrived at Meerut on 19th February, 1847, and was stationed there until 14th February the following year. While here, two officers—Lieutenant Sullivan and Lieutenant Money-Kyrle—died.

The regiment also lost their last Waterloo veteran, by the retirement, on half-pay, of Major George Browne, a brave old officer who had entered the regiment in 1813, fought with it at Quatre Bras and Waterloo, and subsequently much distinguished himself in the affair at Point Peleé island, during the Canadian rebellion.

1848-51.

The first Sikh war was over, and there appeared to be a general calm throughout the land for the first two years after the regiment reached India. In the beginning of 1848, a strong British and native garrison, under Sir John Littler, held Lahore, to protect the chief sirdars from their turbulent fellow-countrymen; and the reconstruction of the government in the Punjaub was progressing, to all appearances, satisfactorily. But mischief was brewing at Mooltan. Negotiations had been going on for some time between the British durbar at Lahore and Moolraj, the dewan or governor of Mooltan, to induce or compel the latter to resign, in favour of Sirdar Khan Singh.

At the request of the Moolraj, two British commissioners—Mr. Vans Agnew, assistant-resident at Lahore, and Lieutenant Anderson, Bombay Fusiliers, had been sent to effect the transfer. They arrived in Mooltan, with a very small escort, on 17th April, 1848; the transfer of the Government was formally completed, the work of the mission done, when the two Englishmen were attacked and desperately wounded. Three days afterwards they were foully murdered, in their place of refuge, without the walls. A revolt at Lahore, and the preaching of a jehad, or holy war followed. Moolraj took the field with five thousand men, but was checkmated by the foresight and indomitable energy of Herbert Edwardes, then a young subaltern employed on revenue duty in the neighbourhood of Mooltan. At the head of a heterogeneous collection of hastily formed levies, in whom he managed to infuse some of his own spirit, he effected a junction with Colonel Van Cortland, commanding at Dhera Isma Khan, and inflicted some severe defeats on the Mooltanese, driving them back under their own walls, where they were kept at bay until the arrival of the British troops, under General Whish, in the following August.

The 32nd Regiment had, on the first intelligence of the assassination, been moved from Umballa to Ferozepore, arriving there on 27th May, having suffered severely from the hot weather on the march. Captain Gardiner died from heat apoplexy, and there were a great many casualties amongst the non-commissioned officers and men. While here the 32nd received orders to join the Mooltan field forces, and marched on 10th August. The excessive heat, both day and night, caused a great number of deaths on this march. Water was scarce and bad. The regiment joined the force under General Whish on 25th August, and formed part of the left column; descended the Sutlej, partly in steamers, partly in native boats, reaching the place of landing the day after the right column which had moved from Lahore. Thence four marches brought them in front of the city of Mooltan.

"The heat during this march," writes an officer of the regiment who was present, "was terrific. The thermometer registered one "hundred and thirty degrees in the men's tents, one hundred and "twenty-seven degrees in the hospital, and one hundred and "eighteen degrees in the officers' tents; and of a detachment of four "and a half companies which reached its halting place before "sunrise one day, there were fourteen men to be buried at sunset."

General Whish, with the right columns, encamped at Seelul-Ke-Maree, six miles distant from Mooltan, on 18th August.

The Ferozepore columns marched next day, as before stated. The siege-train did not arrive until 4th September, when Whish had under his orders a force of eight thousand troops, with thirty-two pieces of siege ordnance and twelve field guns. A motley collection of regular and irregular levies, under Van Cortlandt, Herbert Edwardes, and Lake; and a body of Sikh troops, under Shere Singh, brought up the strength of the besiegers to eight thousand four hundred and seventeen cavalry, and fourteen thousand three hundred and twenty-seven infantry, with forty-five guns of all calibres, and four mortars.* Opposed to these, Moolraj had under his orders in Mooltan a force of ten thousand men, of whom one thousand two hundred were cavalry. The city was surrounded by a wall of burned brick, forty feet high, surmounted by thirty towers, and covered by a ditch, with masonry scarp and counterscarp. The citadel stood upon a mound, and was a formidable work naturally as well as artificially. It was afterwards swept away by the floods consequent on the great storm of 1849, but at the time of the siege was reputed the most regular in design of any fortress in India planned by native engineers.

The village of Ramaneet was occupied on 7th September, and the same night strong working parties of British and Sikhs broke ground against the city of Mooltan. On the day following the enemy was dislodged from some advanced posts without much difficulty. On the 10th a similar attempt was made by detachments of the 10th Regiment and Bengal Native Infantry (chiefly furnished by the relieved picquets), under the command of Lieutenant-Colonel Pattoun, 32nd regiment,

---

* Herbert Edwardes, *A Year in the Punjaub.*

the field-officer of the trenches. The attempt was made with great gallantry, but the position proved more formidable than was expected, and the attacking party was driven back with a loss of fourteen killed and seventy-one wounded. On the 10th, Brigadier Markham, of the 32nd regiment, was wounded while on duty in the trenches, and some desultory fighting took place on that and the succeeding day.

On the 12th the enemy's advanced position was attacked by Brigadier Harvey, with a force consisting of six companies of the 10th Regiment and a like number of the 32nd Regiment, with three regiments of Native Infantry, supported by three squadrons of irregular cavalry and a troop of horse artillery.

The troops paraded at 9 a.m., in two columns; the right, composed of the 32nd Regiment and the 8th Native Infantry, under Colonel Pattoun, 32nd regiment; the left, consisting of the 10th Regiment and 49th Native Infantry, under Colonel Franks, 10th regiment. The position was a strong one, and stoutly defended; and a sanguinary fight ensued, ending in the defeat of the enemy and the capture of all the defensive points on that side of the city, but at a heavy cost. Colonel Pattoun and Quarter-Master Taylor, 32nd regiment, were killed, and three officers wounded, in the contest; the command of the right column devolving on Major Inglis, and that of the 32nd companies on Captain E. D. Lowe—names honourably remembered in connexion with the defence of Lucknow in after years.

Two days afterwards Sirdar Shere Singh went over to the enemy with his five thousand Sikhs; and the commanding engineer—the late Lord Napier of Magdala—being of opinion that the successful conduct of the operations was no longer practicable, General Whish raised the siege and withdrew to a position a few miles distant to await the arrival of fresh troops from Bombay.

On 7th November the enemy's strongly entrenched position on the eastern side of the grand canal, near the village of Soorajkhoond, was carried in a very gallant manner by Brigadier Markham, 32nd regiment, with detachments of 10th and 32nd regiments and some Native Infantry. Four of the enemy's guns were captured. The British loss on this occasion was very small; that of the 32nd being only two men wounded.

On 24th December, a strong body of troops arrived from Bombay, under Brigadier-General the Honble. H. Dundas (afterwards Lord Melville) and Whish, who had now an army of thirty-two thousand men, including Native auxiliaries, and one hundred and fifty guns, and at once resumed the siege of Mooltan.

Siege of Mooltan.

On 27th December the British made a general advance in four columns, the enemy abandoning the suburbs and retiring before them into the city, thereby allowing a position to be taken up within—at some points—a hundred yards of the walls. Three companies of the 32nd Regiment on this occasion formed part of the right centre column, under Colonel Nash, 72nd Native infantry. Three others were subsequently sent down to the support of the column. Major Case,* commanding the 32nd companies, was severely wounded. Numerous batteries were thrown up during the night, and on the 28th a general bombardment commenced.

By the 29th the approaches had been pushed so far that the heaviest guns were firing in breach at eighty yards. Much damage was done by the British shells, and a granary in the citadel and several small magazines were burned.

The bombardment continued, and at 10 a.m. on 30th December a shell from a mortar pierced the supposed bomb-proof dome of the Jumna mosque, in the citadel, which formed the enemy's principal magazine, containing four hundred thousand pounds of powder, and in an instant the sacred edifice and five hundred souls were blown into a thousand fragments. A serious conflagration in the city followed.†

1849-51.

On the morning of 2nd January, 1849, the engineers reported that the breach at the Khonee Bhoorj (bloody bastion) was "practicable, though steep," and that of the Delhi gate was "sufficiently good to allow "of an attempt being made on it for a diversion." ‡ Two columns

---

* Afterwards killed at Chinhutt, in 1857.
† Herbert Edwardes, *A Year in the Punjaub.*
‡ *Corps Papers, Royal Engineers,* p. 419, *et seq.*

were accordingly ordered to assault without delay. What followed is thus related by Brigadier Markham.*

"At one o'clock (p.m.) on the 2nd inst. I proceeded with the "brigade under my orders (Her Majesty's 32nd, 49th, and 72nd "Bengal Native Infantry) to the Mundee Awa, the point of rendezvous "of the left column. At two p.m. we received orders to move on the "Delhi gate, from whence the assault was to be made. At a quarter-"past three, p.m., a salvo being fired from the Delhi gate battery (the "signal agreed on for the assault), the leading companies of the 32nd, "under Captain Smyth, commanding the grenadier company, moved "on to storm the breach. Upon passing the broken ground and "ruined outworks of the gate under a heavy fire of matchlock, they "descended a deep hollow, and found to their surprise the city wall "in front of them unbreached and totally impracticable, being fairly "concealed from view by the nature of the ground until directly upon "it. Captain Smyth immediately, and with great judgment and "promptitude, decided upon retiring, and rejoined the column with "the loss of several men, which loss, however, would have been very "severely increased, both to the leading companies and to the column, "had there been any hesitation on his part.

"I proceeded at once to the breach at Khonee Bhoorj, which I "found had already been entered by the left column, and we made "our way down the ramparts and streets on our right to the Delhi "gate, and thence to that part of the city close to the Dowluit gate, "and directly in front of the fort. The enemy offered considerable "opposition in the narrow streets and on the ramparts, which were "strongly barricaded, but before dark that portion of the city was "in our possession, and we connected our post with those thrown "out by the left column.

"Moolraj had, in fact, retired into the Citadel with three thousand "picked men, closing its gates against the rest of his troops.

"General Whish now resolved to attack the Citadel on two sides at "once; and on the 4th January a brigade of the Bombay Division "moved round to the north side of the Citadel, throwing out picquets

---

* Brigadier Markham's despatch, *London Gazette*, March 23rd, 1849.

"to communicate with the Bengal Division on the east, and Edwardes' "Irregulars on the west. Moolraj, seeing the coils closing round "him, tried to negotiate for terms; but he was given to understand "that only an unconditional surrender would be received. The "approaches were pushed on, and on the 21st, two breaches being "reported ready, arrangements were made for the assault next "morning. The storming parties were ready at their posts, when, "at seven a.m., Moolraj intimated his wish to surrender, and the "firing ceased. Two hours later he surrendered himself and his "garrison unconditionally into the hands of the British general."*

Thus fell the city of Mooltan, at a cost to the British troops of some twelve thousand men, killed and wounded. The loss in the 32nd Regiment from the first commencement of the operations was two officers—Colonel Pattoun and Lieutenant and Quarter-master Taylor—one sergeant, and sixteen men, killed; and eleven officers, three sergeants, one drummer, and one hundred and two men, wounded.

The casualties at Mooltan were as follows:—

Lieut-Colonel Pattoun	killed,	12th September, 1848
Brigadier F. Markham	wounded,	10th September, 1848
Captain Balfour	,,	12th September, 1848
,, King	,,	12th September, 1848
Lieutenant Birtwhistle	,,	12th September, 1848
Ensign Swinburn	,,	12th September, 1848
Major Case	,,	27th December, 1848
Lieutenant Strawbenzee	,,	27th December, 1848
Captain King (2nd time)	,,	2nd January, 1849
,, Smith	,,	2nd January, 1849
,, Brine	,,	16th January, 1849
Lieutenant Maunsell	,,	21st January, 1849

Immediately after the fall of Mooltan, General Whish's troops, carrying Moolraj with them a prisoner, pushed on to join Lord Gough, who, in his entrenched camp at Chillianwallah, had been awaiting the arrival of reinforcements since the battle of 13th January,

---

* *London Gazette*, April 3rd, 1849.

1849. The fort and garrison of Cheniote was surrendered to the force *en route*. The troops reached the head-quarter's camp on the 19th and 20th February, and the same night Lord Gough advanced as far as the village of Shadiwal. The main body of the Sikh army, consisting of sixty thousand Sikh troops, under Sirdar Chuttar Singh and Rajah Shere Singh, with tweve hundred Afghan auxiliaries under a son of Dost Mahomed, and fifty-three guns, had fallen back on Goojerat, a famous place of victory in Sikh annals, and was in position between the walls of that city and the dry beds of the River Dwara, which, in a fashion, covers two of its sides.*

Battle of Goojerat.

At daybreak on 21st February the British line formed for the attack. Dundas' Brigade on the left, Colin Campbell's to the right of it; Gilbert's† division, with the heavy guns, forming the right centre; Harvey's brigade further to the right, with Markham's in support.

"At 7.30 a.m.," wrote the veteran Commander-in-Chief, "the army "advanced in the order described, with the precision of a parade "movement. The enemy opened their fire at a very long distance, "which exposed to my artillery both the position and range of their "guns. Halted the infantry just out of fire, and advanced the whole "of my artillery, covered by skirmishers. The cannonade now "opened upon the enemy was the most magnificent I ever witnessed, "and as terrible in its effects. The Sikh guns were served with "their accustomed rapidity, and the enemy well and resolutely main- "tained his position; but the terrible force of our fire obliged them, "after an obstinate resistance, to fall back. I then deployed the "infantry and directed a general advance, covered by the artillery, as "before. The village of Burrakolra, the left one of those of that "name, in which the enemy had concealed a large body of infantry, "and which was apparently the key to his position, lay in the line to "Sir Walter Gilbert's advance, and was carried in most brilliant style "by a spirited attack by the 3rd brigade, under Brigadier Penny, which

---

* *Corps Papers*, Royal and East India frontier engagements.
† A column to the memory of this officer was erected near Bodmin, **Cornwall**.

"drove the enemy from their cover with great slaughter. A very
"spirited and successful movement was also made about the same
"time against a heavy body of the enemy's troops in and about the
"second, or Chotakolra, by part of Brigadier Harvey's brigade,
"gallantly led by Colonel Franks, Her Majesty's 10th Foot. The
"heavy artillery continued to advance with extraordinary activity,
"taking up successive forward positions, and driving the enemy from
"where they had retired to, while the rapid advance and beautiful fire
"of the Horse Artillery broke the ranks of the enemy at all points.
"The whole line now rapidly advanced and drove the enemy before
"it. The Nullah was cleared, several villages stormed, the guns in
"position carried, the camp captured, the enemy routed in every
"direction; the right wing and Brigadier Campbell's brigade going in
"pursuit to the eastward, and the Bombay column to the westward
"of the city. The retreat of the Sikh army, thus hotly pressed, soon
"became a perfect flight, all arms dispersing all over the country,
"rapidly pursued by our troops for a distance of twelve miles, and
"the track strewed with their wounded, and the arms and accoutre-
"ments they flung away."

Markham's brigade, consisting of the 32nd Regiment, under Lieutenant-Colonel Brooke, and 31st and 72nd Native Infantry had been brought up into the front line during the advance, and on reaching Goojerat was, by Lord Gough's orders, employed collecting the enemy's guns, nineteen of which were at once sent into the headquarter camp. Major Case, 32nd regiment, with three companies of the 32nd and two companies of the 51st Native Infantry, took possession of the eight gates of the city, in which service they captured a Khalsa standard, four guns, and some horses, with the loss of one man killed and one officer wounded. Afterwards, reinforced by the 36th Native Infantry, they occupied the city, various detached portions of the enemy laying down their arms to them, for the most part without resistance. The regimental loss during the day was one man killed, and one officer and four men wounded.

The power of the Sikhs was now completely broken. Shere Singh and the other chieftains submitted, and over sixteen thousand Sikh troops laid down their arms. The Afghans, however, retired towards their own fastnesses, closely pursued by Gilbert and Colin Campbell.

The 32nd Regiment took no part in the pursuit to the Khyber Pass, and, after the conclusion of hostilities was sent to Jellundur. From Jellunder the regiment moved, at the end of 1851, to Peshawar. Colonel Markham, at this time, left the regiment to proceed home on leave.

FIFTH PERIOD.

Indian Mutiny—Return Home.

1852-79.

THE regiment arrived at Peshawar on 8th January, 1852. The head-quarters and service companies formed part of the force employed on field service in the Rannazge valley, with Brigadier-General C. Campbell, from 11th to 27th March. They also formed part of the force employed in the destruction of the villages of Mourdham, Pohangur, and those in the Rannazge valley, from 7th May to 2nd June. The regiment remained at Peshawar the rest of the year.

1853.

The regiment remained quartered at Peshawar until 16th December, 1853, on which date three companies and the women, children, and heavy luggage marched out, *en route* for Kussowlie.

1854.

The head-quarters and six companies marched from Peshawar, *en route* to Kussowlie, on 4th January, 1854.

The three companies which preceded the head-quarters, and an additional one for the left wing, marched to Subathu on 4th March, 1854.

The left wing at Subathu, having been relieved by the 52nd Light Infantry, rejoined head-quarters at Kussowlie, part on 28th July and part on 11th August.

The head-quarters and nine companies marched from Kussowlie on 12th December, from Umballa, and arrived there on 16th December, to form part of the camp of exercise.

1855-58.

On the breaking up of the camp, the regiment returned to Kussowlie, and remained there until the following autumn. Although Kussowlie and Subathu are sanitary stations, the regiment suffered severely from fever and ague. Amongst the casualties were those of Paymaster Garforth and Captain Birtwhistle.

In March of this year Colonel Markham* vacated the command of the regiment, on promotion to major-general. He was succeeded by Colonel Brooke.

The regiment was ordered to Lucknow to relieve the 52nd Light Infantry, and on the march suffered severely from cholera, losing upwards of forty men.

One company, whose melancholy fate the following year is fully recorded on the monument that now covers the celebrated well of that world-renowned city, was left at Cawnpore to form a depôt.

In February of this year Colonel Brooke exchanged to the Grenadier Guards with Colonel Berkeley, and the command of the regiment accordingly devolved on Colonel Inglis.

The Indian Mutiny.

After the Sikh campaigns everything appeared to settle down in India to its usual dulness and monotony. Not that signs were absent of a deep feeling of discontent, but no one desired to heed them; those who offered any suggestion or gave any warning of impending danger were quietly shelved. The gallant old soldier—Sir Charles Napier—was rebuked by the Governor-General for the vigorous manner in which he had suppressed the mutinous spirit which had made itself manifest in the ranks of the Bengal army, and he retired to avoid witnessing with his hands tied the catastrophe which he foresaw. In the face of all these warnings, Lord Dalhousie, on quitting the Government, in 1852, left upon record, in an official despatch, his opinion "that the Indian army was in a condition which *could not be improved.*" Another authority† should be mentioned, who—even before Sir Charles Napier's warning—wrote a pamphlet, proving that the admission of the priestly caste of Brahmins into the ranks of our Indian army, in spite of the positive prohibitions limiting

---

* For Colonel Markham's services see *Appendix*.   † Colonel Hodgson.

their employment, was the occasion of engendering and fomenting discord and sedition among the native troops. Another source of danger, was the way which native officers were promoted who never evinced the slightest consciousness of the duty they owed to their own rank or to the Government, but to all intents and purposes remained in all their feelings and sentiments as ordinary soldiers. The denuding of the native regiments of their European officers was believed to be another cause—whatever it was, or who was to blame, it is difficult to say—the opportunity was taken of the withdrawal of more troops for China than could be spared, the disaffection so long suppressed, but so ominously sending forth muttered warnings, at length broke forth in terrible reality. It was in the month of January, 1857, that the earliest symptoms of revolt manifested themselves. There had been awkward and mysterious movements at work from an earlier period; which, had they been investigated at the time, might have revealed the plot and averted the calamity.

The story of the cakes and the lotus flowers* which was forwarded from regiment to regiment of the Bengal army, was at first laughed at as a practical joke, or an act of unmeaning absurdity. It was too palpable, judging from subsequent events, that it was no joke, but the machinery for setting in operation a deeply organized conspiracy. With respect to the cakes, it was said that after the Sepoys had partaken of them, they were informed that the said cakes contained powdered bones of cows and pigs, and that thus they had lost caste. But another cause of alarm and jealousy was the cartridges served out for the new Enfield rifles, and which, as was industriously rumoured, were greased with pig's fat. There is no question now that all these reports were set in motion by the Mussulman portion of the population, whose object was to destroy the power of the Christians and to resume their long-lost ascendancy.

The first discontents, originating with these unhappy greased cartridges, were in vain met by explanation and assurances of the groundlessness of the offensive suspicions they had given rise to. As no amount of explanation would satisfy the remonstrants, they were

---

* *Illustrated London News*, November, 1857.

permitted to make up their own cartridges; they then transferred their objections to the paper supplied them; and what was at first respectful remonstrance became permanent and growing disaffection. In February, the 19th Native Regiment broke into open mutiny at Berhampore, and was shortly afterwards disbanded. The 34th Native Regiment afterwards displayed the grossest form of mutiny, and shared the fate of the 19th Native Regiment. From this period the Mutiny rapidly extended, and—starting from the neighbourhood of Calcutta—the poison of disloyalty swept like a strong wind up the Ganges and the Jumna; its presence being marked by incendiary fires in many stations and a steady opposition to the use of any cartridges served out by the Government. In May, the whole army was ripe for revolt; yet, in spite of the symptoms which had shown themselves far and wide, the officers of the native regiments continued to repose complete confidence in their men, and to take no precautions against the hideous calamities that already dawned above the horizon of the future.

On 6th May the first overt act of organised rebellion occurred. The 3rd Light Cavalry, stationed at Meerut, were called out on parade and ordered to take these hateful cartridges. Eighty-five of them refused; and, three days afterwards, at a court-martial, were sentenced—some to six years' and others to ten years' hard labour, in pursuance of which they were removed to the neighbouring gaol, shackled and ironed.

Had plenty of firmness and decision been displayed here, instead of weakness, the Mutiny might have been nipped in the bud. The following day was Sunday, and the cavalry joined hands with the infantry, and endeavoured to persuade them to massacre the Europeans whilst they were in church.

Colonel Finnis was shot whilst trying to recall his men to their duty; and, in about an hour, scores of Europeans—men, women, and children—were murdered by the rebels, and the lines of the cantonment were in a blaze. With a fairly large force of Europeans, the general failed to realize the gravity of the position until it was too late; in the meantime the mutineers made off in the direction of Delhi, which was reached on 11th May. They were quickly joined by the men of the three native regiments which were protecting the magazines there; the city became the centre of rebellion, and the puppet king, who years before had been set up in pensioned state, was proclaimed Emperor of India.

It will hardly be believed, but—by some strange infatuation—in spite of repeated warnings the biggest arsenal in India was left entirely under the protection of native regiments, with its hundreds of heavy guns, tens of thousands of stands of arms, millions of cartridges, and piles of munitions of war of all kinds; and the only resistance offered to the frenzied mutineers was at one of the magazines, which Lieutenants Willoughby and Forrest and four subordinates first defended and then blew up. All honour to their gallantry and devotion.

The surprise of the British in the north-west provinces and in central India was complete. For one entire month the rebel flag flaunted unchallenged at Delhi. During that month, and long after, a series of bloody events occurred which defy the imagination in its attempts to realize their horrors, and which fill the heart with horror, pity, and abiding indignation; for, in every direction, during that fearful May, June, and July, lust, murder, and every abomination reigned almost unchecked. Officers were murdered at mess, congregations were butchered in churches, fugitives were caught in their vain attempt at flight and destroyed by hellish torments; some died by the bullet, some by the sword, some in the flames. The revolt soon became universal; the Bengal army had ceased to exist. By the end of June the British held not a single place in Oudh except Lucknow, gallantly kept by Sir Henry Lawrence and the 32nd Regiment; and no place between Allahabad and Delhi, except Agra; and not one post between the Jumna and the Himalaya mountains.

Although we are not concerned here with the Punjaub, it may not be out of place to say that it was saved by the judgment and decision of Sir John Lawrence, who immediately had every native regiment disarmed—where there was a force of Europeans sufficient to accomplish that object—and converted the Punjaub into a base of operations to act against Delhi; and having brought his powerful personal influence to bear on the Sikh nation, who threw in their lot with the British with the same zeal with which they had opposed them only a few years before.

But we must not anticipate further, but let the story unfold itself as we proceed.

The head-quarters of the regiment marched from Kussowlie on 30th October, 1856, to relieve the 52nd Regiment, and arrived at Lucknow, the capital of the newly annexed province of Oudh, under the command of Colonel (afterwards major-general) Sir John Inglis, on 27th December of that year. About Christmas, 1856, cholera broke out, and the regiment lost some fifty men on the march down.

Towards the end of March, 1857, Sir Henry Lawrence arrived at Lucknow to take up the appointment of chief commissioner in Oudh, and noted among the difficulties he encountered :

1.—A general agitation of the empire, from the discontent of the native soldiery.
2.—A weak European force in Oudh, and all its military arrangements defective.
3.—Grievous discontent among various classes of the Oudh population.

The troops in and about Lucknow, at this time, consisted of the 7th Light Cavalry, the 13th, 48th, and 71st Bengal Native Infantry, two regiments of Oudh Local Infantry, and large bodies of irregulars and police ; making altogether a force of over seven thousand native troops of all arms, in whose hands were most of the guns and all the transport. To leaven this mass were the 32nd Regiment (one of only two European regiments then to be found between Meerut and Dinapur) and a weak company of Bengal European Artillery—about seven hundred Europeans in all. It had been part of the Government policy to show that the Dalhousie annexations required no display of (European) armed force.

Lawrence, at his own request, was appointed brigadier-general, which gave him command of all the troops in Oudh. In April, the menacing appearance of the Nana Sahib in the streets of Lucknow announced to those in the secret the impending catastrophe. But all through the month Lawrence, although the attitude of the native troops gave him great anxiety, was striving indefatigably "to pacify "the classes on whom some reliance might be placed, or to redress or "mitigate whatever grievances might admit of remedy or palliation." With the month of May came more anxious and discouraging duties. On the 3rd of that month it was found necessary to disarm the 7th Oudh Infantry, whose lines were about seven miles distant from Lucknow, and who had flatly refused to use the new cartridges. The service was performed by the 32nd Regiment and some native troops from Lucknow the same night.

"It was ticklish work," wrote Lawrence, "taking the 48th Native "Infantry down on Sunday night, but I thought they were safer in "our company than behind us in cantonments. We had to pass for "two miles through the city; indeed, H.M.'s 32nd had four miles of "it. I, therefore, hesitated in moving after dark; but the moon was "in its third quarter, and the first blow is everything. So off we "started, and concentrated from four points, having done the seven "miles in about three hours."

The moon rose in a cloudless sky as the brigade debouched on the 7th's lines, and the mutineers saw their game was up. The word of command was promptly obeyed; many of the Sepoys had expressed their contrition, when a false alarm that the guns were about to open upon them caused a general stampede of the mutineers, of whom only a handful stayed by their European officers. The brigade then collected the arms and accoutrements, and returned to Lucknow shortly after midnight. "The coup, it is said, had a great effect," Lawrence wrote to Lord Canning. But events were hastening. On 7th May the lines of the 48th Native Infantry outside Lucknow were burnt, evidently by an incendiary, and in retaliation for the share borne by the battalion in the business of Sunday night. Within a week the news of the outbreaks at Meerut and Delhi was known far and wide throughout the city. Sir Henry Lawrence lost no time in concentrating supplies at certain points, those selected for the purpose being the Muchee Bowun, a deserted fort occupying rather a commanding position, and the Residency, about three-quarters of a mile from it.

The history of the regiment during the period ensuing is best given in the words of the Report drawn up by Major (afterwards major-general) Lowe, C.B., who commanded the 32nd Regiment at the famous defence of the Residency.

Writing from Cawnpore, on 15th December, 1857, that distinguished officer reports :

" On 16th May last, the regiment being in barracks at Lucknow,
" with a depôt composed of weakly and married men and their
" families at Cawnpore,* orders were received for two companies to
" proceed to the City Residency, under my command, with four guns
" for its protection, and whither the sick and those women (with the
" regiment) were also conveyed. The remainder of the regiment
" marched, early on the 17th, three miles from the city, in which were
" cantoned the Native Infantry regiments, to overawe whom their
" presence was necessary. These moves occurred at the very height
" of the hot season, and from that day the 32nd has, I may say, been
" constantly on duty (until relieved on the 22nd November), sleeping
" in their clothes, their arms by their side, ready for any emergency,
" amidst the most trying weather, the hot winds of May and June,
" and the subsequent heavy rains of the wet season, and from the
" 30th June to 22nd November constantly exposed to the shot and
" shell of the enemy.

" On the 19th May a fort in the city, called Muchee Bowun, was
" occupied by some detachments of Native Infantry and a company
" (subsequently strengthened by another) of the 32nd Regiment from
" cantonments. The morning of the 20th, at three hours' notice, I
" was ordered to Cawnpore, with a party of one subaltern (Lieutenant
" Harmar) and fifty men, an outbreak being expected there. The
" party was conveyed in dâk carriages, and, travelling all day (except
" a halt for cooking), reached Cawnpore at 9 p.m. We were accom-
" panied by two squadrons of Irregular Cavalry, who concealed their
" mutinous intentions on this march ; but subsequently, when detached
" separately towards Delhi, mutinied and killed three officers with

---

* See *Appendix B*.

"them. No outbreak occurred, but we were kept constantly on the
"alert in daily and hourly expectation of one, the whole of the men
"sleeping by the guns every night until 30th May, when, reinforce-
"ments from Calcutta having arrived, and more being daily expected,
"my party was permitted to return to Lucknow that night, and
"thereby escaped the melancholy fate of the depôt of the regiment,
"the details of which will long ere this have reached you. The exact
"number of killed at Cawnpore I, however, enclose herewith.

"The company under my command reached Lucknow on the
"morning of the 31st, in carriages as before. The previous night
"the Sepoys rose in cantonments, burning and plundering whatever
"they could. The 32nd were kept under arms protecting the guns
"and to prevent the mutineers reaching the city and spreading the
"confusion. The garrison of the Residency and fort were on the
"alert all night, and under arms. The guns and head-quarters, of the
"32nd, with a few cavalry, were sent out seven or eight miles in pursuit
"of the mutineers, when several were captured. That evening the
"garrisons of both Residency and fort were strengthened by a
"company from cantonments and more guns.

"Colonel Inglis having been appointed to the command of the
"troops in both these places, Lieutenant-Colonel Case assumed the
"command of the regiment, the head-quarters being still in canton-
"ments.

"The regiment remained now for a month in three detachments, as
"before stated, the duties devolving on them being very harassing,
"whilst towards the close of it cholera made its appearance in the fort,
"fortunately not with much virulence, but tending greatly to dispirit
"the men there. Those in the Residency had a great deal of duty in
"the heat of the day, and barely a relief from the guns at night.
"Those in cantonments slept accoutred every night near the guns
"there.

"On 14th June a party went out from the Residency under Captain
"Bassano (32nd), with two guns and some cavalry, the whole under
"command of Colonel Inglis, in pursuit of some police who had
"deserted, after plundering some houses. They were overtaken, and
"some killed and taken prisoners. The heat during the expedition

"was most overpowering, and one man of the regiment died of
"apoplexy in consequence.

"Towards the end of the month (June, 1857), the Native troops
"having mutinied all over Oudh and the stations, their approach to
"Lucknow was reported in large numbers (the greater portion of the
"Sepoys, who had remained faithful to their colours had been sent
"to their homes on furlough). The head-quarters, 32nd, were sent
"into the fort, detaching another company to join the four already in
"the Residency.

"Such was the position of affairs in Lucknow on 29th June, 1857."

General Lowe further reports :—

"Having been left in command of the remainder of the 32nd in the
"Residency, I am unable to give any details of the action which
"occurred at the village of Chinhut, about eight miles off, but the 32nd
"suffered a very heavy loss for the numbers engaged, the principal
"one being the irreparable and deeply-to-be-lamented loss of
"Lieutenant-Colonel Case.

"The force having returned into Lucknow, were closely followed
"by overpowering numbers of the rebels, who soon commenced
"a heavy fire upon both Residency and fort. We thus found
"ourselves besieged in both places at once, much sooner than
"was anticipated, before the completion of our defences, and
"unfortunately with diminished garrisons, the greater portion of the
"native artillerymen having deserted, in addition to the heavy losses
"of the regiment. It was therefore decided that the fort should be
"blown up, and the garrison make the best of their way to the
"Residency.

"At 12 o'clock on the night of 1st July, the garrison evacuated the
"fort, and reached the Residency, three-quarters of a mile off, with
"their guns all safe, without a shot having been fired at them, or
"their departure being apparently noticed. They had just got
"within the gates when the train they had left reached the magazine
"of the fort, and the ford itself was blown up into the air with a most
"terrific explosion. The accomplishment of this without any
"molestation from the enemy must have arisen either from the rebels

"resting after their two days' previous exertions, or being engaged
"plundering other parts of the city, which is of immense size.
"Though the above was attended with such signal success, it
"unavoidably occasioned most severe losses to the 32nd Regiment,
"whose head-quarters were there. Nearly the whole of the
"regimental records, from 1846 to the present time, the whole of our
"band instruments, a collection of valuable music, and the greater
"part of the paymaster's and quartermaster's books had to be
"abandoned.

"The safe arrival of the garrison at the Residency thus so
"successfully accomplished, raised the spirits of all, and the defences
"now being adequately manned, we prepared for the defence with
"renewed energy.

"The late lamented Sir Henry Lawrence being mortally wounded
"on 2nd July, the command of the garrison devolved upon Colonel
"Inglis, and I had the honour of succeeding to the command of the
"regiment at a most trying time—it having been deprived of its
"former commanding officer, its adjutant, and a great number of the
"oldest and best non-commissioned officers (including three colour-
"sergeants) and soldiers. How nobly the others have followed their
"example during the long siege they have gone through, it will be my
"duty to show.

"The enemy proceeded vigorously with the siege, and the
"regiment was soon deprived of more of its officers and men. On
"6th July a sortie was most gallantly made, led by the late Captain
"Mansfield and Lieutenant Lawrence, to drive the enemy out of a
"house adjoining part of our defences. Great bravery and zeal was
"shown, and the objects in view were accomplished.

"A mine having been sprung on 20th July, with no damage,
"however, resulting, a most determined attack was made by the
"enemy, who, however, were repulsed everywhere, owing to the
"bravery shown by the garrison, who repulsed them with heavy
"loss.

"The enemy kept up for some hours the most tremendous and
"incessant fire of musketry and round shot in every direction. Their
"attention was directed to try and undermine our defences, and the

"services of some Cornish and Derbyshire miners among the men
"were availed of to countermine and throw out listening galleries in
"several places, to frustrate the enemy's intentions. With the
"assistance of the Native Infantry officers and working parties from
"these, the most fortunate results were obtained, as only three mines
"out of twenty were exploded by the enemy with any success, the
"rest having failed, or been destroyed by us under the direction, of
"course, of the engineer officers.

"The enemy's guns were in the meantime doing great damage to
"our defences and outposts, several of which were hardly tenable.
"The Residency itself was reduced to a most ruinous and unsafe
"condition; part of it fell down and buried six men of the 32nd,
"two only of which were extricated alive, and recovered. Men were
"killed and wounded even in the hospital itself.

"A second general atttack was made by the enemy on 10th
"August, which was repulsed as before. On 21st August a house
"from which the enemy annoyed us very much, having been under-
"mined by us, was blown up, and parties of the 32nd and 84th
"detachment, under Captain McCabe and Lieutenant Browne, were
"sent out to spike two guns and destroy a mine of the enemy's.
"This was accomplished in the most gallant manner. Lieutenant
"Browne was the first man up at one of the guns.

"Cholera had made its appearance again during the siege, and
"Captain Mansfield and several men and one woman of the regiment
"fell victims to it.

"Towards the end of September the expectations of relief, so often
"doomed to disappointment, began to be raised again, and on the
"25th of that month the force under Sir H. Havelock arrived at the
"Residency, having cut their way through the city with great loss.

"Thus was concluded the first period of the defence. For
"eighty-seven days, officers and men had been on duty night and
"day; as their numbers were insufficient to admit of regular reliefs,
"it was necessary to change the men daily at some of the more
"exposed posts; besides which, there had been fatigue duties of the
"most incessant and laborious kind, in which officers, soldiers, and
"civilians shared alike.

"After the arrival of the reinforcements, Sir James Outram took up the command, which he had waived in favour of Havelock, and the forces being divided between the Residency and an entrenched position at the Alumbagh, four miles out of the city, the defence proceeded."

Referring to the morning after the arrival of the reinforcements, General Lowe's report proceeds :—

" A party of one hundred and fifty of the 32nd under my command was sent to drive the enemy from the posts they occupied on the river side of the Residency. This was not effected without some loss, and I had to deplore the loss of Captain Hughes, 57th Native Infantry, who had been attached to, and done duty with, the regiment during the siege, and had shown great zeal and attention to his duties. He was mortally wounded in forcing the door of a house occupied by the enemy. The objects he had in view were obtained, and one eighteen-pounder, one nine-pounder, one six-pounder, and three smaller guns were brought in, besides mortars being spiked, and a great number of the enemy shot and drowned in crossing the river. The nine-pounder gun was captured in the most gallant manner by Lieutenant Lawrence and a party of the Light Company, just as the second round was about to be fired at them.

" The same day one hundred men of the regiment under my command, were sent out with Sir H. Havelock's force to reinforce the guard over the heavy guns, ammunition, and baggage which had not been extricated from a dangerous position they had got into the evening before. The enemy commanded their road to the Residency with a heavy fire of musketry and round shot.

" Towards dusk the party of the 32nd was moved to the furtherest end of the position, with orders to remain until the heavy guns and the 90th, who formed the rear guard, had retired, whom we were to follow. This was done towards morning, and, withdrawing my look-out sentries, the 32nd slowly retired, protecting the rear of the whole, without our departure being perceived. The baggage and guns reached the Residency through a palace, which had fallen into

"our hands the day before, and we had not entered the latter long
"before the enemy made a most determined attack upon it. Mount-
"ing the wall of a garden they had occupied unknown to us, they
"began firing down upon the troops below. But the late Captain
"McCabe, with the most distinguised bravery, led a party of volun-
"teers of the 5th, 32nd, and 90th into the garden, and the enemy
"who were inside, very soon paid the penalty of their temerity, very
"few escaping. I, unfortunately, received a wound in the foot very
"soon after, which compelled me to hand over the command of the
"regiment to Captain Bassano, and I could not resume it until after
"our relief by H.E. Sir Colin Campbell's force.

"Several sorties were made from this time to 1st October, in all of
"which the 32nd were engaged and bore a distinguished part.

"On 27th September, the loss of our small party was three killed
"and five wounded. On 29th September three sorties were made
"simultaneously. Captain McCabe, I deeply regret to state, was
"mortally wounded, conducting one—hit in four places, he survived
"but two days. Lieutenant Cook commanded another and was first
"in at an embrasure of the enemy's, whose gun was captured. Lieu-
"tenant Edmondstoune was engaged at another point. His party of
"32nd, joined to 64th and 84th detachments, were most successful
"in spiking six guns, and one, a twenty-four pounder, they were
"enabled to destroy. Lieutenant Edmondstoune was slightly wounded.
"On 1st October, Lieutenant Cook was again out with a party of
"32nd, covering a party employed destroying houses occupied by the
"enemy. The same day a party of 32nd, attached to the Madras
"Fusiliers, went out and remained for two days in possession of
"houses outside, but were eventually withdrawn.

"No more sorties were made after, as the ground by the river was
"no longer occupied by the enemy. Fewer casualties occurred, but
"the long siege had had its effect upon a great number of men, who
"began to show symptoms of scurvy.

"On 18th November the forces under H.E. the Commander-in-
"Chief having cleared the outskirts of the city, a junction was
"effected with the garrison; the sick and wounded and women and
"children were conveyed next day to the camp in the Dilkooshah Park,

"and on the night of 22nd November the Residency and its defences
"were evacuated finally, the regiment coming out under the command
"of Captain Bassano, the enemy offering no molestation, nor being
"apparently aware of our departure. The 32nd Regiment was thus
"relieved of the anxious charge which had devolved principally upon
"them for so many months."

General Lowe then refers to the conduct of the "whole of the
"officers, who nobly sustained the honour of the regiment and their
"character as soldiers," and acknowledges the most unremitting zeal
they evinced and the cheerful support they afforded him on all
occasions. Of the non-commissioned officers and men, he says:—

"Their conduct throughout was most praiseworthy; their duties
"for this long time have been most harassing; their want of the usual
"comforts has been borne with the utmost cheerfulness."

The following were the regimental casualties between the 31st of
May and the 22nd of November, 1857:

KILLED.

	Officers	Sergts.	Drs.	Rk. & File	Total.
Murdered, 31st May	...	...	1	...	1
Killed at Chinhut, 30th June	4	8	2	101	115
Killed during defence	1	3	2	37	43
Died of wounds	6	5	2	59	72
Died of disease	1	8	...	54	63
Killed at Cawnpore	3	7	1	74	85
	15	31	8	325	379

WOUNDED.

	Officers	Sergts.	Drs.	Rk. & File	Total.
At Chinhut, 30th June	1	2	...	33	36
During defence	10	9	7	147	173
	11	11	7	180	209

Brigadier Inglis was given the rank of major-general from 26th
September, 1857, and made K.C.B.; Major Lowe was made brevet
lieutenant-colonel and C.B.; Captains Bassano, Lawrence, Edmondstoune, and Foster were made brevet majors; Lieutenants Cook,

Browne, and Clery were gazetted captains in the then newly raised 100th Royal Canadians; Major Bassano was subsequently made brevet lieutenant-colonel and C.B.

The following letters relate to the before quoted report :—

"Horse Guards, S.W.,
"9th February, 1858.

"Sir,—I have had the honour to lay before the General Commanding "in Chief the very clear and interesting report which you forwarded to "me detailing the services of the 32nd Regiment in the defence of the "Residency of Lucknow, and I am commanded by His Royal Highness "to express to you the high sense which he entertains of the noble "conduct of all the officers and men of the corps during this trying period.

"His Royal Highness had great satisfaction in bringing the conduct of "the troops to the special notice of Her Majesty's Government, and is "greatly gratified to be enabled to inform you that Her Majesty's Govern- "ment have acceded to his recommendations, as announced in Parliament "yesterday evening, that the officers and men shall be allowed to count "one year's service towards their retirement and pension, in acknowledg- "ment of the bravery and endurance which they displayed.

"I have &c.
"*(Signed)* C. YORKE.

"To Major Lowe, 32nd Regiment."

"Horse Guards, S.W.,
"17th February, 1858.

"Sir,—With reference to my letter of the 9th Instant, I have the honour "by direction of the General Commanding in Chief to transmit for your "information the accompanying copy of a letter from Lord Panmure, "conveying the expression of the very high sense entertained by Her "Majesty's Government of the heroic conduct of the regiment under your "command at Lucknow, and concurring in His Royal Highness' proposal "that the officers, non-commissioned officers, and men of the regiment "who served during the siege should be allowed to reckon a year's service "as a special mark of approbation on the part of their Sovereign and "country.

"I have &c.
"*(Signed)* C. YORKE.

"To Major Lowe or Officer Commanding 32nd Regiment."

Major-General Sir J. Inglis, K.C.B.

[COPY OF ENCLOSURE.]

'War Office,
"12th February, 1858.

" Sir,—I have the honour to receive Your Royal Highness' letter of 4th " Inst. enclosing a report from Major Lowe, commanding the 32nd " Regiment, in which he gives a detailed narrative of the services rendered " by that corps during the siege of Lucknow.

" I have perused this report with great gratification and deep emotion.

" I sincerely congratulate Your Royal Highness upon the glory which " this distinguished corps have added to Her Majesty's arms, and I have " to convey to Your Royal Highness an expression of the admiration with " which these heroic achievements have been viewed by Her Majesty's " Government, and the deep sympathy which they entertain for the many " casualties from which the regiment has suffered.

" Her Majesty's Government not only concur in Your Royal Highness' " proposal that the services of this distinguished band of heroes should " reckon, as regards officers, one year's service towards retirement on full " or half-pay ; and, as regards non-commissioned officers and men, one " year's additional service towards pension on discharge ; but that the " same measure should be extended to the surviving officers and men " belonging to any other of Her Majesty's regiments serving in Lucknow " on this memorable occasion.

" I have &c.
"*(Signed)* PANMURE.
" To H.R.H. the General Commanding in Chief."

The 32nd officers present at the Defence of the Residency of Lucknow were as hereunder :

Colonel Inglis, (afterwards Major-General Sir I. Inglis, K.C.B.) commanding garrison, appointed brigadier, *vice* Sir H. Lawrence ; wounded during defence, but not included in Regimental Returns ; died 1861. Major E. W. D. Lowe, (now Major-General E. D. Lowe, C.B.) commanding the 32nd, appointed regimental major, *vice* Colonel Case ; twice wounded, once severely. Captains : Mansfield, died of cholera during defence ; Power, killed in Residency, 2nd July ; Bassano, severely wounded.* Lieutenants : S. Lawrence, (afterwards

---

* The late Major-Generals Bassano, C.B., and McCabe were mortally wounded in the sortie of 29th September.

Captain and Brevet Major Lawrence, V.C., 32nd) since dead; Edmondstoune, (afterwards major and brevet colonel) twice wounded, once severely; Pelham Webb, killed, 2nd August; C. M. Foster, wounded; C. Clery, (afterwards lieutenant-colonel, half-pay, 32nd) since dead; Cook, (afterwards Lieutenant-Colonel Cook, 100th Regiment) wounded. Ensigns: Charlton, dangerously wounded, 13th July, since dead; Studdy, killed, 6th August. Staff-Paymaster Giddings, (afterwards major and paymaster, half-pay) acted as regimental adjutant during the defence, since dead. Surgeon Scott, M.D., (afterwards surgeon-major, M.D., C.B.) principal medical officer in the Residency during the defence, since dead. Assistant-Surgeon Boyd, in medical charge of 32nd Regiment and of European general hospital during defence, since dead. Quarter-Master Wilkinson, 31st, was present as regimental-sergeant-major, 32nd; and Quarter-Master Vaughan, 32nd, as schoolmaster-sergeant during defence, since dead. Attached to 32nd: Captain Hughes, late 57th Native Infantry, and Assistant-Surgeon Darby, E.I.C.S., both killed, and included in 32nd casualties.*

It may be interesting here to give—

SIR HENRY LAWRENCE'S LINE OF DEFENCE.

The line of defence had been formed by Sir Henry Lawrence and his brave associates with consummate skill. It consisted of a ditch and parapet, at the edge of which the ground begins to descend, and a long space of high ground was taken advantage of to construct a battery, named the Redan. The ditch and parapet nearly encircled the Treasury, and ended at the Baillie guard gate, near Doctor Fayrer's house. From this up to the Thuggee gaol the defence consisted of the compound walls, with ditch and palisade inside and barricades across the lanes which separated the compounds. The left corner of the Thuggee gaol was on the prolongation of the Cawnpore road. Here, therefore, a battery was constructed, merely to sweep that

---

* A nominal roll of all officers, members of the uncovenanted service, ladies, European women and children in the Residency during the defence is given in the *London Gazette Extraordinary* of 17th February, 1859, with corrections in subsequent gazettes.

road, its position not enabling it to be put to any other use; the supposition being that our great source of danger was the advance and attack of troops from Cawnpore. The walls of the Thuggee gaol and the native houses, with stockading in front, were the line of defence there; a parapet and ditch and the walls of outhouses encircled Mr. Gubbins' compound. The walls of the Residency out- houses were again the defence there; thence a parapet following the edge of the high ground formed the boundary up to Lieutenant Innes' house, from which point a deep ditch to the Redan completed the line of defence. Most of the houses bordering close on the entrenchments had been levelled, except those on the Cawnpore battery side, but a few that would probably serve to traverse the former from artillery had been left standing. These, and every building within musketry range, became filled with the enemy's sharpshooters, who were able, especially with the eight-inch Howitzers taken some time before at Chinhut, to keep up a most mischievous and deadly fire.

Though symptoms of disaffection had been for some time previously apparent in the vicinity of Lucknow, no military demonstration was made by the British troops until 16th May, 1857. The 32nd Regi- ment was then in barracks, at Lucknow, having a depôt of the weakly and married men, with their families, at Cawnpore.

The sick and women who were with the head-quarters were removed to the Residency, and two companies of the regiment, under the command of Captain Lowe, with four guns, proceeded there for its protection.

The remainder of the regiment marched the following day about three miles out of the city, and encamped at a place called Murrohow, where two native infantry regiments were cantoned, to overawe them, if necessary.

These movements took place at the very height of the hot season, and from this time until relieved—22nd November—the men may be said to have been constantly on duty, sleeping in their clothes, with their arms by their sides. They were ever ready for any emergency that might have arisen, and this, too, when the hot winds of May and June would have been alone sufficient to enfeeble the energies of the stoutest, and when the subsequent heavy rains of the wet season spread fever and dysentry wherever they prevailed. But the exhausting effects of exposure to an Indian climate at its most unhealthy season were by no means the sole evils to which the subsequent defenders of the Residency were to be exposed, for they were soon surrounded by innumerable foes and shut up in a place ill-fortified, and every straggling man who could even crawl to his post was constantly exposed to the shot and shell of an ever-increasing enemy.

On 19th May a fort in the centre of the city, called the Muchee Bawen, was occupied by a company of the regiment and some detachments of native infantry from cantonments. This force was subsequently strengthened by another company of the regiment.

On the morning of 20th May, Captain Lowe proceeded to Cawnpore, on three hours' notice, with a party of one subaltern (Lieutenant Harman) and fifty men, as—from information received—an outbreak was anticipated in that place. The party was conveyed in Dak carriages, and, with the exception of one halt for cooking, travelled all day, reaching Cawnpore about 9 p.m.

They were accompanied by two squadrons of irregular cavalry, who, for the time, concealed their traitorous disposition; but, when separately detached towards Delhi, mutinied and killed three of their officers.

No outbreak occurred at this time at Cawnpore, but the troops were kept constantly on the alert, in hourly expectation that one would take place. The whole of the men slept by the guns at night, so threatening was the attitude of the natives. This continued until reinforcements arrived from Calcutta, on the 30th of the month when the party of the regiment was allowed to return to Lucknow.

The first serious outbreak of the Sepoys in the neighbourhood of Lucknow took place on 30th May. On that night they rose in cantonments and plundered and burned everything within reach The regiment was entirely employed in protecting the guns and preventing the mutineers from nearing the city.

The garrisons of the Residency and fort were kept under arms and on the alert all night. On the following morning the guns and head-quarters of the regiment were sent seven or eight miles in pursuit of the mutineers, of whom several were captured. The same evening the garrisons of both the Residency and fort were each strengthened by more guns and by a company of the regiment from cantonments.

Colonel Inglis was appointed to the command of the troops at both these places, and Lieutenant-Colonel Case assumed command of the regiment; the headquarters being still in cantonments. Thus the regiment continued divided into three detachments for nearly a month.

During this time the duties falling on the men were rendered harassing in the extreme by the constant vigilance everywhere required. Added to this, cholera now appeared in the fort; fortunately, not with very great virulence.

In the Residency the amount of duty to be done in the heat of the day told most heavily, while the number of the garrison was so limited as to be barely sufficient for the relief of guards at night.

The part of the regiment in cantonments was little better off, being kept constantly under arms, and sleeping accoutred by night alongside the guns.

On 14th June, a force, under the command of Colonel Inglis— consisting of a detachment of the regiment under Captain Bassano, three guns, and some cavalry—left the Residency in pursuit of a number of a native police, who deserted and plundered some houses in the city. The deserters were quickly overtaken. Some were killed, but a greater number captured. The heat during this expedition was overpowering. One man of the regiment was struck down by the sun, and died from its effects the following day.

Towards the end of this month the native troops openly mutinied all through Oudh and the neighbouring stations, and their approach in great numbers to Lucknow was reported.

The force in cantonments was accordingly broken up on 29th June, and the Sepoys who had remained faithful were sent to their homes on indefinite furlough.

The head-quarters of the regiment was removed to the fort, one company being detached to join that already in the Residency.

The following morning (30th June) a force, comprising three hundred men of the regiment, commanded by Colonel Case, eleven guns, and some native infantry and cavalry left the city at 6 o'clock, under Sir H. Lawrence, to meet the rebels, who were reported to be then within eight miles of Lucknow. It was the general's design to meet the enemy at a disadvantage, either on its entrance into the suburbs of the city, or at the bridge across the Gokral, a small stream intersecting the Fyzabad road, about half-way between Lucknow and a village called Chinhut.

Misled, however, by the reports of wayfarers—who stated that there were few or no men between Lucknow and Chinhut—he pushed on his force further than he originally intended, and suddenly came in with the enemy, in overwhelming numbers, at Chinhut, concealed behind a long line of trees. The European troops and native infantry, with an eight-inch Howitzer, held the enemy for a time in check, and, had six guns of the Oudh artillery been faithful—and the Sikh cavalry shown a better front—even the immense disparity of numbers would not have saved them from complete discomfiture. But the premeditated treachery (hitherto carefully concealed) of the Oudh gunners was fated to bring disaster on those whose friends they pretended to be. When ordered into action, the drivers overturned the guns into the ditches, cut the traces of their horses, and then abandoned them, regardless of the remonstrances of their own officers, notwithstanding the exertions of the general's staff, headed by Sir Henry himself.

Deprived so unexpectedly of the greater part of its artillery, exposed to vastly superior fire from the enemy, and completely out-flanked on both sides by an innumerable body of infantry and cavalry, the force was compelled to retire, having sustained a heavy loss in killed and wounded, and three pieces of artillery—the result of the treachery of the Oudh gunners.

The heat during this eventful day is said to have been excessive—even for that burning climate—and, in the hurried march back to Lucknow, many who escaped the shot and shell of the enemy sank exhausted under the sun's more destructive influence.

The gun ammunition, too, soon becoming expended—together with the almost total want of cavalry to protect the rear—made the retreat more disastrous. Among the many serious casualties that befel the troops engaged, there were none more irreparable or more deservedly regretted than that of Lieutenant-Colonel Case, who was mortally wounded while gallantly leading the regiment. His high reputation as a most able officer made his loss the more keenly felt in the trying events that soon after followed.

"The village of Ishmaelpore was filled with the enemy's sharp-
"shooters. Colonel Case, at the head of the 32nd men, gallantly led
"them up to it, but fell, struck by a bullet. Had he lived he would
"probably have succeeded in clearing the village; Captain Bassano
"(afterwards General Bassano, C.B.) seeing the colonel fall, went up to
"assist him. 'Captain Bassano,' was the noble speech of the wounded
"hero, 'leave me to die here, your place is at the head of your com-
"pany, I have no need of assistance!' Captain Bassano was
"shortly after this wounded in the leg.

"A man named Johnson, of the Cavalry, formerly a private of the
"32nd, performed a deed of daring, which saved one of the guns.
"Seeing it abandoned in the retreat, he galloped up to it—the enemy, as
"usual, retiring on his approach—dismounted, and making over his
"horse to another soldier, mounted one of the artillery horses, and
"safely brought the gun in. He was recommended for the Victoria
"Cross.

"The Sepoys who had remained faithful to us behaved with the
"greatest gallantry, and assisted in bringing in wounded men of the
"32nd, leaving their own wounded uncared for on the battle field.

"Private Sampson of the 32nd was knocked off his saddle by a
"musket shot in the head." *

When Colonel Case was struck down, the command of the regiment devolved on Captain Stephens, who soon shared his predecessor's fate, as he shortly afterwards received his death-wound. The command of the regiment then fell on Captain Mansfield, who—though he escaped and brought the remnant of the regiment into the Residency—was soon numbered among the cholera victims.

On finding that his force was so immeasurably overmatched, Sir

---

* Rees, *Siege of Lucknow.*

Henry Lawrence immediately commenced to fall back, having despatched a hasty message to Lucknow to have the bridge over-the Goomtee protected, to enable his retiring force to cross over in safety. Lieutenant (afterwards major-general) Edmondstoune, a promising young officer, was sent with his company, and did his work with the utmost gallantry.

Sadly thinned in numbers, the force succeeded in again reaching Lucknow, closely followed by ever-increasing rebels, who quickly opened a heavy and sustained fire on the Residency and fort. The occupants thus found themselves besieged in both places at once much sooner than was anticipated, and, as the defences were still incomplete and the garrisons diminished by the heavy losses the regiment had just sustained, in addition to the desertion of a great part of the native artillery, their isolated position became precarious in the extreme.

Before we proceed further, it would be as well to return to the troops at Cawnpore, and see what had been happening there; for the battle of Chinhut and the final scene at Cawnpore were within two days of one another, namely 30th June and 1st July.

The European troops now left at Cawnpore (not counting European officers and staff of revolted native regiments) consisted of the depôt detachment of Her Majesty's 32nd Regiment, three officers, (Captain John Moore, Lieutenant F. Wainwright, and Ensign Evelyn Hill) seven sergeants, one drummer, and seventy-four rank and file;* detachments of Her Majesty's 84th Regiment and Madras Fusiliers, a few details each; and Bengal European Artillery.†

On Tuesday, 4th June, the 2nd Cavalry broke out into open revolt, and the other native corps speedily followed suit. At dawn on the 6th, the Nana, throwing off all reserve, announced his intention of attacking the British camp. By noon, on Sunday, many guns, drawn from the Cawnpore arsenal, had been placed round at safe distances,

---

* With the 32nd Depôt were four ladies (Mrs. Moore, Mrs. and Miss Wainwright, and Mrs. Hill), forty-one European women, and fifty-four children belonging to the regiment.

† No exact return of numbers has been found.

to rake the entrenchments, and twenty-four-pound shot were crashing through the doors and windows of the two buildings within, every shot being the signal for heartrending shrieks or low wailings, more heartrending still. Within the enclosure, about a quarter of an acre in extent, were gathered all the Christian population of Cawnpore and the districts roundabout, or, rather, all who had eluded the murderous riot of the two preceding days—a mixed and feeble company, to the full sum of a thousand souls. Of these, four hundred and sixty-five were men of all ages and professions (the troops included), and over six hundred women and children. Under European officers, all the men capable of bearing arms were told off to posts in the entrenchment and in certain unfinished "puckah" buildings outside its southwestern angle, one of which, known as "Barrack No. 2," subsequently became the recognised key of the British position—the scene of many an act of unrecorded heroism. Sir Hugh being unequal to the fatigue involved, the active conduct of the defence devolved, informally, on the senior Queen's officer present—Captain Moore,* 32nd regiment, a valiant Irish officer of some sixteen years standing, who had fought with the regiment in the second Sikh war. When once fire was opened, the irremediable defects of the site chosen for the entrenchment became apparent. The Dragoon hospital was en-

---

* The late Colonel Mowbray Thompson, one of the survivors, thus testifies to his worth :—

"Captain John Moore, who was the life and soul of our defence, was a tall, fair " man, with light blue eyes, I believe an Irishman. He was in command of the "invalid Depôt of Her Majesty's 32nd Regiment when the Mutiny broke out. " Throughout all the harassing duties that devolved upon him he never lost deter- " mination or energy. Though the little band of men at his direction was daily " lessened by death, he was cheerful and animated to the last, and inspired all around " him with a share of his wonderful endurance and vivacity. He visited every one of " the picquets daily, and sometimes two or three times a day, speaking words of " encouragement to everyone of us. His never-say-die disposition nerved many a " sinking heart to the conflict, and his affable, tender sympathy imparted fresh patience " to the suffering women. Mrs. Moore sometimes came across with him to our Bar- " rack (No. 2 building), and we fitted up a little hut for her, made with bamboos " and covered with canvas, and there she would sit for hours bravely bearing the " absence of her husband while he was gone on some hazardous enterprise. She, " poor creature, was among the number who unhappily survived the siege and was " afterwards murdered in the House of Horrors."

tirely surrounded by large and solid buildings at distances varying from three hundred to eight hundred yards; buildings from which the assailants derived protection at least as effectual as that afforded to the garrison by their improvised defences.

From roof and window poured a shower of bullets during the hours of daylight, while—after dusk—troops of Sepoys hovered about within pistol shot and made night hideous with incessant volleys of musketry. Sometimes when the enemy became more than usually troublesome, the picquet, which was most hardly pressed, would invite their neighbours to come over, and then the combatant force of some thirty bayonets sallied forth to sweep the line of barracks, chasing the foe before them, killing the boldest or slowest of foot, knocking on the head such as were drunk or asleep, shooting down those who in their anxiety to get a good aim had ensconced themselves too high up to climb down at so short a notice, and driving the rest out and across the plain, at which point the gunners in the entrenchment took up the work and plied the flying multitude with grape and canister.*

By 10th June not a door or window remained in either of the buildings, and the shot coursed freely through and through the bare rooms. Many women and children had already been killed outright, and others seriously wounded by the falling buildings and splinters; all the European gunners had been killed or disabled at their guns. Thus sped the first five days of the defence.

On 12th June the insurgents made their first general attack. The 2nd Cavalry, who a day or two before had been engaged in the more congenial occupation of murdering some boat-loads of European fugitives from Futteghur, at Nawabgunj, led the attack, but these

---

* During one of these early sorties, Mowbray Thompson relates that eleven Sepoy prisoners were taken and lodged in the main-guard; and, as all the available strength of the garrison was required in action, Mrs. Widdowson, wife of Private Thomas Widdowson, 32nd regiment, volunteered to keep guard over them with a drawn sword. They were only secured by a rope passed from wrist to wrist, but they sat motionless on the ground for more than an hour under the Amazonian surveillance to which they were subjected. Presently, when the picquet returned, and they were subject to masculine protection, they all managed to escape. From this time forward it was understood that prisoners were to be left where taken, with the jackal and vulture for their gaolers.—Trevelyan's *Cawnpore*.

heroes soon turned tail; they were followed by the native infantry, who showed rather more resolution, but the attack was repulsed with severe loss to the enemy.

The state of affairs on 14th June is shown in the following letter, which promptly reached Lucknow, secreted on the person of a native bearer :—

"Sir H. Wheeler, to M. Gubbins, Esq.

" My dear Gubbins,—We have been besieged since the 6th by the Nana
"Sahib, joined by the whole of the Native troops, who broke out on the
"morning of the 4th.* The enemy have two 24-pounders and several
"other guns. We have only eight 9-pounders. The whole Christian
"population is with us in a temporary entrenchment, and our defence has
"been noble and wonderful; our loss, heavy and cruel. We want aid, aid,
"aid! Regards to Laurence.

"Yours, &c.,
"(Signed) H. WHEELER.
"June 14th, 1857, 8.15. p.m.
"P.S.—If we had 200 men we could punish the scoundrels and help you."

To this appeal came the following reply from Sir H. Lawrence :—

"Lucknow, June 16th, 1857.

" My dear Wheeler,—I am very sorry indeed to hear of your condition,
"and grieved that I cannot help you. I have consulted with the chief
"officers about me, and all but Gubbins are unanimous in thinking that
"with the enemy's command of the river, we could not possibly get a single
"man into your entrenchment. I need not say that I deeply lament being
"obliged to concur in this opinion, for our own safety is as nearly con-
"cerned as yours. We are strong in our entrenchments, but by attempt-
"ing the passage of the river should be sacrificing a large detachment,
"without the prospect of helping you. Pray do not think me selfish. I
"would run much risk could I see a commensurate prospect of success.
"In the present scheme I see none. Mr. Gubbins, who does not under-
"stand that most difficult of military operations, the passage of a river in
"the face of an enemy, is led away by a generous enthusiasm to desire
"impossibilities. I write not only my own opinion, but that of many ready
"to risk their lives to rescue you.

"Yours, &c.,
"(Signed) H. LAWRENCE."†

---

* Colonel Mowbray Thomson says the 6th, evidently a mistake.

† This letter, by an obvious misprint, is dated from Cawnpore in Sir H. Edwarde's *Life of Sir H. Lawrence.*

On 15th June a carcase set fire to the thatched building in the Cawnpore entrenchment, which—for its more sheltered position—had been selected as a refuge for the sick and wounded, and, despite the efforts made at a rescue, two poor fellows perished in the flames.*

On the 16th, Meer Nawab, a Mussulman of rank, came into Nana's camp with a numerous following, including the Nazidee and Aktaree regiments—late 4th and 5th Oudh Local Infantry—two fine well-drilled corps of Sepoys. The same night, to give early proof that the spirit of the defenders was still unbroken, Captain Moore made a sortie, with fifty picked men, and hurrying down the rebels' line, under cover of the darkness, surprised, in untimely slumber, some native gunners, who never woke again, spiked and rolled over several twenty-four pounders, gratified their feelings by blowing up a piece which had given them special annoyance, and got back safe into camp, carrying in their arms four of their number, and leaving one behind dead.

On 18th June the Oudh men, having had a day's rest, came out to the assault. Charging in a mass across the plain and over the rampart, they bore down the defenders, overthrew a gun, and seemed for a moment to have carried the position. But the volunteer gunners slewed round a nine-pounder gun, and gave them a few stockingsful† of grape, and the picquets coming up with an English rush, sent them back to their master fewer and wiser than they came.

A few hours later the following characteristic letter was written by Moore. Poor Sir Hugh would appear to have been hurt at Lawrence's reply :—

"18th of June, 1857, 10 P.M.

"Sir,

"By desire of Sir Hugh Wheeler, I have the honour to

---

* This day a rifle ball killed Private J. White, 32nd regiment, broke both arms of his wife, who was by his side, and injured one of two children (twins) she held. Mowbray Thompson speaks of the sight of the widowed mother, lying in hospital powerless to move, with a child at each breast, as the most piteous he ever witnessed.

† The ladies in the entrenchment had given up their stockings to serve as cannister-cases for the field guns.

"acknowledge the receipt of your letter of the 16th. Sir Hugh
" regrets that you cannot send him the 200 men, as he believes with
" their assistance he could drive the insurgents from Cawnpore and
" capture their guns. Our troops, officers, and volunteers have acted
" most nobly, and on several occasions a handful of men have driven
" hundreds before them. Our loss has been chiefly from the sun and
" from their heavy guns. Our rations will last a fortnight, and we are still
" well supplied with ammunition. Our guns are serviceable. Report
" says that troops are advancing from Allahabad, and any assistance
" might save our garrison. We, of course, are prepared to hold out
" to the last. It is needless to mention the names of those who have
" been killed or have died. We trust in God, and if our exertions
" here assist your safety, it will be a consolation to know that our
" friends appreciate our devotion. Any news of relief will cheer us.
" By order,
"*(Signed)* J. MOORE, Captain, 32nd Regiment."

A brave letter, worthy of the regiment and the day, but in its hopeful spirit sadly belied by the state of affairs at Cawnpore. Since the destruction of the thatched barrack, dearth of houseroom had forced two hundred of the women and children to spend night and day in the open air. At night they lay on the ground, exposed to every noxious influence and exhalation that was abroad in the air, and in the morning they rose—those among them that rose at all—to endure, bareheaded sometimes and always roofless, the blazing fury of a tropical sun, amidst whirlwinds of dust, under a temperature of one hundred and twenty to one hundred and thirty-eight degrees in the shade. The food supply of the garrison was now reduced to scant allowance of the poorest of native fare, save when a wandering troophorse from the enemy's lines was shot and hauled into camp; their drink was putrid water, fetched by bucketfuls, under a heavy fire, from a well outside. Comforts and appliances for the sick there were none, and day by day the tale of deaths from sickness and wounds increased, and the fire seldom slackened.

On the night of Sunday, 21st June, Major Vibart, 2nd cavalry, transmitted the following lines to Lucknow :

"We have been cannonaded for six hours a day by twelve guns. "This evening upwards of thirty shells (mortars) were thrown into "the entrenchment. This has occurred daily for the last eight days; "an idea may be formed of our casualties, and how little protection "the barracks afford to the women. Any aid to be effective must be "immediate. In the event of rain falling our position would be "intolerable. According to telegraphic despatches received previous "to the outbreak, one thousand Europeans were to have been here "on the 14th instant. This force may be on its way up. Any "assistance you can send might co-operate with it. Nine-pounder "ammunition, chiefly cartridges, is required. . . . We have lost "about a third of our original number. The enemy are strongest in "artillery. They appear not to have more than four hundred or five "hundred infantry: they move their guns with difficulty, by means "of unbroken-in bullocks. The infantry are great cowards, and easily "repulsed.

"By order,
"*(Signed)* G. V. VIBART, Major."

The 23rd June was the centenary of the battle of Plassey—the day originally fixed for a general rising all over northern India. All through the night of the 22nd the defenders of the outlying buildings were kept alert by sounds which betokened that the Sepoys in the adjacent buildings were more than usually numerous and restless. Lieutenant Thompson sent over for a reinforcement, but Moore replied that he could spare no one but himself and Lieutenant Delafosse (53rd native infantry). In the course of a few minutes the pair arrived, and at once sallied forth, one armed with a sword, the other with an empty musket. Moore shouted out, "No. 1 to the front," and the Sepoys, taking it for granted that the well-known word of command would bring upon them a whole company of Sahibs, with fixed bayonets and cocked revolvers, broke cover and ran like rabbits.

Towards morning they returned in force, and attacked with such determination that there remained more dead Hindoos outside the doorway of No. 2 barrack than there were living Europeans within. At the same moment the entrenchment was assaulted by the whole strength of the insurrection. Field-guns, pulled about by horses and bullocks, were brought up within a few hundred yards and pointed at our wall. The troopers, who had bound themselves by the most solemn oaths of their religion to conquer or to perish, charged at a gallop in one direction, while in another advanced a dense array of infantry, preceded by a host of skirmishers, who rolled before them great bundles of cotton, proof against our bullets. It was all in vain. Our countrymen, too, had their anniversary to keep, and kept it in a spirit worthy of those who fought at Plassey and Arcot in the days long gone by. They shot down the teams; they fired the bales; drove the sharpshooters back upon their columns, and sent the columns to the right-about in unseemly haste. They taught the men of the 2nd Cavalry that broken vows and angered gods, and the waters of the Ganges poured fruitlessly on the perjured head, were less terrible than British valour in the last extremity. The contest was short, but sharp. The defeated combatants retired to brag and to carouse; the victors to brood, to sicken, and to starve. That evening a party of Sepoys drew near our lines, made obeisance after their fashion, and requested leave to bury their slain.

A change now came over the spirit of the Nana, and he resolved to cut short the troublesome enterprise he had in hand by a method swifter than famine and surer than open force, to wit—treachery.

On the morning of 25th June a note, attested by no signature, but superscribed "To the subjects of Her most gracious Majesty Queen "Victoria," was brought to the British camp. Its contents, in caricature of a certain Government proclamation, ran thus:

"All those who are in no way connected with the acts of Lord "Dalhousie, and are willing to lay down their arms, shall receive a "safe passage to Allahabad."

The missive was referred to a council, consisting of General Wheeler and Captains Moore and Whiting (Bengal engineers), and after a prolonged debate it was decided to accept the offer. Had the garrison consisted of fighting people only, a dash would have been made for Allahabad, but what could be done with a mixed multitude, in which there was a woman and child to each man, while every other man was incapacitated by wounds and disease? The rains, too, were close at hand, when the entrenchment would be no longer tenable. The stores had dwindled down to a quart a head of nearly uneatable native food. The choice lay between death and capitulation ; and, if the latter were resolved on, it was well that the offer came from the enemy. So it was argued, and at last Sir Hugh gave way. Captains Whiting and Moore and Mr. Roche, the postmaster, were invested with full powers to treat with the Nana's commissioners, and their terms—that our force should march out with sixty rounds of ball-cartridge per man ; that carriages should be provided for the conveyance of the women and sick ; that boats sufficiently victualled with flour should be ready for them—were readily acquiesced in; and Mowbray Thomson states that all due deliberations were observed and every precaution taken to ensure fulfilment of the promises. The morning of 27th June was fixed for the embarkation. A little before 6 o'clock that day the remnant of the heroic little garrison, with bayonets fixed, and Moore at their head, marched out of the camp to the landing place, near to the village of Suttee Chowra, where were drawn up forty boats, of the usual up-country build, to receive the party. How the mixed throng—some on foot, some in doolies, with here and there an elephant—went down the hollow way to the Ghaut; how a mob of peasants at once over-ran the abandoned camp, to find there three brass guns disabled, a bag of flour, and the bodies of eleven Europeans, some still breathing, but dying of gun-shot wounds; how, with much difficulty, the wounded and the women were hoisted on board the boats ; how, at the last moment, the thatch of the boats was treacherously fired, and a storm of grape and musketry broke upon them from either shore ; how but three boats got off, of which two drifted to destruction on the opposite bank, while the third, rudderless and oarless, went down midstream, are matters of history, and need not here be repeated in detail. Indeed, the story, as far as it relates to the 32nd Regiment, is well nigh told.

Captain Moore, with other officers and men, were in the third boat which had taken a large party off one of the sinking boats, and now, with over a hundred persons crowded into a space which could barely hold fifty, alternately stranding and drifting, was tending down stream towards Allahabad at the rate of half-a-mile an hour, under a fire of canister and shells from both banks. Shortly afterwards, in assisting to heave the vessel off a sand-bank, Captain Moore was shot through the heart. Of the two other officers of the 32nd detachment, Lieutenant F. Wainwright had been killed some time before the end of the siege; Ensign Evelyn Hill probably shared the same fate. No details ever reached the regiment, and nothing further can now be learned respecting them.

Meanwhile, some of the women and children whom the flames had spared were collected and brought to land. Among this number, it is said, was poor Mrs. Moore with her infant child. Many were pulled out from under the charred woodwork of boats, and others were driven up from four feet depth of water. Before they emerged from the river, some of the ladies were roughly handled by the troopers, who tore away such ornaments as caught their fancy with little regard to ears or fingers. But when all had assembled, sentries were put round, and no one suffered to molest them. In the evening they were taken to a large building, known as Sevada House, in view of the old entrenchment. They are said to have been one hundred and twenty-five in number. "I saw that many of the ladies were wounded," said one native witness who watched them go by, and whose report was confirmed. "Their clothes had blood on them. Two men were "badly hurt, and had their heads bound up with handkerchiefs. "Some were wet, covered with mud and blood, but all had clothes. "I saw one or two children without clothes. There were no other "men in the party, only some boys of twelve or thirteen years of age."*

The escaped boat continued its way down stream, and at 2 p.m. on the following day, 28th June, struck on a bank off the village of Nussufghur. Straightway the shore was covered with a multitude of feudal militia, intermingled with Sepoys and mounted troopers. A gun was brought forward and unlimbered; but while the artillerymen

---

* Four Englishwomen and three half-castes of this party were seized by the troopers of the 2nd Cavalry, but were at once restored, with a single exception (Miss Wheeler), by order of the Nana, who appears to have regarded the women as useful hostages. It is, perhaps, scarcely necessary to add, that the prurient tales which were rife at the time, afterwards proved to have been utterly devoid of foundation.

were taking their aim, there came down from heaven that unbroken sheet of water for which men had been looking during the past fortnight. The rains had commenced in earnest. The piece could only be discharged once; but the storm did not protect our people from the heavy fusilade, which cost several gallant lives. After five hours of this bitter work, there hove in sight a boat manned by fifty or sixty mutineers, armed to the teeth, who had been deputed by the Nana to follow and destroy the relics of our force. This vessel likewise ran on a sandbank, not altogether against the inclination of her crew, who, probably, did not relish the notion of forming themselves into a boarding party. They liked the idea still less when a score of Englishmen came dashing at them through the shallows. The half-dozen ablest swimmers alone escaped to tell their master that, "after all they had "gone through, those extraordinary Sahibs were the same as ever."

At night the boat floated, but daylight showed that she had drifted into a back-water, whence there was no egress, and the musketry from the shore recommenced. Accordingly, Major Vibart, then dying of his wounds, directed Lieutenants Delafosse (late 53rd native infantry) and Thomson (56th native infantry) to land and drive back the enemy with a party consisting of Sergeant Grady, 32nd regiment, and eleven men of 32nd and 84th regiments, and artillery. They had not departed many minutes when a host of insurgents poured down upon the helpless troop of women and wounded men, and—after a short, but murderous conflict—the boat was captured and escorted to Cawnpore by a strong body of horse and foot.

Thompson and Delafosse, on gaining the shore, drove the enemy in style over a considerable space, but were imperceptibly surrounded in flanks and rear by fresh swarms of rebels. Then they faced about and cut their way back to the spot where they had started, bleeding, but still undiminished in number. The spot they recognised, but the boat was gone. No alternative remained but to retreat down stream. With twenty paces interval between man and man, they slowly retired, firing as best they might on the horde of pursuers, who pressed closer and closer. At the entrance of a small temple, where they sought a few minutes respite, Sergeant Grady was shot through the head. Again the insurgents returned to the attack, and made an unsuccessful attempt to dig up the foundations ; finally, with a view of smoking the besieged out of their citadel, they constructed and set alight a large pile of faggots. It was not until the enemy showed signs of an intention to mend the fire with some bags of gunpowder that the garrison began to be seriously alarmed. They then rushed out, scattering the embers with their bare feet, and leaped the parapet which enclosed the spot of dedicated ground. Six, who could not swim, ran full into the middle of the crowd, carrying their lives for sale to the best market. Seven reached the bank, and flung in their firelocks, and then themselves. The lead in their pouches dragged them so far down that the first flight of bullets passed over them harmlessly. By the time the Sepoys had reloaded, a score of rapid strokes had carried the fugitives well out into the stream. Two were shot through the head; another, overcome with exhaustion, turned over on his back, and was carried by the stream towards a shoal, where his murderers were awaiting him ; the four others, Lieutenants Delafosse and Mowbray Thompson, Gunner Connolly, and Private Murphy, 84th regiment, escaped down stream, and, after many adventures, reached Allahabad in safety.

Meanwhile, the captured boat slowly remounted the now swollen stream, reaching the Suttee Chowra Ghaut again about 10 a.m. on June 30th. There were in her, according to the account of witnesses, sixty-three men, twenty-five women, and four children. Mowbray Thompson states that, after careful enquiry, the only officers shown to be of the party were three of the company's service— Captain Seppings, Lieutenant Masters, and Dr. Boyas. No mention was made of any soldiers. The whole party was slaughtered in cold blood, at the landing-place, by the Nadiree regiment, in the presence of the Nana, immediately afterwards.

Of the thousand persons who had found shelter within General Wheeler's entrenchment four short weeks before, there now remained (besides the four fugitives from Allahabad) only the captives in the Sevada house who, on 1st July, were removed to the small building, afterwards known as the " House of Massacre," about two miles nearer the bridge of boats, on the Lucknow road, where they passed the last fourteen days of their durance.

Of them, individually, no particulars are known. Their names—who died of the pestilence that was among them—who lived to endure the unspeakable agony of the final scene—are secrets of the tomb.

Only, be it said of them, reverently, that they were of the "great "company of Christian people, mostly women and children, who died "at Cawnpore."

To return to Lucknow: it was the original intention that both Residency and fort should be defended to the last, but the disaster at Chinhut seriously affected the strength of the defenders. It was, therefore, quickly determined that one should be sacrificed ; that the fort should be blown up, and the party defending it make their way, as best they could, to their friends in the Residency.

Accordingly, on 1st July, at 12 o'clock at night, the garrison evacuated the fort and reached the Residency, which was about three-quarters of a mile distant, without molestation, their guns and treasures with them ; their departure from the fort being apparently unnoticed.

The train left set for its destruction was so well timed that the evacuating garrison had scarcely entered the gates of the Residency when the Muchee Bawen was blown into the air with a terrific explosion.*

Why the enemy allowed so important a movement to be executed without in any way offering to impede it, can only be accounted for by supposing them either to have been exhausted by the exertions of

---

* On the fort of Muchee Bawen being blown up, it appears one of the garrison, a man of the 32nd regiment who perhaps had been drinking to his country's success a little too freely, concealed himself in some corner where he could not be found when the muster roll was called. On the explosion taking place, after the withdrawal of the garrison, he was thrown into the air, but returned unhurt to mother earth, continuing his too sound sleep the while. The next morning he awoke to find the fort, to his surprise, a mass of deserted ruins. He, therefore, quietly walked to the Residency without being molested by a soul ; and even brought in with him a pair of bullocks attached to a cart of ammunition. On arriving near the Residency the men of the garrison were not a little astonished to hear—in a good old Celtic voice—somewhat husky, the cry of "Arrah, by Jasus, open your gates." They let him in, and his appearance caused much merriment.—Rees, *Relief of Lucknow*, p. 121.

the previous day, or engaged in plundering other parts of the city, which is of immense size. But the successful issue of this operation was of vital importance to the garrison, as, had not the troops in the fort effected a junction with those in the Residency, not one would have probably survived to tell the tale of their subsequent long sufferings.

The Muchee Bawen was commanded from several parts of the town, and very indifferently provided with heavy artillery ammunition. Moreover, the difficulty, hardship, and loss sustained by the Residency garrison in holding that position, even with the reinforcements thus obtained from the fort, sufficiently shows that if the original intention of holding both places had been adhered to, both would have inevitably fallen.

Though the successful evacuation of the fort was in every way a most happy operation, yet it unavoidably entailed serious losses on the regiment, for the head-quarters was at the time stationed in the fort, so that nearly all the Regimental Records, from 1846, the band instruments—with a collection of valuable music, and the greater part of the paymaster's and quarter-master's books had necessarily to be abandoned.

But the losses hitherto sustained by the garrison of Lucknow were comparatively inconsiderable with that which about this time deprived them of their illustrious commander—the guiding spirit of the defence. He to whose foresight in the timely commencement of operations, and great skill in carrying them into effect, the ultimate preservation of the survivors is mainly due, was soon to fall another victim to this lamentable rebellion.

On 1st July an eight-inch shell burst in the room which Sir H. Lawrence was then occupying in the Residency. Though falling close to him, strange to say, he did not receive the slightest injury. Forewarned was, unfortunately, not in this case forearmed, for when implored by his friends to take up other quarters, he jestingly declined to do so, saying that such a thing could never happen twice. But it was otherwise ordained, for on the very next day another shell burst in exactly the same spot, and this time with a more unfortunate result. Sir Henry was mortally wounded, lingering in great agony until the morning of the 4th, when his untimely death, at this critical period, spread consternation through all.

In Sir Henry Lawrence were combined most of those qualities which render a man estimable and a commander influential and beloved. He possessed, to a rare extent, the power of winning the affections of those he governed, so that devotion to the commander became, as it were, a guarantee of zeal for the Government he served. The unbounded confidence reposed in him by all ranks, and the belief in his power to extricate them from their perilous position, made the grief at his loss such as is only felt for a great public benefactor.

On the death of Sir Henry Lawrence, the command of the garrison devolved on Colonel Inglis, 32nd regiment, and Captain Lowe succeeded to the command of the regiment.

At this time there were only two batteries completed in the Residency. Part of the defences were still in an unfinished condition, and the buildings in the immediate vicinity giving cover to the enemy were only partially cleared away. Indeed, the heaviest losses subsequently sustained during the siege were caused by the enemy's sharpshooters stationed in the adjoining mosques and houses, which—from Sir H. Lawrence's desire to spare the holy places and private property—had hitherto been allowed to remain standing.

As soon as the enemy had thoroughly completed the investment of the Residency, they occupied these houses in great force. They rapidly made loopholes on those sides which bore on the post, from which an incessant fire was kept up day and night, causing numerous casualties, there being at one time not less than eight thousand men firing on the position. No spot in the whole works could be considered safe. Several of the sick and wounded lying in the banqueting hall, which had been for the time turned into a hospital, were killed in the very centre of the building, while many women and children were shot dead in a room into which it had not previously been deemed possible that a bullet could penetrate.

Nor were the enemy idle in erecting batteries. From twenty to twenty-five were soon in position, some of them of very large calibre. They were planted all round the post at short distances, some being even within fifty yards of the defence, but so placed that our own guns could not reply to them.

The perseverance of the enemy never relaxed, and their ingenuity in erecting barricades in front of and around their guns in a very short time, rendered all attempts to silence them by musketry entirely unavailable. Nor could they be effectually silenced by shell, on account of their extreme proximity to our position. Besides, the enemy had recourse to digging very narrow trenches, about eight feet deep, in rear of each gun, where the men lay while the shell were falling; and this so effectually concealed them, even while working the gun, that the sharpshooters could only see their heads while in the act of loading.

On 6th July a sortie was made, led by Captain Mansfield and Lieutenant Lawrence, to drive the enemy from a house adjoining that part of the defences. It was performed in the most gallant manner, and the objects in view were entirely accomplished.

On the morning of 20th July the enemy assembled in force all round the position and exploded a mine inside the outer lines of defences of the Water Gate. The mine, which was close to the Redan, and apparently sprung with the intention of destroying that battery, did no harm. The enemy boldly advanced, under cover of a tremendous fire of cannon and musketry, with the object of storming the Redan; but they were received with such a heavy fire, that—after a short struggle—they fell back with much loss. Similar attacks were made at almost every outpost, but were everywhere similarly repulsed, and at 2 p.m. the enemy ceased their attempts to storm the place.

After this failure, the attention of the enemy was directed to undermine the defences. To countermine and throw out listening galleries to frustrate their intentions, the services of some Cornish and Derbyshire men of the regiment* were availed of. With the assistance of the officers and working parties of the Native Infantry Regiment, the most fortunate results were attained, as only three out of twenty mines were exploded with any success by the enemy.

---

* Particular mention should be made of Acting-Sergeants Cullimore, Bannetta, and Farmer, and Corporal Dowling, employed as overseers of miners.

In the meantime their guns were doing great damage to the defences and outposts, rendering several of the latter scarcely tenable. The Residency itself was being rapidly reduced to a ruinous and most dangerous condition, part of it having already fallen in, burying six men of the regiment, two only of whom were extricated alive.

On 10th August the enemy made another assault, having first sprung a mine close to the brigade mess, which entirely destroyed its defences for twenty feet. The breach made was so large that a regiment could have advanced through it in perfect order; and, when the smoke cleared away, some of the enemy came on with great determination. They were met, however, with such a withering flank fire of musketry from the officers and men holding the top of the brigade mess, that they quickly retreated, leaving the more adventurous of their numbers lying on the crest of the breach. While this was going on, another large body advanced on the Cawnpore battery and succeeded in locating themselves for a few minutes in the ditch. They were, however, quickly dislodged from that by hand grenades. At another post they also came boldly forward with scaling ladders, which they planted against the wall. Here, as elsewhere, they were met with the most indomitable resolution; the leaders being slain, the rest fled, forsaking their ladders. They retreated to their batteries and loopholed defences, from which they kept up an unusually heavy cannonade and musketry fire during the rest of the day.

On 18th August the enemy sprung another mine in front of the Sikh lines, and this time with very fatal effect, no less than eleven men being buried alive under the ruins, from whence it was impossible to extricate them, owing to the tremendous fire kept up by the enemy from houses situated less than ten yards in front of the breach. The three officers with this garrison were blown into the air; but, by extraordinary good fortune, returned to earth with no further injury than a severe shaking.

The explosion was followed by a general assault, though of a less determined nature than the two former; and the enemy were consequently repulsed without very great difficulty. They succeeded, however, in establishing themselves under cover of the breach in one of the houses in our position, from which they were driven, in the evening, at the point of the bayonet by some of the 32nd and 84th regiments.

On 21st August a house in the vicinity, from which the garrison had been much annoyed by the enemy, was successfully undermined and blown up. On the same day two parties of the regiment, with a detachment of the 84th, under Captain McCabe and Lieutenant Brown, were sent to spike two guns and destroy one of the enemy's mines. These operations were performed in the most gallant manner.

On 5th September the enemy made their last serious assault on the Residency. Having exploded a large mine, they advanced with scaling ladders, and planted them against the walls, gaining for an instant, the embrasure of a gun; but it was only for an instant, as they were speedily dislodged, with loss, by hand grenades and musketry. A few minutes after, they sprung another mine close to the brigade mess and advanced boldly on that post. Here, again, the accurate and sustained musketry fire from the members of the garrison compelled them to an ignominious flight, leaving their leader—a fine looking old native officer—among the slain.

At other posts similar attacks were made, but everywhere with the same want of success. The enemy's loss on this day must have been very great, as they came on with such determination, and at night were seen bearing large numbers of their killed and wounded over the bridges in the direction of their cantonments.

Though this may be said to have been the last combined assault against the Residency, the siege was still sustained with such vigour by the enemy that not the slightest relaxation was allowed to the incessant vigilance of the defenders.

Exposed to a constant fire of shot and shell, with their battered position fast becoming untenable, they still hoped on for that long deferred relief, never more urgently needed.

At last it appeared to come; for on 25th September the force under General Havelock arrived at the Residency, having cut its way through the city with great loss. But the contrary of relief this, in fact, proved to be; for, insufficient in numbers to extricate the inmates of the Residency, the relieving force, too, became besieged, thus adding fresh comers for the already too limited supply of provisions.

Although nothing hardly was known to the outer world regarding the defence of Lucknow, at this time, as the enemy—by great vigilance—managed to intercept most of the messengers, it may not be out of place to give a short account of the steps that were in progress for their relief by General Havelock and his gallant little force :—

On 12th September, 1857, General Havelock was expecting to be joined by Sir J. Outram, which took place on the 15th, with the 5th Fusiliers, part of the 90th Light Infantry, and some companies of the 78th Highlanders. The following Divisional Order, of the 16th, was published :

" The important duty of first relieving Lucknow has been intrusted " to Major-General Havelock, C.B., and Major-General Outram feels " that it is due to this distinguished officer, and the strenuous and " noble exertions which he has made to effect that object, that to him " should accrue the honour of the achievement.

" Major-General Outram is confident that the great end for which " General Havelock and his brave troops have so long and so " gloriously fought, will now—under the blessing of Providence—be " accomplished. The Major-General, therefore, in gratitude for, and " admiration of, the brilliant deeds in arms achieved by General " Havelock and his gallant troops, will cheerfully waive his rank on " that occasion, and will accompany the force to Lucknow in his " civil capacity as chief commissioner of Oudh, tendering his military " services to General Havelock as a volunteer. On the relief of " Lucknow, the Major-General will resume his position at the head of " the forces."

In acknowledgment of this generous action, the following order was issued, on the same evening, by General Havelock :—

" Brigadier-General Havelock, in making known to the column the "kind and generous determination of General Sir James Outram, " K.C.B., to leave to him the task of relieving Lucknow and rescuing " its gallant and enduring garrison, has only to express his hope that " the troops will strive, by their exemplary and gallant conduct in " the field, to justify the confidence thus reposed in them."

32ND REGIMENT.

Leaving Cawnpore, now in a state of defence, in charge of Colonel O'Brien, Havelock crossed the Ganges on the 19th. This was an arduous affair, for the river, then in flood, was running rapidly, and there were heavy guns, elephants, camels, ammunition waggons, and commissariat stores, as well as long trains of armed men, doolies for the wounded, and troops of burden-bearing coolies, to be got over. At length it was effected, and the march began.

On the previous night, most of the troops had been marched down to the river's bank to await the advance of the morrow. As they moved along, the regimental colours, carried in their dark cloth covering, rose up now and again from the forest of glistening bayonets "like yew trees in a garden." The moon struggled through the rain, which had been falling all the day, and threw a dim light over the river, looming mournfully on the blackened ruin where the brave old soldier—Sir H. Wheeler—and his devoted garrison had closed their last days on earth.

The army was divided into two brigades of infantry; the first comprising the 5th Fusiliers, the 84th Regiment, part of the 64th Foot, and the 1st Madras Fusiliers, under the command of General Neil. The second brigade was formed by the 78th Highlanders, 90th Light Infantry, and the Sikh Regiment of Ferozepore, under the command of Brigadier Hamilton, of the 78th regiment. A third brigade, composed of artillery, consisted of Captain Maude's, Captain Olphert's, and Brevet Major Eyre's batteries, under the command of Major Cope. The cavalry comprised a small body of volunteers and a few irregular horsemen of a native corps, with Captain Burrow in command. A small body of Engineers, under Captain Crommelin, was attached.

After some skirmishing by the river's banks had cleared away the enemy, the wing advanced, by most fatiguing marches; for the Ganges—having acquired its extreme height—had overflowed its banks for several miles on the Oudh side. The water, as in nearly all similar cases, though still, was in some places deep upon the fields, and the sun was beating fiercely on the men. Very few tents had been taken and provisions for only fifteen days brought over; the force was not, therefore, needlessly encumbered with stores; but they had a large park of artillery and an abundant supply of ammunition.

As Havelock advanced, the rebels rapidly retreated, and then of him and his force nothing was heard at Cawnpore for many days. "Since the day that the tail of our army left," says a correspondent of the *Hurkarn*, " no vestige of news has reached us. They ploughed "a way through the tide of rebellion which overflows Oudh, but the "waves closed again, and we have no means of hearing from them or "communicating with them. Yesterday a hundred men, who had been "sent to keep the Lucknow road open, were cut up by the rebels almost "to a man, and our cossids (messengers) have returned with 'no news.'"

Another correspondent wrote : " It seems that many cossids have "been despatched from General Havelock's camp, but the enemy "have kept up such a strict blockade in the rear of his force that to "pass was impossible."

" Havelock found the enemy strongly encamped at Mungarnene, "and after a sharp action he routed them completely ; so much so "that they made no further stand until the Alum Bagh was reached.

" The greatest discomfort was experienced by the gallant little "army, as the rains had set in and their bivouacs were pools of "water. Rest was obtained in a deserted village on the 21st, and on "the 22nd the army continued its march, rain falling heavily. Many "of the coolies, dreading Lucknow, had deserted, which was a "serious loss ; but there was no time to stop and replace them— "Lucknow was in danger, so Havelock and his noble band pressed "on, beset with difficulties, but sustained by the hope of effecting the "object of their march. Another comfortless night was passed in a "deserted village, and a salute of twenty-one guns fired, in the hope "that the beleagured garrison would hear the report and comprehend "its purpose. On the 23rd September Havelock continued his "advance, and found the enemy were determined to dispute every "inch of ground with him. The flower of the rebel army was strongly "posted to resist his further advance, and here he felt what an effort "would have to be made to achieve the object of his march.

" After a struggle, in spite of the strong position of the rebels, "Havelock succeeded in turning their right, and drove them back to "their centre, pounding them with his artillery, finally charging the "position with infantry, capturing village after village, and ultimately

" seizing five guns. The enemy's left, finding that the right and
" centre were turned, fled, followed by Outram and his cavalry. The
" Alum Bagh was won. From this to Lucknow was a series of narrow
" tortuous streets and a wide plain. General Havelock, however,
" knowing the probable tactics of the enemy, would have chosen the
" circuitous route by the Dilkoosha and Martiniere, but was unable,
" owing to the impassable state of the roads. Early on the morning
" of the 25th September, Havelock commenced his forward move,
" leaving his baggage under escort at the Alum Bagh. The
" advance was led by Sir James Outram, who found as he advanced
" what a desperate errand they were on, as every preparation had
" been made for a most determined resistance by the enemy. Not
" only were guns placed, raking the road, but every house was turned
" into a fort and filled with Sepoys, who poured a murderous and
" continuous fire on the little army. The 5th Fusiliers, in a gallant
" charge, took some guns, which formed a battery. No sooner was
" this service performed than another was opened on them, which
" commanded the approach and passage of the Char Bagh, a bridge
" which crosses the Canal and forms one of the entrances to the city
" of Lucknow. The enemy was in great force. The garden enclosures
" had been made temporary fortresses, with loopholed walls, from
" which a constant fire was maintained upon the advancing forces.
" The fire from the heavy guns, which had opened upon them the
" moment they came within range, was kept up with terrible energy.
" With a shout the battery was charged, and, after a brief struggle, was
" taken. Here Sir James Outram was wounded in the arm, but,
" although faint from loss of blood, never dismounted until the
" Residency was reached. During these brilliant affairs the troops
" had been harassed by the incessant fire of musketry from the en-
" closure of the Char Bagh, from the long grass on the left, and from
" the houses on either side of the street at the town end of the bridge.
" It was necessary to clear the garden enclosure and jungle, to enable
" the slow-moving bullocks to bring over the heavy guns and ammuni-
" tion. This was done by the 78th Highlanders, who remained as an
" escort until they could rejoin the advancing column. After advancing
" for nearly two miles it was found that progress in that direction was

" impossible; Havelock therefore left the Cawnpore road and detoured
" along a narrow lane to the right, which skirts the left bank of the
" city canal. This move was successful, and the Kaiser Bagh was
" reached after a march of some hours. It was here necessary to
" tender aid to the party of 78th and guns left in the rear. Aid arrived
" just in time, and at a critical moment the adjutant of the 78th led
" a charge against a battery and seized it in a most gallant style; and
" it was long past noon when the column reached a place of tem-
" porary shelter under the walls of the Furrek Buksh. The troops
" were sorely exhausted. For six weary hours they had struggled in
" deadly fight with a fierce enemy, and all the while under a scorching
" sun. Faint and worn out, they endeavoured to snatch a brief
" respite from this double foe. After much consideration, in spite of
" all the difficulties, it was deemed advisable to continue the advance
" that night, leaving the wounded and baggage and heavy guns, with
" suitable escorts, in the Moolee Mahul and other sheltered places for
" the night. The General placed himself at the head of the High-
" landers and Sikhs, and dashed on for the Residency. No words
" can picture that march of fire and death! Every inch of the road
" was disputed—every house turned into a fortress, from which belched
" forth a continuous stream of fire and lead.

" At last the Residency was reached, with a cheer which only British
" soldiers know how to give. The vanguard of Havelock's 'Column
" of Relief' entered, bringing to the beleagured garrison safety at
" least, if not deliverance. And who shall picture the greetings of that
" night, or describe the joy of those who once more began to hope,
" and the gratitude they felt to that indomitable deliverer, who, for
" nearly a hundred days, had struggled through an overwhelming tide
" of battle, disease, and death, to rescue them from their inhuman
" foes? 'Our reception,' says one 'was enthusiastic; men, women,
" and even infants, pouring down in one sweeping crowd to welcome
" their deliverers.' While another adds, 'Many people were nearly
" mad, and the cheering was deafening.'"*

On the morning following the arrival of this force a party of one

---

* W. Brock, *Biographical sketch of Havelock.*

hundred and fifty of the regiment, under the command of Captain Lowe, were sent out to drive the enemy from the posts they occupied on the side of the river near the Residency. This was effected, but not without a certain amount of loss. One eighteen-pounder, one nine-pounder, and one six-pounder were brought in; two mortars were spiked; and a great number of the enemey were killed and wounded while trying to cross the river. The nine-pounder was captured in a particularly gallant manner by Lieutenant Lawrence and a party of the light company just as a second round of grape shot was being discharged at them.

On the same day a party of one hundred men of the regiment, under Captain Lowe, were sent out with some of Sir H. Havelock's force to strengthen the guard over the heavy guns, ammunition, and baggage, which had not yet been extricated from a dangerous position into which they had fallen the evening before. Their recovery was the more difficult as the enemy, at this time, commanded the road to the Residency with a heavy fire of musketry and round shot. Towards dusk the party of the 32nd regiment was moved to the furtherest end of the position, with orders to hold their ground until the heavy guns and the 90th Regiment, who formed the rear guard, had retired. This they did before morning, and Captain Lowe having withdrawn his look-out sentries, the 32nd slowly retired, protecting the rear of the whole without its departure having been perceived.

The baggage and guns reached the Residency through a palace which had fallen into our hands the previous day; but the troops had scarcely entered when a most determined attack was made upon it by the enemy who—mounting the wall of a garden, which they had managed to occupy unknown to the garrison—poured a deadly fire upon the troops massed in the confined and unsheltered space below. Captain McCabe of the 32nd, with the most distinguished bravery, led a party of volunteers—consisting of the 5th, 32nd, and 90th regiments—into the garden, where he killed or wounded most of those inside, few—if any—escaping.

Soon after this, Captain Lowe was severely wounded in the foot, and, being therefore incapacitated for active duty, the command of the regiment devolved upon Captain Bassano.

Several sorties were made from this time to the beginning of October, in all of which the regiment was engaged and bore a distinguished part.

On 27th September one small party lost three killed and five wounded.

On the 29th, three sorties were simultaneously made, in conducting one of which Captain McCabe* was mortally wounded.

In another, conducted by Lieutenant Cooke, a gun was captured—Lieutenant Cooke being one of the first at the embrasure.

GENERAL EDMONDSTOUNE.

In the third, led by Lieutenant Edmonstoune, consisting of men of the 32nd, 64th, and 84th regiments, they succeeded in spiking six guns, one of which, a twenty-four-pounder, they were unable to destroy on this occasion, Lieutenant Edmondstoune being slightly wounded.

On 1st October, a detachment of the regiment, under Lieutenant Cooke, was sent out to protect parties employed in destroying houses occupied by the enemy.

On the same day another detachment of the regiment, attached to the Madras Fusiliers, went out for the purpose of occupying some houses in the vicinity. After being in possession of them two days they were withdrawn.

No more sorties were made after this, as the enemy ceased to occupy the ground near the river.

The casualties now became fewer, but the privations endured

---

* A most gallant officer, who—even among the many whose valour was conspicuous during the eventful period—was particularly distinguished.

during the long siege began to display its effect on a great number of the men. Symptoms of scurvy became apparent, and its effects on the wounded were pernicious in the extreme.

> NOTE.—The relieving column now occupied the series of palaces, in continuation of the Residency, stretching along the banks of the Goomtee. During the interval between 25th September and the final relief of the garrison, on November 17th, General Havelock continually experienced the extreme difficulty of defending his widely-extended line. With very insufficient means—incessantly harassed as he was by an unwearied and subtle fire—he commenced a system of mining, which, though requiring incessant care night and day, yet were his chief means of defence. General Outram wrote, " I am aware of no parallel to our series of mines "in modern war ; twenty-one shafts, aggregating two hundred feet in " depth, and three thousand two hundred and ninety-one feet of gallery " have been executed." Many scenes of thrilling interest were enacted in these mines and listening galleries, reflecting the greatest credit on all concerned.

At last the gunpowder of the garrison began to fail, and something had to be done to counteract the strategy of the cunning enemy.

A sort of subterranean cordon, or intercepting mine, was constructed around the more advanced and exposed portion of Havelock's position. Numerous shafts were sunk, and from these, listening galleries were constructed, three feet in height and two feet in breadth, of great length, including the whole of that portion of their position open to attack by mining. In these, engineers were placed, constantly listening to discover the approach of the enemy's works, that they might break into their mines, or destroy them by small charges of powder before they could reach Havelock's subterranean boundary. The value of this novel defence, executed under the pressure of an unprecedented exigency, was repeatedly tested, and invariably with the same results.

October had passed, and November was passing apace ; the hopes of the garrison existed on the scanty reports brought in by the spies or communicated to them through a semaphore that had been extemporized upon the roof of the Alum Bagh. News of the advance of Sir Colin Campbell was thus conveyed about the 12th, and of his junction with Brigadier Grant's column, then on its way to Lucknow, and on the same evening they heard of his arrival at the Alum Bagh. On the 15th, the march of the general to the Residency, with a force of five thousand men, was semaphoned, and from that moment everyone was on the watch to mark his progress.

Regardless of the danger, courageous spirits mounted to the tower of the Residency, while not a few joined the look-out on the top of the post-office. Here they were enabled to mark his course, while the smoke and fire indicated plainly his steady advance to their relief.

Instead of crossing the canal at the bridge of the Char Bagh, as Havelock had done, on leaving the Alum Bagh, Sir Colin at once diverged to the right, crossing the country to the Dilkoosha, a small palace surrounded by gardens, about three miles from the Residency. After a running fight of two hours, they drove the enemy down the park to the Martiniere, leaving that building, as well as the Dilkoosha, in the hands of Sir Colin Campbell.

Early next morning Sir Colin began his march on the Sikunder Bagh, a strong square building surrounded by a wall of solid masonry—as usual, loopholed for musketry. It was evident that there would be a tussel for this; a village on the opposite side of the road was likewise held by the enemy, as was also the ground on the left of our advance. The general first cleared the way with his artillery, who were exposed to a merciless fire in reaching the position, and finally launched his infantry—the 53rd Regiment and 93rd Highlanders—at them, who quickly made themselves masters, and drove the enemy flying upon the position across the plain.

"The sight from the Residency," says an eye-witness, "was very "fine. We could observe the enemy retiring, and our guns "advancing through openings in the trees. Occasionally a staff "officer was seen dashing across, and once a group of mounted "officers—supposed to be Sir Colin and his staff—appeared, and "disappeared again. The firing of heavy guns, and the smoke rising "in the clear air, with occasional glimpses of the troops, added "greatly to the effect of a naturally beautiful landscape."

Meanwhile the artillery were pounding away at the walls of the Sikunder Bagh, with little effect. At last a breach was made, or, rather, a hole of two feet square, and then began a charge which for heroic daring has never been surpassed, and rarely equalled. The Highlanders and Sikhs rushed to the wall, and through that hole they dragged themselves in upon the foe. The fight inside lasted the greater part of the day ; the enemy fought like rats in a hole, but were finally overcome. From this the next objective was a mosque— Shah Nujjeef—surrounded by a garden, protected by a strong wall which had been loopholed with great care. After a cannonading of three hours, the 93rd stormed it. The advancing party were aided by the preparations made by the beleagured garrison. To co-operate as much as possible, and with this intention, several mines which had been charged were exploded, and some positions seized which materially assisted Sir Colin.

To quote from Sir Colin's despatch, " on the next day communica- "tions were opened from the left rear of the barracks to the canal, "after overcoming considerable difficulty," in which Captain Peel, Royal Navy, Captains Wolseley, 90th, Hopkins, Guise, and Lieutenant Powlett, took an active part. The last stand was made by the enemy at Motee Mahal, who was overcome in the course of an hour, and communication with the Residency was accomplished.

During the following days the sick and wounded, with the women and children, were conveyed to the camp in the Dilkoosha Park, and on the night of 22nd October the Residency and its defences were finally evacuated. The regiment marched out under the command of Captain Bassano, the enemy again offering no molestation nor being apparently aware of the departure of the garrison.

In terminating this meagre sketch of the principal events that marked the defence of the Residency of Lucknow, no comments more pathetic or illustrative could be added than the following extract from the despatch of Brigadier Inglis, then lieutenant-colonel of the 32nd regiment :

"If further proof be wanting of the desperate nature of the "struggle which we have, under God's blessing, so long and so "successfully waged, I could point to the roofless and ruined houses, "to the crumbled walls, to the exploded mines, to the open breaches, "to the shattered and disabled guns and defences, and—lastly—to

P

"the long and melancholy list of brave and devoted officers and
" men who have fallen. These silent witnesses bear sad and solemn
" testimony to the way in which this public position has been
" defended.

" During the early part of these vicissitudes we were left without
" any information whatever of the position of affairs outside. An
" occasional spy did, indeed, come in with the object of inducing our
" Sepoys and servants to desert, but the intelligence derived from
" such sources was, of course, entirely untrustworthy. We sent our
" messengers daily, calling for aid and asking for information, none of
" whom ever returned until the 26th day of the siege, when a
" pensioner, named Nugud, came back with a letter from General
" Havelock's Camp informing us that they were advancing with a
" force sufficient to bear down all opposition, and would be with us in
" five or six days. A messenger was immediately despatched,
" requesting that on the evening of their arrival on the outskirts of
" the city two rockets might be thrown up, in order that we might
" take the necessary measures in assisting them while forcing their
" way in.

" The sixth day, however, expired and they came not; but, for
" many evenings after, officers and men watched for the ascension of
" the expected rockets with hopes such as make the heart sick.

" We knew not then, nor did we learn until the 29th August, or
" thirty-five days later, that the relieving force, after having fought
" most nobly to effect our deliverance, had been obliged to fall back
" for reinforcements, and this was the last communication we received
" until two days before the arrival of Sir James Outram on the
" 25th September.

" Besides heavy visitations of cholera and small-pox, we have also
" had to contend against a sickness which has almost universally
" pervaded the garrison. Commencing with a very painful eruption,
" it has merged into a low fever, combined with diarrhœa; but,
" although few or no men have actually died from its effects, it leaves
" behind a weakness and lassitude which—in the absence of all
" material substances, save coarse beef, and still coarser flour—none
" have been able entirely to get over.

"The mortality among the women and children—especially the "latter—from these diseases, and from other causes, has been perhaps "the most painful characteristic of the siege.

"The want of native servants has also been a source of much "privation, owing to the suddenness with which we were besieged. "Many of these people—who might, perhaps, have otherwise proved "faithful to their employers, but who were outside the defences at the "time—were altogether excluded; very many more deserted, and "several families were consequently left without the services of a "single domestic. Several ladies had to tend their children and even "wash their own clothes, as well as to cook their scanty meals entirely "unaided. Combined with the absence of servants, the want of "proper accommodation has probably been the cause of much of the "disease with which we have been afflicted.

"I cannot refrain from bringing to the prominent notice of His "Lordship in Council the patient endurance and the Christian "resignation that has been evinced by the women of the garrison. "They have animated us by their example. Many, alas, have been "made widows, and their children fatherless, in the cruel struggle. "But all such seemed resigned to the will of Providence, and many— "among whom may be mentioned the honoured names of Birch "Polehampton, of Barber, and of Gall, have—after the example of "Miss Nightingale—constituted themselves the tender and solicitous "nurses of the wounded and dying soldiers in the hospital."

The following acknowledgments of the heroic services and the gallant conduct of the officers and men of the regiment is extracted from a despatch of the Governor-General in Council :—

"The Good Services of Her Majesty's 32nd Regiment throughout the "struggle have been remarkable. To the watchful courage and sound "judgment of its Commander—Brigadier Inglis—the British Govern- "ment owes a heavy debt of gratitude, and Major Lowe, Captain "Bassano, Lieutenants Edmondstoune, Foster, Harman, Lawrence, "Clery, Cooke, Browne, and Charleton, and Quarter-Master Stribling "are praised by their superior as having severally distinguished "themselves. The Officers here mentioned received the thanks of the

"Governor-General in Council. A further acknowledgment of the "services rendered was made by granting an additional year's service "to every Officer and man engaged in the defence of Lucknow, and by " making the Regiment into Light Infantry."

On evacuating Lucknow the regiment proceeded to Cawnpore, and arrived there on 30th November. It was engaged in the action of Cawnpore and pursuit of the Gwalier Contingent on 6th December, under Sir Colin Campbell.

The regiment remained at Cawnpore from 6th December to the end of the year.

1858.

The regiment was stationed at Cawnpore on 1st January, 1858, and was employed on field service in the district of Calpee, with a column under Colonel Maxwell, C.B., 88th regiment, during February and March. It proceeded with this column to assist the army engaged in the operations against Lucknow, but returned the same month to garrison Cawnpore.

On 15th January, this year, Colonel Inglis was promoted to the rank of major-general for his services during the defence of Lucknow. He was succeeded in the command of the regiment by Colonel Berkeley, who did not, however, long survive his promotion, as he died at Aden, on his way from India, in September of the same year. He was succeeded by Lieutenant-Colonel Carmichael.

In April the regiment was removed from Cawnpore to Allahabad, but again formed part of a column on field service in May, under Colonel Berkely, C.B., 32nd, sent, in co-operation with the Rajah of Benares' force, to protect the villages of Goopegunge and Palee, in the Allahabad district, from being pillaged by the rebel chief—Iwin-Sing—who, at the head of a large force, was threatening both these places. It returned again to Allahabad at the end of the month.

The following memorandum was issued from the Horse Guards:

"14th May, 1858.

"Her Majesty, in consideration of the enduring gallantry displayed in "the defence of the Residency of Lucknow, has been pleased to direct that "the 32nd Regiment be clothed, equipped, and trained as a light infantry "regiment from 26th February last.

" Her Majesty has also been pleased to command that the word " Luck-"now" shall be borne ou the regimental colour of the 32nd Light Infantry, " in commemoration of the enduring fortitude and persevering gallantry "displayed in the defence of the Residency of Lucknow for eighty-seven "days.

" By order of H.R.H. the General Commanding-in-Chief,

"(Signed) G. A. WETHERALL, A.G."

In July the regiment marched from Allahabad and joined the field force, under Brigadier Berkely, at Soroon, in Oudh. It was present at the capture of forts Detreign—July 13th—and Tyrhool—July 17th and 18th.*

The regiment subsequently proceeded to Petabghur, was thence removed to Sultanpore, where it joined the force under Brigadier General Horseford, C.B., and was present with this force at the action of Doadpore and the defeat of the Nusserabad Brigade (Mutineers), October 20th, 1858.

From this time it formed part of the army engaged in the reduction of the province of Oudh, under the personal command of His Excellency the Commander-in-Chief, Lord Clyde, and Major-General Sir H. Grant, K.C.B., until November.

About this time the regiment was detached with a column, under Lieutenant-Colonel Carmichael, 32nd, which (acting in conjunction with the commander in-chief's force) was sent in pursuit of the rebel chief, Beni Maduo, to the banks of the Gogra, across which he was successfully driven.

It was subsequently employed with the same column in disarming the population of the province of Oudh.

1859.

The regiment formed part of the movable column employed on field service in the district of Roy Barielly, under Lieutenant-Colonel

---

* The services of Captain Colls, as field-engineer, were specially mentioned in despatches in connexion with these operations. He subsequently served as deputy-assistant quarter-master-general to Brigadier Pinckney's force in Oudh.

Carmichael, from 1st to 20th January, 1859. It arrived at Roy Barielly on the 21st, and marched, *en route* to Allahabad, on the 22nd, arriving there on the 27th.

The regiment left Allahabad in three detachments by bullock train *en route* to Chinsurah. The first detachment on 10th, the second on 11th, and head-quarters on 12th February. The whole arrived at Chinsurah by the 28th, where the regiment remained until 28th March, when it embarked for England on board the troopship *Albuhera*. It sailed on 24th April, leaving behind six officers and fifty rank and file for whom tonnage had not been taken up.

After being upwards of five months at sea, the regiment disembarked at Portsmouth on 26th August, 1859, and proceeded by rail the same day to Dover, where it remained until August the following year.

Her Majesty having signified her gracious intention to inspect the regiment on disembarkation at Portsmouth, on 26th August, it was drawn up for that purpose in the Dockyard, at 11 a.m., under command of Lieutenant-Colonel Carmichael, C.B., who had met the regiment on arrival.

A few minutes after the time mentioned, Her Majesty arrived, accompanied by the Prince Consort and other members of the Royal Family, being received by a Royal salute, and at once proceeded to inspect the regiment, walking down both ranks, frequently stopping to ask questions relative to the sufferings the regiment had undergone during the siege of Lucknow, in which Her Majesty evinced the warmest interest and sympathy.

The regiment then marched past, and subsequently all the officers and men present who had actually been engaged in the defence of the Residency of Lucknow, were, at the request of Her Majesty, marched to the front, and were most graciously addressed by the Queen, who spoke in the warmest terms of the gallantry of the regiment during the memorable defence of Lucknow, and congratulated the survivors on their safe return.

Her Majesty also congratulated Lieutenant-Colonel Carmichael on the soldierly bearing and clean appearance of his men, remarking that they looked rather as if they had just come from barracks than off a long voyage after an arduous campaign.

Subsequently some of the plate belonging to the mess of the regiment, which had been curiously damaged and twisted by shot and shell during the siege of Lucknow, was graciously accepted by Her Majesty, who commanded Lord Grey to inform the regiment that she should always look upon these objects as among the most interesting of the sort in the collection in the Museum at Windsor Castle, where they were deposited.

1860.

The regiment left Dover on 6th August, 1860, proceeding by rail to Aldershot, where it arrived the same day.

While stationed at Dover the regiment was inspected by H.R.H. the Duke of Cambridge, the commander-in-chief, who expressed himself in the most complimentary manner regarding the efficiency and discipline.

The strength of the headquarters on its arrival in England was only three hundred and forty rank and file, while the depôt—consisting of the 11th and 12th companies, which had moved some months previously from Chatham to Dover—numbered six hundred and thirty-two.

The depôt soldiers were almost all young and untrained, so that reorganising the regiment was attended with nearly as much trouble as raising a new one.

On 25th September, this year, Lieutenant-Colonel Carmichael retired on half-pay, and Major Stapylton succeeded to the command of the regiment.

1861.

The regiment remained stationed at Aldershot until 21st August, 1861, occupying the permanent barracks, South Camp. On that date the head-quarters and six companies, under Lieutenant-Colonel Stapylton, proceeded by rail to Portsmouth, and from thence, in H.M.S. *Magæra*, to Plymouth. The remainder of the regiment, with the exception of one company—detached to Horfield on the 27th—marched from Aldershot to Portsmouth on the 26th, from whence they, likewise, proceeded in the same ship to Plymouth.

While in this station six companies were quartered in the Citadel, Plymouth, three companies in the Raglan barracks, Devonport, and one company at Horfield, near Bristol.

1862.

The regiment remained distributed as before-mentioned until 14th August, 1862, when the company at Horfield was withdrawn, and on the 22nd of the same month the whole of the regiment moved to Raglan barracks, Devonport.

1863.

The regiment remained at Devonport until April, on the 4th of which month the head-quarters and left wing, under Lieutenant-Colonel Stapylton, proceeded, on board H.M.S. *Magæra*, to Dublin, and from thence straight on to the Curragh. The other wing left Plymouth, in the same ship, on the 15th, and arrived at the Curragh on the 17th, where the regiment was stationed until 23rd September. On that date the left wing proceeded by march-route, *via* Naas, to Dublin. The right wing and head-quarters, under Lieutenant-Colonel Stapylton, left by the same route on the 24th, and arrived in Dublin the following day. The regiment was quartered at Richmond barracks, and there remained until May, the following year.

1864.

On 26th of May, 1864, the regiment was again removed to the Curragh. The left wing proceeded thither by march-route, *via* Naas, and the right wing, with the head-quarters, followed the next day. The regiment was quartered in the huts while at the Curragh.

In September the regiment was moved into winter quarters, the head-quarters and one wing to Waterford, the other wing to Kilkenny.

The wings proceeded to their respective stations by march of parties, not more than two companies at a time.

The first two companies of the head-quarter wing left the Curragh on 26th September, two more companies the following day, and the fifth company, with the head-quarters, on the 28th. These parties halted for the night as follows: first night, Athy; second night, Carlow; third night, Bagnalstown; fourth night, Thomastown; and on the fifth day arrived at Waterford. The head-quarter party halted the whole of Sunday at Thomastown, and marched into Waterford the following day. The distance from the Curragh to Waterford is about seventy-five English miles.

The left wing proceeded to Kilkenny in two parties. The first left the Curragh on the 29th, and the other the following day, halting for the night respectively at Athy and Castlecomer, and marching into Kilkenny on the third day.

On 25th November one company, with its officers, was detached from the head-quarter wing to Duncannon Fort.

1865.

On 1st February the depôt companies rejoined the service companies, as regiments stationed at home were no longer allowed to have companies detached at depôts.

On 27th March the regiment was again moved to the Curragh by rail, for the purpose of "formation," prior to embarkation for "foreign service;" it being then under orders to proceed to Gibraltar.

It remained at the Curragh until 28th June, on which day it proceeded by rail to Dublin, thence by rail to Kingstown, and there embarked, on board the troopship *Himalaya*, for Gibraltar. The *Himalaya* sailed immediately the regiment embarked; and, after a fine passage, reached Gibraltar on 3rd July. It disembarked on the following evening, and was encamped at the North Front, pending the embarkation for Canada of the 4th battalion Rifle Brigade, which corps the 32nd Light Infantry had gone out to relieve. On 8th July the regiment moved to Europa Point barracks.

The depôt companies (two in number) under command of Captain H. Priestley, were left at the Curragh camp on the embarkation of the regiment, from whence they proceeded to Cork on 31st June, and were attached to the 14th depôt battalion. On 19th October the depôt, together with the 14th depôt battalion, removed to Buttevant.

1866.

The regiment remained quartered in Europa Point and Buena Vista barracks during the whole of this year. On 10th July, 1866,

Colonel Stapylton retired on half-pay, and Lieutenant-Colonel Johnston, from half-pay, succeeded to the command of the regiment.

The regiment remained in barracks at Europa Point and Buena Vista till 4th May, when it embarked on board the troopship *Orontes* for conveyance to Mauritius, where it arrived on 4th July, and disembarked on the following day. The regiment remained until the 9th in barracks at Port Louis, on which day four companies proceeded to Mahebourg, and the head-quarters and four companies the following day, leaving two companies at Port Louis under the command of Lieutenant-Colonel Bassano.

On 13th July the depôt was removed from Buttevant to Colchester, where it arrived on the 16th, and was attached to the 8th depôt battalion.

1867.

On 18th May, 1867, Brevet Major Edmondstoune assumed command of the depôt, in place of Captain Priestly, who rejoined head-quarters.

1868.

The detachment of the regiment stationed at Port Louis suffered greatly from the malarious fever prevalent in that town, and was consequently reduced to one company; Lieutenant-Colonel Bassano joining the head-quarters of the regiment, which continued at Mahebourg until 14th November, when it proceeded by rail to Port Louis, and embarked on board H.M.S. *Urgent*, to East London, South Africa. It disembarked on the 23rd and 24th November, and marched to fort Beaufort, where it arrived on 7th December, having left one company, under the command of Captain the Honble. R. H. de Montmorency, at East London.

One company—composed of men whose health had suffered to a considerable extent from the Mauritius fever—under command of Captain Hardinge, was sent to the Cape of Good Hope on 12th August, where they continued stationed until the end of the year. Lieutenant-Colonel Johnston proceeded on leave of absence on 12th August, and Colonel Bassano assumed the command of the regiment.

1869.

The regiment embarked on 14th November, 1868, for the Cape, landed on the 24th, and proceeded to fort Beaufort, where it remained until 1st July, 1869, and then marched to Grahamstown.

Lieutenant-Colonel the Honble. B. M. Ward succeeded Lieutenant-Colonel Johnston, the latter officer retiring on full pay on 12th June. Lieutenant Colonel Ward took over the command of the regiment from Colonel Bassano on 19th November, 1869.

On 6th May the depôt was removed from Colchester to Winchester and attached to the 7th depôt battalion.

On 30th September, Captain Stabb assumed command of the depôt in place of Brevet Lieutenant-Colonel Edmondstoune, who rejoined head-quarters.

1870.

On the breaking up of the depôt battalion system, the depôt companies were removed from Winchester, on 22nd March, and arrived in Edinburgh on the 26th, where they were attached to the 90th Light Infantry.

A draft—consisting of two sergeants, one corporal, and fifty privates—embarked at Portsmouth, under the command of Captain Lakin, on board the troopship *Himalaya*, for conveyance to service companies, on 30th April, 1870.

The head-quarters, and " C," " E," " G," and " H " companise, marched from Grahamstown on 15th June, *en route* to Port Elizabeth, embarked on the 21st, on board the *Himalaya*, for conveyance to Natal, and disembarked at Port Natal on 30th June and 1st July; proceeded on 2nd July *en route* to Pietermaritzburg, where it arrived on 5th July, leaving " G " company, under the command of Captain E. Lakin and Lieutenant Phillips, at Durban.

" A," " B," " D," and " F " companies still remained in the Cape Colony, under the command of Brevet Lieutenant-Colonel J. Edmondstoune.

1871.

A draft—consisting of Lieutenant Turnbull, one sergeant, and sixty-nine privates—embarked at Portsmouth, on board the troopship *Tamar*, for conveyance to service companies, on 7th April, 1871.

On 6th June the depôt companies, with the 90th Light Infantry, moved from Edinburgh to Glasgow, where they were quartered in the barracks at Gallowgate.

On 1st November, Captain Cherry assumed command of the depôt, in place of Captain Stabb, who embarked to rejoin service companies.

The head-quarters and four companies of the regiment remained stationed at Natal, and the left-wing—consisting of four companies—at King William's Town, Cape of Good Hope.

On 17th October the head-quarters marched from Pietermaritzburg to Durban, Natal, where it arrived on the 20th, and encamped there until the 5th November, on which day it embarked, on board the troopship *Tamar*, for conveyance to Mauritius, arriving on 16th November, and disembarked the same day. The head-quarters and three companies proceeded by train, the same afternoon, to Mahebourg, there to be stationed.

One company, under the command of Captain J. G. Stopford, and Lieutenant C. F. A. Turnbull, re-embarked, on board the *Tamar*, on 25th November, for passage to the Cape, to join the left wing of the regiment at King William's Town, where it still remained stationed.

On 15th December, Lieutenant-Colonel the Honble. B. M. Ward proceeded on leave of absence, and Major the Honble. R. H de Montmorency assumed the command of the regiment.

1872.

The head-quarters and three companies of the regiment were stationed at Mahebourg, Mauritius, and the left wing—consisting of five companies—at the Cape of Good Hope, on 1st January.

On 1st April the head-quarters and "C" and "G" companies were removed to camp at Point D'Esney, leaving "H" company at Mahebourg, owing to the increased number of admissions to Hospital from malarious fever, where they remained until 31st July, returning to

Mahebourg for the purpose of proceeding to Port Louis on the following day.

A draft—consisting of two sergeants, one bugler, and thirty-five rank and file, under the command of Captain Trueman—left Glasgow on 5th July for embarkation at Queenstown on board the *Himalaya*, which sailed for Mauritius on 9th July.

On 22nd July the depôt companies, with the 90th Light Infantry, moved from Glasgow to Aldershot, arriving on the 27th.

On 1st August—with the exception of one officer and twenty-five non-commissioned officers and men, who remained on detachment at Mahebourg—the head-quarters and " C," " G," and " H " companies proceeded to Port Louis by special train, and were quartered in Line barracks on arrival and until 11th September, when the head-quarters, staff, band, &c., under the command of Major the Honble. R. H. de Montmorency, embarked, on board the *Himalaya*, for the Cape of Good Hope.

The *Himalaya* sailed immediately after embarkation, and—after a fine passage—reached East London on the evening of 19th September. As it was too late to disembark that day, the troops left the ship early on the following morning. The head-quarters and the before-mentioned companies remained at East London until 21st, when they proceeded, by march, to King William's Town, arriving on 24th September.

A detachment from the left wing—consisting of one subaltern, one assistant-surgeon, and thirty-four non-commissioned officers and men, under the command of Major W. J. Anderson—marched from King William's Town on 22nd August, *en route* to East London, where they arrived on 24th August, and embarked the following day, on board the *Himalaya*, for Mauritius, to relieve the head-quarters &c. The *Himalaya* arrived at Mauritius on 6th September, and the detachment disembarked the following day at Cannonier Point, and were placed in quarantine, owing to some cases of fever having occurred during the voyage.

On 20th September it proceeded to Port Louis, and Major W. J. Anderson assumed command of the detachment stationed at Mauritius.

1873.

On 10th March, 1873, the depôt companies ceased to be attached to the 90th Light Infantry, and marched from Aldershot, under command of Captain Hardinge, *en route* to Portsmouth, where they embarked the same day, on board the *Himalaya*, for conveyance to Devonport. They disembarked on 11th March, and marched to Fort Tregantle, being attached to the 2nd Queen's until 26th April, when the 35th Brigade Depôt was formed.

1874.

"A" and "B" companies, under the command of Captains J. Edmondstoune (brevet lieutenant-colonel) and H. R. Hardinge, and Lieutenants C. F. A. Turnbull and W. H. Hammans, embarked at East London, on 7th July, in the hired transport *Elizabeth Martin* for conveyance to Mauritius, for the purpose of relieving the detachment of the regiment there stationed. They arrived at Mauritius on the evening of 17th July, and disembarked on the 20th.

On 22nd July "C" and "H" companies, under the command of Captain Stabb and Lieutenants A. Clarke and C. F. N. Le Queene, embarked at Mauritius for the Cape, arriving at East London on 1st August.

"D" and "F" companies, under the command of Captain A. H. Trueman and Lieutenants R. Phillips, C. E. C. Inglefield, and H. R. Saunders, embarked at East London, on 1st August, for Mauritius, where they arrived on the 10th, and disembarked the following day.

"G" company, under the command of Captains C. E. Le M. Cherry and H. R. Hardinge, and Lieutenants J. J. Glascott and H. S. Woods, embarked at Mauritius for the Cape, on 15th August, and arrived at East London on the 24th. This completed the relief of the detachment, leaving the half-battalion under command of Major W. J. Anderson, and the head-quarter half-battalion under command of Colonel and Lieutenant-Colonel the Honble. B. M. Ward, at King William's Town, Cape of Good Hope.

Authority was granted on 14th December (No. P.C., 32nd Foot, 333) for a special device (the Cornish Arms) to be worn on the collar of the tunic.

1875.

The head-quarters and four companies of the regiment remained at the Cape of Good Hope, and the left half-battalion—viz., four companies—at Mauritius during the year. On 3rd December, Lieutenant-Colonel and Brevet Colonel the Honble. B. M. Ward proceeded on leave of absence, pending retirement, and Major the Honble. R. H. de Montmorency assumed the command of the regiment.

1876.

On 22nd March, Lieutenant-Colonel and Brevet Colonel the Honble. B. M. Ward retired, on half-pay, and on 1st April, Lieutenant-Colonel and Brevet Colonel Thomas Wright Martin, half-pay, 7th Foot, was gazetted lieutenant-colonel, *vice* Honble. B. M. Ward, and retired from the service on 14th June, on which date Major the Honble. R. H. de Montmorency was gazetted lieutenant-colonel of the regiment.

On 19th July the half-battalion stationed at Mauritius, under the command of Major W. J. Anderson, embarked, on board the hired transport *St. Lawrence*, for passage to the Cape of Good Hope. It arrived at East London on the 28th, and disembarked the following day. Three companies proceeded, by rail, to Blaney the same day, marching from thence to King William's Town, where they arrived in the evening and joined the head-quarter half-battalion.

"A" company, with men from other companies to complete the required strength of one hundred non-commissioned officers and men, remained at East London on detachment.

1877.

The regiment remained at the Cape of Good Hope until 13th April, when the left half-battalion—consisting of " B," " C," " E," and " H " companies, under the command of Major W. J. Anderson, proceeded, by rail, to East London and embarked on board the troopship *Himalaya* on the following day for conveyance to England, arriving at Plymouth on 24th May, disembarked on 25th, and proceeded, by march route, to Fort Tregantle the same day, where it was stationed.

The head-quarters of the regiment, and "A," "D," "F," and "G" companies, remained at the Cape of Good Hope until 16th and 17th August, when it embarked, on board the troopship *Orontes*, for conveyance to England, under the command of Lieutenant-Colonel the Honble. R. H. de Montmorency, and arrived at Plymouth on the evening of 22nd September, disembarking on the 24th, when the head-quarters and "F" company proceeded to Fort Tregantle, there to be stationed, and the remaining companies—"A," "D," and "G"--to Raglan barracks, Devonport.

The following order was received by the regiment on arrival in England :

"GENERAL ORDER No. 108.

"Head-Quarters, Cape Town,
" 1st October, 1877.

"His Excellency Lieutenant-General Sir A. T. Cunynghame, K.G.B., "commanding in South Africa, regrets that his absence from Head-"Quarters at a very distant part of his Divisional Command prevented him "from giving expression to his sentiments at the time of the departure for "England of that very distinguished Regiment the Thirty-Second "(Cornwall) Light Infantry.

" The long service of this Regiment in South Africa has been charac-"terised by a constant adherence to its duty.

"Supported by the exertions of the Commanding Officer, the Officers, " N.C. Officers, and men, the Regiment has at all times succeeded in pre-"serving the excellent Regimental System, the pride of our army, doing " credit and honor to themselves and so highly beneficial to the interests "of their Country, and which, as their General, he has such pleasure in " bearing testimony to.

" To Colonel the Honble. R. H. de Montmorency and His Regiment, His " Excellency expresses his warmest wishes for their continued prosperity."

On 29th October a draft of two corporals, one bugler, and seventy-eight privates left Fort Tregantle to join the 46th Regiment--the linked battalion under the new organisation—at Bermuda.

On 1st November the regiment was concentrated in the South Raglan barracks, relieving the 36th Regiment, which proceeded to Pembroke Dock.

1878.

The regiment remained quartered in the South Raglan barracks, Devonport, during the year.

Owing to the serious aspect of affairs in the east of Europe, it was necessary to fill up regiments first on the roster for foreign service, and the 32nd (only just home) was called upon to volunteer, over one hundred men coming forward.

In April the Army and Militia Reserves were mobilized, and the establishment of the regiment increased to one thousand and ninety-six, all ranks. In July these reserves were demobilized, and the Army Reserve men posted to the regiment were retransferred to the Plymouth division, and the Militia Reserve men to the Royal Cornwall Rangers Militia.

Regiments in India falling short of drilled soldiers for carrying on the war against the Afghans, the regiment was called upon to give men, and a number volunteered to join regiments on active service in Afghanistan.

A sad disaster at the Cape of Good Hope, in which the 1st battalion of the 24th Regiment was cut to pieces, rendered it necessary to call again upon the regiment for volunteers, and a number of men came forward for the 1st battalion 24th Regiment, 91st Highlanders, and 94th Regiment.

The difficulties of transport and other duties being so great at the Cape, it was determined to call upon officers to volunteer for special service. Captain C. E. Le M. Cherry and Lieutenant and Adjutant Cochrane embarked on 1st November, and proceeded to the Cape to be employed in that capacity. Shortly after, Lieutenant Cochrane resigned the adjutancy, and Lieutenant C. E. Heath was gazetted to the appointment. On 4th October the second draft, consisting of one sergeant and ninety-eight privates, embarked to join the Linked Battalion at Bermuda.

1879.

On 1st January the establishment was reduced from six hundred to five hundred rank and file.

On 11th March the regiment left Raglan barracks, Devonport, and embarked in the troopship *Assistance* for conveyance to Portland, arriving there on the morning of the 12th, relieving the 2nd battalion 20th Regiment, which left the same day, in the *Assistance*, for Plymouth. The whole regiment was concentrated in the Verne Citadel.

On the departure of the regiment from Devonport, Lieutenant-Colonel the Honble. R. H. de Montmorency received the following complimentary order from Lieutenant-General the Honble. Leicester Smyth, C.B., commanding Western District:

"I am sorry that absence from Devonport has prevented me expressing "in person to the 32nd Light Infantry the regret I feel at their departure "from the Western District, and my satisfaction at their good conduct in "quarters, cleanliness and smartness on parade, and attention to drill and "duties during the time they have been under my command.

"Though it is not long since this Battalion landed from abroad, yet the "changes in its ranks have been very many, necessitating constant exer- "tions on the part of the Officers and Non-Commissioned Officers, and "attention to instruction on the part of the young soldiers who have joined. "The satisfactory condition of the Battalion shows how these conditions "have been fulfilled, and how well it deserves these few words of praise I "now with pleasure send to it.

"Ireland, 12. 3. 79."

In June, the establishment was further reduced from five hundred to four hundred and eighty.

On 30th September a draft—consisting of one sergeant, one corporal, and sixty-four privates—proceeded to Bermuda to join the 46th Regiment, leaving the regiment one hundred and fifty-two below its establishment.

On 17th October the regiment embarked at Portland, on board the troopship *Assistance*, for Jersey, and disembarked at Gorey, on the north-east end of the island, on 21st and 22nd October, having been detained on board four days on account of the tempestuous state of the weather. On the evening of the 21st, two companies, under command of Major and Brevet Lieutenant-Colonel J. Edmondstoune, disembarked, and marched to St. Peters, there to be stationed. The head-quarters landed the following morning and marched to Fort Regent, St. Heliers.

During November and December the regiment was made up to its establishment, receiving over two hundred recruits in those months.

SIXTH PERIOD.

Home—Malta—India.

1880.

In 1880 the regiment was stationed at Jersey, head-quarters at Fort Regent and detachment at St. Peters, under the command of Brevet Major G. C. Swiney.

On 24th February thirty-two volunteers left to join the 2nd battalion 17th and 48th regiments in India.

Major H. Sparke Stabb, from special duties at the Cape of Good Hope, on termination of the Zulu Campaign, rejoined the regiment in May.

On 15th September a draft of eighty-three men embarked to join the 46th Regiment, which left the strength one hundred and eighteen below the establishment.

On 12th October thirty-one recruits joined from the 35th Brigade Depôt.

On 20th November instructions were received that the regiment was to be held in readiness for Aldershot, and to embark at Gorey on Thursday, the 25th. The heavy baggage was packed up in readiness by the 24th, but the regiment did not embark until the 29th, the transport (H.M.S. *Assistance*) having been delayed by stress of weather at Portsmouth, with the relieving regiment (the 2nd battalion 12th) on board. The regiment disembarked at Portsmouth on 30th November, and was conveyed by special train to Aldershot, where it was attached to the 1st Brigade, and quartered in the " L," " P," " Q," and " S " Lines, South Camp.

On 22nd December twenty men arrived from the 35th Brigade Depôt to form part of a draft, then in course of preparation for the 46th Regiment, to embark on 1st January.

1881.

The regiment remained at Aldershot, quartered in "L," "P," "Q," and "S" Lines, South Camp, and attached to 1st Brigade.

On 1st January one hundred and forty-three non-commissioned officers and privates proceeded from Aldershot, and embarked at Portsmouth in the troopship *Himalaya*, to join the linked battalion (46th Regiment), stationed at Gibraltar.

Lieutenant-Colonel and Brevet Colonel the Honble. R. H. de Montmorency, having completed five years' service as regimental lieutenant-colonel, was, in consequence, placed on half-pay on 14th June. In succession to the vacancy thus caused, Major and Brevet-Colonel J. Edmondstoune was gazetted lieutenant-colonel; but, retiring on half-pay on the 29th of the same month, the command of the regiment devolved upon Major H. S. Stabb, who was promoted to the rank of lieutenant-colonel on the latter date.

On 18th June, Sergeant G. J. T. Webb obtained a commission as 2nd lieutenant in the North Staffordshire Regiment, after a service of three years.

Major-General J. B. Spurgin, C.B., C.S I., inspected the regiment on 21st July, and subsequently a communication was received from H.R.H. the Field-Marshal Commanding-in-Chief, expressing complete satisfaction with the result.

Her Majesty having approved of the formation of Territorial Regiments—to be composed of four battalions, and designated by territorial titles—the 32nd Light Infantry became, on 1st July, the 1st battalion Duke of Cornwall's Light Infantry, the 2nd battalion being formed by the 46th Regiment, and the 3rd battalion by the Royal Cornwall Rangers Militia. The 4th battalion has not yet been formed.

The head-quarters of the regimental district remain at Bodmin, but is renumbered, "32."

The regiment has had to deplore the loss of Quarter-Master, Captain E. Vaughan, who died on 24th September, 1881, after a continuous service in the regiment of thirty years and five months.

He was the oldest member of the regiment, and had distinguished himself during the ever-memorable defence of Lucknow, having been recommended for the Victoria Cross for his gallant conduct. He was succeeded in his appointment by Regimental Sergeant-Major J. Conway, who was gazetted quarter-master on 30th November.

1882.

On 21st March, 1882, whilst stationed at Aldershot, a draft of sixty-three men was despatched to the 2nd battalion at Gibraltar.

On 1st April the establishment of the 1st battalion was raised to six hundred and fifty rank and file.

In consequence of this increase, recruiting had been very active throughout the year, and the regiment received thirty-three men from the 2nd battalion Middlesex (Edmonton) Royal Rifle Regiment (militia), when that corps was dismissed, after completion of its annual training.

The average number of recruits that joined the battalion between June and December was about fifty-one per month. The majority were posted from the recruiting parties and sent direct to the regiment. Among them were very few West countrymen, and of these but a small number from Cornwall. They were principally from the county or neighbourhood in which the regiment had lately been stationed, viz., from Surrey and London. A few recruits were, however, derived from the Midland counties.

The death occurred, in London, on 12th September, of Major-General Bassano, C.B., aged 56 years. The deceased had passed the whole of his regimental career in the 32nd regiment, the command of which devolved upon him on its withdrawal from the Residency, after the relief of the garrison of Lucknow by General Sir Colin Campbell.

On 31st December the strength of the 1st battalion was seven hundred and ninety-eight.

1883-84.

On 15th September, 1883, Brevet Major Cochrane resigned the appointment as adjutant to the 1st battalion, being gazetted brigade-major at Hong-Kong.

Lieutenants J. T. Bowles and A. D. Homfray, 1st battalion, volunteered, and embarked for service with 2nd battalion, in Egypt, on 4th December, 1884.

1885.

The 1st battalion remained stationed at Richmond barracks, Dublin, with a musketry detachment at the Curragh.

Between January and May, three hundred and thirty-seven recruits joined from the depôt. They were raised in all parts of the country, and—on the whole—were of fairly good physique. With the exception of a draft of one hundred and fifty, which joined in February, and which contained about eighty Irishmen, the recruits had a fair proportion of West countrymen, a few being natives of Cornwall. Early in April the sad intelligence was conveyed to the 1st battalion, by telegraph, of the death of Lieutenant A. D. Homfray, which had taken place while he was on active service with the 2nd battalion in the Soudan. This was subsequently confirmed by a letter from the officer commanding 2nd battalion, in which he stated that Lieutenant Homfray had died of enteric fever, at Tami, on 2nd April, 1885.

Lieutenant A. E. Bassano proceeded for service with the depôt at Bodmin, on 9th May, 1885, in relief of Lieutenant H. P. Garnett, who, on joining head-quarters, was ordered to the Curragh, in charge of the musketry detachment.

On 13th April, 1885, H.R.H. the Prince of Wales presented the battalion with new colours. The ceremony took place in the Castle Gardens, where the battalion was formed in review order, with every available man in the ranks. His Royal Highness addressed the battalion as follows:

" Colonel Stabb, Officers, Non-commissioned Officers, and men of
" the Duke of Cornwall's Light Infantry.—I consider it a high honor
" to be permitted to present New Colours to such a distinguished
" Regiment—one which, ever since it was raised in 1702, has as
" brilliant a record of service in the field as any Regiment in Her
" Majesty's army. You first served with the great Duke of Marl-
" borough in Flanders and then in America. Dettingen is the first
" name inscribed on your colours. In the great Peninsular war you
" specially distinguished yourselves, and suffered heavy loss at Corunna

"and Salamanca. At Quatre Bras and Waterloo you lost more than
"any other corps engaged, and the gallant Sir Thomas Picton was
"killed at the head of the Regiment. Your next service was in India,
"where you took part in the Punjaub campaign. Later, in 1857, you
"greatly distinguished yourselves in the suppression of the Indian
"Mutiny, and gallantly held the Residency of Lucknow during its
"defence, from June to November. You were on that occasion com-
"manded by Brigadier-General Inglis, who for these services was
"created Major-General and Knight Commander of the Bath, while
"you received the honor of being made Light Infantry. You,
"Colonel Stabb, are, I believe, the only officer now present that served
"during the Mutiny. When, nine years ago, I visited the remains of
"the Residency of Lucknow, my attention was called specially to the
"services of this Regiment. On your return the Queen and my father
"inspected the Regiment, and personally thanked the Officers, non-
"commissioned officers, and men for their gallant conduct at Lucknow,
"and I feel doubly proud, as their son, to have the honor of present-
"ing these new colours to you to-day. The latest records on your
"colours are Egypt and Tel-el-Kebir. A Second Battalion, serving at
"this moment in the Soudan, has recently been added to you, which,
"with the Royal Cornwall Rangers Militia, of which I am Honorary
"Colonel, and two Volunteer Battalions, make up the Duke of
"Cornwall's Light Infantry. From the title I bear, I am especially
"proud to be connected with this fine regiment, and, in confiding
"these colors to your care, I feel sure that the honor of your Sovereign
"and your Country will ever be before you, as on former occasions,
"and that in the future, as in the past, the roll of honorable
"distinctions will ever increase."

Lieutenant-Colonel Stabb, commanding the battalion, said, in reply:

"May it please your Royal Highness. In the name of every
"officer, non-commissioned officer, and man belonging to the 1st
"Battalion Duke of Cornwall's Light Infantry, I have to offer our
"most grateful thanks for the high honor you have this day done the
"Regiment in presenting them with new colors. Your Royal Highness
"has alluded in most gracious terms, to the past services of the

"Regiment, and I think your Royal Highness will consider that I
"cannot express a better hope—and I do so with great confidence—
"that, should occasion offer, these new colors may be as faithfully
"guarded and as gallantly defended as were those carried by the
"regiment at Waterloo and Lucknow. Could further incentive be
"wanted by a Regiment bearing a title so closely connected with your
"Royal Highness to faithfully and gallantly perform its duty to Queen
"and Country, that incentive has this day been given by the high
"honor you have just conferred upon the Regiment, and which will
"be handed down amongst its most cherished records. This honor
"will, I know, be also fully appreciated by the 2nd and 3rd battalions
"of the Regiment, and, I believe, every soldier in the Army. Again,
"your Royal Highness, I beg to thank you, in the name of the
"regiment, for the great honor you have done us."

After the conclusion of the ceremony, the old colors were, by his special request, given to His Royal Highness, and graciously accepted.

They were escorted to the Castle by "B" company, accompanied by the band of the battalion, under the command of Major D. Bond, and—having been received by Their Royal Highnesses The Prince and Princess of Wales—were conveyed to the Royal yacht *Osborne*, at Kingstown, for transmission to Marlborough House.

Between June and December twenty-nine recruits joined from the depôt at Bodmin. The musketry training of the battalion was carried out at the Curragh Camp, where the companies were conveyed by rail in succession; the course lasted from May until September, and on 24th November the permanent detachment, under command of Lieutenant H. P. Garrett, was withdrawn.

The following drafts embarked on the dates specified to join the 2nd battalion, still employed on the Nile Expedition, in Upper Egypt: on 17th October, two sergeants, two corporals, and one hundred and forty-six privates, in charge of Captain R. Eden and four subalterns of the 2nd battalion, proceeded by rail to Queenstown and embarked on the 20th on board the freight ship *Lewada;* on 28th November, one sergeant, two corporals, and one hundred and nineteen privates, in charge of Major F. H. A. Disney Roebuck and Lieutenant

Martyn, proceeded by rail to Queenstown and embarked on 2nd December on board the steam ship *Deccan.*

Orders were received on 14th August that the battalion was to be held in readiness to embark for Malta, on or about 1st September, and preparations were accordingly in progress; when, on 18th August, orders were received by telegram that the embarkation was to be suspended.

On 7th December orders were again received by telegram, from Adjutant-General, Horse Guards, to hold the battalion in readiness to embark for Malta on or about 17th December. The battalion, accordingly, on that date, proceeded to Kingstown by rail, and embarked on board the hired transport *India*, and sailed at nightfall, arriving at Gibraltar—after an uneventful passage—on the 22nd, where the vessel took on board 6/1 Battery Cinque Ports Royal Artillery, which had returned from Barbadoes in the troopship *Tamar.* On the 24th the transport *India* sailed for Malta, and—after a fine passage down the Mediterranean—arrived at that fortress on the 28th, on which date the whole battalion, except "C" company, disembarked. The strength of the battalion, on embarking, was as follows: two lieutenant-colonels, two majors, one captain, nine subalterns, two staff, one warrant officer, forty-four sergeants, fourteen buglers, and five-hundred and ninety-five rank and file. There were also three officers' wives, eight officers' children, forty-two soldiers' wives, and fifty-five soldiers' children. Left at Dublin, time expired, etc.: one warrant officer, two sergeants, one bugler, and sixty-nine privates, with eleven women and ten children.

The head-quarters proceeded to Fort Ricasoli; "B" company (and "C" company on the 29th) to Fort Salvatora, in command of Major W. J. Alexander; and "E" company, in charge of Captain C. F. M. le Quesne, to Zabbor Gate, these stations being then vacant.

The sad news of the death of Lieutenant-Colonel C. E. le M. Cherry, which resulted from heat apoplexy, whilst in command of a brigade at Suakim, was conveyed to the battalion in July. The event was greatly regretted in the regiment, where he had served for twenty-five years.

During the extreme heat of the summer, or from July to September, a great percentage of the battalion suffered from the slow continued fever so prevalent in Malta during these months, the average daily number of sick being fifty, out of a strength of nine hundred and twenty. Owing to this and other reasons, chiefly sanitary, two detachments were ordered to forts Ta Silc and Delemara. The former, under Lieutenant F. H. Chapman, and the latter, in charge of Captain W. Francis, marched on 2nd August, and the detachments rejoined head-quarters on 30th September.

1886.

In April, 1886, Colonel Stabb proceeded on leave to England, and took final leave of the battalion, previous to being placed on half-pay on 1st July. He was universally esteemed by all ranks, and had served in the regiment during his whole career, with the exception of a special service appointment during the Zulu War. Colonel G. C. Swiney then assumed command. The regiment was moved from Fort Ricasoli to Verdala barracks, and while in that fort entertained Admiral H.R.H. the Duke of Edinburgh, Commander-in-Chief of the Mediterranean Squadron, and staff, on Friday, 26th November. A guard of honour—composed of Captain Verschoyle, Lieutenants Marriott and Walker, with one hundred rank and file and the band—was drawn up opposite the entrance to the mess, in the Verdala barracks, and received His Royal Highness with a Royal salute, the band playing "God save the Queen."

Great improvements in the messing of the men were effected during the next few months. They were given an early cup of cocoa before morning parades, which had a wonderful sustaining effect and shewed a marked improvement in the health of the battalion.

The battalion was moved to Pembroke camp, where they were all together. The health of the regiment was further improved during their stay there.

1887-88.

On March 18th, 1887, being the anniversary of the birthday of H.R.H. Princess Louise, Marchioness of Lorne, a full-dress brigade parade was held, when Her Royal Highness, who was present on the occasion, received a Royal salute, and afterwards rode down the line.

On 21st June the battalions forming the brigade, together with the Royal Engineers and Royal Artillery and Naval Brigades, were concentrated near Fort Manuel for the celebration of Her Majesty's Jubilee. The regiments present were: the 32nd, 42nd, 51st, 75th; the battalion of the 32nd Regiment was highly complimented, both by His Excellency the Governor-General, Sir Lintorn Simmons, and Major-General J. Davis, commanding the infantry brigade, on their smart and soldierlike appearance.

On 1st July, Colonel G. C. Swiney completed his period of command, was placed on half pay, and was succeeded by Lieutenant-Colonel Stopford.

Whilst stationed at Pembroke camp in October, news reached the battalion of the death of Lieutenant J. T. Bowles, which took place on the 1st of that month whilst he was on leave of absence in England. This officer succumbed after a long illness, contracted whilst on active service in Egypt, and thus another name was added to the long list of those who have lost their lives in the service of their Queen and Country.

On 6th December the battalion was shocked by the sudden death of Lieutenant A. E. Bassano, on which melancholy occasion the commanding officer (Lieutenant-Colonel J. G. B. Stopford) caused the following order to be published :—

" The Commanding Officer announces to the Battalion, with deep
" regret, the death of Lieutenant A. E. Bassano, at 7.25 p.m. on the
" 6th instant, from the effects of an accidental fall from the staircase
" at the Officers' Mess, Floriana. The distinguished career of this
" officer's father, the late Major-General Bassano, in the 32nd Light
" Infantry, will not soon be forgotten, and has associated the name in
" a peculiar manner with the Regiment."

On 24th January, 1888, the commanding officer issued the following battalion order :—

" Lieutenant-Colonel J. G. B. Stopford informs the battalion that
" he received yesterday, from Mr. Henry Bowles, of Myddleton
" House, Waltham Cross, Herts, a cheque for £100 which his son,

"the late Lieutenant John Bowles, before he died, expressed a wish
"should be given as a donation to the Regimental Shooting Club.

"The Regiment will recognise with gratitude, in this munificent
"present, that the latest thoughts of this lamented officer were
"directed to its welfare.

"It is a thing of which a Regiment may well be proud, that these
"who serve in it should come to regard it with such feelings of
"affection; and the piece of plate which Mr. and Mrs. Bowles and
"their sons are, in accordance with their son's dying wish, presenting
"to the Officers' Mess will long remain a memorial of an officer who
"was a thorough soldier and devoted to his profession and his corps."

On 12th December, 1887, the battalion received orders to hold itself in readiness to embark, on 18th February, in the troopship *Crocodile*, for Bombay, and, accordingly, embarked on that date; having marched to the Custom House, where the battalion was inspected by the Princess Louise and the Marquis of Lorne, accompanied by His Excellency the Governor of Malta.

About 12 noon the *Crocodile* left her moorings, and—after a very calm passage—arrived in Bombay on 7th March, 1888. Major-General the Honble. R. H. de Montmorency, (commanding the troops at Alexandria,) who commanded the battalion from 1st April, 1876, to 14th June, 1881, came on board at Port Said, having travelled from Alexandria to visit his old regiment, and remained until off Ismalia.

On arriving at Bombay, orders were received that the battalion would be stationed at Bellary and Madras.

The battalion disembarked on 7th March and proceeded to Poonah by rail, arriving on the 8th. The battalion was inspected at Poonah on the 10th by Major-General S. Flood, commanding Poonah district.

Sergeant Thomas Morris was promoted to a 2nd lieutenancy in the Lincolnshire Regiment on the 18th July.

On 31st October Captain H. G. Morris proceeded to Bombay, for embarkation for the depôt, in relief of Brevet Major G. A. Ashby, who had completed his tour of duty there.

The sad news of the death of Colonel H. S. Stabb, who was in command of the battalion from 29th June, 1881, to 28th June, 1886, was received on 11th November. He died suddenly from heart disease, at Natal, where he was in command of the troops. The event was greatly regretted by the officers and men of the regiment, whose confidence he had won by his excellent qualities as a commanding officer and by his popularity in private life.

His Excellency the Commander-in-Chief of the Madras army, Sir C. G. Arbuthnot, K.C.B., made his inspection of the battalion on 8th November.

On 13th November, Captain H. C. Perkins, at the expiration of a year's leave, went on half-pay.

Correspondence between the two wings was closely kept up during their separation, and men from Madras took furlough to visit their comrades in Bellary, and *vice versa*.

The Madras wing was always made a good deal of; and on the occasion of the Proclamation of Lord Lansdowne, as Viceroy of India, after a grand parade of all the troops in garrison by His Excellency Lord Connemara, was highly complimented for its smart appearance and the way in which it marched past. A ball, on 1st December, given in honour of the Governor, will long be remembered.

A fund, to raise a memorial tablet to Colonel Stabb, was organized; also one to the officers and men who lost their lives during the Egyptian campaign was set on foot.

The following is a description of the window which was placed in the Parish Church, December, 1890, contributed by the Rev. W. Iago:

MILITARY MEMORIAL WINDOWS IN BODMIN CHURCH.

" Since Bodmin has been constituted the Depôt centre of the Western
" Military District, and the home station of the Duke of Cornwall's Light
" Infantry, its ancient church (St. Petroc's), the largest in Cornwall, has,
" very properly, been selected as the most fitting edifice in which to erect
" memorials to such of the officers and other soldiers as die in the service
" of their country.

"A handsome stained glass window, the first of a series, has just been
"inserted in the South Aisle with the following inscription:—

"'In memory of Colonel Henry Sparke Stabb, who served for thirty years in
"the 32nd Light Infantry, now the 1st Battalion the Duke of Cornwall's Light
"Infantry, which he commanded from 1881 to 1886, and, whilst commanding the
"troops at Natal, died at Pietermaritzburg, on the 22nd October, 1888, from the
"effects of his devotion to duty in the suppression of the Zulu rebellion of that
"year. Erected by the Officers, Non-commissioned Officers, and men who have
"served in the Regiment, 1890.'"

"The old stonework of the window is of perpendicular architecture.
"The glass, an excellent art production, is from the manufactory of Messrs.
"Claydon and Bell, London.

"There are four long lower lights of 5-foil cusping, three principal
"upper lights in the tracery, similarly cusped, and several smaller openings
"between.

"The central light, in the head of the window, displays the Cornwall
"County shield:—*Sable, 15 bezants in pile, 5, 4, 3, 2, 1*, and the motto
"*One and All* beneath. Above the shield is a label inscribed *Duke of
"Cornwall's Light Infantry*, showing that these insignia have now also
"been adopted as the regimental badge.

"To right and left, a little lower, each of the adjacent main lights
"displays *beneath a crown and upon a foliated background a sword and
"shield, the latter overlying the blade of the former, which is inclined
"diagonally, point upward;* each such group being arranged in the
"manner of a military trophy. The shield towards the West is charged
"with the personal arms of the late colonel, viz.:—*Ermine, between cottises
"in bend 3 martlets argent, with a canton or;* impaling those of his wife:—
"*Sable, a fesse or between 3 squirrels, 2 and 1, argent.* The shield, east-
"ward, emblazoned:—*Gules, a cross argent*, is without special significance,
"unless we regard it as suggestive of bearing a cross of purity on a
"sanguinary field. Each of the intervening small openings contains a con-
"ventional *rose or, with its leaves proper.*

"Between the main mullions of the window the four long lights are filled
"with large figures of saints standing beneath Gothic canopies backed with
"gules and azure alternately. Each saint has a nimbus, and, on a label
"above him, his name in English. Beneath each is a group of small figures
"illustrative of his career. At the foot of the window, under these groups,
"the inscription, quoted above, extends in three lines of lettering across the
"entire width.

Window in Bodmin Church,

Erected to the Memory of Colonel Sparke Stabb.

"In saints' effigies, in stained glass, anachronisms as to costume are
"allowable ; and such occur in the present instance, as in early examples.
"Of the four chief figures, the outer ones represent St. George and
"St. Alban, the inner ones, St. German and St. Mawes. They, and the
"groups at their feet, may be thus described in detail :—

"No. 1 (in Easternmost light), "*S. George,*" patron Saint of England and
"of Warriors. He is helmed and clad in full armour of gold and silver hues, with
"fluted breastplate and red surcoat. He holds in his right hand his sword erect,
"on his left arm his shield charged " *Argent, a Cross gules*" (S. George's Cross),
"his left foot is advanced, trampling on the prostrate green dragon. In the group
"below, S. George is shown in combat slaying the dragon. The Saint's legendary
"history (describing his exploits in Egypt, &c.) with its symbolism of valour and
"the triumph of Christianity over evil, is too well known to need insertion here.
"A very remarkable S. George Window, of Mediæval date, is in St. Neot's
"Church.

"No. 2 "*S. Germain, Bp.*" He was a famous champion in his day.
"The church of S Germans in Cornwall is dedicated to him. He was Bishop of
"Auxerre, and is shown in Episcopal habit, mitred, bearing in his right hand a
"church (his emblem) ; in his left, a pastoral staff, crook outward. His rich vest-
"ments are elaborately represented. The ends of his stole are seen depending,
"below which the skirt of the alb reaches to his feet. His shoes are of gold colour,
"his gloves green, and the other portions of his attire are delicately shaded in gold,
"white, and blue. Beneath, he appears giving instruction in church to a mixed
"congregation.

"No. 3 "*S. Mawes.*" Leland, when writing more than 300 years ago,
"recorded concerning this saint '*at the fischar town caullid St. Maw's* [in Corn-
"wall] *is a chapel of hym, his chair of stone, and his well. He was a Bishop in
"and* [was] *paintid as a scholemaster.*' The saint is now shewn in that capacity
"in the Bodmin window. In his right hand he holds a pen ; in his left, a book.
"On his head is a white coif. His outer garb (cape, coat, sash, shoes, &c.) are of
"red moroon, mauve, white and golden colours, over a scarlet cassock reaching to
"his feet. In the group he is depicted at his desk in some sacred building teach-
"ing four youths.

"No. 4. "*S. Alban.*" This valiant warrior, styled the Protomartyr of England,
"is, by the artist, made to harmonize with, and yet be in contrast to, the other mil-
"itary saint—S. George, in the first light. His full suit of armour is handsomely
"delineated, the different parts of it resembling brass and steel, or the more
"precious metals. His head-piece is coronal in form, his breast-plate is fluted, and
"from beneath this extends an habergeon of chain-mail. In his right hand he
"carries a slender cross. By his left side his sword rests point-downward in the
"scabbard, tastefully ornamented with blue. The group below this effigy com-
"pletes the set. S. Alban is therein figured as about to be beheaded for his devotion
"to his Lord. He is still clad in armour, but with head and neck bare. Kneel-
"ing in the presence of military witnesses he joins his hands in prayer, whilst the
"executioner strikes the blow which hastens the spirit of the brave soldier of Christ
"to its glorious rest."

1889.

On 15th March, Lieutenant S. Custance completed his term of service as adjutant to the regiment, and, being succeeded by Lieutenant C. N. Evelegh, relieved that officer in the acting appointment in Madras.

On 19th November, H.R.H. Prince Albert Victor, K.G., arrived at Madras, and stayed at Government House. The wing, with Captain Garnett in command, and Lieutenants C. B. Jervis-Edwards and P. E. Vyvyan, found a guard of honour. The wing also lined the road from Government House gates to the Residence. On the 21st the wing found a guard of honour at the State ball given at the banqueting hall.

1890.

It was not till May, 1890, that the regiment, going to Burmah, appeared to be settled. Three years in two bad stations were to be followed by three years in a new semi-civilized country like Burmah; yet, such is the restlessness of the soldier, the idea of change was welcomed by all ranks, and by privates especially.

The sojourn of the battalion in the Madras Presidency was drawing to a close, and on 23rd September the battalion received orders to hold itself in readiness to embark, on 31st December, in H.M. Indian mail ships *Mayo* and *Dalhousie* for Rangoon, *en route* to Mandalay, in Burmah.

1891.

The *Mayo* was the first to steam out of the harbour, followed by the *Dalhousie*. After a very calm passage, the battalion arrived at Rangoon on 5th January, 1891, disembarking the following morning. Still maintained as two wings, the battalion started by rail the same evening for Mandalay. The journey was broken at Toungoo, Mandalay being reached on the morning of the 8th.

The regiment was not destined to remain long inactive in its new station. On 16th February the Tsawbaws of Wunthoo (father and son) having revolted, and having attacked and burnt Kawlin, an outlying post, an order was received for fifty non-commissioned officers and men of the mounted infantry, under Captain S. Custance, and fifty dismounted men, under Lieutenant S. Nicholson, to proceed at once to the seat of the rebellion. They had scarcely been despatched, with the least possible delay, when a further order was received the same day for fifty more men, Lieutenant C. B. Jervis-Edwards being put in command. Again there was another demand on the battalion for another fifty men; Captain and Adjutant C. N. Evelegh, with Lieutenant L. P. H. Bliss, being detailed. Three days later, 2nd Lieutenant the Honble. W. J. H. de Montmorency, together with fifty more of the mounted infantry, followed. Lieutenant R. N. S. Lewin also accompanied the Expedition, and Major H. E. C. Kitchener, who had gone up the Chindwin river on a reconnaissance, rode across from Mingin to Wunthoo, a distance of one hundred and fifty miles, in three days, joining the column there. There was thus a total of eight officers and two hundred and fifty-five non-commissioned officers and men out with the Wunthoo Expedition. The various detachments returned to Mandalay between 1st April and the middle of May.

The casualties during the Expedition consisted of one officer, one sergeant, and five men, all of whom died from the effects of the bad climate and exposure to the sun.

The outbreak of the Manipur disaster occurred on 27th March, 1891. Major H. E. C. Kitchener and Lieutenants J. J. B. Jones-Parry and R. A. S. Lewin did duty with the Manipur field force, the two former as transport officers, the latter in charge of the treasure chest.

On 30th June, Colonel J. G. B. Stopford having completed his four years in command of the battalion, Major Disney-Roebuck, second in command of the home battalion, was gazetted as his successor.

Lieutenant Lambe, who had proceeded home on sick leave, was reported to have died at sea.

His Excellency the Commander-in-Chief, Major-General Sir James

Dormer, inspected the battalion on 14th November, and expressed his entire appreciation of the appearance and general turn-out of the battalion.

Two hundred rifles, under the command of Captain F. G. G. Griffin, with Lieutenants Lambe and the Honble. W. J. H. de Montmorency, proceeded to Bhamo on 23rd November for frontier duty.

1892.

Lieutenants Percy Vyvyan and Hill, two very promising young officers, succumbed to an attack of enteric fever, to the great regret of the whole battalion.

The Brigadier-General commanding Mandalay District made his annual inspection of the battalion on 4th, 5th, and 8th January, and expressed himself satisfied generally with the efficiency and interior economy of the battalion.

On 14th February a draft of one sergeant, one corporal, and seventy-four privates joined from the 2nd battalion, under the command of Captain R. Stewart, Lieutenants Newbury and Tremayne also accompanying the draft.

His Excellency the Commander-in-Chief in India (Lord Roberts) inspected the battalion on 16th February, and expressed his entire satisfaction, both as regarded its efficiency and interior economy.

No. 1,045, Corporal Harry Richardson, was promoted sergeant in recognition of services rendered in the field whilst doing duty with the Irrawaddy Column, Upper Burmah.

On 27th April a draft of one sergeant, four boys, and forty-six privates joined from the 2nd battalion.

The sad news was received on 27th April of the death of Lieutenant H. J. G. Lambe, who was drowned off Perim whilst *en route* to England on leave of absence.

Major-General R. Stewart, commanding Burmah District, inspected the battalion on 13th June, and expressed himself highly satisfied with the state of the battalion.

On 27th June the commanding officer announced to the battalion, with deep regret, the death of Lieutenant P. E. Vyvyan, which occurred at the Station Hospital on 26th June, from enteric fever.

On 2nd July another sad announcement was made to the battalion in the death of 2nd Lieutenant B. U. Hill, which occurred in the Station Hospital from remittent fever.

It was resolved to devote a portion of a sum of £100, left by the late Lieutenant Lambe in his will, as a mark of regard for his old regiment, in the purchase of a cricket shield, to be designated the "Lambe Challenge Cricket Shield," to be played for annually, and held by the winning team for the year.

Services of the Second Battalion,

1882-92.

The 2nd battalion landed at Alexandria on 23rd July, 1882, being the third British battalion to reach Egypt. It landed at once, and marched to Resetta Gate, the eastern entrance to the city. On 2nd August they marched to Ramleh, within a few miles of Kafr Dowar, where the main body of rebels had assembled under Arabi Pasha, and took part in the reconnaissance in force on 5th August.

They were amongst the first troops that landed at Ismalia, and were present at the engagements of El-Magfar, Tel-el-Mahuta and Massameh. The battalion formed part of the advance guard, under command of General Graham, who were sent on to protect the lock at Kassassin, and took part in both engagements there, in the first of which Major Forster, Captain Reeves, Lieutenants Carden and Cunningham, and about forty rank and file were wounded. It was here, on 28th August, that Private Harris (who was serving with the mounted infantry) distinguished himself by gallantly defending a wounded officer, after being severely wounded himself, for which he received the VICTORIA CROSS.

The battalion was also engaged at Tel-el-Kebir, where Colonel Richardson and several men were wounded. They subsequently formed part of the Army of Occupation, being stationed at Cairo and Alexandria until July, 1884, when it was ordered up the Nile, and formed part of the river column under General Earle, returning to Cairo in July, 1885, after a year's hard service, during which time a large number of all ranks died from sickness.

The 2nd battalion returned to England, leaving a large draft with the 1st battalion at Malta (when the two battalions were together for two days.) It landed from H.M. troopship *Tamar* at Plymouth in June, 1886, and was quartered in Raglan Barracks, Devonport.

Colonel Grieve, having completed his period of command, was succeeded by Lieutenant-Colonel Roberts (late 7th Royal Fusiliers,) who was brought in from half-pay, on 31st July, 1889.

The 2nd battalion proceeded to Pembroke Dock in April, 1889, and from thence was removed to Dublin, in December, 1891.

[245]

NOTES ON THE COSTUME AND EQUIPMENTS.

1708-1881.

THE early years of the regiment were passed in the Marine service, and it was not until after the treaty of Utrecht that it was placed on the Irish establishment as an ordinary regiment of foot.

No evidence is forthcoming as regards its early uniform, excepting that, like all other similar corps, it was clothed in the usual red uniform. Tradition says the facings were always white. Facings generally meant the lining of the coat, which shewed on the cuffs and skirts when turned back. The first really authentic information is obtained from the work entitled " *The Cloathing of His Majesty's Troops, etc., etc., 1742* " (copy in the British Museum). Collars—at least for the infantry—were not then in use, and the regiment, in common with a few others, had no chest lapels buttoned back (see illustration, page 30), the coat simply single-breasted, of considerable amplitude, and having voluminous skirts. The cuffs alone were white; the skirts, and, possibly, the coat itself, lined green. This divergence was, at the time, quite rare. In every other infantry regiment the whole exposed part of the lining, lapels, cuffs, or skirts was of one and the same colour. Reference must be made to the colour-striped white lace with which the coat cuffs and button-holes were bound. Whether it was intended to strengthen the coat is uncertain, but it was ornamental and characteristic. Most corps had different patterns, which, together with the various hues of the facings, was about all that distinguished one regiment from another—no numbers as yet shewing on the buttons.

The reader of these notes will observe that from time to time the exact pattern of lace worn by the regiment was changed—possibly to suit the taste of the colonel. He it was who provided the clothing, and—at all events, up to 1768, when some sort of regularity was established, met with little interference from the authorities.

In 1742 the private soldier's lace was of white worsted, about half-an-inch wide, with a green stripe on one side and a red worm pattern on the other.

The next information is found in the oil picture of a grenadier of the regiment at Windsor Castle, by David Morier, who executed a great number of military pictures for the king, about 1750-52. The illustration, page 44, represents the picture in question. The tall mitre-shaped cap forms a most distinctive feature. All grenadiers wore this high cap, having on the lower part a red flap, thereon the "White Horse" of Hanover, with the motto "*Nec aspera terrent.*" The upper part was of cloth, the colour of the regimental facings embroidered with worsted crewel work ; in this case it took the form of the royal cipher in red, surmounted by a crown ; on each side a spray of roses and rose leaves, this latter being quite peculiar to the 32nd grenadier cap, giving it a noticeable and distinctive character.

The cuffs still continue very large, and the white chest lapels appear for the first time. The lace also, it will be noticed, has changed in pattern, being white, a black stripe at each side, and a black zig-zag down the centre, the broader cuff lace having two black zig-zags. The lace on the red waistcoat is plain white, and the loops bastion shaped, whereas those on the coat are square-headed. These details are not trivial—they served, indeed, to distinguish one regiment from another at a period before numbers were displayed, or, indeed, much used.

Though called grenadiers, their occupation as such was gone ; no hand grenades had been thrown for twenty years or more. Originally the tallest and strongest men were selected, the high caps being for the purpose of giving them still greater height. Evelyn, in his diary, under date June, 1678, mentions the new sort of soldiers called grenadiers : "They had furred caps, with sloping crowns, like "janizaries, which made them look very fierce."

Very little alteration had been made in the accoutrements since 1742, but the brass match case may be observed, however, fastened into the front of the shoulder belt. It was a cylinder, some four inches long, pierced with holes to allow air for the ignited slow match inside, now, as we have seen, out of use, but lingered on as a special mark of distinction for many years—indeed, the grenadiers of one distinguished infantry regiment only discarded it in 1830. Grenadier companies, with some little distinction in dress, lasted until about thirty years ago.

Unless the evidence of family portraits should be forthcoming, we have no exact information as to the officers' uniform in 1751. No doubt a voluminous wide-skirted coat, with white facings, like that of the private men, was worn, laced with narrow gold lace, sword suspended from a waistbelt under the waistcoat, a crimson silk sash over the left shoulder, and a gold aiquillette on the right shoulder. The battalion officers, like the men, had three-cornered cocked hats, but laced with gold, and displaying on the left side the black cockade of the reigning House of Hanover. Grenadier officers wore a cap, in shape like that of the men, but handsomely embroidered in gold and silver.

Annual regimental inspections by general officers had been instituted as far back as 1709, but the earliest *recorded* inspection of the regiment—then still known as Leighton's—took place at Glasgow, 18th August, 1762; the inspecting officer observing, amongst other matters, "The colours in good order; officers' uniform good and "rich; the regiment has two remarkably good fifers; the private men, "no swords."

Though regiments appear to have been officially numbered since 1742 (see Millan's *Succession of Colonels* of that date), and that an order of precedence had been definitely established, in accordance with a royal warrant issued in 1713 (*War Office Miscellany Books*), yet regimental numbers seemed to find no favour with inspecting officers or the authorities furnishing clothing; but, it being found desirable to have an additional form of distinction beyond the facings and lace, a warrant was issued, 21st September, 1767, requiring that the number of the regiment should appear on the buttons—hitherto quite plain.

By Warrant in 1768, the cloth grenadier cap was abolished, and a new one of bear-skin introduced, having in front the badge of the King's crest (lion and crown) in white metal on a black ground.

This, it may be mentioned, was common to all grenadiers, and not a purely regimental distinction.

The illustration, page 46, represents a grenadier of the regiment in the uniform conformable to the new regulations of 1768, taken from a MS. work in the Prince Consort's Library, Aldershot. The large and roomy coat of the Hogarthian period has given place to a more closely fitting garment. The turned down collar, or cape, as it was then called, has appeared, the coat only just meeting across the chest, leaving the white waistcoat exposed, the lapels across the chest very much smaller than before; indeed, serving little more than to show off the lace-looped button-holes on them. The Royal Warrant, 19th December, 1768, is very explicit and full of detail on every point connected with the uniform of the infantry, both men and officers.

The private soldier's lace also became a matter of strict regulation, which was not departed from in pattern until the black striped lace was abolished in 1836. The *Official Army List* for 1769, for the first time, gave particulars of the various regimental laces, under the heading "Succession of Colonels"—the 32nd lace being described as white, with a black worm, and a black stripe (see illustration, page 46), being one stripe less than in 1751.

There were several methods of wearing the lace loops round the button-holes. Some regiments wore them square headed, some pointed, and a few had what was called the bastion, or flowered loop; the first pattern was that adopted by the 32nd, and worn equidistant until towards the close of the century, when they were worn by twos, and so continued long after the black stripes were lost, until 1855, in fact, when the tunic came into use.

Officers' costume was as follows:—scarlet coats, lapelled to the waist with white cloth; lapels, three inches wide, fastened back with gilt buttons (having the regimental number) placed at equal distances; the cape, or collar, of white cloth, turned down, and fastened by one button-hole to the top button of the lapel; small round white cuffs, three and a half inches deep, having four buttons and button-holes; cross pockets, in line with the waist, having four buttons; skirts, lined and turned back white. Whatever may have been the case previously, no gold lace was now worn by the officers; everything was remarkably plain. The regiment may be described, up to 1829, as being a non-laced one, as far as the officers were concerned. Where no actual button-holes were required, as in the cuffs and pocket, a neat "dummy," or false button-hole, edging of white silk was used.

Officers of the grenadier company wore an epaulet of gold lace and fringe on each shoulder; battalion officers, one on the right shoulder only, white waistcoat and breeches, black linen gaiters, with black buttons, crimson silk sash tied round the waist (until recently worn over the shoulder), a gilt gorget, with the King's arms engraved thereon, fastened to the neck with white silk rosettes and ribbons, hats laced with gold, and the usual black cockade.

Grenadier officers wore the black bear-skin cap, like the men, but on the plate the King's crest was in gilt, upon the black metal; they carried fusils, and had white shoulder belts and pouches. Battalion officers carried the espontoon, a light steel-headed pike, with a small cross-bar below the blade, seven feet in length, used with graceful effect in the salute. Sergeants had buttons of white metal, and narrow loops of plain white tape, hats laced with silver, silk shoulder knots, and crimson and white worsted sashes. They carried swords and halberds, the latter a light ornamental kind of battle axe with a long shaft.

The uniform of 1768 remained almost unchanged until about 1790. Cross belts were, however, introduced, that is the bayonet belt removed from the waist to the shoulder, and a brass breastplate, as an ornament, affixed to the latter.

The officers' swords were also ordered to be suspended in a white shoulder belt over the right shoulder, and, in their case also, a gilt breastplate came into use, though of what design, in the absence of any authority, we cannot arrive at.

The inspection returns of last century, preserved at the Record Office, are singularly meagre of information regarding the regiment. At one inspection, however—Dublin, 12th September, 1777—the inspecting general reports "the light infantry accoutrements wrong, "being made of buff instead of tan."

PRIVATE SOLDIER'S
BUTTON,
1795.
(ENLARGED.)

The private soldier's button was made of the usual metal, pewter, and quite flat. The illustration represents a specimen in the possession of the author.

1784. Fuzees ordered to be used by sergeants of the grenadier and light company.*

The light companies not having been very long formed, it appeared desirable, in view of their peculiar duties, that the sergeants should discard the pike, so as to be able to take some part in the skirmishing and light infantry movements then being developed. The grenadiers, with the light companies, received the name of flank companies, and were frequently detached together for light advanced operations.

The illustration, page 48, represents an officer, 1792. The outline of the figure, and all details of dress, are taken from E. Dayes' beautiful series of coloured engravings of the regiments of foot, in the British Museum. It will be noticed that the gaiters are shorter than formerly, only reaching to the knee; the collar also is worn turned up, the button and loop, originally used to fasten it down, still retains on it, only as an ornament however, destined—as will be afterwards seen—to develop into two buttons and two loops, of gold lace, and to remain on the officer's coat collar until 1855, nearly a century after its original purposes and uses had lapsed! The coat had become still more scanty, the waistcoat also shrinking quite up to the waist. The private soldier's uniform was extremely like that of the officer's in cut, but with loops of the regimental lace to all the button-holes.

Towards the end of the century, following civilian, or, more probably Prussian military fashion, it was decided to fasten the coat in front down to the waist, completely hiding the waistcoat. The Warrant of 1796 directed that for officers the lapels were to be continued down to the waist, and to be made either to button over occasionally (making what now would be called a double-breasted coat), or to fasten close

---

* These companies were introduced about 1771, armed with a lighter kind of musket or fuzee. Powder horns and hatchets formed part of the equipment, and small round leather caps were worn.

with hooks and eyes all the way to the bottom, in which case the white lapel would show, being buttoned back; stand up collar, very high and roomy, to admit the large neck-cloth then coming into fashion. The new jacket for the rank and file was single-breasted, having ten buttons down the front, most probably arranged in twos, and not at equal distances as before—ten regimental lace loops, about three inches long, on each breast, serving no other purpose but ornament. The old white woollen waistcoat, with sleeves, became practically the shell jacket, worn for undress or fatigue duties, though then, and for many years afterwards, called the "waistcoat."

Horse Guards Warrant, dated 22nd April, 1799, directed officers and men of infantry (except the flank companies) to wear their hair queued, to be tied a little below the upper part of the collar of the coat, and to be ten inches in length, including one inch of hair to appear below the binding.

The cocked hat worn by the men was discontinued by General Order, dated February, 1800, and a cylindrical shako, with peak, introduced. This head-dress was made of lacquered felt, ornamented with a large oblong brass plate in front, about six inches high, thereon engraved the regimental number, with the King's crest, surrounded by a trophy of drums, standards, etc. A red and white worsted tuft was fixed in front, rising from a black cockade. Officers, however, still retained the old cocked hat, using it all through the earlier stages of the Peninsular War, and at least one year after the order was issued for its discontinuance.

The illustration, page 58, represents an officer of the regiment, 1808, the same costume being also worn up to 1811. As a general rule, the large cocked hat was worn fore and aft, the top of the coat lapel turned back to show the colour of the facing. Bright blue pantaloons were much worn, and it will be noticed that the old-fashioned knee boot had given way to that of the Hessian pattern with tassels.

Major Ross-Lewin, 32nd regiment, in his lively work, entitled *Life of a Soldier*, states that during the harassing retreat from Burgos, in the autumn of 1812, "one of the queerest figures observed was an "eccentric subaltern of my corps. Besides enveloping his form in a "blanket, and wearing the hinder flap of his cocked hat down, he was "mounted on a cart dragoon horse, sixteen hands high, gaunt and "rawboned in the extreme," thus proving beyond doubt that the cocked hat was, up to that date, still worn by the officers of the 32nd, notwithstanding that an order for its discontinuance was issued in December, 1811. No doubt, however, the officers were all provided with shakos before the opening of the campaign in 1813.

Chevrons for the non-commissioned officers were introduced in consequence of a General Order, dated July, 1802; sergeant-majors to be distinguished by four, sergeants by three, and corporals by two chevrons on the right arm; the first, of silver lace; the second, of plain white tape lace; and the third, of the black striped regimental lace. For a very long period the sergeant-majors and staff sergeants had worn silver lace on their coats. This was the universal custom in all infantry regiments (whether the officers wore gold lace or not), and was so kept up until 1855.

By the year 1808 it became pretty clear to the authorities that too much time was taken up in making the queue—time far better spent at drill, now that soldiers were so much wanted at the front. To the joy of the sufferers, the troublesome queue was abolished by an order dated July 20th, 1808 : " The hair to be cut short in the neck, and a "small sponge added to the list of the soldier's necessaries, for the "purpose of frequently washing his head."

Let Major Ross-Lewin relate his experiences : " As a great alter-"ation was effected here (Vimiera) in the personal appearance of our "troops, I cannot leave it unnoticed. The short queues that were "worn, both by officers and men, were cropped on the field this day, "in obedience to orders that had arrived from England. When I "joined the militia, in 1793, all military men wore their hair clubbed; "that is, each had a huge false tail attached by means of a string "that passed round the upper part of the head, and over it the hair "was combed and well thickened with powder or flour. A plastering "of pomatum or grease was then laid on; a square bag of sand was "next placed at the extremity of the tail, rolled up with the assistance "of a small oblong iron until it touched the tail, and tied with a

"leathern thong and rosette, so as to confine it in a proper position.
"After the arrangement of the tail, the officer's fore tops were rubbed up
"with a stick of pomatum—a most painful operation, especially on
"cold mornings; when this was over, the frisseur retired a pace or
"two for the purpose of frosting, which was effected by means of
"an elastic cylinder, filled with powder, and so constructed as to
"expel and let fall upon the hair a light shower of it; and, lastly,
"the powder knife prepared the head for parade, by arching the
"temples and shaping the whiskers to a point. In this agreeable
"manner half-an-hour of every morning was consumed. The men
"only powdered on 'dress days,' as Sundays, Thursdays, and days of
"duty were called. Each dressed his comrade's hair, so that an hour
"was lost in dressing and being dressed. Hair powder was used by
"the army as late as 1806. The flank companies wore the hair
"turned up behind, and made to rest on pieces of glazed leather,
"which were called flashes."

December, 1811. A War Office order authorised infantry officers to wear a cap of a pattern similar to that worn by the men, also permitting them to wear a regimental coat or jacket to button over the breast and body (double-breasted, in fact) and a grey overcoat, also grey pantaloons or overalls, with short boots, as the private men. This was the service dress used by officers during the later Peninsula and Waterloo campaigns.

1814. The general costume of the regiment was as follows:—
Officers: long-tailed scarlet coat for parade, levees, etc.; white lapels, buttoned back by ten gilt buttons, and white silk twist holes set on by pairs; the button, slightly convex, ornamented with the regimental number, within a garter, having a strap, but no buckle; the garter itself bearing no device, but of a simple fluted pattern; a crown over the garter—an uncommon pattern, used only at the time by one other regiment— the 43rd. There have been many changes in regimental buttons from time to time, but the regiment adhered to this design (with one or two

OFFICER'S GILT BUTTON, 1815. (ENLARGED.)

alterations in the size) until regimental numbers were done away with, quite recently. The coat collar of white cloth, with one button and twist hole at each side; cuffs with four loops and buttons by pairs, cross pockets (in line with the waist) with the same; skirts turned back white, the skirt ornaments (where the points of the turnbacks met, replacing, in fact, the buttons absolutely necessary with the old voluminous skirts) being gold embroidered single bullion bows; the pockets of the coat and side seams of the tails edged with a white piping. White breeches and black leggings for home, and grey trousers for active service.

OFFICER'S BREASTPLATE, 1815.

As before mentioned, the service dress was a short-tailed jacket, cuffs and collar as above, but buttoned across the chest, with no lapels. The long, straight sword, black leathern scabbard, gilt mounting, with crimson and gold sword knot, was worn according to regulation, suspended in a frog, from a white buffalo leathern shoulder belt, the latter ornamented with the regimental breastplate—at this period gilt metal, of a square shape, the corners just rounded off; thereon, in raised silver, the number "32," within a silver garter, having a buckle and strap, on the garter "Cornwall," and surmounting it a silver crown.

Officers of the light company carried the curved light infantry sabre, suspended by slings from the shoulder belt. Generally on service, however, this weapon was carried by all officers. A crimson silk sash was worn round the waist.

Officers' rank distinguished by the epaulettes, according to the instructions laid down in General Order dated February, 1810. Field officers wore two; a colonel having a crown and a star on the strap; a lieutenant-colonel, a crown; major, a star. Captains and subalterns, including the quarter-master, wore one epaulet on the right shoulder; officers of the flank companies, two shoulder wings, with grenades or bugles thereon respectively; the adjutant wore, in addition to this epaulet, an epaulet strap, without fringe, on his left shoulder. The epaulettes of field officers and captains, together with the wings of captains of flank companies, were edged with gold bullion; those of the subalterns, with gold fringe. Paymaster and surgeon wore the regimental coat single-breasted, without epaulettes or sash, the sword being suspended by a plain waist belt under the coat. In those days there never could be the slightest difficulty in defining an officer's rank; epaulettes were constantly worn, and, fitting very close to the shoulder, with the strap of flexible lace, were comfortable and never in the way, at the same time forming a handsome addition to the dress. The 32nd, indeed, required something of the kind, as, excepting their single epaulettes, the captains and junior officers had no lace whatever on their coats. The light infantry officers' wings, compared with the rich and ornate wings worn by corresponding officers of other regiments, were of an exceedingly simple description, being described as gilt narrow round curb chain wings, with solid silver bugles, mounted on scarlet, and edged all round with gilt jack chain (whatever that may have been). Some regiments in the army had a superabundance of gold and silver lace, whilst many very distinguished regiments were perfectly content, like the 32nd, to have absolutely none at all.

Private soldiers had single-breasted short red cloth jackets, laced across the breast with square headed loops of regimental lace, four inches long, set on in pairs (the lace pretty much as before, black stripe on one side and a line of black spots on the other); white pewter buttons, with the regimental number; lace round the high white collar, showing a white frill in front; white shoulder straps, edged with lace, terminating with a small white worsted tuft; in the flank companies, terminating with a wing of red cloth, trimmed with stripes of lace, edged with an overhanging fringe of white worsted, gaiters, breeches, and trousers as officers. (See illustration, page 102.)

Sergeants dressed like privates, but in finer cloth, having the chevrons of their rank on the arm, which, together with their coat lace, was of fine white tape; sash, crimson worsted, with a white stripe. They carried a straight sword in a shoulder belt, with a brass breastplate, as worn by the men, their other weapon being the halberd, having a plain steel spear-head with crossbar, not unlike the "espontoon" formerly carried by the officers, the old battleaxe-headed halberd having fallen into disuse about 1792.

The head-dress for officers was a light felt cylindrical shako, with black leathern peak, a black cockade, and small red and white tuft on the left side (green or white, for light infantry and grenadiers respectively), a gilt oval plate in front, surmounted by a crown, thereon the cipher "G.R.," with the regimental number; across the front a festoon of red and gold cord, with tassels on the right side. That for the men was of similar make, and the cords and tassels of white worsted. On service, cap covers were worn, of black japanned material.

Judging from specimens still preserved, this head-dress must have been comfortable to the wearer, very much more so than the huge flat-topped shako which so soon succeeded it. Our troops saw every variety of foreign military dress at Paris during the occupation, and it soon became evident to onlookers that the small head-dress of our troops did not look so imposing as those worn by the Prussian and Russian troops. Upon the occasion of the second grand review at Paris, when the four sovereigns were present, Major Ross-Lewin remarks: "The French officers gave it as their opinion that the "English troops had the advantage over the others, as well in "appearance, as in other respects; but our grenadiers would have "looked better than they did, had they had their dress caps. The "rest of the British infantry were disfigured by the small caps they "wore."

In 1816 the neat and serviceable felt cap was laid aside, and the broad-topped heavy shako introduced, its shape being more in accordance with foreign fashion then—as before—our chief guide in such matters. It was eleven inches in diameter at the top, and seven and a half inches deep; brass chin scales, which, when not required could be fastened up to the cockade in front, ornamented with an upright white feather, twelve inches high, and a brass plate in front with the regimental number. The light company had a green feather. Grenadier companies on home service and in cold climates were directed to wear high bear-skin caps, a head-dress which, during the busy war time had fallen into disuse.

The officers' shakos had gold lace two inches wide round the top, and a three-quarter inch gold lace round the bottom. On the lace, immediately below the high feather, appeared the black cockade, in the form of an oval boss, of black cord, a regimental button in the centre; the ornament in front taking the form of a small circular gilt burnished plate, having 32 in raised silver in the centre over two silver laurel leaves; above, a neat silver scroll, with " Peninsula;" and below, a similar one, with " Waterloo." Over the gilt plate, and immediately under the cockade, a gilt crown. The honours— " Peninsula," " Waterloo "— having quite recently been granted to the regiment to be displayed on

OFFICER'S SHAKO PLATE, 1816-24.

the colours and worn on the appointments, were as a consequence placed on the officer's new breastplate. This ornament, of the same shape as its predecessor, was gilt, having 32 in foliated figures, surrounded by a laurel wreath, all of silver, in centre; above the wreath a Peninsula, and below it a Waterloo, scroll of silver; a gilt crown above the higher label.

Short-tailed coats or jackets for all ranks were abolished in 1820, and two years afterwards the breeches and leggings.

OFFICER'S BREASTPLATE, 1817-28.

The same year a circular was issued, calling attention to the fact that " the gorget formed part of the officer's equipment." This ancient ornament seemed falling into disuse; whether this circular restored it to its former position is very doubtful, it is difficult to find any evidence from portraits or miniatures that it was worn at all; finally, in 1830, it was obligingly abolished.

In 1826 the private soldier's coat altered in shape, the lace loops across the chest made broader at the top, tapering down narrower towards the bottom, and the lace taken off the skirts.

T

1827. Officer's costume.—Shakos as before described, but half an inch higher, the gold lace round the top a handsome pattern, viz., "*Fleur de lis and wave*;" the gilt plate had disappeared, and a star substituted; the star rays of silver, with five battle honours displayed on them—"Peninsula," "Waterloo," "Salamanca," "Nivelle," "Nive." Four more, viz., "Roleia," "Vimiera," "Pyrenees," "Orthes"—had recently been authorized (January, 1826), but do not appear to have as yet been placed on this particular shako-plate. In the centre of the star the numerals 32, surrounded by a garter with Cornwall on it, the whole enclosed in a laurel wreath, surmounted by a crown—all these latter ornaments gilt.* Long-tailed coats, the skirt ornament being gold embroidered stars, with 32 in the centre on scarlet cloth. The general cut of the coat much as in 1814, excepting that the white lapels were cut rather broader, forming what was known as the cuirass breast. The collar also was of the so-called Prussian shape, cut square, and fastened up the front, precluding the possibility of wearing the shirt collar and large black neck-cloth so conspicuous only a few years before. Cross pockets were used, that is, pockets in line with the waist, and they were edged with white piping. Epaulettes were under the same regulations as in 1814, but had become much larger, the strap of gold lace (fine check pattern) two and a half inches wide, octagon top, and corded round; large corded crescent, fitted in bullion, the fringe some three and a quarter inches deep. The wings worn by the officers of the flank companies very handsome, strap and crescent as battalion officers, thereon silver grenades or bugles. The wing part (over the shoulder at right angles to the strap) twelve inches long, tapering to points at each end, was made of scarlet cloth, edged with three-quarter inch gold "fine check" lace (as 3rd Guards)—the usual gold bullion or fringe on the outside. The skirt ornaments worn by these officers were gold embroidered grenades or bugles respectively. The dress trousers worn very full, cossack shape, of light bluish-grey cloth, trimmed down the seams with one-inch gold lace.

---

* An almost similar star to this was placed on the officer's shako plate of 1830. See illustration on the next page.

A new regulation cut and thrust sword had been adopted, and was worn in the frog of a white shoulder belt. A new breastplate also had just been introduced, which was worn by the officers, without change, until the Crimean war. The plate was square, gilt, ornamented with a silver star, having the authorized battle honours, eight in number, on the star rays.

Light company officers wore whistles and chains. A blue "great coat," otherwise frock coat, was authorized for undress, the crimson sash worn with it, and the sword suspended in a frog from a black leathern waist-belt. For balls, levees, etc, the coatee was worn with white kerseymere breeches, silk stockings, and shoe buckles; the sword being carried in a belt under the coat. (See illustration, page 142.)

OFFICER'S BREASTPLATE, 1824-54.

December 1828. The officer's shako was considerably altered, being reduced to six inches in height, all the gold lace removed ; and, to the surprise of many, the time honoured Hanoverian black cockade also disappeared ; never since this date worn as shakos, it still lingers in a modified form on the cocked hats of the staff. The only ornament in front of the new shako was a " universal pattern " gilt star plate, with crown over, about six inches by five. In the centre, regiments were allowed to place their own devices, and the 32nd used the silver star which did duty with the old shako (from which device or pattern the star on the new breastplate was taken). Gold cord cap lines were introduced, having a heavily braided festoon in front, terminating in two tassels looped up to one of the

OFFICER'S SHAKO PLATE, 1830-45.

coat buttons. The men had similar shakos, with a small brass star plate, with white, and the light company green, cap lines.

A month afterwards the feather was ordered to be white for the whole, light infantry excepted, still remaining twelve inches high.

It has been mentioned that the officers of the 32nd wore no lace on their coats, but many regiments wore a superabundance of gold or silver lace, of various, and in some cases, fantastic design, altered from time to time by the whim of the commanding officer, or perhaps the suggestion of the army tailor.

To such an extent had this practice grown, that the authorities determined to introduce a universal pattern coatee, hence the warrant of February, 1829, authorizing the well-known double-breasted coatee, which remained, with scarcely any alteration, the dress of officers until the Crimean war. The coatee worn by the 32nd had two rows of gilt buttons down the front, in pairs. A white collar, Prussian shape, on each side two loops of regimental gold lace and small buttons. White cuffs with a scarlet slash, thereon four gold loops and buttons in pairs; white turnbacks to the skirts, the tails still ornamented with the embroidered star as before; scarlet slashed pockets on the skirts, placed obliquely, with lace loops in pairs, the pocket edge of white piping—this latter minor distinction contrary to the dress regulations, but allowed in consequence of having been a regimental custom so long.

Large gold epaulettes worn "on both shoulders" by all ranks of officers (for the first time in the case of captains and subalterns of infantry), excepting the grenadiers and light infantry, who wore large curb chain wings strictly according to the new regulation. The epaulette fringe varied a little according to rank, the field officers being distinguished by silver crowns and stars on the strap, which was of vellum pattern, with white silk stripes. To carry out these instructions it became necessary to choose a pattern for the new regimental gold lace; this was done, and a wave vellum lace, with one edge scolloped, adopted, the wave on the lace being a lightly marked zigzag.

The regiment was not altogether unfamiliar with the pattern, it having been, with two scolloped edges, the regulation lace for the bottom of all officers' shakos since 1816. This lace was used for fifty years, in fact until the introduction of the territorial scheme. Two other regiments adopted it likewise, the 30th and the 91st.

The new Oxford mixture was now substituted for the old blue-grey trousers, and a blue forage cap with a broad stiff top was, for the first time, authorized. Great varieties of this head dress had been previously worn. A plain scarlet shell jacket was ordered to be adopted by officers at certain stations. Except in tropical climates, officers had to sit down to mess in the full dress coatee with epaulettes.

1830. A red fatigue jacket was substituted for the white one hitherto worn by the rank and file, which had originally, in its turn, sprung from the old white waistcoat with sleeves. Fusils were also substituted for the halberds so long carried, of one shape or another, by the sergeants.

The recently introduced cap lines evidently found little favour, for they were abolished by the comprehensive warrant of 1830, marking the accession of William the Fourth. The tall feathers were reduced to eight inches; a green ball tuft ordered to be worn by the light infantry; musicians to be dressed in white; the gorget formally abolished; and, lastly, the regular army ordered to wear gold lace. Up to this time, perhaps, one half the army and militia had worn silver appointments, the other half gold.

1832. Field officers ordered to use brass scabbards. A red seam down the trousers authorized January, 1833. Next year a new forage cap adopted by the officers, of blue cloth, with a black silk band (oak leaf pattern); 32, in gold embroidery, in the centre.

The officer's undress uniform now presented a handsome appearance. The blue single-breasted frock coat, with gilt buttons, had shoulder straps edged with gold lace, terminated in gilt metal crescents; grenadier officers wearing a silver grenade, and light infantry officers a silver bugle in the centre of the crescent; the sword carried in the frog of the black waistbelt, over the crimson sash.

At the first half-yearly inspection, 1834, whilst the regiment was stationed in Canada, a curious circumstance came to light. The inspecting officer remarked, "Turnbacks of skirts on the sergeants' " coats have a narrow black stripe, sanctioned by long custom."

It is easy to gather from a study of these "Returns" that inspecting officers were becoming very stringent indeed as regards any departure from the clothing regulations; consequently this innovation was quite enough to warrant special notice. What could it mean? Evidently an old regimental custom, probably in use years and years, it may have been worn in conjunction with the black stripes on the lace as a mourning memento of some valued officer, who knows? At all events, we never hear of it again; the black stripes also were improved away very shortly after.

These apparently trivial details, old customs no doubt, keeping in remembrance old and almost forgotten stories, perhaps stirring deeds, all go to make up their share of the regimental *esprit de corps*, developed to its greatest extent in the long-service days, when a man's life was spent in his regiment, his home.

By Royal Warrant, dated October 10th, 1836, the colour-striped lace so long worn by the rank and file of the infantry was abolished, and a plain white tape lace took its place; but each regiment was to retain its peculiar method of wearing it. The 32nd, therefore, continued to wear its loops square-headed and by pairs, though it lost its special distinction—the black stripe and black worn laces.

Sergeants were directed to wear double-breasted coatees, without any lace across the chest, white epaulettes or wings. Coloured lace was still worn by the drummers, the pattern being white, with a broad stripe down each side, each stripe composed of small checks of black and red, besides the ordinary parts of the coat being laced after the manner of the coatees worn by the rank and file; the back and side seams, the arm seams, and the skirts were also covered with this lace. Very large wing tufts were worn, of white, red, and black worsted.

The officer's uniform of 1840 is well represented in the illustration, page 148. It is on too small a scale to show the elaborate details of the shako and breastplate, the centre of both being blue enamel. The same year the new percussion muskets were generally introduced.

In 1844 a new shako for the infantry was authorized, often called the "Albert" hat, six and three-quarter inches high, one quarter inch less in diameter at top than at bottom, thus completely altering the appearance of the head-dress. Grenadier fur caps were also abolished, but, as changes of this kind must necessarily be gradual, it may have been a year or two before the change affected the regiment.

Officers lost the fine handsome plate worn with the old shako, a smaller one sufficing, consisting of a universal gilt star, crown over, four and a half inches in diameter; regimental devices, all gilt, in the centre; the number, surrounded by a girdle, "Cornwall" on it; a label, with "Peninsula" above; another, with "Waterloo" below; all surrounded by a laurel wreath. On the eight larger star rays appeared the other battle honours. The men still continued to use the old cap ornament, a small circular brass plate, with the regimental number, crown over.

OFFICER'S SHAKO PLATE, 1845-55.

1845. The sergeants lost their red and white sashes; others, of plain crimson, introduced.

Just before the regiment embarked for India, in 1846, the bandsmen were dressed as follows:—Shako like the privates; coatee of white cloth, double-breasted; red collar, shoulder straps, and shoulder tufts or crescents; red cuffs and slash, with four buttons and plain white tape loops by twos; red turnbacks to the coat tails, and white trousers; a white leathern waistbelt carried in a frog; a long brass scabbard, brass-handled sword. This was strictly according to regulation. Many regimental bands, especially on arriving from foreign service, wore fanciful additions to their uniform.

1848. The undress uniform of infantry officers was altered very considerably in appearance by the discontinuance of the blue frockcoat, with shoulder scales, and the adoption of a plain shell jacket of scarlet cloth, the collar and cuff of regimental facing. Possibly this change may not have affected the officers of the 32nd to any great extent, as the regiment was in India, and it is believed that shell jackets had been worn in that country for some time. A black patent-leathern sling sword-belt was ordered to be worn with the shell jacket, and a great-coat of grey cloth adopted.

1850. A plain shoulder belt, without breastplate, to carry the men's pouches, was authorised, the bayonet being hung in a frog from a waist-belt. This change, however, was not carried out at once; in many cases the cross-belts were worn for a few years afterwards. The illustration, page 156, represents a private of the light company, immediately before the old cross-belts were removed. The grenadiers wore exactly the same dress, the ball of the shako, however, being white. The battalion companies had red and white shako balls, and plain shoulder straps, with a small white worsted tuft at the extremity, crescent shape.

1855. The coat tails of the whole army disappeared, and frock coats or tunics took the place of the old coatee. The first issue was double-breasted, the buttons of brass, placed at equal distances; no lace used, excepting round the buttons on the cuffs and skirts, the coat edging piped all over with white cloth; dark blue trousers, with a red welt introduced; the shako made smaller and lighter; officers' and sergeants' sashes worn over the left and right shoulders respectively.

At the next issue the tunic was single-breasted. Officer's rank was now distinguished by the amount of gold lace worn, and by crowns and stars on the collar. A captain had an edging of the regimental gold lace round the top of the collar and the top of the cuff; four loops of lace, diamond shape, round the buttons on the cuff slash; the same loops round the skirt buttons; a crown and star on the collar. Lieutenants and ensigns, a crown or star respectively. Field officers had additional lace in the bottom of the collar, round the cuff, the cuff slash, and on the skirts behind; colonels, a crown and star on the collar; lieutenant-colonels and majors, crowns or stars respectively. A double-breasted blue frock coat adopted for undress, with the gilt regimental buttons and a plain stand-up collar; the crimson silk sash worn over the left shoulder; sword carried in a white sling belt.

By *Horse Guards Circular*, dated 14th May, 1858, the regiment was "directed to be clothed, equipped, and trained as a light infantry "regiment." This, however, involved no very great change in the equipment; for the balls in the shakos, green horsehair plumes, "drooping from them five inches high," were substituted; whistles and chains were adopted by the sergeants, worn on the pouch-belt; the chevrons of the non-commissioned officers were displayed on both arms, and finally the drummers gave up their drums and became buglers. The regimental number, with a bugle, was worn on the forage cap of both officers and men.

The illustration, page 214, taken from a picture drawn for Her Majesty the Queen, by Thomas, gives a very good representation of a sergeant's dress at this period.

1866. The peculiar drummer's lace, used by the regiment from the early part of the century, was done away with, and the universal pattern (white, with red crowns) adopted.

1867. The officer's black sword scabbard replaced by steel ones, and a patrol jacket substituted for the blue frock coat.

1868. The slashed cuff on the tunic discontinued, and pointed cuffs introduced. For levees, etc., officers were authorized to wear a gold and crimson sash, gold-laced trousers, and sword belt; the shako was ornamented with gold lace; the old star replaced by a garter and crown; the number inside surrounded by a wreath of laurel in high reliefs; the green plume also reduced in size.

About 1873, white clothing, so long used by the band, was discontinued; and, soon after, the shell jackets, worn by the men, abolished, and loose scarlet frocks adopted for undress.

1880. The helmet introduced, also a round undress forage cap for officers, with circular peak over the forehead; the number and bugle in gold embroidery; badges of rank removed from the collar and displayed on the shoulder straps.

1881.—Signalized by the introduction of the territorial system, when the officers lost their peculiar pattern of gold lace, and the regimental distinctions of the 32nd became merged in those of another distinguished regiment—the 46th—together forming the Duke of Cornwall's Light Infantry.

S. M. MILNE.

APPENDIX.

Battle of Chinhut, 1857.

Mr. John Lawrence gives the following account of the unfortunate affair at Chinhut, which was written within two or three days of its occurrence, namely, 30th June, 1857 :—

"At 4 a.m. this morning, a force—consisting of two hundred and "fifty of the 32nd Queen's; the Sikh Cavalry, some one hundred "sabres; Volunteer Horse, some thirty-five; some of the 13th "Native Infantry, and a batch of Carnegie's gallant Burkundauzes— "were ordered to Chinhut. We had also one eight-inch Howitzer, "drawn by elephants, and some ten field-guns, native gunners, and "drivers. The morning was very close and suffocating when we set "out. The big gun was rather an inconvenience, for the elephants "literally crawled along the road. We got up to the village of "Ishmaelgunge, on the Chinhut road, about 9 a.m. Here we drew "up in battle array : the 32nd lay in the hollow of the road, to the "left, under the village, with some of the 13th Native Infantry as "skirmishers. In the centre of the road was the eight-inch, to the "right the light field-guns, Sikhs and ourselves to the extreme right "of all. We opened fire ; and the sound of the nine-pounder yet "rang in our ears when the artillery of the rebels opened with "beautiful precision—every shot flew slap into us. Our guns "hammered away manfully for an hour ; and as for the Europeans "working the Howitzer, their conduct was beyond praise. The fire "was awful ; the enemy's cavalry now commenced pouring at us in "one unceasing tide towards our right in the Lucknow direction, "evidently outflanking us.

"After an hour's cannonade, the opposite artillery ceased its fire ; "in a few minutes rolling volleys of musketry from the village of "Ishmaelgunge showed that Jack Sepoy was there. The Volunteer

" Cavalry was ordered to move further to the right, and then, for the
" first time, I got a view of the plain between Ishmaelgunge and
" Chinhut. It was one moving mass of men. Regiment after
" regiment of the insurgents poured steadily towards us, the flanks
" covered with a foam of skirmishers, the light puffs of smoke from
" their muskets floating from every ravine and bunch of grass in our
" front. As to the mass of the troops, they came on in quarter-distance
" columns, the standards waving in their places, and everything
" performed as steadily as possible. A field day on parade could not
" have been better, and what was to hinder the enemy from doing just
" as they pleased? Our artillery ceased its fire, but beyond might be
" heard the crashing roll of musketry in Ismaelgunge, where the 32nd,
" outnumbered by myriads, still maintained a struggle. Our side was
" perfectly passive ; Carnegie's invincibles had deserted, and while I
" was looking about for them, a bustle in my rear attracted my
" attention ; the rascally gunners were cutting their traces and were
" galloping away ; the elephants for the Howitzer gone ; the Sikh
" Cavalry flying at full speed on the Lucknow road. A few European
" gunners, the Volunteer Cavalry, and the 32nd remained, but now
" the enemy pressed on more closely. He unlimbered his guns, and
" swept us with grape and canister ; the deadly mitraille of musketry
" poured in one leaden shower from the swarming skirmishers. And
" now the valiant few of the 32nd are beaten near the village, and
" come upon the road, their gallant colonel (Case) falls dead as he
" approaches ; some of our guns are spiked and abandoned (the
" Howitzer among them), four are limbered ; and the gun-carriages,
" covered with wounded men, gallop towards Lucknow. The 32nd
" also retreat ; mixed up with them are some of the braves of the 13th
" Native Infantry—noble fellows, who were seen carrying wounded
" soldiers to the gun-carriages, abandoning their own wounded
" comrades on the ground. The Volunteer Cavalry form upon the
" left of the road ; the rest of the handful of England's army is in
" retreat. A cloud of insurgent cavalry is gathering on the far rear
" to the left of our retreating column. Do they mean to charge
" down among those staggering, half-dead heroes, who can scarcely
" walk along? The red and blue flags thicken among them, when

"the tremendous voice of our leader (Captain Radcliffe, of the 7th
"Light Cavalry), is heard—'Three's right!' 'Trot!' and we sweep
"out of the trees, and off the road, and we are within a quarter of a
"mile of our opponents. Their 'gole' still forms heavy and dark,
"and now two light guns open on us; but the nine-pounder scarce
"whistled overhead when the stentorian 'Charge' was heard; the
"notes of our trumpet sounded sharp above the din of the fight, and
"we rode straight at them; the cowards never bided the shock; they
"galloped like furies from the spot. Five hundred cavalry and two
"guns to be hunted by thirty-five sabres; it was a miserable fact!
"The guns got under the shelter of a regiment of the line, which we
"dared not charge, for the first volley they gave us emptied two
"saddles; so sabring up the scattered skirmishers, we wheeled and
"galloped to the rear of our slowly moving columns.

"The battle of Chinhut was done; the line of our retreat was
"marked by the bodies of the 32nd, their arms, their accoutrements:
"men were falling untouched by ball; the heat of a June sun was
"killing more than the enemy. Hard upon our heels they followed;
"and as we got into the Residency so did the round shot of the
"pursuing foe whistle in the air. The siege then virtually commenced.
"How to end, the Lord alone can tell. In one fatal day the 32nd
"have left three officers and one hundred and sixteen men to tell the
"tale of British heroism; but, alas! also of British failure."

THE BURMESE BELL AT BODMIN.

With regard to the large bell recently presented to the town of Bodmin by the men of the 1st Battalion of the Duke of Cornwall's Light Infantry, full particulars have now been ascertained by the Rev. W. Iago on behalf of those interested in the gift.

By corresponding with those acquainted with the circumstances attending its acquisition in Burmah, and by making careful copies of its inscription, in manuscript and by a rubbing, Mr. Iago has elicited from reliable sources the bell's history here given :—

"The WUNTHO BELL" may be accepted as its descriptive title, for it was originally presented with great ceremony to a new Pagoda Temple, in the town of that name, by the Prince and his family who ruled and dwelt there.

It is a modern bell, and the following is the account of its passing into the hands of the British. An officer writes :—

"On the 16th of February, 1891, without warning of any kind, the "storm of invasion broke on the peaceful villages of Upper Burmah. "The Swabwa of Wuntho declared war in the usual Oriental fashion, "viz., by advancing unexpectedly into our country, burning villages "and destroying life wherever unopposed.

"Brigadier-General Wolseley, C.B., A.D.C., with a force composed "of detachments of the Devons, Cornwalls, military police, and some "artillery, was soon in movement, and by the 20th had driven the "enemy back to his own territory, and was advancing on Wuntho, "his capital.

"News was brought in on the 21st that the enemy were strongly "stockading themselves on the Wuntho road.

"Captain Davis, in command of the advance, did not wait for the "artillery, the forward movement commending itself, and the attack "on the morrow was decided on.

"At the first streak of dawn the column advanced, the mounted "infantry moving to the flanks to cut off the enemy's retreat, while

"the Devons sent forward a reconnoitring party, under Lieutenant
" Holman, to ascertain the position and strength of the foe.

"This they were not long in doing, for about three miles from
" Kawlin and five from Wuntho they exchanged shots with the out-
" posts, and, driving them in, found themselves in front of a steep
" hill, surmounted by a strongly stockaded ' Poungee Kyaung ' (priest's
" house and temple), protected at the base of the hill by a rapid
" stream.

" The advanced party now came under a hot fire, and two men
" (out of the leading section of 11) fell dead, three being severely
" wounded. Notwithstanding this loss of nearly half their number, the
" section passed across the stream and took what cover they could in
" the wooded slope to await the arrival of the stormers.

" During this time Lieutenant Holman had two bullet holes drilled
" through his helmet, one an inch from his head, the other grazing his
" temple. Surgeon Anderson, who has had a good deal of experience
" of this class of fighting in other Burmah wars and in Egypt, was
" close at hand, but before he could reach Holman, who had been
" temporarily rendered insensible by the blow, the latter was again on
" his legs, and leading the stormers (who had now come up) straight
" on the Poungee Kyaung.

" Though the Devon men were all young soldiers, and dropping
" fast under the heavy fire poured upon them, they never hesitated
" until they reached the stockade, and here, while some fired through
" the chinks, others cut and hacked at the buildings until an entrance
" was forced.

" During the attack the Burman war-gong kept up a continual clang,
" and the leaders were heard shouting ' Slay ! Slay the dogs ! '

" Directly, however, an entrance was forced the real fighting was
" practically over. The Swabwa's men did not appear to relish the
" idea of cold steel, and fled down the reverse slope of the hill, to fall
" into the hands of the Cornwall men, who—all picked shots, and
" judiciously posted by Captain Custance—opened upon them a deadly
" fire.

" Seventy-six dead bodies were counted, and the neighbouring
" villages were said to contain numbers of wounded.

"Among the dead were found the bodies of two of the Swabwa's "body-guard, recognisable by the red velvet breeches, which they "alone are allowed to wear; also one of the Swabwa's Ministers, "identified by his breeches, in this case of green velvet. This last "gentleman was bowled over by a volley from six of the Cornwall's at "a range little short of one thousand yards.

"After the fight was supposed to be at an end, and the men were "re-forming after the pursuit, a volley was fired into them from some "low jungle. A rush was made for it, and some 40 more Burmans "were found, in rifle pits, in the low scrub.

"A short, sharp struggle followed, and shots of friends and foes "whizzed in all directions; but the result was never in doubt, and in "a short time the men fell in, and were ready to march on Wuntho, "which was now defenceless."

Having entered the town and occupied it, our troops converted the Prince's new Pagoda and Temple (in which Buddhist rites were celebrated) into a Post-office. There, the day after the fight, they found the large bell. It still bears traces of having been richly gilded.

On quitting Wuntho, they took the bell with them, and had considerable trouble, on account of its weight, in conveying it over the Mangandine Pass (two thousand feet high), which lies between Wuntho and the great river Irrawaddy. Lives having been sacrificed on both sides in the advance upon Wuntho, the soldiers regarded its bell as a war-trophy, and, as soon as possible, forwarded it to their home barracks in Bodmin, desiring to present it to the town.

After it had arrived at the barracks, and been handed over to the Mayor and Corporation, a letter of thanks in ackowledgment of the thoughtfulness of the gift was sent to the donors.

The bell itself must now be described:

It weighs about two hundred-weight. The bell-metal is cast a considerable thickness. A blow or fall, however, received probably in the course of its long journey to Bodmin, has, unfortunately, caused a crack in it, which, although not conspicuous, has entirely deprived the bell of its note.

In form the bell is—like other Burmese bells—narrow at the mouth compared with its height, open at the crown, and without clapper. Dragons, forming loops or canons for its suspension, adorn the top.

Such bells, depending from a cross-beam supported by two side posts, are set up outside the Buddhist temples, a deer's horn or two being placed near them.

A worshipper, having recited his prayers, takes up a deer horn and strikes the bell with it, generally on the rim, with the idea, it is said, of communicating a share of the merit he has acquired by praying, to all who are within earshot of the sound and hear the same in a right state of mind. When a deer's horn is not used, any hard piece of wood may be used as a mallet. Deer horn is preferred, as being hard but not likely to injure. An iron striker should be avoided.

On the exterior, partly round the haunch of the bell, runs an inscription, neatly incised in six lines of small writing, consisting of semi-circles, circles, and other curves and dashes, more or less connected.

General Ardagh, of the Imperial Institute, South Kensington (some of whose words have already been quoted with reference to the sounding of Burmese bells), has obligingly translated the Rev. W. Iago's copy of the legend; the date which occurs in it, having been verified also by Mr. Cecil Bendall, of the British Museum, and by Dr. Rost, librarian of the India-office.

The following is the translation of the inscription on the bell :—

"In the year 1239, on the 11th waxing of the moon Thadingyoot
"(that is, on the 18th of October, 1877), the Prince of the town of
"Woontho, the Tsawbwa Gyee Raza (or Rajah, ruler) of high
"descent, THOHONBWA, and the Princesses THOOWOONA-KAYA, Maha
"Daewee, and Thoowoona-Roopa Maha Daewee, his Royal spouses,
"with all their sons and daughters, gave this copper bell, weighing
"7,750 viss, in accordance with what was suitable, 205, 2 moos and
"1 pai. If the price be told it was given in silver rupees. And they
"consecrated it, as an offering in front of the Pagoda, having regard
"to the excellent Incomprehensible, and desiring Norwana (Heaven).

"On account of this good deed, may they throughout all ages, be
"blessed with the characteristics of excellent men and with the

"precious endowments of good people, and be conspicuous and "abound with the Ten Cardinal Virtues, and be able to avoid from "afar and shun all evil demerits and bad deeds, and be able to come "out of, and rise up from, the future state of punishment and hell. "And may they be filled with the gift they ought to wish for, and "long for, out of the three excellent gifts, viz., the gift of the knowledge "belonging to a professed (Buddhist) disciple, and that of a semi- "Boodh, and the omniscience of a Boodh. And may they arrive at "the excellent golden land of Nerwana, and the resting place of the "great golden country of the true Nerwana."

The inscription reads from left to right, and the numerals follow the same order, and are placed according to the decimal system of notation, just as ours are, the commencing words, &c., being:—"Thekkareet 1,239 Khoo, Thadingyoot," &c.

The legend is written in the Burmese and Pali languages, some parts being repeated, so that one language may serve as a key to the other. The date is that of the Burmese ordinary era, which commences with A.D. 638, the epoch of a certain famous ruler. The Burmese religious era is reckoned from B.C. 543, the date of the death of the fourth Buddha, whose images and supposed relics the Burmese worship.

There are in Burmah some immense bells which have been described in Vincent's *Land of the White Elephant.* From the facts now brought together it will be seen that the bell at Bodmin was PRINCE THOHONBWA'S FAMILY GIFT, IN 1877, TO THE BUDDIST PAGODA-TEMPLE OF WUNTHO, the capital of one of the Shan States of Upper Burmah, and that, after a sharp fight with the Prince's followers, it was taken by our troops, in repelling the Prince's invasion of our territory.

ROLL OF OFFICERS AND MEN

WHO WERE

PRESENT DURING THE WATERLOO CAMPAIGN.

Obtained from a Roll in the possession of Mr. W. C. MURPHY, Hazlewood, Deacon Road, Kingston-on-Thames, who kindly placed it at the Author's disposal.

The Roll was certified to and signed by—

    J. MAITLAND, *Lieutenant Colonel*,
    SAMUEL LAWRENCE, *Adjutant*,
    THOMAS HART, *Paymaster.*

Dated at Guernsey, 25th May, 1816.

RETURN OF OFFICERS,
NON-COMMISSIONED OFFICERS, DRUMMERS, AND PRIVATES
OF THE 32ND REGIMENT

Who were present in the Battles of the 16th, 17th, and 18th June, 1815.

Rank.	Name.	Remarks.
Brevet Lieutenant-Colonel	John Hicks	
,, ,, ,,	Felix Calvert	
Brevet Major	Charles Haines	
,, ,,	Henry Ross Lewin	
,, ,,	W. H. Toole	
Captain	John Crowe	
,,	Jacques Boyse	Died of wounds, 16th June
,,	Thomas Cassan	Died of wounds, 16th June
,,	Edward Whitty	Killed
,,	Hugh Harrison	
,,	Charles Wallet	
Paymaster	Thomas Hart	
Surgeon	William Buchanan	
Lieutenant	H. W. Brooks	
,,	George Barr	
,,	M. W. Meighan	
,,	S. H. Lawrence	
,,	Theobald Butler	
,,	John Boase	
,,	Thomas Ross Lewin	
,,	Henry Butterworth	
,,	James Colthurst	
,,	James Robinson	
,,	R. T. Belcher	
,,	James Fitzgerald	
,,	Thomas Horan	
,,	Edward Stevens	
,,	Henry Quill	
,,	Jonathan Jago	
,,	George Small	
Ensign	Jasper Lucas	
,,	James McCouchy	
,,	Henry Metcalf	
,,	John Birtwhistle	
,,	Alexander Stuart	
,,	George Browne	
,,	William Bennet	
,,	Charles Dallas	
Adjutant	David Davies	
Quarter-Master	William Stephens	
Assistant Surgeon	R. Lawder	
,, ,,	H. McClintock	

APPENDIX.   277

Rank.	Name.	Company.	Remarks.
Sergeant-Major	William Peppnal	Whitty's	
" "	George Ode	Whitty's	
Qr.-Mr. Sergt.	John Meadmibree	Whitty's	
" "	John Barton	Whitty's	
Schoolmaster Sergt.	George Berkley	Whitty's	
Sergt.-Armourer	William Glanville	Whitty's	
Drum-Major	Saml. Pollard	Whitty's	
Sergeant	Adwicke, John	Crowe's	
"	Barnett, Thomas	Harrison's	
"	Battenby, Jas.	Boyse's	
"	Bottonely, Joseph	Harrison's	
"	Broad, Saml.	Haines'	Died 19th June, 1815
"	Brown, William	Haines'	
"	Clarke, Francis	Crowe's	
"	Colwell, William	Wallett's	
"	Corrigan, Michl.	Toole's	
"	Courtney, Thomas	Dillon's	
"	Dobble, William	Crowe's	
"	Duffy, James	Wallett's	
"	Fagan, David	Cassan's	
"	Glynn, William	Dillon's	
"	Hills, James	Harrison's	
"	Horford, John	Toole's	
"	Jarrett, Mark	Harrison's	
"	Larken, John	Harrison's	
"	Leslie, John	Whitty's	
"	McCormick, Wm.	Ross Lewin's	
"	McGowan, Jno.	Dillon's	
"	Millar, John	Toole's	
"	Nichols, James	Dillon's	
"	O'Brien, Patrick	Wallet's	
"	Pimlett, John	Harrison's	
"	Pringle, John	Boyse's	
"	Seery, Patrick	Haines'	
"	Slater, James	Cassan's	Died 27th June, 1815
"	Sheppard, John	Haines'	
"	Spence, John	Ross Lewin's	
"	Stephenson, Robt.	Cassan's	
"	Switzer, Christr.	Cassan's	
"	Smalden, Richd.	Whitty's	
"	Virtue, James	Crowe's	
"	Warren, Joshua	Ross Lewin's	
"	Webster, John	Cassan's	
"	Wilson, Charles	Boyse's	
Corporal	Bingham, Peter	Ross Lewin's	
"	Bonney, John	Dillon's	Killed 16th June, 1815
"	Bryan, Charles	Harrison's	
"	Britt, Patk.	Toole's	
"	Carpenter, Joseph	Haines'	
"	Carracher, John	Dillon's	
"	Clark, Jos. (first)	Whitty's	
"	Clark, Jos. (second)	Ross Lewin's	
"	Colbeck, John	Ross Lewin's	
"	Cooper, William	Wallett's	

APPENDIX.

Rank.	Name.	Company.	Remarks.
Corporal	Croskins, Richard	Cassan's	
,,	Davey, William	Boyse's	Died 19th June, 1815
,,	Dodd, John Thomas	Boyse's	Killed 18th June, 1815
,,	Dore, James	Whitty's	Died 19th June, 1815
,,	Gynnen, William	Dillon's	
,,	Hanlan, James	Harrison's	
,,	Henry, William	Wallett's	
,,	Hunchliff, Thomas	Haines'	
,,	Jennett, James	Boyse's	
,,	Jones, Stephen	Crowe's	
,,	Jones, William	Crowe's	Died 5th July, 1815
,,	Lawey, William	Crowe's	Died 19th June, 1815
,,	McGill, William	Harrison's	Died 7th July, 1815
,,	Martinscroft, Samuel	Boyse's	Killed 18th June, 1815
,,	Miller, Hugh	Harrison's	
,,	Moore, James	Ross Lewin's	
,,	Murphy, Patrick	Toole's	
,,	Nowland, Dennis	Crowe's	
,,	Nowland, James	Crowe's	
,,	Pritchard, Richard	Haines'	
,,	Ramsdon, John	Ross Lewin's	
,,	Ramsey, William	Whitty's	Died 28th July, 1815
,,	Reynolds, John	Boyse's	
,,	Richardson, George	Boyse's	
,,	Shanklin, Andrew	Harrison's	
,,	Sommers, John	Haines'	Killed 16th June, 1815
,,	Sutton, William	Whitty's	
,,	Turner, William	Ross Lewin's	
,,	Webb, Richard	Dillon's	
,,	White, James	Dillon's	
,,	Williams, John	Wallett's	Died 5th October, 1815
,,	Williams, William	Whitty's	Died 19th June, 1815
Drummer	Bealty, William	Toole's	
,,	Cornelius, Peter	Dillon's	
,,	Cullen, Andrew	Wallett's	
,,	Dowling, Stephen	Harrison's	
,,	Fisher, John	Crowe's	
,,	Logdon, Thomas	Haines'	
,,	Mahon, James	Wallett's	
,,	Metcalf, Thomas	Cassan's	
,,	Murray, James	Boyse's	
,,	Reid, John	Ross Lewin's	
,,	Reid, Thomas	Crowe's	
,,	Rodgers, John	Wallett's	
,,	Spry, Henry	Boyse's	
Private	Athers, Joseph	Crowe's	
,,	Allison, John	Whitty's	
,,	Annear, John	Boyse's	Killed 16th June, 1815
,,	Andrews, Joseph	Boyse's	
,,	Annear, William	Cassan's	
,,	Astier, John	Whitty's	
,,	Astor, John	Dillon's	
,,	Arnold, Valentine	Boyse's	
,,	Atkins, Caleb	Haines'	

APPENDIX. 279

Rank.	Name.	Company.	Remarks.
Private	Baisley, William	Harrison's	
,,	Banfield, William	Ross Lewin's	
,,	Bannister, William	Ross Lewin's	
,,	Bannew, Daniel	Toole's	
,,	Barker, James	Crowe's	
,,	Barrow, Joseph	Crowe's	
,,	Batty, John	Crowe's	
,,	Batley, Benjamin	Dillon's	
,,	Bartle, James	Dillon's	
,,	Barry, William	Dillon's	
,,	Barrett, Thomas	Dillon's	
,,	Barrett, Robert	Harrison's	
,,	Bamfield, John	Haines'	
,,	Barber, Drew	Haines'	
,,	Beamish, John	Ross Lewin's	
,,	Bealtie, Thomas	Cassan's	
,,	Benson, Henry	Cassan's	
,,	Beer, William	Boyse's	
,,	Bible, Francis	Crowe's	Died at Corfu
,,	Bigwood, John	Boyse's	Killed 18th June, 1815
,,	Birch, John	Dillon's	Died 9th June, 1815
,,	Birch, Henry	Harrison's	
,,	Bingham, John	Toole's	
,,	Birch, Francis	Crowe's	
,,	Blackwell, William	Dillon's	
,,	Blizzard, Thomas	Toole's	
,,	Blake, Lewis	Crowe's	
,,	Blake, Lewis	Crowe's	
,,	Blunn, Moses	Crowe's	
,,	Bond, John	Cassan's	Killed 18th June, 1815
,,	Bowell, Robert	Wallett's	Died at Corfu
,,	Bottomley, Joseph	Whitty's	
,,	Bowles, John	Dillon's	
,,	Boyle, Neale	Wallett's	
,,	Boyd, Robert	Cassan's	
,,	Boyton, George	Toole's	
,,	Browne, John (first)	Toole's	
,,	Browne, John (second)	Crowe's	
,,	Browne, John (third)	Ross Lewin's	Died of wounds 16th Jan., [1816
,,	Browne, James (fourth)	Whitty's	
,,	Bennett, John	Toole's	
,,	Brookes, George	Crowe's	Killed 18th June, 1815
,,	Brutton, Joseph	Whitty's	
,,	Brennan, Andrew	Dillon's	
,,	Bray, William	Ross Lewin's	
,,	Brophy, John	Toole's	
,,	Bruncaid, William	Boyse's	
,,	Bryan, John	Harrison's	
,,	Bryan, Daniel	Wallett's	
,,	Bryan, Edward	Ross Lewin's	
,,	Brinkworth, Robert	Toole's	
,,	Burke, John	Whitty's	
,,	Burne, James	Whitty's	
,,	Butler, Thomas	Haines'	Died at St. Maura

Rank.	Name.	Company.	Remarks.
Private	Burnes, James	Harrison's	
,,	Burnes, Patrick	Dillon's	
,,	Burnet, William	Boyse's	
,,	Byrne, James	Boyse's	
,,	Carnes, William	Whitty's	
,,	Cohill, John	Haines'	
,,	Carpenter, Benjamin	Haines'	
,,	Carnell, Henry	Haines'	Died 9th July, 1815
,,	Carnell, Thomas	Harrison's	Died 19th June, 1815
,,	Carrow, Simon	Dillon's	
,,	Carty, Owen	Dillon's	
,,	Caddell, Joseph	Wallett's	
,,	Cadden, Michael	Toole's	
,,	Cano, James	Cassan's	Died 9th July, 1815
,,	Carson, George	Cassan's	
,,	Carr, Peter	Cassan's	
,,	Cavanagh, Lawrence	Cassan's	
,,	Caulfield, Thomas	Cassan's	Killed 16th June, 1815
,,	Carmoody, James	Ross Lewin's	
,,	Charters, John	Crowe's	Killed 18th June, 1815
,,	Challis, Thomas	Crowe's	Died 19th June, 1815
,,	Clarke, Samuel	Boyse's	Killed 18th June, 1815
,,	Chappel, Thomas	Boyse's	Killed 16th June, 1815
,,	Clifford, Alexander	Cassan's	
,,	Cleew, Philip	Toole's	
,,	Cluff, Francis	Ross Lewin's	
,,	Coughran, Samuel	Whitty's	
,,	Couto, Stephen	Haines'	
,,	Cooper, Stephen	Harrison's	
,,	Corcoran, John	Harrison's	Died 1st July, 1815
,,	Colrick, Samuel	Harrison's	
,,	Collier, Richard	Harrison's	
,,	Costello, Thomas	Harrison's	
,,	Cooper, John	Wallett's	
,,	Cove, Jonathan	Wallett's	
,,	Cornish, John	Ross Lewin's	
,,	Coburne, William	Toole's	
,,	Collier, William	Toole's	
,,	Cootes, Charles	Toole's	Killed 16th June, 1815
,,	Couharn, John	Cassan's	
,,	Cooke, James	Cassan's	
,,	Coles, Daniel	Boyse's	
,,	Crow, William	Boyse's	
,,	Cock, James	Crowe's	
,,	Coleman, William	Crowe's	
,,	Conway, John	Whitty's	Killed 18th June, 1815
,,	Crozier, Robert	Whitty's	
,,	Crompton, George	Haines'	
,,	Craig, William	Wallett's	
,,	Cripps, John	Ross Lewin's	
,,	Crowley, William	Toole's	
,,	Dalton, Richard	Harrison's	Died at St. Mama
,,	Dauce, Joseph	Wallett's	
,,	Dagg, Thomas	Ross Lewin's	

APPENDIX. 281

Rank.	Name.	Company.	Remarks.
Private	Davies, Edward	Boyse's	
,,	Davies, John	Boyse's	
,,	Dellamore, Thomas	Toole's	Died 29th June, 1815
,,	Delaney, Patrick	Ross Lewin's	Killed 16th June, 1815
,,	Devlin, John	Boyse's	
,,	Devlin, James	Boyse's	Died 15th October, 18'5
,,	Devlin, Henry	Cassan's	
,,	Dixon, Richard	Wallett's	
,,	Doherty, John	Whitty's	
,,	Donohue, Edward	Whitty's	
,,	Donnelly, James	Whitty's	
,,	Downey, James	Haines'	
,,	Donovan, Jeremiah	Dillon's	
,,	Dovey, John	Dillon's	
,,	Donnelly, John	Wallett's	Died 19th June, 1815
,,	Doyle, James	Wallett's	[1815
,,	Deane, Thomas	Ross Lewin's	Died of wounds, 9th July,
,,	Douglas, George	Boyse's	Died of wounds, 26th July,
,,	Donlaw, Patrick	Crowe's	[1815
,,	Downey, John	Crowe's	
,,	Dumphy, Michael	Whitty's	
,,	Dunsheath, James	Haines'	
,,	Dunsheath, Nathaniel	Wallett's	
,,	Dunbar, John	Wallett's	
,,	Dunne, Lawrence	Boyse's	
,,	Dunne, William	Boyse's	
,,	Durmew, Phillip	Crowe's	Killed 16th July, 1815
,,	Drew, Nicholas	Harrison's	
,,	Dyer, Saml. William	Ross Lewin's	
,,	Eastman, William	Whitty's	
,,	Eagan, Gilbert	Harrison's	
,,	Eastman, Thomas	Wallett's	
,,	Ellison, John	Wallett's	
,,	Emsley, Benjamin	Ross Lewin's	
,,	Eccles, Thomas	Crowe's	
,,	Elliott, George	Crowe's	
,,	Faneks, George	Crowe's	
,,	Fagan, Edward	Cassan's	
,,	Farrell, Francis	Dillon's	
,,	Fleming, William	Whitty's	
,,	Fleming, John	Dillon's	
,,	Flatley, John	Wallett's	
,,	Fitzsimmons, Daniel	Harrison's	
,,	Forster, Thomas	Harrison's	
,,	Faley, Timothy	Ross Lewin's	
,,	Francis, Charles	Ross Lewin's	
,,	Freestone, Edward	Cassan's	Died 1st July, 1815
,,	Freeman, James	Boyse's	
,,	Francis, David	Crowe's	
,,	Turnifall, David	Harrison's	Killed 18th June, 1815
,,	Garner, John	Wallett's	
,,	Garner, Thomas	Crowe's	
,,	Gilbert, Thomas	Whitty's	Died 19th June, 1815
,,	Gilded, Michael	Cassan's	

APPENDIX.

Rank.	Name.	Company.	Remarks.
Private	Gordon, Thomas	Haines'	
,,	Golding, Henry	Dillon's	
,,	Gadson, Oliver	Toole's	Died 19th June, 1815
,,	Gould, Isaac	Toole's	
,,	Gormby, Thomas	Cassan's	Died 19th June, 1815
,,	Goddard, John	Dillon's	Killed 18th June, 1815
,,	Grier, Patrick	Whitty's	
,,	Grigg, Joseph	Whitty's	
,,	Graham, Robert	Whitty's	
,,	Grimes, John	Haines'	
,,	Greenwood, William	Harrison's	Died 19th July, 1815
,,	Greenslade, William	Dillon's	
,,	Grey, Richard	Dillon's	
,,	Granfield, John	Wallett's	
,,	Grimes, Samuel	Cassan's	
,,	Groves, John	Toole's	Killed 18th July, 1815
,,	Groom, Edward	Harrison's	Killed 18th July, 1815
,,	Haines, Richard	Whitty's	
,,	Hargroves, William	Whitty's	
,,	Hawkes, William	Whitty's	
,,	Hall, John	Haines'	
,,	Hall, Charles	Harrison's	
,,	Hamilton, Francis	Harrison's	
,,	Hands, Thomas	Harrison's	
,,	Harding, James	Harrison's	Killed 18th July, 1815
,,	Harding, John	Toole's	
,,	Hanley, Elijah	Dillon's	
,,	Hart, Thomas	Wallett's	
,,	Hancock, William	Ross Lewin's	
,,	Halligan, Stephen	Cassan's	
,,	Hannon, Thomas	Boyse's	
,,	Harford, John	Boyse's	
,,	Hamilton, William	Crowe's	
,,	Handcock, William	Crowe's	
,,	Hanslam, Samuel	Crowe's	
,,	Hawkes, James	Cassan's	
,,	Hawkes, Edward	Wallett's	Killed 18th June, 1815
,,	Heady, John	Crowe's	
,,	Herd, George	Crowe's	
,,	Healy, Thomas	Boyse's	
,,	Hennessy, John	Cassan's	
,,	Head, William	Ross Lewin's	
,,	Heale, Jacob	Wallett's	
,,	Higgins, Joseph	Dillon's	Killed 16th June, 1815
,,	Hinds, James	Whitty's	Died at Zant
,,	Higgs, Thomas	Crowe's	
,,	Holland, James	Crowe's	
,,	Hoy, Michael	Crowe's	
,,	Holleron, Thomas	Boyse's	
,,	Hopkins, Thomas	Boyse's	
,,	Hopham, Thomas	Cassan's	Killed 18th June, 1815
,,	Hope, John	Toole's	
,,	Hoskins, Thomas	Toole's	
,,	Hozie, Paul	Toole's	

APPENDIX.   283

Rank.	Name.	Company.	Remarks.
Private	Hookway, John - -	Toole's	
,,	Horne, James - -	Ross Lewin's	
,,	Holfand, Thomas -	Wallett's	
,,	Hook, William - -	Wallett's	
,,	Holbert, William -	Dillon's	
,,	Howell, Robert - -	Dillon's	
,,	Hollant, John - -	Harrison's	
,,	Howee, Timothy -	Haines'	
,.	Holmes, George - -	Whitty's	
,,	Hughes, Joseph - -	Whitty's	
,:	Huntley, David - -	Whitty's	
,.	Huston, Boyle - -	Harrison's	
,,	Hutchinson, Thomas -	Ross Lewin's	
.,	Hughes, William -	Toole's	Died at St. Mama
,,	Hulse, Joseph - -	Boyse's	
,:	Humpherson, John -	Boyse's	Died 5th September, 1815
,.	Hynes, Daniel - -	Haines'	Killed 18th June, 1815
,,	Ingram, John - -	Harrison's	
,,	Ingram, Thomas -	Boyse's	Died 6th July, 1815
,,	Ireland, William -	Crowe's	
,,	James, James - -	Whitty's	
,,	James, Thomas - -	Haines'	
,,	Jackson, William -	Toole's	
.,	Jenkins, William -	Whitty's	Killed 16th June, 1815
,,	Jeffries, John - -	Wallett's	
,,	Jonas, John - -	Haines'	
.,	Jones, Thomas (first) -	Harrison's	
,,	Jones, Thomas (second)	Crowe's	
,,	Jones, Daniel - -	Toole's	
.,	Johnstone, Edgar -	Ross Lewin's	
,.	John, Evan - -	Boyse's	
,,	Jordan, James - -	Boyse's	Died 1st July, 1815
,,	Kennon, John - -	Whitty's	Killed 18th June, 1815
,,	Kerr, Henry - -	Haines'	
,,	Kennedy, John - -	Harrison's	
,,	Kelly, Dominick -	Ross Lewin's	
,,	Kennedy, James -	Cassan's	
,,	Kirby, Jonathan -	Whitty's	Died 30th October, 1815
,,	King, Elijah - -	Whitty's	
,,	Kimbre, William -	Toole's	
,,	Kimbre, Nathaniel -	Dillon's	
,,	Kiernan, Michael -	Crowe's	
,,	Kirkwood, William -	Crowe's	Died 14th August, 1815
,,	Kibby, Richard - -	Wallett's	Died 23rd July, 1815
,,	Kirbess, Edward -	Harrison's	Died 12th July, 1815
,,	Kirby, John - -		Died 25th May, 1815
,:	Kinsley, James - -	Harrison's	Killed 18th June, 1815
.,	Knowles, Samuel -	Cassan's	
,,	Knox, Andrew - -	Boyse's	
,:	Lacey, William - -	Whitty's	
.,	Lawles, Daniel - -	Whitty's	
,,	Lamsden, William -	Haines'	
,,	Lamb, Thomas - -	Harrison's	
,,	Lawton, Robert - -	Dillon's	

Rank.	Name.	Company.	Remarks.
Private	Lanscombe, William	Ross Lewin's	
,,	Lawton, Robert	Boyse's	
,,	Langley, John	Crowe's	
,,	Lancaster, John	Harrison's	
,,	Leonard, Patrick	Dillon's	
,,	Lee, Joseph	Boyse's	
,,	Linnox, James	Harrison's	
,,	Leiton, William	Haines'	
,,	Little, John	Whitty's	
,,	Linegen, John	Wallett's	
,,	Lidwell, James	Toole's	Died at Albany Barracks
,,	Lockley, James	Whitty's	
,,	Lobb, William	Boyse's	Killed 16th June, 1815
,,	Leaford, William	Ross Lewin's	Killed 18th June, 1815
,,	Lewis, James	Cassan's	Killed 16th June, 1815
,,	Logan, John	Haines'	
,,	Looney, William	Wallett's	
,,	Lukes, Richard	Ross Lewin's	
,,	Mackery, William	Whitty's	
,,	Manley, John	Whitty's	
,,	Mahon, John	Haines'	
,,	Magwood, John	Haines'	
,,	Maison, John	Harrison's	
,,	Maddon, John	Dillon's	
,,	Mackle, Charles	Ross Lewin's	
,,	Marley, Miles	Ross Lewin's	
,,	Marshall, William	Ross Lewin's	
,,	Martin, Robert	Cassan's	Died at St. Mar
,,	Mayne, Cornelius	Boyse's	
,,	Masfield, John	Boyse's	
,,	Marks, Thomas	Crowe's	
,,	Maniar, Samuel	Crowe's	
,,	Marshmew, John	Crowe's	
,,	McCool, John	Boyse's	Killed 16th June, 1815
,,	McGuire, Hugh	Ross Lewin's	Killed 16th June, 1815
,,	McKiernan, Luke	Crowe's	Killed 16th June, 1815
,,	McGuire, James	Crowe's	Killed 18th June, 1815
,,	McDonagh, Dennis	Toole's	Killed 18th June, 1815
,,	McJeroy, William	Wallett's	Killed 18th June, 1815
,,	McGarn, Owen	Haines'	Died 24th July, 1815
,,	McLelland, Robert	Whitty's	
,,	McHoin, William	Haines'	
,,	McGarn, Michael	Haines'	
,,	McKenny, Patrick	Haines'	
,,	McLoughlin, David	Haines'	
,,	McLuade, James	Haines'	
,,	McCarrell, William	Dillon's	Died 19th June, 1815
,,	McCarroll, James	Wallett's	
,,	McCarthy, David	Wallett's	
,,	McCarthy, Henry	Ross Lewin's	
,,	McCarthy, Jeremiah	Boyse's	
,,	McCeiver, James	Ross Lewin's	
,,	McPhatridge, John	Ross Lewin's	
,,	McManus, Edward	Ross Lewin's	

APPENDIX. 285

Rank.	Name.	Company.	Remarks.
Private	McCann, Terence	Toole's	
,,	McHood, Edward	Toole's	
,,	McCabe, Peter	Cassan's	
,,	McGarvey, Thomas	Cassan's	
,,	McHarry, James	Cassan's	
,,	McDole, Smith	Cassan's	
,,	McAffee, John	Boyse's	
,,	McGuire, John	Boyse's	
,,	McDonald, Timothy	Crowe's	
,,	McMamara, John	Crowe's	
,,	Meighan, John	Harrison's	
,,	Millar, Thomas	Haines'	
,,	Milton, James	Haines'	
,,	Moore, Thomas	Harrison's	Killed 16th June, 1815
,,	Millen, William	Dillon's	
,,	Mitton, James	Wallett's	
,,	Mitchell, Thos. (first)	Toole's	
,,	Mitchell, Thos. (second)	Boyse's	
,,	Mitchell, Robert	Boyse's	
,,	Mitchell, Silus	Cassan's	Died 19th June, 1815
,,	Miles, Michael	Cassan's	
,,	Mills, Joseph	Cassan's	
,,	Mortimore, Alexander	Whitty's	
,,	Moulton, John	Haines'	
,,	Morris, John	Harrison's	
,,	Moore, James	Dillon's	Killed 15th June, 1815
,,	Moore, Robert	Dillon's	
,,	Moore, Samuel	Cassan's	
,,	Morris, Charles	Dillon's	
,,	Mortgatroyd, Matthew	Dillon's	
,,	Morrow, William	Wallett's	
,,	Montgomry, James	Cassan's	
,,	Morris, Matthew	Boyse's	
,,	Morley, Thomas	Crowe's	
,,	Mortimor, Joseph	Crowe's	
,,	Murray, James	Whitty's	
,,	Murray, William	Whitty's	
,,	Murray, Michael	Boyse's	
,,	Murray, John	Crowe's	
,,	Mullins, Thomas	Harrison's	
,,	Mullolland, Arthur	Wallett's	
,,	Mullins, James	Ross Lewin's	Died at Corfu
,,	Mullewey, John	Cassan's	
,,	Murphy, Michael	Cassan's	
,,	Neilly, John	Whitty's	
,,	Newman, William	Haines'	Killed 18th June, 1815
,,	Nesbitt, John	Wallett's	
,,	Noonan, Timothy	Dillon's	
,,	Oates, James	Ross Lewin's	Died 29th June, 1815
,,	Odgers, John	Wallett's	
,,	Ogden, James	Boyse's	
,,	Oliver, James (first)	Boyse's	
,,	Oliver, James (second)	Whitty's	
,,	Onions, William	Cassan's	

Rank.	Name.	Company.	Remarks.
Private	Painter, Solomon	Dillon's	
,,	Palmer, Wm. (first)	Dillon's	
,,	Palmer, Wm. (second)	Toole's	
,,	Palmer, Roger	Cassan's	
,,	Parsons, Richard	Boyse's	
,,	Patrick, William	Ross Lewin's	
,,	Pascoe, Robert	Wallett's	
,,	Pearcy, Thomas	Haines'	
,,	Pearce, Benjamin	Harrison's	
,,	Pearce, James	Crowe's	
,,	Jewe, John	Harrison's	
,,	Peglar, George	Boyes's	
,,	Perry, William	Boyse's	
,,	Perry, James	Cassan's	
,,	Perkins, Joseph	Cassan's	
,,	Peyton, John	Wallett's	
,,	Philips, John (first)	Haines'	
,,	Philips, John (second)	Harrison's	
,,	Philips, Thomas	Harrison's	
,,	Planner, Anthony	Boyse's	
,,	Porter, Henry	Whitty's	
,,	Powers, Jonn	Haines'	
,,	Polkinstone, John	Wallett's	
,,	Pogus, George	Wallett's	
,,	Poxton, William	Crowe's	
,,	Pritchard, William	Toole's	
,,	Prudom, John	Haines'	
,,	Pritting, Isaac	Wallett's	
,,	Probitt, William	Toole's	
,,	Purser, Isaac	Ross Lewin's	
,,	Pullen, Thomas	Whitty's	
,,	Pugh, William	Toole's	
,,	Purnell, William	Cassan's	
,,	Prime, John	Cassan's	
,,	Potters, Thomas	Wallett's	Killed 16th June, 1815
,,	Pinker, Thomas	Harrison's	Killed 18th June, 1815
,,	Luigly, Patrick	Cassan's	Killed 16th June, 1815
,,	Rawlings, William	Whitty's	Died 19th June, 1815
,,	Rawdon, George	Toole's	
,,	Rawlins, William	Crowe's	
,,	Restrick, David	Cassan's	
,,	Rectmond, Hugh	Whitty's	
,,	Reed, Joseph	Whitty's	
,,	Reed, Samuel	Whitty's	
,,	Reed, William	Harrison's	
,,	Romsay, William		Died 28th July, 1815
,,	Reedman, Thomas	Dillon's	
,,	Reynolds, John	Whitty's	
,,	Reynolds, James	Harrison's	
,,	Rea, James	Haines'	
,,	Reilly, John	Haines'	Died 4th July, 1815
,,	Reilly, Miles	Dillon's	
,,	Riddle, Joseph	Harrison's	
,,	Rodgers, William	Whitty's	

APPENDIX.

Rank.	Name.	Company.	Remarks.
Private	Rodgers, John	Haines'	
,,	Rodgers, Frederick	Harrison's	
,,	Roskelly, William	Toole's	
,,	Rooney, John	Haines'	
,,	Roberts, Charles	Harrison's	
,,	Roche, Michael	Dillon's	
,,	Rowley, James	Dillon's	
,,	Rodgerson, Robert	Wallett's	
,,	Rowen, Stephen	Toole's	
,,	Rowe, John	Cassan's	Died 6th July, 1815
,,	Rollison, George	Boyse's	Died 14th July, 1815
,,	Richards, John	Boyse's	
,,	Roecliffe, John	Crowe's	
,,	Reedken, Henry	Toole's	
,,	Reesden, Henry	Crowe's	
,,	Rutherforce, Joseph	Crowe's	
,,	Rafter, John	Crowe's	Killed 16th June, 1815
,,	Sanderson, George	Haines'	
,,	Sanders, Thomas	Wallett's	
,,	Sanders, William	Ross Lewin's	
,,	Saubrook, Benjamin	Ross Lewin's	
,,	Sadler, Samuel	Ross Lewin's	
,,	Safeguard, George	Ross Lewin's	
,,	Salsbury, John	Ross Lewin's	
,,	Savage, Richard	Toole's	
,,	Serjeant, John	Crowe's	Died 19th June, 1815
,,	Scott, William	Harrison's	
,,	Sennett, Moses	Wallett's	Died
,,	Schackleton, William	Toole's	Killed 16th June, 1815
,,	Sheer, Luke	Boyse's	
,,	Shephard, Nathaniel	Crowe's	
,,	Sherry, William	Boyse's	
,,	Sheridan, John	Dillon's	
,,	Shannon, Samuel	Harrison's	
,,	Simms, George	Haines'	
,,	Simmonds, John	Dillon's	Killed 16th June, 1815
,,	Skilling, William	Dillon's	Died 15th January, 1816
,,	Skalling, George	Wallett's	
,,	Slade, John (first)	Crowe's	Killed 18th June, 1815
,,	Slade, John (second)	Wallett's	
,,	Slade, Thomas	Crowe's	
,,	Sly, Thomas	Ross Lewin's	
,,	Sneyd, Thomas	Crowe's	
,,	Smith, James (first)	Haines'	Died 19th June, 1815
,,	Smith, James (second)	Boyse's	
,,	Smith, John (first)	Boyse's	
,,	Smith, John (second)	Harrison's	
,,	Smith, Thomas	Haines'	
,,	Smith, Daniel	Dillon's	
,,	Smith, William	Dillon's	
,,	Smith, Benjamin	Wallett's	Died 18th June, 1815
,,	Smith, Louis	Ross Lewin's	
,,	Smith, Vere	Toole's	
,,	Solomon, Robert	Harrison's	

APPENDIX.

Rank.	Name.	Company.	Remarks.
Private	Sommerton, John	Toole's	
,,	Southall, John	Cassan's	
,,	Stanley, Ralph	Haines'	
,,	Stanley, Thomas	Cassan's	
,,	Sternaway, Thomas	Crowe's	
,,	Stanfield, John	Crowe's	Died at Corfu
,,	Stephens, Isaac	Crowe's	Killed 18th June, 1815
,,	Stuke, Edward	Cassan's	
,,	Strong, William	Toole's	
,,	Stuart, James	Crowe's	
,,	Stuart, Thomas	Toole's	
,,	Sullivan, Patrick	Whitty's	
,,	Sullivan, John	Dillon's	
,,	Sullivan, James	Boyse's	
,,	Sutton, Joseph	Dillon's	
,,	Swain, James	Harrison's	
,,	Swain, Thomas	Harrison's	
,,	Sweeny, John	Toole's	
,,	Short, Samuel	Dillon's	
,,	Tatlock, Matthew	Crowe's	Died at Bristol
,,	Thomas, Joseph	Whitty's	
,,	Thomas, Robert	Haines'	
,,	Thomas, John	Harrison's	
,,	Thomas, William	Dillon's	
,,	Thomas, George	Dillon's	
,,	Thornton, William	Crowe's	
,,	Thornton, Patrick	Harrison's	
,,	Tiley, Jonathan	Wallett's	
,,	Toole, Patrick	Boyse's	
,,	Tomlinson, James	Boyse's	
,,	Trevain, Thomas	Boyse's	Died at Ostend
,,	Tomlinson, Frederick	Haines'	
,,	Townley, George	Toole's	
,,	Touks, William	Ross Lewin's	
,,	Tregilgns, John	Whitty's	
,,	Trewhela, Henry	Dillon's	
,,	Trescott, George	Crowe's	
,,	Tredwin, Henry	Boyse's	
,,	Travers, George	Boyse's	
,,	Trotter, John	Dillon's	
,,	Taylor, Peters	Wallett's	
,,	Upton, Thomas	Harrison's	
,,	Underwood, Benjamin	Toole's	
,,	Vennard, John	Toole's	
,,	Verinder, Benjamin	Wallett's	
,,	Vagus, Robert	Harrison's	
,,	Valt, Thomas	Harrison's	
,,	Vereker, Dennis	Haines'	
,,	Wales, Thomas	Harrison's	
,,	Ward, Daniel	Wallett's	
,,	Watley, William	Ross Lewin's	
,,	Walker, George	Cassan's	
,,	Waterhall, George	Crowe's	
,,	Webber, William	Cassan's	

APPENDIX.

Rank.	Name.	Company.	Remarks.
Private	Webber, John	Dillon's	
,,	Webber, George	Whitty's	
,,	Westwood, Thomas	Whitty's	
,,	White, Benjamin	Haines'	
,,	Whimpey, William	Toole's	
,,	Whicham, James	Boyse's	
,,	Whenton, George	Crowe's	
,,	Willets, Samuel	Toole's	Killed 18th June, 1815
,,	Wilkes, George	Toole's	
,,	Willis, William	Haines'	
,,	Williams, John	Haines'	
,,	Williams, Edward	Harrison's	
,,	Williams, Hugh	Ross Lewin's	
,,	Williams, Joseph	Cassan's	
,,	Williamson, Charles	Harrison's	
,,	Wilkinson, John	Wallett's	Died 19th June, 1815
,,	Winters, Patrick	Wallett's	
,,	Woods, Peter	Toole's	
,,	Woolley, John	Ross Lewin's	
,,	Worrail, Thomas	Harrison's	
,,	Wright, Charles	Boyse's	
,,	Wood, William	Crowe's	
,,	Wynne Peter	Ross Lewin's	Died 9th July, 1815
,,	Yardley, George	Cassan's	
,,	Young, Joseph	Haines'	
,,	Young, John	Whitty's	

BATTLE OF SALAMANCA.

(From the Casualty Returns, 32nd Regiment, 1812.)

KILLED IN ACTION.

23rd and 24th June.—Privates Robert Greenway, William Lacey, Andrew Harman, Michael Courtney, Edward James, James Lear, Robert Tate, William Paul, James Doherty.

22nd July.—Sergeant John Keyes; Privates Charles Matthews, Henry Collins, Thomas Armstrong, Samuel Reed, Benjamin Walsh, Edward Dunne, John Neagle, Thomas Phillips, Peter Henshaw, Robert Seggerson, Timothy Wilkins, John Peilley.

DIED OF WOUNDS.

June.—Corporal John Tibbs; Private James Mould.

From July to August.—Sergeant James Payne: Privates Edward Kite, John Weakly, Thomas Allen, Thomas Bickerton, Thomas Glover, John Hobbs, John Fogarty, Richard Hardcastle, Thomas Colesby, Stephen Tyther, Richard Owen, Samuel Reeves, John Courtney, Samuel Sheppard, Edward Morgan, James Cantling, George Browne, Moses Nettle, Thomas Higginson, Joseph Turner.

NOTES ON THE SERVICES OF THE 32ND REGIMENT IN THE DEFENCE OF LUCKNOW, 1857.*

LIST OF THE OFFICERS ENGAGED IN THE DEFENCE:

T. Inglis, colonel, brigadier
Lieutenant-Colonel Case - - - - - Killed
Major Lowe - - - - - - Wounded
Captain Steevens (or Stevens) - - - - Killed
Captain Mansfield - - - - - Killed
Captain Power - - - - - - Killed
Captain Bassano - - - - - - Wounded
Captain McCabe - - - - - - Killed
Lieutenant Lawrence
Lieutenant Edmondstoune, 2nd battalion - - Wounded
Lieutenant Webb - - - - - Killed
Lieutenant Foster - - - - - Wounded
Lieutenant Clery
Lieutenant Brown
Lieutenant Brackenbury - - - - - Killed
Lieutenant Harmar - - - - - - Wounded
Lieutenant Cook - - - - - - Wounded
Ensign Charlton - - - - - - Wounded
Ensign Studdy - - - - - - Killed
Paymaster Giddings
Quarter-Master Stribbling
Surgeon Scott, M.D.
Assistant-Surgeon Boyd

LADIES CONNECTED WITH THE 32ND REGIMENT IN LUCKNOW DURING THE SIEGE:

Mrs. Case and sister; Mrs. Steevens; Mrs. Giddings.

The officers and sixty men of the 32nd Regiment were instructed in gun-drill, as there were only a very few artillery in the garrison.

---

* The Editor is indebted to Major Shanks, R.M.L.I., for these interesting Notes.

June 30th.—A reconnaissance was made by Sir H. Lawrence, the troops comprising three hundred men of the 32nd regiment, being commanded by Lieutenant-Colonel Case; the advance guard was commanded by Captain Steevens, 32nd regiment. The enemy was found to be in overwhelming strength; our force met with heavy losses and was compelled to retire. Colonel Case and Captain Steevens were killed in this affair.

July 4th.—Five privates of the 32nd regiment went out and spiked a nine-pounder gun which the enemy had placed very near the gate of Inne's post; they also shot four of the rebels, who were taken completely by surprise while at their dinner.

July 5th.—On this day a private of the 32nd regiment was seen to kill five of the enemy with ten shots, while he was under a very severe musketry fire.

July 7th.—A sortie was made by fifty men of the 32nd regiment and twenty Sikhs, led by Captain Mansfield and Lieutenant Lawrence, of the 32nd regiment, and Ensign Studdy of the same corps; the object was to discover if the enemy were driving mines; it was perfectly successful, and some twenty of the enemy were killed. Our loss was one of the 32nd regiment, severely, and one slightly, wounded.

July 13th.—Ensign Charlton, of the 32nd Regiment, was dangerously wounded in the head while in the Church.

July 19th.—About 9.30 a.m. a large shot passed through a room in the Residency, in which the officers were at breakfast; Lieutenant Harmar, 32nd regiment, had a leg broken by the shot, but no one else was touched.

July 22nd.—(The twenty-third day of the siege). The 32nd regiment had now lost fifty-one men, not including officers, since the siege began.

August 3rd.—A soldier of the 32nd regiment was shot dead this morning in the centre room of the hospital, showing how little safety there was anywhere from the enemy's fire.

August 6th.—This morning a twenty-four-pounder shot carried off the arm of Ensign Studdy, just as he sat down to breakfast in the Residency.

August 7th.—A shell from one of the enemy's batteries burst close to the Residency this morning, and mortally wounded a colour-sergeant and an orderly-room-clerk of the 32nd regiment.

August 9th.—Ensign Studdy (wounded on the 6th) died this day.

August 10th.—Captain Power, 32nd regiment, (wounded early in the siege) died this day.

August 12th.—A sortie was made by twelve men of the 32nd regiment, under Lieutenant Clery, in order to see what the enemy was doing; but the guards of the trenches were so strong and well on the alert that our people had to retire without discovering anything.

August 20th.—Captain Lowe, 32nd regiment, had a very narrow escape to-day; an eight-inch shell burst close to him and slightly wounded him in the hand, while it carried off the arm of a soldier standing beside him.

August 21st.—A sortie was made by fifty men of the 32nd regiment, under Captain M'Cabe and Lieutenant Browne, of the 32nd regiment; they took the enemy by surprise, spiked two of their guns and held Johannes' house while the engineers made preparations for blowing it up. Two privates were wounded in this service, which was most successfully carried out.

August 22nd.—By this day (the fifty-fourth of the siege) the 32nd Regiment had lost one hundred and one men, besides several officers.

August 27th.—The property of the late Brigadier General Sir Henry Lawrence, K.C.B., were sold by auction to-day. Brandy fetched £16 a dozen; beer, £7 a dozen; sherry, £7 a dozen; hams, £7 10s. each; a bottle of honey, £4 10s.; small cakes of chocolate, £3 to £4 a dozen.

September 5th.—An eighteen-pounder shot to-day passed right through the whole length of the hospital, which was crowded with patients; it slightly wounded Ensign Charlton and a private of the 32nd who were lying there wounded, but touched no one else.

September 10th.—At the sale to-day of the effects of an officer recently killed, a single bottle of brandy fetched 34s.

September 12th.—Captain Mansfield, 32nd regiment, died on this day. Enormous prices offered in the garrison for all kinds of supplies—a small fowl was to-day purchased by a gentleman, for his sick wife, for £2; a bottle of Curaçoa fetched 32s.; sugar, 16s. a pound. The garrison has been without tobacco for six weeks now— since the 8th or 9th August—and had taken to smoking dried leaves of any kind.

September 19th.—A new flannel shirt to-day, at an auction, fetched £4; and five old ones brought in £11 4s. for the lot. A bottle of brandy, £2.

September 25th.—Siege (which had lasted eighty-seven days) was terminated this afternoon by the arrival of Sir J. Outram's force. That force left Cawnpore two thousand six hundred strong, but one-third of the number were killed or wounded on the way, and being so weakened could do nothing for the relief of the Lucknow garrison. The rebels, therefore, renewed the siege, which then lasted to the 22nd November, when the garrison was finally relieved by the army under the commander-in-chief.

"Captain M'Cabe, 32nd regiment, was killed at the head of his "men, while leading his fourth sortie."—*Extract from Brigadier Inglis' despatch.*

All the officers of the 32nd regiment were mentioned conspicuously in the despatches.

"I have the pleasure of bringing the splendid behaviour of the "soldiers of the 32nd Foot . . . . &c., to the notice of the "Government of India. The losses sustained by the 32nd show that "they know how to die in the cause of their countrymen. Their "conduct under the fire, the exposure, and the privations which they "had to undergo, has been throughout most admirable and praise-"worthy."—*Extract from Brigadier Inglis' despatch.*

NUMBER OF OFFICERS OF THE VARIOUS CORPS IN LUCKNOW DURING THE SIEGE,

Shewing the strength and losses in each case.

	Officers.	Killed.	Wounded and recovered.	Not wounded.	Total.
Artillery	9	5	3	1	9
Engineers	3	1	...	2	3
7th Light Cavalry	10	6	2	2	10
32nd Regiment	18	8	7	3	18
84th Regiment	2	...	1	1	2
13th Native Infantry	9	3	2	4	9
41st Native Infantry	10	2	3	5	10
48th Native Infantry	13	3	5	5	13
71st Native Infantry	10	3	2	5	10
Oudh Brigade	10	5	...	5	10
Oudh Irregulars	21	10	3	8	21
Civil Service	9	2	2	5	9
Uncovenanted Service	126	22	14	90	126
Totals	250	70	44	136	250

Percentage of officers present killed, 28·00 ; Ditto in 32nd Regt., 44·4
Percentage of officers present wounded, 17·6 ; Ditto in 32nd Regt., 38·8
Percentage of officers present not wounded, 54·4 ; Ditto in 32nd Regt., 17·0
Percentage of officers present killed or wounded, 45·6 ; Ditto in 32nd Regt., 83·3

EXTRACT

From a report in the *Standard* newspaper, of 25th September, 1891, of the "Lucknow Dinner."

Surgeon-General Lee, speaking on behalf of the old 78th, now the Seaforth Highlanders, confirmed the statement that the regiment marched to Lucknow with their pipes, and said that "Jessie Brown, "who in her fever declared that she heard them, was the wife of a "corporal in the 32nd Regiment."

APPENDIX.

EXPENSES OF A MARINE REGIMENT IN 1702.

(From Gillespie's History of the Marine Corps.)

	Per diem.
	£ s. d.
FIELD AND STAFF OFFICERS:	
Colonel, as Colonel	0 12 0
Lieutenant-Colonel, as Lieutenant-Colonel	0 7 0
Major, as Major	0 5 0
Chaplain	0 6 8
Adjutant	0 4 0
Chirurgeon	0 4 0
One Mate to ditto	0 2 6
	£2 5 2
ONE COMPANY:	
Captain	0 8 0
1st Lieutenant	0 4 0
2nd Lieutenant	0 3 0
2 Sergeants, each 1/6	0 3 0
3 Corporals, „ 1/-	0 3 0
59 Privates, „ 8d.	1 19 4
	£3 2 4

10 Companies, total cost per year ... ... £12,513 8s. 4d.

NOTE.—In the Marine Corps, 2nd Lieutenants took the place of Ensigns.

ESTABLISHMENT AND RATES OF PAY, 32ND REGIMENT, IN 1762.

	Per diem.		For 365 days.
	s. d.	£ s. d.	£ s. d.
FIELD AND STAFF OFFICERS:			
Colonel, as Colonel	12 0		
In lieu of his servant	2 0		
		0 14 0	
Lieutenant-Colonel, as Lieutenant-Colonel		0 7 0	
Major, as Major		0 5 0	
Chaplain		0 6 8	
Adjutant		0 4 0	
Quarter-Master	4 0		
In lieu of his servant	0 8		
		0 4 8	
Surgeon		0 4 0	
2 Mates, each 3/6		0 7 0	
		£2 12 4	£955 1 8

ESTABLISHMENT AND RATES OF PAY, 1762—*continued*.

	s.	d.	Per diem. £ s. d.	For 365 days. £ s. d.
ONE COMPANY:				
Captain	8	0		
In lieu of his servant	2	0		
			0 10 0	
2 Lieutenants, each 4/-	8	0		
In lieu of their servants	1	4		
			0 9 4	
Ensign	3	0		
In lieu of his servant	0	8		
			0 3 8	
4 Sergeants, each 1/6			0 6 0	
4 Corporals, ,, 1/-			0 4 0	
2 Drummers, ,, 1/-			0 2 0	
100 Private men ,, 8d.			3 6 8	
			5 1 8	1,855 8 4
Allowance to the { Widows			0 1 4	
Colonel			0 1 2	
Captain			0 1 0	
Agent			0 0 6	
			5 5 8	1,928 8 4
7 Companies more, of the same numbers and rates as the company above mentioned			36 19 8	13,498 18 4
ONE COMPANY OF GRENADIERS:	s.	d.	£ s. d.	£ s. d.
Captain	8	0		
In lieu of his servant	2	0		
			0 10 0	
3 Lieutenants, each 4/-	12	0		
In lieu of their servants	2	0		
			0 14 0	
4 Sergeants, each 1/6			0 6 0	
4 Corporals, ,, 1/-			0 4 0	
2 Drummers, ,, 1/-			0 2 0	
2 Fifers, ,, 1/-			0 2 0	
100 Private men, ,, 8d.			3 6 8	
			5 4 8	1,910 3 4
Allowance to the widows, colonel, captains, and agent, as before			0 4 0	73 0 0
Total for the Regiment			£50 6 4	£18,365 11 8

THE 32ND REGIMENT CONSISTED OF 10 COMPANIES IN 1775.

1 Colonel and Captain	1 Chaplain	30 Sergeants
1 Lieut.-Col. and Captain	1 Adjutant	30 Corporals
1 Major and Captain	1 Quarter-Master	20 Drummers
7 Captains more.	1 Surgeon	2 Fifers
12 Lieutenants	1 Mate	560 Private men
8 Ensigns		

Total ... . 677.

ROLLS OF OFFICERS

OF

THE 32ND REGIMENT,

From the Monthly Army Lists of

1708, 1740, 1748, 1755, 1760, 1783, 1790, 1801, 1807, 1812,
1815, 1822, 1838, 1850, 1860, 1870 ;

And of the 1st, 2nd, and 3rd Battalions of the

DUKE OF CORNWALL'S LIGHT INFANTRY,

1881 AND 1882.

APPENDIX. 299

FROM PRESENT STATE, 1708.

COLONEL BORR'S REGIMENT.

Jacob Borr, Esquire	Colonel
R. Cobham, Esquire	Lieut.-Colonel
Francis Foulks, Esquire	Major

ARMY LIST, 1740.

Colonel	Simon Descury	1st Lieutenant	Peter Parr
Lieut.-Colonel	Bernard Dennet	,,	Hugh Farquhar
Major	Sam. Stone	,,	John Munro
Captain	Mel. Guy Dickens	,,	Chas. Douglas
,,	Will. Redsdale	,,	John Roper
,,	Christ Adams	,,	Thos. Barlow
,,	John Graydon	2nd Lieutenant	John Kendall
,,	Hugh Jones	,,	Chas. Bailie
,,	Geo. Gordon	,,	Sir George Suttie
,,	John Butler	,,	Peter Desbusay
Capt. Lieut.	Peter Margarett	,,	William Douglass
1st Lieutenant	Dawney Sutton	,,	James Weyms
,,	William Bryans	,,	Andrew Agnew
,,	Knowles Kensey	,,	John Macdonald
,,	Robert Graydon	,,	Henry Descury

REGISTER, 1748.

32ND REGIMENT.

Colonel (vacant)		Major	Sir George Suttie
Lieut.-Colonel	Christ. Legard	Agent	Mr. Adair

ARMY LIST, 1755.

Colonel	Francis Leighton	Lieutenant	Hugh Powell
Lieut.-Colonel	Richmond Webb	,,	Robert Farquhar
Major	W. Taylor	,,	John Wilkins
Captain	W. McDougal	,,	John Kelsey
,,	R. Murray	Ensign	Isaac Barre
,,	Ed. Fuller	,,	Chas. Ross
,,	Jas. Seton	,,	Mont. Agnew
,,	Archibald McNab	,,	Humphrey Hooper
,,	John Meslin	,,	John Bruce
,,	Henry Descury	,,	Lawrence Norcop
Capt. Lieut.	John Lindesay	,,	Bethel Robinson
Lieutenant	Robert Rogers	,,	Reuben J. Green
,,	Geo. T. Ridsdale	,,	J. Harcourt Wodehouse
,,	Patrick Blake	Chaplain	David Tanqueray
,,	James Stuart	Adjutant	John Wilkins
,,	Geo. Farquhar	Qr.-Mr.	John Lindesay
,,	Rawlins Hillman	Surgeon	Peter Mackenzie

300   APPENDIX.

ARMY LIST, 1760.

Colonel	-	Francis Leighton	Lieutenant	-	Andrew Armstrong
Lieut.-Col.	-	Will. McDowall	,,	-	Will. Southwell
Major	-	Jas. Seton	,,	-	Will. Sherren
Captain	-	Arch. McNab	,,	-	Lewis Ray
,,	-	J. Meslin	,,	-	Geo. Barclay
,,	-	Henry Descury	,,	-	Burnet Minisie
,,	-	John Quinchant	,,	-	George Swiney
,,	-	Hans Hamilton	,,	-	John Atkinson
,,	-	Chas. Ross	Ensign	-	Will. Ogilvie
,,	-	J. Kelsee	,,	-	Edmund Vero
Capt. Lieut.	-	G. Farquhar	,,	-	Henry Cordwell
Lieutenant	-	R. Farquhar	,,	-	John Drake
,,	-	Isaac Barre	,,	-	W. Duffey Cane
,,	-	J. Nugent	,,	-	F. Bridges-Schaw
,,	-	Humphrey Hopper	,,	-	Sir C. Bond, Bart.
,,	-	Milo Bagot	,,	-	Alex. Burrowes Irwin
,,	-	Anthony Pujolas	Chaplain	-	David Tanqueray
,.	-	Will. Mackay	Qr.-Mr.	-	Humphrey Hopper
,,	-	Will. Rickman	Surgeon	-	Peter Mackenzie
,,	-	Lawrence Norcop			

ARMY LIST, 1783.

Colonel	-	Ralph, Earl of Ross	Lieutenant	-	F. Crofton
Lieut.-Colonel	-	J. Fletcher Campbell	,,	-	J. McCartney
Major	-	Edmund Strachan	,,	-	J. Grant Butler
Captain	-	Stuart McEvan	,,	-	Nicholas Colthurst
,,	-	Edward Edwards	,,	-	Charles Adams
,,	-	Fred. Booth	,,	-	Anthony Waters
,,	-	Richard Northey	,,	-	Jas. O'Donnell
,,	-	Robert Riddell	,,	-	S. Madden West
,,	-	Hon. Vesey Knox	,,	-	Anth. Foster Tisdal
,,	-	George Vesey	,,	-	Rich. Roberts
Capt. Lieut.	-	Edward Williams	,,	-	Thos. Wallis
Lieutenant	-	Edward Brookes	Ensign	-	Will. Russell
,,	-	Thos. Hifferman	,,	-	Jas. Mansergh
,,	-	J. Chilton L. Carter	,,	-	Edw. Hoare Reeves
,,	-	Thos. Gape	,.	-	W. Campbell Healtey
,,	-	Jenkin Lewis	,,	-	Henry McMahon
,,	-	Osborne Wilson	,,	-	Foster Scott
,,	-	Edmund Kelly	,,	-	Ralph Smith
,,	-	Thos. Ormsby	Chaplain	-	Richard Freeman
,,	-	Will. Butler	Adjutant	-	Edward Brookes
,,	-	Robert Knox	Qr.-Mr.	-	J. Cuthbert
,,	-	Anthony Lane	Surgeon	-	W. Kennedy

APPENDIX. 301

ARMY LIST, 1790.

Colonel	-	Ralph, Earl of Ross	Lieutenant	-	C. Maddison
Lieut.-Colonel	-	J. Fletcher Campbell	,,	-	J. Boland
Major	-	Edward Edwards	,,	-	J. White
Captain	-	Fred. Booth	,,	-	R. G. Chitter
,,	-	E. Williams	,,	-	J. Hicks
,,	-	R. Northey	Ensign	-	E. Baynes
,,	-	R. Riddell	,,	-	A. D. Robertson
,,	-	Hon. Vesey Knox	,,	-	J. Buchannan
,,	-	Anth. Lane	,,	-	R. Shaw
,,	-	J. Macartney	,,	-	E. E. Colman
Capt.-Lieut.	-	J. Chilton L. Carter	,,	-	W. L. Wooldridge
Lieutenant	-	E. Kelly	,,	-	G. Godfrey
,,	-	Thos. Wallis	,,	-	Thomas Lord Blayney
,,	-	F. Scott	Chaplain	-	I. Purcell
,,	-	J. Mansergh	Adjutant	-	J. C. L. Carter
,,	-	B. Bunbury	Qr.-Mr.	-	A. Wilson
,,	-	A. Graham	Surgeon	-	T. Taylor

ARMY LIST, 1801.

Colonel	-	Ralph, Earl of Ross	Lieutenant	-	Alex. Chancellone
Lieut.-Col.	-	Richard Northey	,,	-	John Trotter
,,	-	J. A. Stuart	,,	-	Will. Hopkins
Major	-	W. Wentworth Maxwell	,,	-	Peter McDougal
,,	-	Samuel Venables Hinde	,,	-	J. Haverfield
Captain	-	W. Augustus Johnson	,,	-	Ed. Burroughs
,,	-	J. Wood	Ensign	-	Will. Northey
,,	-	J. Hicks	,,	-	E. Bourne
,,	-	J. White	,,	-	-- Power
,,	-	G. Evans	,,	-	Will. O'Dogherty
,,	-	J. Bennet	,,	-	C. H. Strode
,,	-	J. Priestley	,,	-	Rowland Dunscombe
,,	-	C. Hames	,,	-	W. C. Bruce
,,	-	J. Crawley	,,	-	J. Sontar
,,	-	J. Bird	,,	-	J. Crowe
Capt.-Lieut.		Robert Coote	,,	-	J. Wood
Lieutenant	-	— Sherston	,,		H. Gore
,,	-	J. Rowland	Paymaster	-	A. Gore
,,	-	W. Harrison	Adjutant	-	— Wright
,,	-	J. Short	Qr.-Mr.	-	J. O'Brien
,,	-	Henry Ross-Lewin	Assist.-Surg.	-	Jas. Dalzel

ARMY LIST, 1807.

Lieut.-Col.	-	R. N. Hopkins
,,	-	S. V. Hinde
,,	-	Manley Power
Major	-	W. A. Johnson
,,	-	John Wood
,,	-	John Hicks
,,	-	John Bennet
Captain	-	Robert Coote
,,	-	C. Hames
,,	-	J. Rowland
,,	-	H.W. Sherdon (Sherston?)
,,	-	G. W. Barr
,,	-	N. B. Tucker
,,	-	Jonathan Short
,,	-	Henry Ross-Lewin
,,	-	H. Richardson
,,	-	J. Gerrard
,,	-	W. H. Toole
,,	-	Wm. Gibson
,,	-	W. N. Hopkins
,,	-	D. Gregory
,,	-	Dennis Hogan
,,	-	John Crowe
,,	-	Joseph Wood
,,	-	Patk. McDougal
,,	-	W. O. Dogherty
,,	-	Dennis O'Kelly
Lieutenant		Arthur Molloy
,,	-	Wm. Grundy (Adjutant)
,,	-	Thos. Jones
,,	-	G. Mauritzy
,,	-	W. Trueman
,,	-	A. Grayes
,,	-	J. W. Sweetman
,,	-	J. C. Dennis
,,	-	E. Whitty
Lieutenant	-	C. O'Dogherty
,,	-	C. Coleridge
,,	-	G. W. Paty (Party?)
,,	-	R. Oriel Singer
,,	-	A. R. Blake (Adjutant)
,,	-	G. Eason
,,	-	M. Kilkelly
,,	-	A. Disney
,,	-	R. Dillon
,,	-	Wm. Hinde
,,	-	Thos. Rose
,,	-	Chas. Wallet
,,	-	W. H. Thornton
,,	-	R. Robinson
,,	-	H. W. Brooks
,,	-	H. Harrison
Ensign	-	W. J. Rea
,,	-	T. O'Neale
,,	-	Geo. Barr
,,	-	Daniel Kirk
,,	-	M. W. Meighan
,,	-	S. H. Lawrence
,,	-	W. French
,,	-	Theo. Butler
,,	-	S. Whear
,,	-	C. Seymour
,,	-	Thos. Ross-Lewin
,,	-	John Munton
,,	-	John Sinclair
Qr.-Mr.	-	J. O'Brien
,,	-	— Stephens
Surgeon	-	Wm. Buchanan
,,	-	George Bell
Asst.-Surg.	-	Dillon Jones
,,	-	David Lynn
,,	-	W. Waters

APPENDIX. 303

ARMY LIST, 1812.

Lieut.-Col.		S. V. Hinde	Lieutenant	-	J. H. K. Chapman
,,	-	Manley Power	,,	-	Theo. Butler
,,	-	W. A. Johnson	,,	-	John Boase
Major	-	John Wood	,,	-	Chas. Seymour
,,	-	John Hicks	,,	-	Thos. Ross-Lewin
,,	-	John Bennet	,,	-	John Munton
,,	-	H. Richardson	,,	-	H. Butterworth
Captain	-	Robert Coote	,,	-	J. S. McCulloch
,,	-	C. Hames	,,	-	J. R. Colthurst
,,	-	H.W. Sherdon (Sherston?)	,,	-	M. Dennis
,,	-	G. W. Barr	,,	-	Bayle Hill
,,	-	Henry Ross-Lewin	,,	-	Jas. Jarvey
,,	-	W. H. Toole	,,	-	N. Sherlock
,,	-	Wm. Gibson	,,	-	J. Robinson
,,	-	John Crowe	,,	-	Geo. Brock
,,	-	P. McDougal	,,	-	Thos. Hillas
,,	-	G. Purcell	,,	-	R. T. Belcher
,,	-	Jaques Boyse	,,	-	J. Fitzgerald
,,	-	G. W. Paty (Party?)	,,	-	T. H. Turquhand
,,	-	Thos. Jones	Ensign	-	E. Stephens
,,	-	Thos. Cassan	,,	-	Henry Quill
,,	-	G. Mauritzy	,,	-	H. Newton
,,	-	Fra. Savage	,,	-	A. Wood
,,	-	M. O'c. Caulfield	,,	-	E. F. Roberts
,,	-	Ed. Whitty	,,	-	T. Horan
,,	-	W. Trueman	,,	-	R. U. Fitzgerald
,,	-	Robt. Dillon	,,	-	Wm. Peyton
Lieutenant		A. Grayes	,,	-	T. Lawder
,,	-	J. C. Dennis	,,	-	J. Jagoe
,,	-	George Eason	,,	-	F. Lloyd
,,	-	Micl. Kilkelly	,,	-	G. Sayer
,,	-	Wm. Hinde	,,	-	W. Blood
,,	-	Thos. Rose	,,	-	Wm. Crawley
,,	-	Chas Wallet	Paymaster	-	Thos. Hart
,,	-	W. H. Thornton	,,		Jacob Dudden
,,	-	R. Robinson	Quarter-Master		W. Stephens
,,	-	H. W. Brooks	,,	-	E. Charles
,,	-	H. Harrison (Adjutant)	Surgeon	-	W. Buchanan
,,	-	T. O'Neale	,,	-	George Bell
,,	-	D. Davies (Adjutant)	Assist.-Surgeon		D. Jones
,,	-	Geo. Barr	,,	-	R. Sandford
,,	-	Daniel Kirk	,,	-	R. Lawder
,,	-	M. M. Meighan	,,	-	T. Howell
,,	-	S. H. Lawrence			

ARMY LIST, 1815.

Colonel	- A. Campbell (General)	Lieutenant	-	R. T. Belcher
Lt.-Col.	- J. Maitland	,,	-	J. Fitzgerald
Major	- John Hicks (Bt. Lt.-Col.)	,,	-	T. H. Horan
,,	- F. Calvert (Bt. Lt.-Col.)	,,	-	E. Stephens
Captain	- C. Hames (Bt. Major)	,,	-	H. Quill
,,	- H. Ross-Lewin (Bt. Major)	,,	-	J. Jagoe
,,	- W. H. Toole (Bt. Major)	,,	-	G. Small
,,	- J. Crowe	,,	-	B. R. O'Connor
,,	- R. Dillon	,,	-	H. Newton
,,	- H. Harrison	,,	-	J. Peyton
,,	- C. Wallett	,,	-	J. Lucas
,.	- S. Cane	,,	-	J. M'Couchy
,,	- H. W. Brookes	,,	-	H. Metcalfe
,,	- D. Davies	Ensign	-	J. Birtwhistle
,,	- G. Barr	,,	-	A. Stewart
Lieutenant M. W. Meighan		,,	-	G. Brown
,,	- S. H. Lawrence	,,	-	W. Bennett
,,	- Theo. Butler	,,	-	C. Dallas
,,	- John Boase	,,	-	S. Mackay
,,	- T. Ross-Lewin	,,	-	F. Short
,,	- H. Butterworth	,,	-	J. Morris
,,	- J. S. M'Culloch	Paymaster	-	T. Hart
,,	- J. R. Colthurst	Adjutant	-	S. H. Lawrence (Lieut.)
,,	- Boyle Hill	Qr.-Mr.	-	W. Stephens
,,	- J. Jarvey	Surgeon	-	W. Buchanan
,,	- J. Robinson	Assist.-Surg.		R. Lawder
,,	- G. Brock	,,	-	H. M'Clintock

Agents—Messrs. Hopkinson and Son.

The regiment was then styled "The Cornwall," but the Militia Regiment of the county was at that time called "The Royal Cornwall."

Lieutenant Brock was recruiting at Wells at this time, the only two recruiting stations in Cornwall—Bodmin and Redruth—being occupied by an officer of the 41st and 48th Regiments respectively.

ARMY LIST, 1822.

Colonel	- Alex. Campbell	Lieutenant	-	Hector W. B. Munro
Lieut.-Col.	- Hon. J. Maitland	,,	-	J. Birtwhistle
Major	- J. Hicks	,,		Alex. Stuart
,,	- R. Dillon	,,	-	George Moore
Captain	- Henry Ross-Lewin	,,	-	Geo. Browne
,,	- J. Crowe	,,	-	Ed. Shervell
,,	- Hugh Harrison	Ensign	-	Stuart Mackay
,,	- D. Davies	,,	-	J. G. Campbell
,,	- G. Elliot	,,	-	J. Palk
,,	- J. William	,,	-	Otto Ives
,,	- R. Tresillian Belcher	,,	-	Thos. Calder
,,	- Hon. R. P. Arden	,,	-	A. Gray Slacke
,,	- Michael W. Meighan	,,	-	Manley Power
Lieutenant	- Sam. Hill Lawrence	Paymaster	-	H. G. Eagar
,,	- Thos. Ross-Lewin	Adjutant	-	George Moore
,,	- Jas. Robert Colthurst	Qr.-Mr.	-	W. Pepperel
,,	- Jas. Robinson	Surgeon	-	Thomas Bulkeley
,,	- J. H. Wingfield	Assist.-Surgeon		Geo. Griffin
,,	- H. Stephens Olivier			

APPENDIX. 305

OFFICERS OF THE 32ND REGIMENT, SEPTEMBER, 1838.

Colonel	Sir R. Macfarlane, K.C.B. & G.C.H. (Gen.)	26th Sept.,	1837
Lieut.-Colonel	Hon. J. Maitland (Colonel)	26th March,	1818
Major	T. H. Wingfield	3rd June,	1828
,,	John Palk (Depôt)	16th April,	1829
Captain	Henry Reed (Major)	25th July,	1821
,,	J. Birtwhistle (Major)	13th May,	1824
,,	J. Swinburn (Major, Depôt)	15th Aug.,	1810
,,	F. Markham	16th April,	1829
,,	G. Browne (Major)	10th Feb.,	1832
,,	Thomas Calder	16th Feb.,	1833
,,	John Thomas Hill (Depôt)	13th Feb.,	1835
,,	H. V. Brooke	22nd May,	
,,	J. H. Evelegh	20th Jan.,	1832
,,	Robert Bradfute	27th March,	1828
Lieutenant	Thomas White	25th Aug.,	1824
,,	Alexander Gardner	20th July,	1815
,,	F. J. Griffin	12th June,	1828
,,	George Oke (Depôt Paymaster)	26th June,	1828
,,	E. O. Broadley	29th Sept.,	1829
,,	Cuthbert A. Baines (Depôt)	8th Oct.,	1830
,,	John Dillon (Depôt)	10th Feb.,	1832
,,	John Grogan	20th April,	
,,	R. Campbell (Depôt)	2nd Aug.,	1833
,,	S. B. Hayes	13th Feb.,	1835
,,	Thomas Forsyth (Depôt)	22nd May,	
,,	William Case	9th Feb.,	1838
,,	T. D. Kelly (Adjutant)	10th Feb.,	1838
Ensign	J. Ernle Money	18th April,	1833
,,	J. E. W. Inglis	2nd August,	
,,	Willam Dillon	13th Feb.,	1835
,,	S. A. Dickson	22nd May,	
,,	Rhys Jones	2nd Sept.,	1836
,,	Thomas Robins (Depôt)	7th Oct.,	
,,	E. W. D. Lowe (Depôt)	20th May,	1837
,,	George Samuel Moore	9th Feb.,	1838
Paymaster	G. Moore	19th Oct.,	1826
,,	,. (Lieutenant)	6th Dec.,	1813
Adjutant	Thomas Daniel Kelly (Lieutenant)	12th April,	1833
Quarter-Master	Thomas Healey	29th Nov.,	1827
Surgeon	W. Bampfield	21st Jan.,	1813
Assist. Surgeon	Duncan M'Gregor	4th Jan.,	1833
,,	Alexander M'Grigor	31st May,	

x

OFFICERS OF THE 32ND REGIMENT, JANUARY, 1850.

Rank	Name	Date	Year
Colonel	Sir John Buchan, K.C.B.	12th June,	1843
Lieut.-Colonel	F Markham, C.B.	22nd July,	1842
,,	Hen. V. Brooke, C.B	13th Sept.,	1848
Major	J. E. Wilmot Inglis	23rd Feb.,	1848
,,	W. Case	13th Sept.,	1848
Captain	Jas. D. Carmichael Smyth	18th April,	1845
,,	E. W. D. Lowe	23rd April,	1845
,,	J. P. Pigott (Depôt)	19th Dec.,	1845
,,	A. L. Balfour (Instr. of Musketry)	31st May,	1839
,,	Cha. Tho. King	25th Feb.,	1848
,,	Fred. Yard	25th Feb.,	1848
,,	Wm. Bell	2nd July,	1841
,,	G. S. Moore	24th May,	1848
,,	H. W. Hough	10th April,	1846
,,	A. G. Brine	13th Sept.,	1848
Lieutenant	T. Maunsell	23rd May,	1845
,,	H. J. Davies	13th Feb.,	1846
,,	Geo. Jeffrey	18th June,	1841
,,	Rob. S. Colls	24th April,	1843
,,	Wm. Cumming	3rd May,	1844
,,	Jas. H. Wemyss	3rd April,	1846
,,	John Moore	3rd April,	1846
,,	Wm. Airde Birtwhistle	3rd April,	1846
,,	J. Wm. Boissier	3rd April,	1846
,,	Chas. Clapcott	12th June,	1846
,,	R. E. L. H. Williams	23rd Sept.,	1847
,,	W. Patterson	14th April,	1846
,,	Hen. D. O'Callaghan	10th Dec.,	1847
,,	W. Garforth (Adjutant)	24th Feb.,	1848
,,	B. Van Straubenzee	25th Feb.,	1848
,,	Wm. Power	25th Feb.,	1848
,,	A. Bassano	24th May,	1848
,,	Wm. Rudman	11th Feb.,	1848
,,	H. Wm. Sibley	9th Feb.,	1848
,,	J. Birtwhistle	3rd Sept.,	1849
,,	Wm. Harris	13th August,	1847
,,	B. McCabe	11th April,	1849
,,	S. H. Lawrence	22nd Feb.,	1860
Ensign	W. L. Ingles	21st Jan.,	1848
,,	John Hedley	25th Feb.,	1848
,,	H. K. Drury	26th Feb.,	1848
,,	W. J. Anderson	13th August,	1848
,,	J. A. Shortt	20th Oct.,	1848
,,	P. J. Dunbar	8th Dec.,	1848
,,	A. D. Kirkwood	10th April,	1849
,,	Edm. de L. Joly	30th March,	1850
Paymaster	Geo. Moore	19th Oct.,	1826
Adjutant	Wm. Garforth (Lieutenant)	3rd April,	1846
Qr.-Master	J. Giddings	13th Sept.,	1848
Surgeon	C. Scott, M.D.	9th May,	1845
Asst. Surgeon	Ed. Moorhead, M.D.	2nd August,	1842
,,	Alex. P. Cahill, M.D.	3rd April,	1846
,,	J. Dunlop, M.D.	3rd April,	1846

APPENDIX. 307

OFFICERS OF THE 32ND REGIMENT, JANUARY, 1860.

Rank	Name	Date
Colonel	Sir Willoughby Cotton, G.C.B. & K.C.H.	17th April, 1854
Lieut.-Colonel	J. D. Carmichael, C.B.	26th Nov., 1857
Major	Wm. Bell	23rd March, 1858
,,	,, (Brevet Lieutenant-Colonel)	16th Jan., 1859
Captain	R. S. Colls	20th Feb., 1855
,,	A. Bassano	15th Oct., 1856
,,	William Rudmun	15th May, 1857
,,	H. Priestley	3rd April, 1857
,,	John Birtwhistle	28th June, 1857
,,	W. J. Anderson	11th Aug., 1857
,,	Charles R. Ricketts	14th Sept., 1857
,,	John Edmondstoune	2nd Oct., 1857
,,	Charles M. Foster	26th Nov., 1857
,,	Edward Harmar	23rd March, 1858
,,	R. H. Magenis	25th Feb., 1855
,,	Edward A. T. Cunynghame	11th March, 1859
Lieutenant	H. E. Bennett	29th April, 1856
,,	H. S. Stabb (Adjutant)	1st Aug., 1856
,,	James Strachan	1st July, 1857
,,	Charles Edward Lane-Bluett	5th Feb., 1858
,,	Edmund Lakin	5th Feb., 1858
,,	Alexander J. Bagley	8th Jan., 1858
,,	John Garforth	6th Feb., 1858
,,	H. M. Gilby	9th Nov., 1855
,,	J. T. Gray	30th April, 1858
,,	A. R. W. Thistlethwayte	26th Oct., 1855
,,	George Walker	27th Nov., 1857
,,	S. B. Noble	23rd March, 1858
,,	Timothy Morris	9th Aug., 1858
,,	Charles G. Stanley	26th Sept., 1858
,,	C. F. Clery	3rd June, 1859
Ensign	A. Bishop	12th Feb., 1858
,,	William T. Goad	13th Feb., 1858
,,	Charles E. Le M. Cherry	23rd March, 1858
,,	W. P. Walshe	31st March, 1858
,,	H. R. Hardinge	14th May, 1858
,,	F. A. Horridge	2nd July, 1858
,,	David Bond	7th Sept., 1858
,,	F. N. Golding	29th Oct., 1858
,,	Charles H. Trueman	29th Oct., 1858
,,	H. W. M. Cathcart	3rd June, 1859
Paymaster	John Giddings	28th Nov., 1858
Adjutant	H. S. Stabb (Lieutenant)	9th Aug., 1858
Instr. of Mus.	Edmund Lakin (Lieutenant)	27th Aug., 1859
Quarter-Master	F. Stribling	28th Nov., 1856
Surgeon	William Boyd	27th Sept., 1858
Assist. Surgeon	W. H. Harris	10th March, 1855
,,	W. Bradshaw (V.C.)	15th Aug., 1854

OFFICERS OF THE 32ND REGIMENT, JANUARY, 1870.

Rank	Name	Date	Year
Colonel	Lord Frederick Paulet, C.B.	3rd Aug,	1868
Lieut.-Colonel	Hon. B. M. Ward	12th June,	1869
Major	Alfred Bassano	16th March,	1868
,,	Hon. R. H. de Montmorency	25th Sept.,	1869
Captain	W. J. Anderson	11th Aug.,	1857
,,	John Edmondstoune	2nd Oct.,	1857
,,	,, (Brevet Major)	24th March,	1858
,,	,, (Lieut.-Colonel)	18th March,	1869
,,	H. S. Stabb	5th Nov.,	1861
,,	C. F. Clery	16th Jan.,	1866
,,	G. C. Swiney	15 May,	1865
,,	Charles Le M. Cherry	16th Oct.,	1866
,,	John George Stopford	2nd Oct.,	1866
,,	R. N. C. Foll	23rd June,	1865
,,	H. R. Hardinge	22nd Feb.,	1868
,,	David Bond	16th Sept.,	1868
,,	Edmund Lakin	12th June,	1869
,,	Charles H. Trueman	25th Sept.,	1869
Lieutenant	W. J. Alexander	16th Jan.,	1866
,,	A. E. Havelock	18th April,	1866
,,	J. F. Ballard	17th April,	1866
,,	Robert Phillips	16th Oct.,	1866
,,	A. C. Tawke	3rd April,	1867
,,	W. H. Iremonger	21st Aug.,	1867
,,	J. J. Glascott (Adjutant)	22nd Feb.,	1868
,,	F. A. Garden	21st March,	1868
,,	Chas. F. A. Turnbull	22nd July,	1868
,,	L. F. Knollys	2nd Sept.,	1868
,,	Albert Clarke	16th Sept.,	1868
,,	William F. D. Cochrane	2nd Dec.,	1868
,,	Chas. F. N. Le Quesne	12th June,	1869
,,	A. W. Hammans	25th Sept.,	1869
,,	L. B. Beaumont	20th Oct.,	1869
Ensign	F. Trevelyan	21st August,	1867
,,	A. J. M. Sillery	22nd Feb.,	1868
,,	L. E. C. Inglefield	21st March,	1868
,,	Ed. G. C. Cregoe	16th Sept.,	1868
,,	C. R. Glyn	28th Oct.,	1868
,,	A. S. Woods	2nd Dec.,	1868
,,	C. B. Down	20th Oct.,	1869
,,	E. M. Glegg	30th Oct.,	1869
Paymaster	John Mahony	5th March,	1867
Adjutant	J. J. Glascott (Lieutenant)	2nd Dec.,	1868
Quarter-master	Ed. Vaughan	3rd April,	1867
Surgeon	R. C. Lofthouse, M.D.	9th March,	1867
Assist.-Surgeon	A. Sanderson	12th Jan.,	1859

APPENDIX. 309

OFFICERS OF DUKE OF CORNWALL'S LIGHT INFANTRY, JANUARY, 1882.

Colonel (1st Batt.)		Gen. Sir Wm. Jones, K.C.B.	2nd Jan.,	1871
,, (2nd Batt.)		Gen. Charles Stuart	20th June,	1870

Commanding 32nd Regimental District:

Lieut.-Col.		A. F. Warren, C.B.	4th June,	1881
,,		,, (Colonel)	1st Oct.,	1877

FIRST AND SECOND BATTALIONS.

Lieut.-Col.	1	Hen. Sparke Stabb	29th June,	1881
,,	2	Wm. S. Richardson	1st July,	1881
,,		,, ,,	1st May,	1880
,,	1	Geo. Clayton Swiney	1st July,	1881
,,	2	Thomas John	26th July,	1881
Major		C. E. Le M. Cherry	29th June,	1881
,,		,, ,,	30th Jan.,	1880
,,	1	John G. B. Stopford	29th June,	1881
,,		,, ,,	1st Jan.,	1880
,,	1	David Bond	1st July,	1881
,,	2	Frank Grieve	1st July,	1881
,,	2	John J. F. Grant	1st July,	1881
,,	2	Fra. Henry A. Disney-Roebuck	1st July,	1881
,,	1	Wm. Jas. Alexander	1st July,	1881
,,	2	Jas. Fitz E. Forster	30th Nov.,	1881
,,		,, ,,	1st July,	1881
Captain	2	John Maxwell Low	28th March,	1874
,,	2	H. Horatio Newman	5th June,	1875
,,	2	William Farwell	21st July,	1875
,,		H. E. C. Kitchener (P.S.C., M.C.)	13th Nov.,	1875
,,	1	John Fane Ballard	14th June,	1876
,,	2	W. Barrington Browne	1st July,	1876
,,		Hen. T. W. Allatt (P.S.C., M.C.)	26th July,	1876
,,	1	Robert Phillipps	31st Jan.,	1877
,,	2	John Reeves	26th Sept.,	1877
,,		Art. Christian Tawke	29th Jan.,	1879
,,	1	Fra. Wm. S. Grant	13th Sept.,	1879
,,		,, ,,	26th March,	1873
,,	1	Chas. F. A. Turnbull (Staff)	26th May,	1880
,,	1	Albert Clarke	26th May,	1880
,,	1	W. F. D. Cockrane	14th June,	1881
,,	1	Chas. F. N. Le Quesne	14th June,	1881
,,	1	Arthur Wm. Hammans	29th June,	1881

310 APPENDIX.

List of Officers for 1882—(continued).

Rank		Name	Date	Year
Lieutenant	1	L. B. Beaumont (Instr. of Musketry)	20th Oct.,	1869
,,	1	Ernest H. Studdy	13th Nov.,	1872
,,		,, ,,	10th Jan.,	1872
,,	1	Fredk. Geo. Vigor	24th Sept.,	1873
,,		,, ,,	11th Sept.,	1873
,,	2	H. P. Carden (Instr. of Musketry)	13th June,	1874
,,		Arthur H. Dumaresq	19th June,	1874
,,		Chas. Ernest Heath	9th August,	1874
,,	2	Keith H. St. G. Young	4th Dec.,	1874
,,	2	John H. Verschoyle	13th June,	1875
,,	2	J. Montagu R. Eden	27th June,	1875
,,	2	H. Westenra Carden	28th August,	1875
,,		,, ,,	21st Sept.,	1874
,,	2	Geo. Ashby Ashby (Adjutant)	20th Nov.,	1875
,,	2	Wolstan Francis	5th Jan.,	1876
,,		,, ,,	20th Nov.,	1875
,,		G. R. MacMullen (prob.)	11th Sept.,	1876
,,	2	Edmund J. Hollway	11th Sept.,	1876
,,	2	Fredk. Wm. Steele	11th Nov.,	1876
,,	2	Hewlett C. Perkins	29th Nov.,	1876
,,	2	John Alex. W. Falls	29th Nov.,	1876
,,	1	Henry Percy Garnett	21st August,	1878
,,		,, ,,	20th Nov.,	1875
,,	1	Richd. S. Ireland	2nd Feb.,	1881
,,	2	Wm. Lueg Harvey	18th June,	1881
,,	2	Hen. Gage Morris	1st July,	1881
,,	2	Arthur Morrison	1st July,	1881
,,	1	Ralph J. Wilbraham	1st July,	1881
,,		Piers R. Legh (prob.)	1st July,	1881
,,	1	Edward J. J. Teale	1st July,	1881
,,	2	Cyril G. Martyr	1st July,	1881
,,	1	John T. Bowles	1st July,	1881
,,	1	Alfred E. Bassano	1st July,	1881
,,	1	C. Newman Evelegh	1st July,	1881
,,	1	Jas. D. Vyvyan	1st July,	1881
,,	1	Sidney Custance	22nd Oct.,	1881
,,	2	Henry J. G. Lloyd	22nd Oct.,	1881
,,	2	G. G. Cunningham	22nd Oct.,	1881
,,	2	Percy Holland	22nd Oct.,	1881
,,	1	Wm. Geo. Hatherell	22nd Oct.,	1881
,,	1	Evan Fredk. Maberly	22nd Oct.,	1881

APPENDIX. 311

List of Officers for 1882—(continued).

Paymaster	-	2	T.G.Booth (Hon. Capt.) Pymstr., A.P.D.		
,,		1	A.H.Hyslop(Ret.Major) Pymstr.,A.P.D.		
Instr. of Mus.		1	L. B. Beaumont (Lieutenant) -	25th April,	1881
,,		2	H. P. Carden (Lieutenant) - -	20th June,	1881
Adjutant	-	2	G. A. Ashby (Lieutenant) - -	10th Feb.,	1877
Qr.-Mr.	-	2	Geo. Styles - - - - -	11th July,	1874
,,		1	John Conway - - - -	30th Nov.,	1881

THIRD BATTALION.

Hon. Colonel	Field-Marshall H.R.H. Albert Edward Prince of Wales, K.G., K.T., G.C.B., K.P., G.C.S.I., G.C.M.G., A.D.C. - -	28th April, 1875
Lieut.-Colonel -	Harry R. S. Trelawny - - -	4th May, 1872
Major - -	Sir John St. Aubyn, Bart., (Hon. L.C.)	5th May, 1866
,,	E. St. Aubyn (Hon. L.C.) - -	22nd May, 1872
Captain - -	Hon. Chas. Eliot - - - -	11th Dec., 1869
,,	Sir Wm. W. R. Onslow, Bart. -	9th Jan., 1875
,,	Thomas E. J. Lloyd - - - -	6th Oct., 1877
,,	Hugh H. Ley - - - -	11th March, 1879
,,	Ernest de M. Lacon - - - -	26th Nov., 1879
,,	Edward C. Kendall - - -	12th March, 1881
,,	George E. Blake-Aughton - - -	9th May, 1881
,,	R. A. H. Bickford Smith - -	5th Oct., 1881
Lieutenant -	John Littleton - - - -	21st May, 1879
,,	Arthur A. H. Inglefield - -	29th Feb., 1872
,,	Wm. M. Marland - - - -	17th Nov., 1880
,,	A. S. B. Washbourn - - -	22nd Dec., 1880
,,	Herbert R. Vyvyan - - - -	12th March, 1881
,,	Hugh J. G. Arathoon - - -	1st July, 1881
,,	Claude D. J. Carmichael - - -	1st July, 1881
,,	John G. O. Aplin - - - -	1st July, 1881
,,	Edmund B. Hawker - - - -	15th Oct., 1881
,,	Henry Percy Uniacke - - -	19th Nov., 1881
Quarter-Master	Thomas Chivers - - - -	1st April, 1877
,,	,, ,, (temp. Q.M. in Army)	1st April, 1878
Medical-Officer	Thomas Q. Couch (Surgeon-Major) -	1st March, 1873

312　APPENDIX.

OFFICERS OF DUKE OF CORNWALL'S LIGHT INFANTRY, JANUARY, 1892.

Colonel (1st Batt.)	Gen. John Thomas Hill	8th April,	1890
„	„　　　„　　　„	24th Oct.,	1872
„ (2nd Batt.)	Gen. Charles Stuart	20th June,	1870

Commanding 32nd Regimental District.

Colonel	G. C. Swiney	7th March,	1888
„	„　(Colonel)	1st July,	1885

FIRST AND SECOND BATTALIONS.

Rank	Bn.	Name	Date	Year
Lieut.-Colonel	2	William E. Roberts (Com. Bn.)	31st July,	1887
„	1	Francis H. A. Disney-Roebuck	1st July,	1891
Major	2	H. E. C. Kitchener (P.S.C.)	26th July,	1885
„	1	W. Barrington Browne	26th July,	1885
„		„　　　„	18th Nov.,	1882
„	2	Henry T. W. Allatt (P.S.C.)	1st Jan.,	1886
„	2	Charles F. A. Turnbull	5th April,	1886
„		W. F. D. Cochrane (Staff)	29th June,	1886
„		„　　　„	18th Feb.,	1882
„	1	Charles F. N. Le Quesne	29th June,	1886
„	1	Arthur Wm. Hammans	14th Dec.,	1887
„	2	Frederick G. Vigor	1st July,	1891
Captain	1	Henry P. Carden	8th May,	1883
„		„　　„　(Brevet Major)	15th June,	1885
„	1	John H. Verschoyle	29th Dec.,	1883
„	1	Geo. Ashby Ashby	1st Jan.,	1886
„		„　(Brevet Major)	2nd Jan.,	1886
„		Wolstan Francis	17th Feb.,	1886
„		Edmund J. Hollway	2nd May,	1886
„	2	Wm. Lueg Harvey	1st July,	1887
„		Henry G. Morris	14th Nov.,	1887
„	2	Ralph J. Wilbraham	14th Dec.,	1887
„	2	Edward John J. Teale	11th April,	1888
„		Cyril G. Martyr	14th August,	1889
„	1	C. Newman Evelegh (Adjutant)	14th August,	1889
„		Sidney Custance	14th August,	1889
„		Henry M. Sidney	14th August,	1889
„	1	Rupert Stewart	23rd April,	1890
„	1	Frederic H. Chapman	23rd May,	1890
„	2	Wm. J. S. Fergusson	29th June,	1890
„	1	F. C. Griffiths Griffin	14th Jan.,	1891
„	2	Francis M. J. D. Rhodes	4th March,	1891
„		„　　　„	20th July,	1888
Lieutenant	1	Harold B. Walker	14th May,	1884
„	1	Robert N. S. Lewin	23rd August,	1884
„	1	Bertram A. Newbury	23rd August,	1884
„	2	Ernest S. Burder (Adjutant)	7th Feb.,	1885
„	1	George Wm. T. Prowse	7th Feb.,	1885
„	2	Richard C. E. Marriott	28th Feb.,	1885
„	1	Hugh John G. Lambe	6th May,	1885
„	1	James M. A. Kennedy	9th May,	1885
„	1	Cecil B. Jervis-Edwards	29th August,	1885
„	2	George B. M. Rawlinson	25th Nov.,	1885

APPENDIX.   313

List of Officers for 1892—(continued).

Lieutenant	1	Eustace Scott Williams	27th Jan.,	1886
,,	1	Percy Edmund Vyvyan	30th Jan.,	1886
,,	1	John J. B. Jones-Parry	14th August,	1889
,,	1	Sutherland H. Bradford	4th Jan.,	1890
,,	1	Leonard P. H. Bliss	26th Jan.,	1890
,,	2	Edgar Penrose Mark	23rd April,	1890
,,	2	Ernest A. Shakerley	23rd May,	1890
,,	1	Henry A. Tremayne	29th June,	1890
,,	1	Hon. Willoughby J. H. de Montmorency	20th April,	1891
,,	2	Hon. George B. Molesworth	13th May,	1891
2nd Lieutenant	1	Thomas L. Trethewy	23rd March,	1889
,,	2	Paul B. Norris	23rd March,	1889
,,	1	Beauchamp U. Hill	9th Nov.,	1889
,,	2	Arthur St. C. Holbrook	21st Dec.,	1889
,,	2	Robert H. F. Standen	29th March,	1890
,,	1	Frank L. Orman	3rd May,	1890
,,	2	Alexander G. W. Grant	28th June	1890
,,	2	John H. Mander	16th July,	1890
,,	1	Martin N. Turner	23rd July,	1890
,,	2	Walter K. Buck	29th Nov.,	1890
,,	2	Bernard S. Streeten	2?rd May,	1891
,,	2	Vincent F. W. Tregear	23rd May,	1891
Paymaster	1	E. S. Williams (Lieutenant, acting)		
Adjutant	1	C. N. Evelegh (Captain)	1st March,	1889
,,	2	E. S. Burder (Lieutenant)	26th Jan.,	1890
Qr.-Master		Geo. Styles	11th July,	1874
,,		,, ,, (Hon. Captain)	11th July,	1884
,,	1	J. Conway (Hon. Captain)	30th Nov.,	1891
,,	2	H. C. Hart (Hon. Lieutenant)	10th June,	1882

THIRD BATTALION.

Hon. Colonel	Field-Marshal H.R.H. Albert Edward, Prince of Wales, K.G., K.T., K.P., G.C.B., G.C.S.I., G.C.M.G., G.C.I.E., A.D.C.	28th April,	1875
Lieut.-Colonel	Hon. Chas. G. C. Eliot (Hon. Colonel)	29th June,	1889
Major	Thos. Edwd. J. Lloyd	4th May,	1885
,,	Hugh H. Ley	10th August,	1889
Captain	Hugh C. F. Luttrell (Hon. Major)	6th July,	1887
,,	Henry John Greame Lloyd	22nd Oct.,	1887
,,	Arthur Fras. Salmon	5th Nov.,	1887
,,	Gerald Marcell Conran	12th Nov.,	1887
,,	John G. A. Aplin	4th April,	1888
,,	Hugh Molesworth St. Aubyn	22nd June,	1889
,,	Viscount P. A. H. Valletort	23rd March,	1891
Lieutenant	John Claude L. Tremayne	6th Nov.,	1886
,,	Fitzroy D. Marshall	29th May,	1889
,,	J. H. T. Cornish-Bowden	22nd June,	1889
,,	Charles E. Wyld	4th March,	1891
,,	John C. Michell	4th May,	1891
2nd Lieutenant	Stuart J. Bevan	25th Jan.,	1890
,,	Richard T. Vyvyan	9th March,	1891
,,	Reginald W. C. Fenton	23rd March,	1891
,,	James E. S. Trelawny	30th Dec.,	1891
Inst. of Musketry	Wolstan Francis (Captain and Adjutant)	3rd Jan.,	1887
Quarter-Master	George Styles,	1st April,	1882
,,	,, ,, (Hon Captain)	11th July,	1884

THE REGIMENTAL MARCH.

"ONE AND ALL."

Very little information can be ascertained of the origin of the Regimental March "One and All." It is stated to have been written by a lady residing near Bodmin, and to have been adopted by the regiment early in the year 1811.

The Cornish arms and motto, "One and All," are supposed to have originated during the time of the Crusaders. The story is, that a Duke of Cornwall was taken prisoner by the Saracens and held to ransom for fifteen bezants; on the news reaching Cornwall, the whole of the population subscribed. The fifteen bezants are represented by fifteen balls in the shield of the Cornish arms, with the motto "One and All," meaning, it is presumed, that all subscribed.

VICTORIA CROSS ROLL.

BRADSHAW, SURGEON WILLIAM. Granted 23rd September, 1858.

LAWRENCE, BREVET MAJOR S. H. Granted 21st November, 1859.

DOWLING, PRIVATE W.* Granted 21st November, 1859.

BROWNE, LIEUTENANT-COLONEL H. G. Granted 20th June, 1862.

HARRIS, PRIVATE. Granted 1882.

---

* William Dowling was rightly styled in the *Catholic Times*, which announced his death, as a "Lucknow hero." During his lifetime he underwent many perils and endured much suffering on the battle-field. He particularly distinguished himself during the Indian Mutiny, 1857-58. He took part in the siege of Mooltan, and the engagements of Lucknow, Cawnpore, Beyrout, and Dinapur, receiving many distinctions, and the Victoria Cross for his gallantry at Lucknow. Men such as these make the history of a regiment.

BIOGRAPHIES OF COLONELS.

Edward Fox (1702-4.)
Appointed 12th February, 1702.

Edward Fox's first commission was dated at Windsor, 1st September, 1679, by which he was appointed lieutenant to Captain John Richardson, in the King's Holland Regiment,* commanded by the Earl of Mulgrave.

Some twenty-three years later, Colonel Fox was appointed to raise and command a regiment for the Marine service. His commission as colonel, together with those of his field officers, were signed by William III. on 12th February, 1702, and were renewed by Queen Anne on 22nd August of the same year, at Bath.

Granting the commissions of the other officers of Fox's Marines in March, 1702, was one of the first official acts of Queen Anne's reign, and from that date Fox's Regiment of Marines commenced its existence.

Colonel Fox commanded the rear guard of the army in the retreat from Rota, after the Duke of Ormond's unfortunate attempt upon Cadiz in August, 1702, and, owing to his skilful dispositions, the re-embarkation of the troops was effected with little or no loss.

He took part with his regiment in October of the same year in the successful capture of French men-of-war and store-ships at Vigo, and in the surprise of Gibraltar in August, 1704. At the commencement of the first defence of Gibraltar, in which British arms were employed, he was brigadier-general in command of the Marines; and during this siege he met his death, being killed in action on 9th November, 1704.

Jacob Borr (1704-23.)
Appointed 5th December, 1704.

Major, Fox's Marines, 12th February, 1702; colonel, 29th October, 1704; brigadier-general, 1st January, 1709-10.

---
* Afterwards the 3rd Buffs.

From lieutenant-colonel of Fox's Marines, Jacob Borr was appointed to the command of that regiment in recognition of his gallant services during the defence of Gibraltar in 1704, the appointment being dated 5th December, 1704.

In November of the same year, owing to the deaths of senior officers, the command of the English troops in Gibraltar devolved upon him. Contemporary writers are united and enthusiastic in their admiration of the gallant defender of Gibraltar and his lieutenant, and it is not too much to say that it is to these two men—Prince George of Hesse Darmstadt and Colonel Borr—that Great Britain to-day owes the possession of the Rock. For eight months the siege lasted; with a garrison of two thousand men, soon to be reduced by casualties to half that number, with inferior armament on battered fortifications, they held the place against a besieging army of twelve thousand men and a formidable fleet. By their staunch soldierly qualities in the presence of a hostile population, and that worst of foes—internal dissention—they kept their worn-out troops together and enemies without the lines until the arrival—long deferred—of a relieving force, when the siege was raised.

In 1705 Colonel Borr proceeded to Barcelona in command of his regiment, but on landing he had the misfortune to kill Lieutenant-Colonel Rodney, of Holt's Marines, in a duel. It is not improbable that on this account he took no part in the operations before that town. Colonel Borr was not with his regiment at Almanza. On 5th June, 1706, he was appointed quarter-master-general of an expeditionary force, under Richard Earl Rivers, destined for a descent near the mouth of the Charente.

Brigadier-General Borr died on 8th July, 1723.

CHARLES DUBOURGAY (1723-32.)
Appointed 28th June, 1723.

Captain in Sir George St. George's Regiment of Foot (afterwards 17th Regiment), 1st January, 1693, his first commission; captain of Grenadier company in Sir Matthew Bridge's regiment (afterwards 17th Regiment), 14th March, 1700-1; brevet lieutenant-colonel, 2nd June, 1707; colonel, 1708; brigadier-general, 11th March, 1726-27.

Colonel Dubourgay acted as quarter-master-general under the Earl of Galway in Spain in 1706. In the following year he commanded, as a temporary measure, General Blood's regiment (afterwards 17th Foot.) Subsequently he was given the command of a regiment of foot, thirty-fourth in seniority, which was disbanded at the end of 1712. In July, 1715, he was appointed colonel of the 46th, one of the thirteen additional regiments of foot raised in that year to repress rebellion and threatened invasion. This regiment was disbanded in Ireland in 1718. On the death of General Borr, General Dubourgay was selected to command the 32nd Regiment, from 21st June, 1723.

Brigadier-General Doubourgay was employed in the diplomatic service in Hanover and also at the Court at Berlin,* from which he retired on account of ill-health in 1730. He also held the position of Lieutenant-Governor of Jamaica, and it was shortly after his return from that island that he was appointed to the command of the 32nd Regiment. He died on 11th July, 1732, at Edinburgh.

THOMAS PAGET (1732-38.)
Appointed 28th June, 1732.

First commission ante, 1701; captain, 8th March, 1706; lieutenant-colonel, 8th Horse (now 7th Dragoon Guards), 1st August, 1710; colonel, 28th July, 1732; brigadier-general, 1739.

Thomas Paget served for many years in the 8th Horse, and saw with that regiment much active service. He was subsequently lieutenant-colonel of the second, or Scotch Troop, of the (Horse) Grenadier Guards. On 28th July, 1732, he was appointed colonel of the 32nd Regiment, from which, on the death of General Moyle, in 1738, he was removed to the command of the 22nd Regiment.

It is interesting to note that General Paget was the great grandfather of that distinguished soldier, Field Marshal the Earl of Anglesea.

He was a groom of the bed chamber to His Majesty George II., and Governor of the Island of Minorca. He died 28th May, 1741.

---

* For some account of his services at Berlin, see Carlyle's *Friedrich II. of Prussia.*

Although Colonel Paget's appointment was ante dated to 28th July, it was not made until December, 1732. On the death of Major-General Dubourgay, Lieutenant-Colonel Sir Adolphus Oughton, Bart., K.B., M.P., Coldstream Guards, was nominated to succeed in the command of the 32nd Regiment, but the appointment appears to have been cancelled. Subsequently Sir Adolphus Oughton commanded the 8th Light Dragoons (now 8th Hussars.)

SIMON DESCURY (1738-40.)
Appointed 16th December, 1738.

Simon Descury entered the army as a lieutenant in February, 1701-1702, and was appointed to command the 32nd Regiment from lieutenant-colonel, 13th Foot, on 15th December, 1738. He died 4th October, 1740.

JOHN HUSKE (1740-43.)
Appointed 25th December, 1740.

Ensign, 1st Foot Guards, 20th August, 1707; captain, Coldstream Guards, 22nd July, 1715; second major, 30th October, 1734; first major and brevet colonel, 5th July, 1730; colonel, 32nd Regiment, 25th December, 1740; brigadier-general, 18th February, 1741-42; major-general and colonel, 23rd Royal Welsh Fusiliers, 28th July, 1743; lieutenant-general, 11th August, 1747.

Colonel Huske was promoted, from the Coldstream Guards, to command the 32nd Regiment on 25th December, 1740. He served with distinction at the battle of Dettigen, on 27th June, 1743, as brigadier, and was severely wounded. In recognition of his services on that occasion, he was promoted to major-general and given the command of the 23rd Regiment.

On the breaking out of the rebellion in 1745, General Huske assisted in forming the camp in the North of England under the command of Field Marshal Wade. He was second in command at the battle of Falkirk, on 17th January, 1747, where, by the firm front he showed the rebels, he all but recovered the fight and secured the retreat of the Royal forces at Linlithgow. To quote the *General Advertiser:* "That composed and bold officer, Major-General Huske, "with only four regiments, beat the left wing of the rebels and drove "them up the hill, remaining master of the field, and then retired to "the camp." He also distinguished himself on 16th April at the head of a division, at the battle of Culloden, which crushed the rebellion. On the partition of Scotland into military districts, he was appointed second in command under Lord Albemarle at Edinburgh.

General Huske commanded the 23rd Regiment during the defence of Minorca against the French in 1756. He held the appointment of Governor of Hurst Castle in 1721, and was Governor of Jersey at the time of his death, which occurred on 3rd January, 1761.*

HENRY SKELTON (1743-45.)

Appointed, 27th August, 1743.

First commission, captain, 23rd December, 1708; major and lieutenant-colonel, 3rd Foot Guards, 1739; lieutenant-colonel, April, 1743;† brigadier-general, 25th February, 1743-44; colonel, 32nd Regiment, 27th August, 1743; major-general, 1745; lieutenant-general, 1747.

Henry Skelton served two campaigns in the Netherlands, and was for many years in the 3rd Foot Guards. He acted as brigadier at the battles of Dettingen and Fontenoy; after the latter fight he was given the command of a flying column, to observe the movements of the French. On the death of Colonel Duroure, of wounds received at the battle of Fontenoy, he was removed to the command of the 12th Foot. His name does not appear in official reports in connection with any of the battles of 1745; but, when Scotland was divided into military districts, he commanded that having head-quarters at Perth. He held the position of Governor of Portsmouth, and died on 9th April, 1757, leaving his property to his former aide-de-camp, Captain

---

* The provisions of his will are given in the *Gentleman's Magazine* for 1761. He left a considerable portion of his property to the Regimental Agent of the Welsh Fusiliers.

† Cannon's 12th Foot.

Jones, 3rd Foot Guards, who had saved the life of his general during the War of the Austrian Succession.

⁎ Captain Jones' heir took the name of Skelton on succeeding to the estates in Cumberland—Branthwaite Hall &c.—in accordance with the will of General Skelton.—*London Gazette*, 24th November, 1774.

WILLIAM DOUGLAS (1745-47.)
Appointed 29th May, 1745.

First commission, captain, 15th May, 1709; captain, Coldstream Guards, 9th June, 1720; second major, 29th December, 1740; first major, 27th April, 1743; colonel, 32nd Regiment, 27th May, 1745.

Shortly after 1715, the year in which the regiment was raised, Captain Douglas joined Croft's Light Dragoons (now 9th Lancers), from which, in 1720, he was appointed to the Coldstream Guards. He served with distinction in the War of the Austrian Succession, and was given the command of the 32nd Regiment soon after Fontenoy.

Iu August of the same year (1745) conjointly with the Hanoverian general, Zastrow, he was entrusted with the construction of entrenchments along the Vilvorden Canal, behind the line of which the army had retired. The 32nd Regiment was one of the first to be hurried home on the breaking out of the rebellion in Scotland, and in the advance to the north, in December, Colonel Douglas was given the command of a brigade. He returned to the low countries in time to take part as brigadier in the disastrous battle of Roucoux, near Liege, on 11th October, 1746, and in the two days' fight at Val, or Laffelt, on 20th and 21st June, 1747.

Brigadier-General Douglas died at Brabant on 5th August, 1747, falling a victim to the unhealthiness of the climate.*

FRANCIS LEIGHTON (1747-73.)
Appointed 1st December, 1747.

First commission, captain, 16th June, 1737; lieutenant-colonel, 6th July, 1737; colonel, 32nd Regiment, 1st December, 1747;

---

* Brigadiers Price, Houghton, and Douglas died within a short time of one another, probably at Breda, from effects of climate.

major-general, 5th February, 1757 ; lieutenant-general, 6th April, 1759; general, 25th May, 1772.

Lieutenant-Colonel Leighton's name appears in connection with the history of the campaign in Scotland in 1715, where, as lieutenant-colonel of Blakeney's (27th Foot), he was sent from Perth to hold the important outpost of Castle Menzies, with a considerable force. From lieutenant-colonel of the 27th he was appointed to command the 32nd Regiment, on 1st December, 1747. General Leighton died on 9th June, 1773.

ROBERT ROBINSON (1773-75.)
Appointed 11th January, 1773.

Captain, 18th Royal Irish, 20th September, 1745; major, 20th Foot, 2nd September, 1756; lieutenant-colonel, 67th Foot, 26th February, 1758; colonel, 18th April, 1763; colonel, 32nd Foot, 11th June, 1773.

Lieutenant-Colonel Robinson was serving in the 2nd battalion of the 20th Regiment in April, 1758, when it was formed into the 67th, from which, on 11th June, 1773, he was appointed to command the 32nd Regiment. He resigned the command for the governorship of Pendennis Castle. Lieutenant-Colonel Robinson was for many years aide-de-camp to the King.

WILLIAM AMHERST (1775-81.)
Appointed 18th October, 1775.

Ensign, 3rd Foot Guards, 7th June, 1753; lieutenant and captain, 21st September, 1757; captain-lieutenant, 12th June, 1765; captain and lieutenant-colonel, 12th June, 1765; brevet lieutenant-colonel, 1759; colonel, 6th August, 1766; colonel 32nd Regiment, 18th October, 1775; major-general, 29th August, 1777; lieutenant-general, 19th February, 1779.

Major-General Amherst was appointed to command the 32nd Regiment on 18th October, 1775. During his distinguished military career he held the appointments of Lieutenant-Governor of Portsmouth, Governor of St. John's, Newfoundland, and adjutant-general

Y

at head-quarters. General Amherst was aide-de-camp to the King. He died 13th May, 1781.

RALPH, EARL OF ROSS (1781-1802.)
Appointed 17th May, 1781.

Captain, 33rd Regiment, ante 1747. Lieutenant-colonel, 92nd Donegal Light Infantry, 1st January, 1760; colonel, 92nd, 25th May, 1772. Major-general, 29th August, 1777. Lieutenant-general, 20th November, 1782. General, 3rd May, 1796.

Lord Ross served with much distinction in Flanders, where, as a company officer of the 33rd Regiment, he fought, and lost his right arm at Fontenoy. After the battle of Val, or Laffelt, he was personally thanked by the Duke of Cumberland at the head of his regiment, which, as a junior captain, he had brought out of action. He subsequently retired from the 33rd Regiment, presenting his company to the son of Colonel Simon Descury, of the 32nd Regiment. In 1760 he was appointed lieutenant-colonel-commandant of the 92nd Donegal Light Infantry, a corps some nine hundred strong, which he had raised and equipped in four months, entirely at his own expense, and with which he served under the Count de Lippe in Portugal. This regiment was disbanded at the peace of 1768. General Lord Ross succeeded Sir W. Augustus Pitt as commander-in-chief in Ireland. His portrait at page 46, is from a picture now in the possession of the Right Honble. the Earl Rosse, K.P. He died in 1802.

JAMES OGILVIE (1802-13.)
Appointed 4th September, 1802.

Lieutenant, 4th Regiment, 20th December, 1757; captain, 30th March, 1764; major, 22nd April, 1774; lieutenant-colonel, June, 1777; colonel, 20th November, 1782; major-general, 12th October, 1793; lieutenant-general, 1st January, 1798; colonel, 89th Regiment, 28th March, 1801; colonel, 32nd Regiment, 4th September, 1802; general, 23rd September, 1803.

Major-General Ogilvie was appointed to command the 32nd Regiment from the colonelcy of the 89th Regiment. Until he was promoted into the latter regiment he had served only in the 4th King's Own. He saw much service in North America. In August, 1776, he commanded his regiment at the capture of Long Island, and also in the actions of Chad's Ford, Germanstown, and White Marsh, in 1777. As brigadier-general in 1793 he commanded the expeditionary force despatched to capture Miquelon and St. Pierre, but the Governor of these islands surrendered to him at discretion.*

General Ogilvie died in London on 14th February, 1813, in his seventy-third year.

ALEXANDER CAMPBELL (1813-32.)
Appointed 15th February, 1813.

Ensign, 42nd Regiment, April, 1769; lieutenant, 2nd battalion Royals, 1770 ; captain, 50th Regiment, August, 1772 ; transferred to 62nd Regiment in September, 1772 ; major, 74th Regiment, 1777 ; lieutenant-colonel, 62nd Regiment, 31st December, 1782 ; colonel, 3rd Foot Guards, 12th October, 1793 ; major-general, 26th February, 1795; colonel, 7th West India Regiment, 10th November, 1796; lieutenant-general, 29th April, 1802 ; colonel, 13th Foot, 11th July, 1804; general, 1st January, 1812 ; colonel, 32nd Regiment, 15th February, 1813.

Alexander Campbell joined the 42nd Regiment in Ireland, and was shortly afterwards promoted in the Royals at Minorca. He obtained a company in the 50th Regiment, which he never joined, being transferred to the 62nd Regiment. This regiment he joined in Ireland, and embarked with it for Canada, where he served as captain of light infantry under General Carleton, in the campaigns of 1776, and of 1777 under General Burgoyne. After the surrender of the army at Sarratoga, in the end of the year 1777, having procured a majority in the 74th Regiment and an exchange from the Americans, he was appointed to serve as major in the 1st battalion of Light Infantry at New York. In this capacity he served two campaigns, and at the end of the war commanded at Penobscot. He obtained a lieutenant-

---

* *Vide* Brigadier-General Ogilvie's despatch to the Right Hon. Henry Dundas, *London Gazette*, 2nd July, 1793.

colonelcy in the 62nd in 1782, and remained with that regiment in Scotland and Ireland until 1789, when he exchanged into the 3rd Guards, in which he served as captain of light infantry, the campaign of 1793 and part of 1794, under the Duke of York; but having got the rank of colonel, in 1793, and having raised the 116th in 1790, he served, first as brigadier-general, and afterwards as major-general, on the staff of what was called Lord Morra's Army. He served in the West Indies under Sir Ralph Abercromby, in 1796, and there was given the command of the 7th West India Regiment. He served on the staff at Newcastle, in 1797; in Ireland, in 1798, and subsequently in Scotland; and as lieutenant-general again in Ireland and Scotland. He was appointed colonel of the 13th Foot in 1804, and colonel of the 32nd Regiment 15th February, 1813. He died February, 1832.

Sir Samuel Venables Hinde, K.C.B. (1832-37.)
Appointed 28th February, 1832.

Ensign, 25th Regiment, 24th January, 1788; lieutenant, 25th Regiment, 28th March, 1792; captain, 25th Regiment, 3rd April, 1795; brevet major, 25th Regiment, 6th July, 1797; major, 32nd Regiment, 5th November, 1800; brevet lieutenant-colonel, 29th April, 1802; lieutenant-colonel, 32nd Regiment, 1st April, 1804; brevet colonel, 4th June, 1811; major-general, 4th June, 1814; lieutenant-general, 22nd July, 1830; colonel, 32nd Regiment, 28th February, 1832.

Sir S. V. Hinde, K.C.B.—the son of Robert Hinde, of Hunsdon, Herts,—like many other linesmen of his generation, received his education at the Royal Military Academy, and through the instrumentality of the Master-General of Ordnance (the Duke of Richmond) obtained a commission in the 25th Regiment. Whilst serving on Marine duty in the fleet in the Mediterranean, he took part in the capture and subsequent evacuation of Toulon, and afterwards at the reduction and occupation of Corsica. In 1797, when on board H.M.S. *St. George*, Captain Hinde was instrumental in suppressing a mutiny among the ships company, which was on the point of breaking out, for which service he received the special thanks of Admiral Lord

APPENDIX. 325

St. Vincent, and was rewarded with a brevet majority. In 1799 Major Hinde served in Holland, and was wounded at the battle of Alkmaar. In 1804 he commanded the experimental light battalions formed of the light companies of certain line and militia regiments at the Curragh. He embarked in command of the 32nd Regiment, in 1807, and took part in the expeditions to Copenhagen and the capture of the Danish fleet. He commanded the battalion in Sir Brent Spencer's expedition in 1808, and in the retreat to and battle of Corunna, in the Walcheren expedition, and proceeded with it to Spain in 1811, when Major-General Bowes was killed in action before the forts of Salamanca. Colonel Hinde succeeded to that officer's brigade, which he commanded at the battle of Salamanca and at the siege of and retreat from Burgos. In 1813 he commanded the 2nd brigade of the 6th Division in the advance into Spain, and being in rear of the army after the battle of Vittoria, prevented the recapture of that city by General Clausel. He also commanded the same brigade at the investment of Pampeluna and in the battle of the Pyrenees. Being relieved by Major-General Lambert, he reverted to the command of the 32nd Regiment, and on 7th October he received a wound, which compelled him to return to England. He died at Hitchin, on 20th September, 1837, and was buried in the parish church, where there is a monumental inscription to his memory.

⁎ There is a tradition in Hertfordshire to the effect that a member of the Hinde family—one of Marlborough's soldiers—furnished Sterne with a model for his "Uncle Toby." Cassan, however, in his *History of Hertfordshire*, puts this story in a somewhat different light.

Sir Robert Macfarlane, K.C.B., G.C.H. (1837-43.)

Appointed 26th September, 1837.

Ensign, 59th Regiment, 26th May, 1789; lieutenant, 59th Regiment, 26th May, 1793; captain, 59th Regiment, 25th September, 1793; major, 113th Regiment, 12th November, 1794; lieutenant-colonel, 113th Regiment, 19th December, 1794; lieutenant-colonel, 72nd Regiment, 13th September, 1798; colonel, 1st January, 1800; major-general, 25th April, 1808; lieutenant-general, 4th January, 1813;

colonel, 96th Regiment, 1816; general, 26th July, 1830; colonel, 32nd Regiment, 26th September, 1837.

Sir Robert Macfarlane entered the Army in 1789 as an ensign, and was in 1794 appointed major in the newly raised 113th Regiment (the Loyal Londonderry). When the regiment was disbanded, he was transferred to the 72nd. He held a brigade command in the expedition to Copenhagen in 1807, and his name was included in the vote of thanks from Parliament. He was second in command at Sicily, under Lord William Bentinck. After the capture of Genoa, in 1814, he commanded there, and at Marseilles, until the British troops were finally withdrawn in 1816. He was a member of the Consolidated Board of General Officers, and Grand Cross of the Neapolitan Order of St. Ferdinand and Merit. He died in London, 1843, aged seventy-three.

Sir John Buchan, K.C.B. (1843-50.)

Appointed 12th June, 1843.

Ensign, Scotch Brigade (94th Regiment), 29th July, 1795; lieutenant, Scotch Brigade, 21st October, 1795; captain, 2nd Ceylon Regiment, 15th March, 1802; major, 2nd Ceylon Regiment, 30th June, 1804; lieutenant-colonel, 4th West India Regiment, 30th March, 1809; colonel, 12th August, 1819: major-general, 22nd July, 1830; colonel, 95th Regiment, 1838; lieutenant-general, 23rd November, 1841, colonel, 32nd Regiment, 12th January, 1843.

Sir John Buchan was actively employed in the Mysore War, and was present at the battle of Mallavelly, and at the assault of Seringapatam. In 1800 and 1801 he was employed with the flank companies of the Scotch Brigade (the old 94th Regiment) in the operations against the Southern Poligars, on which occasion he relinquished a staff appointment to join his company in the field. He was promoted captain in the 2nd Ceylon Regiment, formed in 1802 out of a part of the Dutch Native Infantry taken into British pay on the transfer of that island, and held different detached commands in Ceylon during the Kandian War. In 1809 he was appointed lieutenant-colonel of the 4th West India Regiment, and held a command at the attack and capture of Quadaloupe. Subsequently he was appointed to the command of the 7th Portuguese Regiment, and was present at the battles of Vittoria, Pyrenees, Nivelle, Nive, Orthes, and Toulouse. Sir John Buchan received the medal for Quadaloupe, and a cross and one clasp for the Peninsular campaign. In 1838 he was given the command of the 95th Regiment, being transferred to the 32nd Regiment in 1843. He died in London in 1850.

Sir Richard Armstrong, K.C.B. (1850-54.)
Appointed 25th June, 1850.

Ensign, 32nd Regiment, 23rd June, 1796; lieutenant, 5th November, 1799; captain, 9th Battalion of Reserve, 9th July, 1803; major, 97th Foot, 30th May, 1811; lieutenant-colonel, 26th August, 1813; colonel, 22nd July, 1830; major-general, 23rd November, 1841; lieutenant-general, 11th November, 1851. Colonel, 32nd Regiment, 25th June, 1850.

Sir Richard Armstrong was the only son of Lieutenant-Colonel Armstrong, of Lincoln, attached to the Portuguese Army. Served in the Peninsula from August, 1808, to the end of that war in 1814, including the capture of Oporto, battle of Busaco, actions at Pombal and Reeinha, defence of Alba de Tormes, battles of Vittoria, the Pyrenees (severely wounded through the arm), and Toulouse, besides a great many minor actions and skirmishes. He continued in the service of Portugal for six years after the conclusion of the war. As brigadier he took part in the campaigns of 1825 and 1826 in Burmah, and was present at the storming and capture of the stockades near Prome, on 1st and 5th December, 1825. He served on the staff in Canada as major-general. In 1851 he was appointed Commander-in-Chief in Madras, but shortly after taking up his duties in India, he resigned his command owing to impaired health. He died 3rd March, 1854, aged seventy-two, on the homeward voyage. He received the gold medal and two clasps for the battles of Busaco, Vittoria, and the Pyrenees, and the silver war medal with one clasp for Toulouse. Besides his British decorations he was a Knight Commander of the Portuguese Order of the Tower and Sword and of St. Bento d'Avis.

SIR WILLOUGHBY COTTON, G.C.B., G C.H., &C. (1854-60.)

Appointed 17th April, 1854.

Ensign, 3rd Guards, 31st October, 1798; lieutenant and captain, 25th November, 1799; captain and lieutenant-colonel, 12th June, 1811; colonel, 25th July, 1821; major-general, 22nd July, 1830; lieutenant-general, 23rd November, 1841; general, 20th June, 1854; colonel, 32nd Regiment, 17th April, 1854.

Sir W. Cotton, the only son of Admiral Cotton, was born in 1783, and was educated at Rugby. Served with the 3rd Guards on the expedition to Hanover, in 1805; and on that to Copenhagen in 1807, where he was appointed deputy assistant-adjutant-general to the reserve under Sir A. Wellesley, and was present at the battle of Kioge. In 1809 he accompanied Sir A. Wellesley to Spain, and served as deputy assistant-adjutant-general to the light division during the whole of the campaign of the retreat to Torres Vedras and the subsequent advance, the former containing a series of skirmishes, and the battle of the Coa. Returned to England on promotion in 1811, and rejoined the Peninsular army in 1813. He was present at the battle of Vittoria, commanded the light companies at the passage of the Adour, and the pickets of the second brigade of guards at the repulse of the sortie from Bayonne. He commanded a division of Sir Archibald Campbell's army in the Burmese war, and there became acquainted with Havelock, who was afterwards his aide-de-camp. He was appointed to the command of the 1st Division of the Bengal Army in the Afghan war in 1838-39, under Sir Henry Fane, and afterwards under Lord Keane in Afghanistan, and was present at the assault and capture of Ghuznee on 23rd July, 1839, at which he commanded the reserve which entered the city after the storming party had established themselves inside. His name was most honourably mentioned in the despatches of Sir John Keane, and those of the Governor-General, Lord Auckland. In October, 1839, he relinquished the command of the Bengal forces, then encamped near Cabul, to assume the command within the Bengal and Agra presidencies. Sir Willoughby was commander-in-chief at Bombay from 1847 to 1850, and was second member of council in that presidency. For his services he had received the order of the Bath of all grades, being nominated a Grand Cross of that order in 1840. He was made a Knight Commander of the Royal Hanoverian Guelphic Order in 1830, and had conferred on him the order of the Doranèe empire of the first class at Cabul in September, 1839. The colonelcy of the 98th Foot was given to him in 1839, from which he was removed to the 32nd Regiment in 1854. He was groom of the bedchamber to H.R.H. the Duke of Gloucester. Sir W. Cotton died 4th May, 1862, aged seventy-six.

SIR JOHN EARDLEY WILMOT INGLIS, K.C.B. (1860-62.)
Appointed 5th May, 1860.

Ensign, 32nd Regiment, 2nd August, 1838; lieutenant, 19th January, 1839; captain, 29th September, 1843; major, 25th February, 1848; brevet lieutenant-colonel, 7th June, 1849; lieutenant-colonel, 20th February, 1855; colonel, 5th June, 1855; major-general, 26th November, 1857; colonel, 32nd Regiment, 5th May, 1860.

Sir John Inglis (son of the Right Rev. John Inglis, D.D., Bishop of Nova Scotia) joined the 32nd Regiment in 1833, and it is not a little remarkable that he served in every grade, "one and all," from ensign to full colonel in that regiment. He served in Canada, during the rebellion in 1837, and was present in the actions of St. Denis and St. Eustache; also in the Punjaub campaign of 1848-49, and was present at the first and second siege operations before Mooltan, including the attack on the enemy's position in front of the advanced trenches on the 12th September, where, after the death of Lieutenant-Colonel Pattoun, he succeeded to the command of the right column of attack; commanded the 32nd at the action of Soorjkoond; and was also present at the storm and capture of the city and surrender of the fortress of Mooltan, surrender of the fort and garrison of Cheniote, and battle of Goojerat, for which services he received the brevet rank of lieutenant-colonel (medal with clasps). Was promoted to the rank of major-general and nominated a K.C.B. "for his enduring fortitude and persevering "gallantry in defence of the Residency of Lucknow,* for eighty-seven

---

* Lady Inglis, who was with her husband during the siege, subsequently received the decoration of the Crown of India.

"days, against an overwhelming force of the enemy." In 1862 he held the command of the troops in the Ionian Islands, and on 27th September of the same year he died at Homburg, aged forty-seven, his health having been affected by the long anxiety and desperate privations of the defence of Lucknow.

HENRY, VISCOUNT MELVILLE, G.C.B.

Appointed 17th October, 1862.

Ensign and lieutenant, Coldstream Guards, 18th November, 1819; lieutenant and captain, Coldstream Guards, 1st April, 1820; major, unattached, 11th July, 1826; lieutenant-colonel, 83rd Regiment, 3rd December, 1829; colonel, 28th November, 1841; major-general, 20th June, 1854; lieutenant-general, 5th May, 1860; colonel, 100th Regiment, 22nd June, 1858; colonel, 32nd Regiment, 17th October, 1862; colonel-commandant, 60th Foot, 5th May, 1863; general, 1st January, 1868.

Henry Dundas, the eldest son of Robert Viscount Melville, K.T., was born on 25th February, 1801. Having served some years in the Coldstream Guards, he commanded the 83rd Regiment during the suppression of the insurrection in Lower Canada in 1837, and also in repealing the attacks of the American brigands, who landed near Prescott, in Upper Canada, 1838. He commanded the Bombay column of the army throughout the Punjaub campaign of 1848-49, and was present at the siege and storm of the town and capture of the citadel of Mooltan, the battle of Goojerat, and subsequent operations. For his "indefatigable zeal and exertions" in that campaign he received the Order of the Bath and the thanks of Parliament. Lord Melville commanded the forces in Scotland in 1856, became Governor of Edinburgh Castle in 1860, and was also vice-president of the Council of the Royal Archers of Scotland. In 1863 he was appointed colonel-commandant of the 60th Rifles. Lord Melville died at Melville Castle, near Edinburgh, 1st February, 1876. He was aide-de-camp to William IV. and Her Majesty the Queen.

RIGHT HON. SIR GEORGE BROWN, G.C.B., K.H. (1863-65.)

Appointed 1st April, 1863.

Ensign, 43rd Regiment, 23rd January, 1806; lieutenant, 8th September, 1806: captain, 3rd Garrison Battalion, 20th June, 1811; major, 85th Regiment, 26th May, 1814; lieutenant-colonel, 29th September, 1814; colonel, 6th May, 1831; major-general, 23rd November, 1841; lieutenant-general, 11th November, 1851; general, 7th September, 1855; colonel, 32nd Regiment, 1st April, 1863; colonel-in-chief, Rifle Brigade, 18th April, 1863.

Sir George Brown, the third son of George Brown, Provost of Elgin, was born at Linkwood, near Elgin, on 3rd July, 1790. He was educated at Elgin Academy, and at the age of sixteen obtained an ensigncy in the 43rd Regiment. He served at the siege and capture of Copenhagen in 1807; in the Peninsula, from August, 1808, to July, 1811, and again from July, 1831, to May, 1814, during which periods he was present at the following engagements: The battle of Vimiera, passage of the Douro and capture of Oporto, with the previous and subsequent actions; the battle of Talavera, where he was severely wounded in both thighs; action of the light division at the bridge of Almeida, battle of Busaco, the different actions during the retreat of the French army from Portugal, action of Sabugal, battle of Fuentes d'Onor, siege of San Sebastian, battles of Nivelle and Nive, and the investment of Bayonne. He served afterwards in the American war, and was present at the battle of Bladensburg and the capture of Washington. He was slightly wounded, and so severely at Bladensburg, that his life was despaired of. He received the war medal with seven clasps. In 1824 Lieutenant-Colonel Brown exchanged from the 59th Regiment to the Rifle Brigade. In 1850 he was deputy assistant-adjutant-general and deputy adjutant-general under Lord Hill, subsequently adjutant-general under the Duke of Wellington. Lieutenant-General Brown commanded the light division throughout the Crimean campaign, and was present at the battles of the Alma, where his horse was shot under him, Balaclava, Inkerman, in which battle he was severely wounded (shot through the arm), and at the siege of Sebastopol (medal and four clasps, G.C.B., Grand Cross of the Legion of Honour, first class of the Medjidie, Sardinian, and Turkish medals). In 1860 he was appointed to command the forces in Ireland, and on 18th April, 1863, colonel-in-chief of the Rifle Brigade. He died on 27th August, 1865, aged seventy-five, at Linkwood, where he was born.

Sir George Brown was a soldier of the Wellington School, and consequently a strict disciplinarian. His manner was thought by some to be too abrupt and peremptory, and he was by no means a popular character whilst he held office at the Horse Guards; but those who knew him intimately were aware that much of this roughness was merely assumed under the idea of supporting discipline.*

WILLIAM GEORGE GOLD (1865-67.)
Appointed 28th August, 1865.

2nd lieutenant, 7th April, 1825; lieutenant, 53rd Regiment, 26th June, 1828; captain, 53rd Regiment, 29th June, 1832; major, 53rd Regiment, 10th February, 1843; lieutenant-colonel, 53rd Regiment, 26th July, 1844; colonel, 20th June, 1854; major-general, 17th October, 1859; colonel, 32nd Regiment, 28th August, 1865.

Major-General Gold served, as lieutenant-colonel of the 53rd Regiment in the campaign on the Sutlej, including the affair of Buddiwal and the battles of Aliwal and Sobraon, where he was wounded. He commanded his regiment during the subsequent operations, receiving the war medal and clasp.

SIR GEORGE BELL, K.C.B. (1867-68.)
Appointed 2nd February, 1867.

Ensign, 34th Regiment, 14th March, 1811; lieutenant, 34th and 45th Regiments, 17th February, 1814; captain, 1st Royals, 7th August, 1828; brevet major, 1st Royals, 20th March, 1839; major, 1st Royals, 14th July, 1843; lieutenant-colonel, 1st Royals, 5th December, 1843; colonel, 20th June, 1854; major-general, 4th

---

* For a characteristic anecdote of Sir G. Brown, see *Gentlemen's Magazine*, September, 1865.

April, 1859; colonel, 104th Regiment, 23rd October, 1863; colonel, 32nd Regiment, 2nd February, 1867.

George Bell was appointed by the Duke of York to the 34th Regiment, and accompanied F. M. Lord Strafford soon after to the Peninsula, where he served from July, 1811, to the end of the war in 1814, and was engaged in the action of Arroyo de Molino, under the command of General Hill; the last siege of Badajoz; the capture of Fort Napoleon and bridge at Almaraz; retreat from Burgos and Madrid: battles of Vittoria, the Pyrenees; pass of Maya, and Roncesvalles; actions of the 30th and 31st July, 1813, against D'Erlon's corps, in the mountains near Pampluna; battles of the Nivelle, Nive, Bayonne, St. Pierre (contusion of the head), Orthes, Tarbes, and Toulouse (slightly wounded); and with many other affairs and skirmishes.

He afterwards served in Ceylon and in the East Indies, in the Burmese war, and in the West Indies. He was stationed with his regiment for seven years in Canada, and was actively employed during the rebellion in Canada in 1837-38, particularly in the capture of St. Charles and St. Eustache. He commanded the fort and garrison of Coteau-du-lac, an important position on the river St. Lawrence, and received the thanks of the commander of the forces and the brevet of major for his exertions in recovering the guns of the fort and shot, which had been sunk by the rebels in the river. The guns were twenty-four-pounders, sixteen of which—and four thousand shot—he brought to the surface, in the depth of a Canadian winter, and unspiked and mounted the guns when their recovery was reported impracticable.

He served in the Crimea in 1854-55, and commanded the 1st Royals in the battles of Alma and Inkerman, and the siege of Sevastopol, where he was wounded; he subsequently commanded a brigade. Mentioned in despatches, C.B., Knight of the Legion of Honour, and fourth class Medjidie.

Having seen much service in the 34th and 45th Regiments, he served thirty consecutive years in the 1st Royals. After commanding that regiment for eleven years he was appointed colonel and inspecting field officer for the Northern district.

Colonel Bell was given the command of the 104th Bengal Fusiliers, from which he was removed to the 32nd Regiment, on 2nd February, 1867.

Under the title of *Rough Notes by an old Soldier*, he published the history of his military career; this autobiography contains his portrait and many interesting reminiscences of the campaigns in which he took part.

LORD FREDERICK PAULET, C.B. (1868-71.)
Appointed 3rd August, 1868.

Ensign and lieutenant, Coldstream Guards, 11th June, 1826; lieutenant and captain, 21st September, 1830; captain and lieutenant-colonel, 8th May, 1846; colonel, 20th June, 1854; major, 20th February, 1855; lieutenant-colonel, 26th October, 1858; major-general, 13th December, 1860; lieutenant-general, 12th February, 1870; colonel, 32nd Foot, 3rd August, 1868.

Lord Frederick Paulet, the youngest son of Charles, thirteenth Marquis of Winchester, was born May 12th, 1810, and at an early age entered the Coldstream Guards as ensign. He served in the Crimean campaign of 1854, and up to 26th May, 1855, with that regiment, including the battles of Alma (where he had a horse shot under him), Balaclava, and Inkerman, and the siege of Sevastopol. He served on the staff in North America, having commanded the Brigade of Guards sent to that country in 1861. Lord Frederick Paulet was equerry and comptroller to H.R.H. the Duchess of Cambridge. He died on 1st January, 1871, aged sixty.

THE DUKE OF CORNWALL'S LIGHT INFANTRY.

SIR WILLIAM JONES, K.C.B. (1871-90.)

Appointed 2nd January, 1871.

Already colonel of the 32nd Regiment. Became colonel of the 1st battalion Duke of Cornwall's Light Infantry on the formation of the Territorial Regiment in August, 1881.

Ensign, 61st Regiment, 10th April, 1825; lieutenant, 12th December, 1826; captain, 24th November, 1835; major, 26th July, 1844; lieutenant-colonel, 29th December, 1848; colonel, 28th November, 1854; major-general, 1st April, 1863; lieutenant-general, 31st December, 1871; general, 1st October, 1877. Colonel, 32nd Foot, 2nd January, 1871.

Sir William Jones was the son of William Jones, of Glan Helen, Co. Carnarvon. He was educated at Sandhurst, and saw all his regimental service in the 61st Foot. Served through the Punjaub campaign of 1848-49, was present at the passage of the Chenab, and in the battles of Sadoolapore and Chillianwallah; after which he commanded the regiment at the battle of Goojerat; he also commanded a portion of Sir Walter Gilbert's field force, consisting of a troop of Bengal Horse Artillery, and the 61st Regiment in pursuit of the enemy to the Khyber pass in March, 1849 (medal with two clasps, and C.B.). Commanded, as brigadier, the 3rd infantry brigade at the siege of Delhi, in 1857, and repulse of the sortie of the 9th July; commanded the 2nd column at the assault on the 14th September, during which the command of the 1st column devolved on him, on the fall of General Nicholson, and he continued in command of the both columns during the six days' fighting within the city, until its final capture on the 20th September (mentioned in despatches, medal with clasp, reward for distinguished services, 1858, and K.C.B.) He died at Dublin, 8th April, 1890, aged eighty-two.

APPENDIX.

CHARLES STUART (1870-92).

Appointed 20th June, 1870.

Already colonel of the 46th Regiment. Became colonel of the 2nd battalion Duke of Cornwall's Light Infantry on the formation of the Territorial Regiment in August, 1881.

Ensign, 46th Regiment, 30th December, 1826; lieutenant, 31st December, 1828; lieutenant and captain, 26th July, 1832; captain and lieutenant-colonel, 15th April, 1845; colonel, 20th June, 1854; major-general, 28th January, 1860; lieutenant-general, 1st May, 1868; general, 29th May, 1875. Colonel 46th Foot, 20th June, 1870.

JOHN THOMAS HILL.

Appointed colonel 1st battalion 8th April, 1890, and became colonel of the three battalions, September, 1892.

Ensign, 32nd Regiment, 13th March, 1827; lieutenant, 19th April, 1829; captain, 13th February, 1835; major, 12th March, 1841; lieutenant-colonel, 21st Regiment 3rd April, 1846; colonel, 20th June, 1854; major-general, 30th July, 1860; lieutenant-general, 14th June, 1869. Colonel 75th Foot, 24th October, 1872. Colonel 1st battalion Duke of Cornwall's Light Infantry, 8th April, 1890. Colonel Duke of Cornwall's Light Infantry, September, 1892.

MEMOIRS OF OFFICERS.

Major Felix Calvert.

MAJOR FELIX CALVERT was born 1790. He was the eldest son of Nicholson Calvert, of Hunedon, M.P., Herts. Served, as major of 32nd Regiment, at Waterloo, where he had three horses shot under him. Promoted lieutenant-colonel, 15th July, 1815.

Major Henry Ross-Lewin.

HENRY, the eldest son of George Ross-Lewin, formerly of the 14th Dragoons, entered the Limerick Militia in 1793, and joined the 32nd Regiment as ensign, 4th November, 1795. He saw much active service in St. Domingo and other parts of the West Indies in 1796-97. In 1804, when battalions were formed of the light companies in Ireland, Captain Ross-Lewin was selected as adjutant of the battalion commanded by Colonel Colman, of the Guards. He was present at the following general engagements and sieges:—The siege of Copenhagen and the capture of the Danish fleet in 1807; the battles of Roleia and Vimiera in 1808; the siege and capture of Flushing in 1811; the capture of the forts of Salamanca and the battle of Salamanca, where he was severely wounded, during the last charge, a musket ball, at short distance, passing through the left arm near the shoulder, from the effects of which he never thoroughly recovered.

In June, 1814, he received his majority by brevet, and in the following year was present at the battles of Les Quatre Bras and Waterloo. On his father's death, Major Ross-Lewin retired from the service. At home he was largely instrumental in restoring tranquility to the disturbed districts in the West of Ireland, and his exertions were rewarded by a graceful acknowledgment from Dublin Castle.

In 1834 he published his autobiography, under the title of "*The Life of a Soldier.*" This work has been largely quoted in the present volume. He received the Waterloo medal, but he died in 1843, before the distribution of the war medal, granted for the Peninsula. When the medals were given to the survivors of that campaign, his family was denied the melancholy satisfaction of receiving one.

Lieutenant-General William Augustus Johnson.

WILLIAM AUGUSTUS JOHNSON, the eldest son of Rev. Robert Augustus Johnson, having raised men for rank, obtained a commission as captain at the age of sixteen, 23rd April, 1794. He was transferred from the 2nd Queen's to the 32nd Regiment on 7th January of the following year, and was promoted major, 2nd April, 1803.

He commanded the companies of the 32nd Regiment that in 1808 were ordered to Sicily. Having been recalled to Spain, he was present with his regiment at the battles of Roleia, Vimiera, and Corunna, and received the war medal with the three clasps for those engagements. The anxieties and privations of the retreat to Corunna had the effect of turning his hair grey, although he was only thirty years of age. Major Johnson served through the Walcheren expedition in 1809, being promoted lieutenant-colonel, 17th May, 1810, and colonel, by brevet, 12th August, 1819, He went on half-pay of the 3rd Ceylon Regiment, 18th August, 1814. He was Sheriff of Lincolnshire in 1830, and represented Boston in Parliament 1821-26, and Oldham, 1837-47. He finally retired with the rank of lieutenant-general, 23rd November, 1841, and died 26th October, 1863, at his residence, at Wytham-on-the-Hill, at the advanced age of eighty-six.

Lieutenant Thomas Ross-Lewin.

THOMAS ROSS-LEWIN, the younger brother of Major Ross-Lewin, joined the 32nd Regiment as ensign in 1807, and saw much active service in the Peninsula, France, and Belgium. He was wounded at Sarrogin, and again at Waterloo, where Sir William Ponsonby's "Union Brigade" rode over him as he was lying wounded on the field. He was invalided at Corfu, and retired on half-pay. He died in 1857, having received the Waterloo war medal with eight clasps.

Captain Thomas Cassan.

THOMAS CASSAN, a gallant youth, was wounded in the battle of Quatre Bras, 16th June, 1815, but concealed his situation, and continued in the field with that manly resolution, intrepidity, and disregard for personal danger which always distinguished him. His fall was deservedly regretted by his brother officers and all who knew him. He was the son of the late John Cassan, Esq., captain 56th Regiment, and had been in the 32nd Regiment from ensign to lieutenant and captain, and had served in the East Indies.

Major-General Frederick Markham, c.b.

FREDERICK MARKHAM was the youngest son of Vice-Admiral John Markham, M.P. for Portsmouth, and grandson of William Markham, Archbishop of York. His mother was Maria, daughter of G. Rice, Esq., and the Baroness Dynover. General Markham was born at Ades, his father's seat, in Sussex, on August 16th, 1805. He was educated at Westminster school, leaving it in 1824, when he obtained a commission in the 32nd Regiment. Served in Canada, in command of the light company of the 32nd, during the rebellion in 1837, and was very severely wounded in the action of St. Denis. He served also in the Punjaub campaign of 1848-49, having commanded the 2nd Infantry Brigade at the first and second siege operations before Mooltan (wounded 10th September, 1848); the division, at the action of Soorjkoond, when the enemy's position was carried and seven guns taken; and the Bengal column, at the storming and capture of the city of Mooltan, on 2nd January, 1849; he was also present at the surrender of the fortress of Mooltan, on 22nd January, and at the surrender of the fort and garrison of Cheniote, on 9th February. On 20th February he joined the army of the Punjaub with his brigade, and commanded it at the battle of Goojerat the following day, for which services he was nominated a Companion of the Bath, received Punjaub medal with clasps, C.B., Mooltan and Goojerat, and aide-de-camp to the Queen.

In 1852 he published a "Journal of sporting adventures and travel in Ladak, Tibet, and Cashmere."

Appointed adjutant-general in India, March, 1854; major-general, 28th November, 1854. In the Crimea commanded the second division as lieutenant-general; commanded that division at the attack on Redan, and witnessed the fall of Sevastopol. And here a passing tribute must be paid to the memory of one of the best and most popular of the many good officers the corps has produced. The scion of a good fighting stock, Frederick Markham joined the 32nd, in which all his regimental service was passed, in May, 1824. As captain of the light company he signalized himself during the Canadian rebellion, especially in the affair with the insurgents at St. Denis, on which occasion his "romantic gallantry," to quote the words of an eye-witness, was conspicuous, and he received four severe wounds. He became lieutenant-colonel of the regiment, by purchase, in July, 1842. He commanded the 2nd Infantry Brigade throughout the second Sikh war (wounded, repeatedly mentioned in despatches, C.B.), and was afterwards adjutant-general of Queen's troops in India, from the time of his return to India from leave, up to November, 1854, when he was promoted to the rank of major-general, and appointed to the division at Peshawur. When within two days journey of his new command, he was recalled to take command of a division in the Crimea. Performing the journey down in the unexampled short space of eighteen days at the hottest season of the year, he arrived in the Crimea in March, 1855, and took over the second division (with the local rank of lieutenant-general), commanding it at the last attack upon the Redan. He was just able to witness the fall of Sevastopol, when his health, which had been in a very precarious state, broke down altogether, and necessitated his return to England. He died in London, on 21st November, 1855, and was buried at Morland. A white marble monument to his memory was erected by officers of the 32nd Regiment. His death, at the age of fifty, deprived the country of an officer who appeared destined to attain to the highest distinction.

Major-General Thomas Maunsell, c.b.

Thomas Maunsell served in the 32nd Regiment throughout the Punjaub campaign of 1848-49, and was present at the first and second siege operations before Mooltan, including the attack on the enemy's strong position in front of the advanced trenches on 12th September, 1848 (slightly wounded); the action of Soorjkoond; storm and capture of the city (where he was personally engaged at one time with two Sikh soldiers, one of whom he killed), and surrender of the fortress; afterwards present at the capture of the fort and garrison of Cheniote, and at the battle of Goojerat (medal and two clasps); was severely wounded at Mooltan on 21st January, 1849 (by a splinter of shell on the left shoulder and arm).

Served in the Eastern campaign of 1854, and up to 20th February, 1855, in the 28th Regiment, including the battles of Alma and Inkerman and siege of Sevastopol, during which time he commanded the Volunteer Sharpshooters of the third division for seventy-six days (for which most perilous service he volunteered), until severely wounded (bullet through left arm, bone broken), on 30th December, 1854, for which service he was honourably mentioned in Division Orders of 3rd January, 1855. He joined his regiment again in the Crimea, and served with it there until after the war, when the regiment embarked for Malta (medal and three clasps, Sardinian and Turkish medals, and fifth class of the Order of the Medjidie); promoted brevet-major 2nd November, 1855; served in India during the latter part of the Mutiny of 1858-6c, during which time (nearly two years) he commanded the 28th Regiment when a detachment of the regiment was employed with the Okamundel Field Force at the storming and capture of the fort of Beyt, and at the siege and occupation of Dwarka.

Nominated a Companion of the Order of the Bath, 29th May, 1875.

SERVICES OF THE OFFICERS, 32ND REGIMENT

AND THOSE OF THE

DUKE OF CORNWALL'S LIGHT INFANTRY,

(THREE BATTALIONS).

ALEXANDER, WILLIAM JAMES. Ensign, 32nd Regiment, 12th March, 1861; lieutenant, 16th January, 1866; captain, 19th October, 1872; major, 1st July, 1881; retired, with rank of lieutenant-colonel, 12th February, 1887.

ALLATT, HENRY THOMAS WARD. Ensign, 46th Regiment, 30th October, 1866; lieutenant, 22nd October, 1870; captain, 26th July, 1876; major, 1st January, 1886. Passed staff college.

ANDERSON, WILLIAM JAMES. Ensign, 32nd Regiment, 15th August, 1848; lieutenant, 16th September, 1851; captain, 11th August, 1857; major, 27th March, 1872; lieutenant-colonel, 25th June, 1878; colonel, 23rd July, 1879. Served in the operations against the hill tribes on the Peshawar frontier in 1851-52, and was present at the affairs of Prunghur and Sharkote (medal and clasp.)

APLIN, JOHN G. O. Captain, 3rd battalion Duke of Cornwall's Light Infantry, 4th April, 1888.

ASHBY, GEORGE ASHBY. Lieutenant, 32nd Regiment, 20th November, 1875; captain, 1st January, 1886; brevet major, 2nd January, 1886. Served as adjutant with the 2nd battalion Duke of Cornwall's Light Infantry throughout the Egyptian war of 1882, and was present in the engagements at El Magfar and Tel-el-Mahuta, in the two actions at Kassasin, and at the battle of Tel-el-Kebir (mentioned in despatches, medal with clasp, 5th class of the Medjidie, and Khedive's star). Served with the Nile expedition, in 1884-85, with the 2nd battalion of the Duke of Cornwall's Light Infantry, and took part in the operations of the advance column under Major-General Earle (mentioned in despatches, brevet of major, clasp).

BACE, HENRY WILLIAM. Ensign, 32nd Regiment, 15th February, 1833; lieutenant, 27th July, 1838; captain, 7th July, 1848.

BADGLEY, ALEX. JAMES. Ensign, 32nd Regiment, 1st June, 1855: lieutenant, 8th January, 1858. Served during the Indian mutiny in 1858-59, and was present at the action of Doadpore, and throughout the Oudh campaign (medal).

BALLARD, JOHN FANE. Ensign, 32nd Regiment, 8th January, 1864; lieutenant, 17th April, 1866; captain, 14th June, 1876; major, 1st July, 1881; retired, with rank of lieutenant-colonel, 14th December, 1887.

BARNETT, CAREW. 2nd lieutenant, Duke of Cornwall's Light Infantry, 16th November, 1887; lieutenant, 28th February, 1889. Now wing officer, 3rd Madras Native Infantry.

BASSANO, ALFRED. Ensign, 32nd Regiment, 3rd April, 1846; lieutenant, 24th May, 1848; captain, 15th October, 1856; brevet major, 24th March 1858; brevet lieutenant-colonel, 16th March, 1860; major, 27th July, 1866; colonel, 16th March, 1868. Served with the 32nd Regiment at the first and second siege operations before Mooltan, including the attack on the enemy's position in front of the advanced trenches on 12th September, 1848, the action of Soorjkoond, storm and capture of the city, and surrender of the fortress; also present at the surrender of the fort and garrison of Cheniote, and at the battle of Goojerat (medal with two clasps). Served during the Indian mutiny, in 1857-59; was in action at Chinhut, on 30th June, 1857, (severely wounded), and from that date engaged in the defence of the Residency of Lucknow, until its final relief by Lord Clyde, on 24th November, 1857; engaged in a sortie on

26th September, when seven guns were captured, and was in command of the regiment from 27th September to 24th November (mentioned in despatches by Sir John Inglis and the governor general, brevets of major and lieutenant-colonel ; also engaged in the defeat of the Gwalior rebels at Cawnpore, on the 6th December, 1857, and in part of the subsequent campaign at Oudh (medal with clasp, and grant of a year's service for Lucknow.)

BASSANO, ALFRED ERNEST. 2nd lieutenant, 32nd Regiment, 22nd January, 1881 ; lieutenant, 1st July, 1881. Died at Malta.

BAYLY, GEORGE C. Lieutenant, Royal Artillery, 1st March, 1863 ; captain, 8th December, 1875 ; brevet major, 1st March, 1883 ; paymaster, Duke of Cornwall's Light Infantry, 13th September, 1882. Served in the Afghan war of 1878-80 (medal). Served with the Nile expedition in 1884-85 (medal with clasp, and Khedive's star).

BEAUMONT, LINDESAY BEAUMONT. Ensign, 32nd Regiment, 3rd April, 1867 ; lieutenant, 20th October, 1869 ; captain, 1st July, 1881. Retired.

BELL, WILLIAM. Ensign, 32nd Regiment, 30th November, 1815 ; lieutenant, 26th April, 1828 ; captain, 2nd July, 1841 ; brevet major, 20th June, 1854 ; major, 23rd March, 1858 ; brevet lieutenant-colonel, 16th January, 1859. Was present at the battle of Goojerat (medal and clasps).

BELL, PERCY TAYLOR. Lieutenant, Duke of Cornwall's Light Infantry, 30th January, 1886.

BENNETT, HENRY ELKINS. Ensign, 32nd Regiment, 14th September, 1855 ; lieutenant, 29th April, 1856. Served during the Indian mutiny in 1857-59, and was present at the capture of the forts Dehaign and Tyrhool, action of Doadpore, and throughout the Oudh campaign (medal).

BEVAN, STUART J. 2nd lieutenant, 3rd battalion Duke of Cornwall's Light Infantry, 25th January, 1890.

BICKFORD-SMITH, R. A. H. Captain, 3rd battalion Duke of Cornwall's Light Infantry, 5th October, 1881.

BIRTWHISTLE, WM. AIRDE. Ensign, 32nd Regiment, 12th December, 1843; captain, 3rd April, 1846. Served at the first and second siege operations before Mooltan, including the attack on the enemy's position in front of the advanced trenches on 12th September, 1848, the action of Soorjkoond, storm and capture of the city, and surrender of the fortress. Also present at the surrender of the fort and garrison of Cheniote, and at the battle of Goojerat (medal and clasps). Was wounded at Mooltan, 12th September, 1848.

BIRTWHISTLE, JOHN. Ensign, 32nd Regiment, 11th December, 1847; lieutenant, 3rd September, 1849; captain, 28th June, 1857. Served with the 32nd Regiment in the Punjaub campaign of 1848-49, including the second siege operations before Mooltan, the storm and capture of the city and surrender of the fortress; also at the surrender of the fort and garrison of Cheniote and battle of Goojerat (medal and clasps).

BISHOP, ARTHUR. Ensign, 32nd Regiment, 12th February, 1858.

BLAKE-AUGHTON, GEO. E. Captain, 3rd battalion Duke of Cornwall's Light Infantry, 9th May, 1891.

BLISS, LEONARD PHILIP HENRY. 2nd lieutenant, Duke of Cornwall's Light Infantry, 4th May, 1887; lieutenant, 26th January, 1890.

BLUETT, CHARLES EDW. LANE. Ensign, 55th Regiment, 15th January, 1856; lieutenant, 32nd Regiment, 5th February, 1858; captain, 25th September, 1860; captain, 22nd Regiment, 25th September, 1867; brevet major, 22nd August, 1873; major, 13th March, 1878; lieutenant-colonel, 21st April, 1882; commanded 22nd Regiment, 21st April, 1886.

BOND, DAVID. Ensign, 32nd Regiment, 7th September, 1858; lieutenant, 22nd January, 1864; captain, 16th September, 1868; major, 1st July, 1881; lieutenant-colonel, 29th June, 1886; brevet colonel, 29th June, 1890. Retired.

APPENDIX. 347

BOWLES, JOHN TREACHER. 2nd lieutenant, 46th Regiment, 23rd October, 1880; lieutenant, 1st July, 1881. Served with the Nile expedition in 1884-85 (medal with clasp). Died, 1886.

BOYD, WILLIAM. Assistant surgeon, 12th March, 1852; surgeon, 7th September, 1858. Served during the Indian mutiny, in 1857-59, and was engaged in the defence of the Residency of Lucknow from 30th June until its final relief on 24th November by Lord Clyde, during which time he officiated as medical officer in charge of the European garrison hospital, besides having charge of the 32nd Regiment—was promoted surgeon " for eminent services " rendered throughout the whole siege of Lucknow, and mentioned in despatches by Sir John Inglis and the governor general; present also at the defeat of the Gwalior rebels at Cawnpore, on 6th December, and accompanied the 32nd Regiment in several minor excursions after the mutineers, both before and subsequent to the siege of Lucknow (medal and clasp).

BRADFORD, SUTHERLAND HENRY. 2nd lieutenant, Duke of Cornwall's Light Infantry, 4th May, 1887; lieutenant, 4th January, 1890.

BRADSHAW, WILLIAM, (V.C.) Assistant surgeon, 15th August, 1854. Served with the 50th Regiment at the siege and fall of Sebastopol, from 8th November, 1854 (medal and clasp, and Turkish medal). Served with the 90th Light Infantry during the Indian campaign of 1857-58, and was present with Havelock's column at the actions of the 21st and 23rd September (wounded), relief and subsequent defence of Lucknow, defence of the Alumbagh under Outram, and fall of Lucknow (medal and clasps, and Victoria Cross).

BROOKE, HENRY VAUGHAN, C.B. Ensign, 32nd Regiment, 12th July, 1827; lieutenant, 11th June, 1830; captain, 22nd May, 1835; major, 22nd July, 1842; lieutenant-colonel, 13th September, 1848. Served in the Punjaub campaign of 1848-49, in command of the 32nd, and was present at the first and second siege operations before Mooltan (including the action of

Soorjkoond, in command of the left column of attack), storm and capture of the city and surrender of the fortress of Mooltan, surrender of the fort and garrison of Cheniote, and battle of Goojerat, for which services he was nominated a Companion of the Bath (medal and clasps).

BROWNE, HENRY GEORGE, (V.C.) Ensign, 32nd Regiment, 31st August, 1855 ; lieutenant, 15th October, 1856 ; captain, 1st June, 1858 ; major, 1st February, 1868 ; lieutenant-colonel, 27th February, 1877 ; colonel, 1st July, 1881. Served in the 32nd Regiment during the Indian mutiny, in 1857-58, and was present at the action of Chinhut and defence of Lucknow Residency from June to November, 1857. Also with Maxwell's force in the Suregon campaign of 1855. Was twice wounded—once severely. Thanked in general orders by Sir J. Outram, Sir J. Inglis, and by the governor general (Victoria Cross, medal with clasp, with a year's service) ; was awarded the V.C. " for conspicuous bravery in having, on the 21st August, 1857, " during the siege of the Lucknow Residency, gallantly led a " sortie, at great personal risk, for the purpose of spiking two " heavy guns which were doing considerable damage to the " defences. It appears from the statements of the non-" commissioned officers and men who accompanied Captain " Browne on the occasion, that he was the first person who " entered the battery, which consisted of the two guns in " question, protected by high palisades, the embrasures being " closed with sliding shutters. On reaching the battery, " Lieutenant Browne removed the shutters and jumped into the " battery. The result was that the guns were spiked, and it is " supposed that about one hundred of the enemy were " killed."

BROWNE, WILLIAM BARRINGTON. Ensign, 46th Regiment, 8th January, 1868 ; lieutenant, 16th March, 1870 ; captain, 1st July, 1876 ; brevet major, 18th November, 1882 ; major, 26th July, 1885. Served in the Egyptian war of 1882, and was present in the engagements at El Magfar and Tel-el-Mahuta, at the two actions at Kassasin, and at the battle of Tel-el-Kebir (mentioned in despatches, brevet of major, medal with clasp, and Khedive's star).

BUCK, WALTER KEATS. 2nd lieutenant, Duke of Cornwall's Light Infantry, 29th November, 1890.

BURDER, ERNEST SUMNER. Lieutenant, Duke of Cornwall's Light Infantry, 7th February, 1885 ; adjutant, 2nd battalion, 26th January, 1890.

CANTAN, HENRY T. 2nd lieutenant, Duke of Cornwall's Light Infantry, 18th May, 1892.

CARDEN, HENRY PARRY. Lieutenant, 81st Regiment, 13th June, 1874 ; captain, 8th May, 1883 ; brevet major, 15th June, 1885. Served with the 2nd battalion Duke of Cornwall's Light Infantry throughout the Egyptian war of 1882, and was present in the engagements at El Magfar and Tel-el-Mahuta, in the actions at Kassasin, on 28th August (wounded) and 9th September, and at the battle of Tel-el-Kebir (medal with clasp, and Khedive's star). Served in the Nile expedition in 1884-85 with the 2nd battalion of the Duke of Cornwall's Light Infantry, and took part in the operations of the advance column under Major-General Earle (mentioned in despatches, brevet of major, 3rd class of the Medjidie, clasp).

CARDEN, HENRY WESTENRA. Lieutenant, 46th Regiment, 21st September, 1874 ; captain, 13th December, 1884. Served with the 2nd battalion of the Duke of Cornwall's Light Infantry throughout the Egyptian war of 1882, and was present in the engagements at El Magfar and Tel-el-Mahuta, in the two actions at Kassasin, and at the battle of Tel-el-Kebir (medal with clasp, and Khedive's star). Served with the Nile expedition in 1884-85 (clasp). Transferred to Army Pay Department, 17th November, 1885.

CARMICHAEL, CLAUDE D. J. Lieutenant, 3rd battalion Duke of Cornwall's Light Infantry, 6th September, 1890.

350   APPENDIX.

CARMICHAEL, JAMES DODINGTON, C.B. Ensign, 32nd Regiment, 12th July, 1839; lieutenant, 11th May, 1841; captain, 18th April, 1845; major, 20th February, 1855; brevet lieutenant-colonel, 1st February 1856; lieutenant-colonel, 26th November, 1857. Served with the 32nd Regiment at the first and second siege operations before Mooltan, and was at the action of Soorjkoond; led the right column of attack at the storm and capture of the city of Mooltan (wounded), and was present at the surrender of the fortress, as also at the surrender of the fort and garrison of Cheniote, and at the battle of Goojerat (medal and clasps). Commanded the regiment in the Indian campaign at the attack and capture of the forts of Dehaign and Tyrhool, under Brigadier Berkeley; again at the action of Doadpore and defeat of the Nuseerabad mutineers, under Brigadier Horsford, and was thanked in that officer's despatch "for the able "manner in which he commanded the infantry." Served in the campaign for the reduction of Oudh—commanded a movable column, which, acting under the orders of, and in conjunction with, Lord Clyde's force, was sent in pursuit of the rebel chief Beni Maddoo, to drive him and his troops across the river Gogra, which object the column successfully accomplished—mentioned in Lord Clyde's despatch as "distinguished for the "decision and celerity of his movements" (C.B., medal).

CARPENTER, GEORGE WILLIAM WALLACE. Ensign, 32nd Regiment, 17th June, 1851; lieutenant, 27th January, 1854; captain, 12th January, 1855; major, 13th May, 1859. Appointed to the reserve, 7th July, 1880. Served with the 7th Fusiliers in the Eastern campaign of 1854, and was wounded at the battle of Alma (medal with clasp, and Turkish medal).

CASE, WILLIAM. Ensign, 32nd Regiment, 10th February, 1832; lieutenant, 9th February, 1838; captain, 25th February, 1842; major, 13th September, 1848. Served at the first and second siege operations against Mooltan, part of the time as major of brigade to the 2nd Infantry Brigade, including the assault on the suburbs of Mooltan, 27th December, 1848, on which

APPENDIX. 351

occasion he commanded the companies of the 32nd that were engaged, and was very severely wounded. He was afterwards present at the surrender of the fort and garrison of Cheniote, and at the battle of Goojerat (medal and clasps). Lucknow, 1857. Killed at battle of Chinhut.

CATHCART, HUGH W. MORT. Ensign, 32nd Regiment, 3rd June, 1859.

CHAPMAN, FREDERIC HAMILTON. Lieutenant, Duke of Cornwall's Light Infantry, 6th February, 1884 ; captain, 23rd May, 1890.

CHARLTON, JAMES WOLFE. Ensign, 32nd Regiment, 8th July, 1856 ; lieutenant, 28th June, 1857.

CHERRY, CHARLES E. LE M. Ensign, 32nd Regiment, 23rd March, 1858 ; lieutenant, 25th September, 1860 ; captain, 16th October, 1866 ; major, 30th January, 1880 ; lieutenant-colonel, 1st July, 1886. Served through Zulu war (medal) ; Egypt, 1885. Died, as commander-in-chief, at Suakim.

CLAPCOTT, CHARLES. Ensign, 32nd Regiment, 18th April, 1845 ; lieutenant, 12th June, 1846 ; captain, 23rd July, 1852 ; major, 26th September, 1858. Served with the 32nd Regiment at the first and second siege operations before Mooltan, including the attack on the enemy's position in front of the advanced trenches on 12th September, 1848 ; the action of Soorjkoond, storm and capture of the city, and surrender of the fortress ; also present at the surrender of the fort and garrison of Cheniote, and at the battle of Goojerat (medal and clasps).

CLARKE, ALBERT. Ensign, 32nd Regiment, 10th April, 1866 ; lieutenant, 26th September, 1868 ; captain, 26th May, 1880. Retired.

CLERY, CORNELIUS FRANCIS, C.B. Ensign, 32nd Regiment, 5th March, 1858 ; lieutenant, 3rd June, 1859 ; captain, 16th January, 1866 ; major, 20th March, 1878 ; lieutenant-colonel, 29th November, 1879 ; colonel, 21st May, 1884. Commandant of Staff College, with rank of brigadier-general. Served in South African war, 1879 ; Zulu campaign, battles of Isandhlwana and Ulundi (despatches, *London Gazette*, 15th March and 21st

August, 1879 ; medal with clasp, brevet of lieutenant-colonel) ;
Egyptian campaign, 1884 ; Soudan (assistant-adjutant-general);
battles of El Teb and Tamai (despatches, *London Gazette*, 27th
March and 6th May, 1884 ; two clasps and C.B.)

COCHRANE, WILLIAM FRANCIS DUNDONALD. Ensign, 32nd
Regiment, 31st August, 1866 ; lieutenant, 2nd December, 1868 ;
captain, 14th June, 1881 ; brevet major, 18th February, 1882 ;
major, 29th June, 1886. Served in the Zulu war of 1879, and
was present in the engagement at Isandhlwana, on 22nd
January, as orderly officer to Colonel Durnford ; served afterwards with Wood's column in command of the Natal native
horse, taking part in the engagements at Inhlobana Mountains,
Kambula, and Ulundi (brevet of major, medal with clasp).
Served as assistant-adjutant-general (principal staff officer) to
Cape colonial forces during the Basuto war, in 1880-81, and
was present at the capture of Lerothodi's stronghold and several
minor engagements. Served in the Egyptian war of 1882, with
the commissariat and transport corps (medal and Khedive's
star). Assistant military secretary, South Africa. Appointed to
command brigade, Egyptian army, 1893.

COLLS, ROBERT STACY. Ensign, 32nd Regiment, 14th February,
1840 ; lieutenant, 24th April, 1843 ; captain, 20th February,
1855 ; major, 26th April, 1859 ; lieutenant-colonel, 1st April,
1866. Served with the 39th Regiment in the battle of Maharajpore (medal). Served with the 32nd in the Punjaub campaign
of 1848-49, and was present at the second siege operations
before Mooltan, including the storm and capture of the city, and
surrender of the fortress ; also present at the surrender of the
garrison of Cheniote, and at the battle of Goojerat (medal and
clasps). Served during the Indian mutiny, in 1857-59, and
present as field engineer to the force under Brigadier Berkeley
at the capture of the forts of Dehaign and Tyrhool (mentioned
in despatches) ; also as deputy assistant quarter-master general
to Brigadier Pinckney's force during the campaign in Oudh
(brevet of major, medal).

CONRAN, GERALD MARCELL. Captain, 3rd battalion Duke of Cornwall's Light Infantry, 12th November, 1887.

CONWAY, JOHN. Hon. lieutenant and quarter-master, Duke of Cornwall's Light Infantry, 30th November, 1881 ; hon. captain, 13th November, 1891.

CORNISH-BOWDEN, JAMES H. T. 2nd lieutenant, Duke of Cornwall's Light Infantry, 23rd March, 1892.

CREGOE, EDWD. GARLAND COLMORE. Ensign, 32nd Regiment, 16th September, 1868.

CROWDY, WILLIAM MORSE. Ensign, 32nd Regiment, 27th June, 1851.

CROZIER, BURRARD, RAWSON. First commission, 32nd Regiment, 12th December, 1868 ; paymaster, 2nd March, 1885. Transferred to Royal Scots Fusiliers 1882.

CUMMING, WILLIAM. Ensign, 32nd Regiment, 8th April, 1842 ; lieutenant, 3rd May, 1844.

CUNNINGHAM, GEORGE GLECAIRN. Lieutenant, Duke of Cornwall's Light Infantry, 22nd October, 1881 ; captain, Derbyshire Regiment, 14th August, 1889 ; brevet major, 15th August, 1889. Served in the Egyptian war of 1882, and was present in the engagements at El Magfar and Tel-el-Mahuta, and in the action at Kassasin on 28th August—twice wounded (mentioned in despatches, medal, 5th class of the Mejidie, and Khedive's star.) Served in the Nile expedition of 1884-85 with the 2nd battalion of the Duke of Cornwall's Light Infantry, and took part in the operations of the advance column under Major-General Earle (clasp). Now serving with the Egyptian army.

CUNYNGHAME, EDW. AUG. T. Ensign, 32nd Regiment, 9th October, 1855 ; lieutenant, 26th February, 1856 ; captain, 11th March, 1859. Retired. Now Sir Edward Cunynghame, Bart.

CUNSTANCE, SYDNEY. Lieutenant, Duke of Cornwall's Light Infantry, 22nd October, 1881 ; captain, 14th August, 1889 ; adjutant,

AA

1st battalion. Served in Burmah in Mounted Infantry, 1891 (mentioned in despatches.)

DE MONTMORENCY, THE HONBLE. WILLOUGHBY JOHN HORACE. 2nd lieutenant, Duke of Cornwall's Light Infantry, 22nd August, 1888; lieutenant, 20th April, 1891. Served in Burmah with Mounted Infantry, 1891.

DISNEY-ROEBUCK, FRANCIS HENRY A. Ensign, 46th Regiment, 26th February, 1864; lieutenant, 17th April, 1867; captain, 9th April, 1870; major, 1st July, 1881. Served in the Nile expedition in 1884-85 with the 2nd battalion of the Duke of Cornwall's Light Infantry, and took part in the operations of the advance column under Major-General Earle (medal with clasp, and Khedive's Star). Commanding 1st battalion, 1st July, 1891.

DUCAT, RICHARD. 2nd lieutenant, Duke of Cornwall's Light Infantry, 13th August, 1892.

DUMARESQ, ARTHUR HEMERY. Lieutenant, 32nd Regiment, 19th June, 1874; captain, 1st October, 1883. Served in the Nile expedition in 1884-85 with the 2nd battalion of the Duke of Cornwall's Light Infantry (medal with clasp).

EARY, CHARLES J. Hon. lieutenant and quarter-master, 2nd battalion Duke of Cornwall's Light Infantry, 3rd August, 1892.

EDEN, JOHN MONTAGU RODNEY. Lieutenant, 46th Regiment, 27th June, 1875; captain, 26th January, 1884. Served in the Egyptian war of 1882, and was present in the engagements at El Magfar and Tel-el-Mahuta, in the two actions at Kassasin, and at the battle of Tel-el-Kebir (medal with clasp, and Khedive's star). Served in the Nile expedition in 1884-85, and was present with the river column under Major-General Earle and Brigadier General Brackenbury (clasp). Also served in the operations in 1885-86, under Sir Frederick Stephenson, as special service officer on the staff.

EDMONDSTOUNE, JOHN. Ensign, 32nd Regiment, 15th October, 1850; lieutenant, 5th January, 1855; captain, 2nd October,

1857 ; brevet major, 24th March, 1858 ; brevet lieutenant-colonel, 18th March, 1869 ; major-general, 1st April, 1882. Served with the 32nd Regiment during the Indian mutiny, in 1857-59 ; defended the iron bridge over the river Gomtee, with fifty men to cover the retreat from Chinhut, on 30th June, 1857, and from that date engaged in the defence of the Residency of Lucknow until its final relief, on 24th November, by Lord Clyde ; led a sortie on 29th September, and was twice severely wounded—on 20th July and 29th September (mentioned in despatches by Sir John Inglis and the governor general, brevet of major) ; and subsequently engaged in the defeat of the Gwalior rebels at Cawnpore, on 6th December, at the capture of the forts of Dehaign and Tyrool, and throughout the Oudh campaign, during part of which he served as staff officer to the movable column, under Lieutenant-Colonel Carmichael (medal with clasp, and grant of a year's service for Lucknow ; recommended for Victoria Cross).

ELIOT, HONBLE. CHAS. G. C. Hon. colonel, commanding 3rd battalion Duke of Cornwall's Light Infantry, 29th June, 1889. Late lieutenant and captain Grenadier Guards.

EVELEGH, CHARLES NEWMAN. 2nd lieutenant, 32nd Regiment, 19th February, 1881 ; lieutenant, 1st July, 1881 ; captain, 14th August, 1889 ; adjutant, 1st battalion, 1st March, 1889.

FALLS, JOHN ALEXANDER WRIGHT. Lieutenant, 32nd Regiment, 29th November, 1876 ; captain, 12th February, 1887. Captain, Army Service Corps, 1st April, 1889. Served in the Egyptian war of 1882, and was present at the action at Kassasin on the 28th August (mentioned in despatches), and at the battle of Tel-el-Kebir (mentioned in despatches, medal with clasp, and Khedive's star).

FARWELL, WILLIAM. Ensign, 46th Regiment, 29th September, 1865 ; lieutenant, 12th December, 1868 ; captain, 21st July, 1375. Served in the Egyptian war of 1882, and was present at the battle of Tel-el-Kebir (medal with clasp, and Khedive's star).

FAULKNER, STAFFORD BETT. Captain, 3rd battalion Duke of Cornwall's Light Infantry, 2nd February, 1889.

FENTON, REGINALD W. C. 2nd lieutenant, 3rd battalion Duke of Cornwall's Light Infantry, 23rd March, 1891.

FERGUSSON, WILLIAM JAMES SMYTH. Lieutenant, Duke of Cornwall's Light Infantry, 6th February, 1884; captain, 29th June, 1890. Served with the Nile expedition in 1884-85, with the 2nd battalion of the Duke of Cornwall's Light Infantry, and took part in the operations of the advance column under Major-General Earle (medal with clasp, and Khedive's star).

FOLL, RICH. NATHANIEL CARTWRIGHT. Ensign, 32nd Regiment, 23rd April, 1858; lieutenant, 6th January, 1860; captain, 23rd June, 1865. Retired.

FORSTER, JAMES FITZEUSTACE. Ensign, 46th Regiment, 19th December, 1862; lieutenant, 14th September, 1866; captain, 16th September, 1868; major, 1st July, 1881; brevet lieutenant-colonel, 21st May, 1884; colonel, 26th May, 1888. Served in the Egyptian war of 1882, and was present in the reconnaissance in force from Alexandria on the 5th August, in the engagement at El Magfar, and at the action at Kassasin on the 28th August—severely wounded (medal, and Khedive's star). Served with the transport department in the Soudan expedition in 1884 (mentioned in despatches, brevet of lieutenant-colonel, and clasp). Served in the Nile expedition in 1884-85 with the 2nd battalion Duke of Cornwall's Light Infantry, and took part in the operations of the advance column under Major-General Earle (clasp).

FORSTER, THOMAS HENRY BURTON. Lieutenant, 81st Regiment, 23rd March, 1872; captain, 10th November, 1880; major, Royal Warwick Regiment, 16th December, 1891. Was deputy assistant-adjutant-general, Belfast, 25th September, 1888.

FOSTER, CHARLES MARSHALL. Ensign, 32nd Regiment, 18th April, 1851; lieutenant, 14th April, 1855; captain, 26th November,

1857 ; major, 24th March, 1858. Served in the Indian mutiny in 1857-58, and was in action with the rebel force at Chinut on the 30th June, 1857, and from that date engaged in the defence of the Residency of Lucknow until its final relief by Lord Clyde on 24th November—was severely wounded during the siege, and mentioned in despatches by Sir John Inglis and the governor general ; was subsequently engaged in the defeat of the Gwalior rebels at Cawnpore, on 6th December, 1857 (medal and clasp, and brevet of major).

FRANCIS, WOLSTAN. Lieutenant, 32nd Regiment, 20th November, 1875 ; captain, 17th February, 1886. Served with the 2nd battalion Duke of Cornwall's Light Infantry throughout the Egyptian war of 1882, and was present at the reconnaissance in force from Alexandria, on the 5th August, in the engagements at El Magfar and Tel-el-Mahuta, in the two actions at Kassasin, and at the battle of Tel-el-Kebir (medal with clasp, and Khedive's star). Was adjutant, 3rd battalion, 3rd January, 1887.

FRANKFORT DE MONTMORENCY, VISCOUNT RAYMOND HARVEY. Ensign, 33rd Regiment, 18th August, 1854 ; lieutenant, 12th January, 1855 ; captain, 29th March, 1861 ; major, 25th September, 1869 ; lieutenant-colonel, 14th June, 1876 ; colonel, 14th June, 1881 ; major-general, 30th November, 1889. Served with the 33rd Regiment in the Crimea in 1855, including the siege and fall of Sevastopol and attack of the Redan on the 8th September (medal with clasp, Sardinian and Turkish medals). Commanded a detachment of the 33rd against the rebels, and, after the death of the senior officer, commanded the Dohud field force in suppressing the insurgent Bheels in the Rewa Kanta, Guzerat. Served with a wing of the regiment at the siege and occupation of Dwarka, Okamundel. Served in the Abyssinian campaign of 1867-68 (medal). Commanded the Frontier Field Force during the operations in the Soudan, in 1886-87 (Khedive's star). Commanding 1st class District in India.

FRASER, WALTER SIMON. 2nd lieutenant, Duke of Cornwall's Light

Infantry, 23rd March, 1887 ; lieutenant, 3rd March, 1888. Now officiating squadron officer, 19th Bengal Cavalry.

GARDEN, FRANCIS ANTHONY. Ensign, 32nd Regiment, 5th January, 1866 ; lieutenant, 21st March, 1868. Retired.

GARFORTH, WM. Quarter-master, 32nd Regiment, 28th June, 1844 ; ensign, 3rd April, 1846 ; lieutenant, 24th February, 1848 ; paymaster, 16th April, 1852. Served with the 32nd Regiment in Canada during the rebellion in 1837, and was present at the action of St. Eustache. Served as adjutant during the first and second siege operations before Mooltan, including the action of Soorjkoond, storm and capture of the city, and surrender of the fortress. Also at the surrender of the fort and garrison of Cheniote, and at the battle of Goojerat (medal and clasps).

GARFORTH, JOHN. Ensign, 32nd Regiment, 19th June, 1857 ; lieutenant, 6th February, 1858. Served during the Indian mutiny in 1858-59, including the Oudh campaign (medal). Now Rev. J. Garforth, rector of Spexhall, Halesvork, Suffolk.

GARNETT, HENRY PERCY. Lieutenant, 32nd Regiment, 20th November, 1875 ; captain, 12th February, 1887. Retired.

GIDDINGS, JOHN. Quarter-master, 32nd Regiment, 13th September, 1848 ; paymaster, 28th November, 1856. Served at the first and second siege operations before Mooltan, including the action of Soorjkoond, storm and capture of the city, and surrender of the fortress ; also at the surrender of the fort and garrison of Cheniote, and battle of Goojerat (medal and clasps). Served during the Indian mutiny, in 1857-59, and was engaged in the defence of the Residency of Lucknow from 30th June until its final relief on 24th November by Lord Clyde, during part of which time he acted as adjutant of the regiment, and was also in temporary charge of posts in addition to other duties ; was subsequently engaged in the defeat of the Gwalior rebels at Cawnpore on 6th December, 1857 (medal and clasp).

APPENDIX. 359

GILBY, HENRY MANT. Ensign, 32nd Regiment, 17th August, 1855: lieutenant, 9th November, 1855. Served with a detachment of the 88th Regiment in the operations at Cawnpore, under General Windham, and was severely wounded at the attack against the Gwalior contingent on 26th November, 1857 (medal).

GLASCOTT, JAMES JOCELYN. Ensign, 32nd Regiment, 9th May, 1865; lieutenant, 22nd February, 1868; captain, Manchester Regiment, 9th July, 1879; hon. major, 13th September, 1886.

GLEGG, EDWARD MAXWELL. Ensign, 32nd Regiment, 30th October, 1869.

GLYN, CHARLES ROBERT. Ensign, 32nd Regiment, 28th October, 1868.

GOAD, WILLIAM TRICKETT. Ensign, 32nd Regiment, 13th February, 1858. Served during the Indian mutiny in 1858-59; as a volunteer, with the 79th Highlanders, at the siege and capture of Lucknow by Lord Clyde; subsequently with the 32nd Regiment at the capture of the forts of Dehaign and Tyrhool, action of Doadpore, and throughout the Oudh campaign (medal and clasp).

GOLDING, HARRY. Ensign, Duke of Cornwall's Light Infantry, 31st December, 1861; lieutenant, 5th December, 1862; captain, 18th December, 1875; major, 1st July, 1881; hon. lieutenant-colonel, 18th July, 1886.

GOLDING, FRED. NASSAU. Ensign, 32nd Regiment, 29th October, 1858.

GRANT, FRANCIS WILLIAM SEAFIELD. Ensign, 2nd West India regiment, 4th July, 1865; lieutenant, 9th November, 1866; captain, 26th March, 1873; captain, 96th Regiment, 11th November, 1875; captain, 32nd Regiment, 13th September, 1879; major, 13th December, 1884. Served throughout the Ashantee war of 1873-74, and commanded the detachment 2nd West India regiment at the repulse of the Ashantee army at Abrakrampa, during the 5th and 6th November, 1873, and led it in two charges against an advanced party of the enemy—wounded; conduct of the detachment mentioned in despatches (Medal with clasp). Was aide-de-camp to governor, Bahamas, 27th May, 1869, to 7th July, 1870. Fort adjutant, Sierra Leone, 27th August, 1870, to 16th September, 1872. Aide-de-camp to governor, West Africa settlement, 1st April to 10th September, 1874.

GRANT, ALEXANDER GEORGE WILLIAM. 2nd lieutenant, Duke of Cornwall's Light Infantry, 28th June, 1890.

GRANT, JOHN JOSEPH FORSYTH. Ensign, 32nd Regiment, 25th April, 1858; lieutenant, 17th July, 1860; captain, 25th December, 1867; major, 1st July, 1881.

GRAY, JAMES THOMAS. Ensign, 32nd Regiment, 17th November, 1857; lieutenant, 30th April, 1858. Served during the Indian mutiny in 1858-59, including the Oudh campaign (medal).

GRIEVE, FRANK. Ensign, 46th Regiment, 20th February, 1855; lieutenant, 6th July, 1855; captain, 19th October, 1868; major, 1st July, 1881; brevet lieutenant-colonel, 18th November, 1882; lieutenant-colonel, 26th July, 1885; colonel, 18th November, 1886. Served with the 46th Regiment in the Crimea from the 3rd September, 1855, to the 20th May, 1856, including the siege and fall of Sevastopol (medal with clasp, and Turkish medal). Served with the 2nd battalion Duke of Cornwall's Light Infantry in the Egyptian war of 1882, and was present at the reconnaissance in force from Alexandria, on the 5th August, in command of the half battalion; in the engagements at El Magfar and Tel-el-Mahuta; at the action at Kassasin on the 28th August (mentioned in despatches), and at the battle of Tel-el-Kebir (brevet of lieutenant-colonel, medal with clasp, and Khedive's star); also served in the Nile expedition, in 1884-85, with the river column under Major-General Earle (clasp); in 1885 he was employed on the staff of the line of communications as commandant at Kaboddie. Commanded the 2nd battalion Duke of Cornwall's Light Infantry, 26th July, 1885.

APPENDIX. 361

GRIFFIN, FREDERICK GERALD GRIFFITH. 2nd lieutenant, 10th Foot, 22nd January, 1881 ; lieutenant, 1st July, 1881 ; captain, Duke of Cornwall's Light Infantry, 14th January, 1891.

GREEN, RICHARD MEAD. 2nd lieutenant, Duke of Cornwall's Light Infantry, 21st December, 1889. Transferred to Prince Consort's own Rifle Brigade.

HAMMANS, ARTHUR WILLIAM. Ensign, 32nd Regiment, 18th December, 1866 ; lieutenant, 25th September, 1869 ; captain, 29th June, 1881 ; major, 14th December, 1887. Now Commandant, Wellington Depôt.

HARDINGE, HERBERT RICHARD. Ensign, 32nd Regiment, 14th May, 1858 ; lieutenant, 22nd February, 1861 ; captain, 22nd February, 1868 ; major, 26th May, 1880 ; lieutenant-colonel, 1st July, 1881. Retired.

HARMAR, EDWIN. Ensign, 23rd March, 1855 ; lieutenant, 15th June, 1855 ; captain, 23rd March, 1858. Served during the Indian mutiny in 1857-58, and was in action with the rebel force at Chinut on 30th June, 1857, and from that date engaged in the defence of the Residency of Lucknow until its final relief on 24th November by Lord Clyde (severely wounded, leg fractured by a round shot, mentioned in despatches by Sir John Inglis and the governor general, medal and clasp).

HARRIS, WILLIAM HENRY, M.R.C.S., L.S.A. Assistant surgeon, 10th March, 1855 ; surgeon, 15th February, 1868 ; hon. brigade surgeon, 2nd May, 1880. Served in the Crimea from 22nd May, 1855, including the siege and fall of Sevastopol, the attack of the 18th June, and battle of the Tchernaya (medal and clasp). Also served during the Indian mutiny in 1857-59, including the Oudh campaign (medal).

HART, HENRY C. Hon. lieutenant and quarter-master, 2nd battalion Duke of Cornwall's Light Infantry, 10th June, 1882 ; hon. captain, 10th June, 1892. Served in the Egyptian war of 1882, and was present at the battle of Tel-el-Kebir (medal with clasp, and Khedive's star); also served with the Nile expedition in 1884-85 (clasp).

HARTLEY, JAMES. Ensign, 5th Fusiliers, 29th December, 1857; lieutenant, 24th December, 1858; captain, 32nd Foot, May, 1886. Retired, 1886.

HARVEY, WILLIAM LUEG. Ensign, 46th Regiment, 30th January, 1878; lieutenant, 18th June, 1881; captain, 1st July, 1887. Served with the 2nd battalion Duke of Cornwall's Light Infantry in the Egyptian war of 1882, and was present at the battle of Tel-el-Kebir (medal with clasp, and Khedive's star). Served in the Nile expedition in 1884-85 with the 2nd battalion Duke of Cornwall's Light Infantry, and took part in the operations of the advance column under Major-General Earle (clasp).

HATHERELL, WILLIAM GEORGE. Lieutenant, Duke of Cornwall's Light Infantry, 22nd October, 1881. Now wing officer, 22nd Bombay Native Infantry.

HAVELOCK, HIS EXCELLENCY SIR ARTHUR ELIBANK, K.C.M.G. Captain, 32nd Foot. Retired, 1877. Late chief civil commissioner for the Seychelles Islands, 1879. Governor and commander-in-chief of the West African Settlements, 1881-84; of Trinidad, 1881-85; of Natal, 1885-89; and of Ceylon since 1890.

HAWKER, EDMUND B. Lieutenant, 3rd battalion Duke of Cornwall's Light Infantry, 15th October, 1881.

HEATH, CHAS. ERNEST. Sub-lieutenant, 32nd Regiment, 9th August, 1873; lieutenant, 9th August, 1874; adjutant, 1st October, 1878, to 17th March, 1881; captain, 1st October, 1883; captain, Army Service Corps, 1st April, 1889; deputy assistant-adjutant-general, Malta, 11th December, 1888.

HEATHCOAT-AMORY, HARRY W. L. H. Lieutenant, 3rd battalion Duke of Cornwall's Light Infantry, 4th March, 1891; 2nd lieutenant, Coldstream Guards, 5th December, 1891.

APPENDIX. 363

HILL, BEAUCHAMP URQUHART. 2nd lieutenant, Duke of Cornwall's Light Infantry, 9th November, 1889. Died at Burmah, 2nd July, 1892.

HOLBROOK, ARTHUR ST. CLAIR. 2nd lieutenant, Duke of Cornwall's Light Infantry, 21st December, 1889; lieutenant, 3rd July, 1892.

HOLLAND, PERCY. Lieutenant, Duke of Cornwall's Light Infantry, 22nd October, 1881. Served in the Egyptian war of 1882, and was present in the engagements at El Magfar and Tel-el-Mahuta, at the two actions at Kassasin, and at the battle of Tel-el-Kebir (medal with clasp, and Khedive's star). Served with the Burmese expedition in 1885-87 (twice mentioned in despatches, medal with clasp). Now wing officer, 5th Punjaub Infantry.

HOLLWAY, EDMUND JOHN. Lieutenant, 46th Regiment, 11th September, 1876; captain, 2nd May, 1886. Served with the 2nd battalion Duke of Cornwall's Light Infantry throughout the Egyptian war of 1882, and was present at the reconnaissance in force from Alexandria on the 5th August, in the engagement at Tel-el-Mahuta, in the two actions at Kassasin, and at the battle of Tel-el-Kebir (medal with clasp and Khedive's star). Was adjutant, 1st volunteer battalion Duke of Cornwall's Light Infantry, November, 1887, to 1892.

HOLT, ERNEST WILLIAM LYONS. Lieutenant, Duke of Cornwall's Light Infantry, 23rd August, 1884. Served in the Nile expedition in 1884-85 with the 2nd battalion of the Duke of Cornwall's Light Infantry, and took part in the operations of the advance column under Major-General Earle (medal with clasp).

HOMFRAY, AUGUSTUS D. 2nd lieutenant, Duke of Cornwall's Light Infantry, 30th May, 1883. Served in Egyptian campaign, 1884-85. Died on service.

HORRIDGE, FRANK A. Ensign, 32nd Regiment, 2nd July, 1858.

INGLEFIELD, ARTHUR A. H. Lieutenant, 3rd battalion Duke of Cornwall's Light Infantry, 29th February, 1872; captain, 109th

Regiment, 1881. Served in Egyptian campaign, 1884-85. Died on service.

INGLEFIELD, LOFTUS EDWARD COORE. Ensign, 32nd Regiment, 21st March, 1868.

IRELAND, RICHARD SAMUEL. Ensign, 32nd Regiment, 15th September, 1877; lieutenant, 2nd February, 1881; captain, 9th March, 1887. Retired.

IREMONGER, WILLIAM HENRY. Ensign, 32nd Regiment, 11th April, 1865; lieutenant, 21st August, 1867. Retired.

JAY, HARVEY BROWNRIGG. 2nd lieutenant, Duke of Cornwall's Light Infantry, 16th November, 1887. Retired.

JEFFREY, GEORGE. Ensign, 32nd Regiment, 4th June, 1839; lieutenant, 18th June, 1841; captain, 15th March, 1853. Served as a captain in the Anglo-Spanish legion, and was present at the operations on the heights of Arlaban, in Alava, on the 16th, 17th, and 18th January; in the general actions in front of San Sebastian, on the 5th May (severely wounded, medal) and 1st October (severely wounded), 1836; 10th, 12th, (wounded), 14th, 15th, and 16th March, storm and capture of Irun, 16th and 17th May (medal), 1837. He served with the 32nd before Mooltan, during all the operations from September, 1848, till the surrender of the fortress, 22nd January, 1849, after which he was present at the battle of Goojerat (wounded), (medal and clasps).

JERVIS-EDWARDS, CECIL BRADNEY. Lieutenant, Duke of Cornwall's Light Infantry, 29th August, 1885.

JOHN, THOMAS. Ensign, 46th Regiment, 10th June, 1853; lieutenant, 1st December, 1854; captain, 24th May, 1861; major, 8th July, 1874; lieutenant-colonel, 26th July, 1881; colonel, 26th July, 1885; major-general, 9th December, 1885. Served with the Queen's in the campaign of 1860, in China, and was present at the action of Sinho, taking of Tangku, and the inner Taku fort (medal with clasp). Served with the 2nd battalion

Duke of Cornwall's Light Infantry throughout the Egyptian war of 1882, and was present in the engagements at El Magfar and Tel-el-Mahuta, in the two actions at Kassasin, and in command of the battalion at Tel-el-Kebir after Lieutenant-Colonel Richardson was wounded (mentioned in despatches, medal with clasp, 4th class of the Osmanieh, and Khedive's star). Also served with the Nile expedition in 1884-85 (clasp).

JOHNSTON, PATRICK. Ensign, 32nd Regiment, 20th November, 1838; lieutenant, 18th July, 1841; captain, 17th February, 1851; brevet major, 9th November, 1862; lieutenant-colonel, 1st April, 1866; colonel, 12th June, 1869. Commanded the light company of the 99th at the storming of Kawiti's Pah, at Ohaeawas, on the 1st July, 1845 (where he was slightly wounded on the forehead), and destruction of the same on the 10th July; again at the destruction of Arratua's Pah on 16th July; also at the destruction and capture of Kawiti't Pah at Ruapekapeka, in January, 1846 (medal).

JOLY, EDM. DE LOTBINIERE. Ensign, 32nd Regiment, 15th March, 1850; lieutenant, 23rd July, 1852.

JONES, OSWALD ROUTH. Ensign, 32nd Regiment, 3rd September, 1870.

JONES-PARRY, JOHN JEFFREYS BULKELEY. 2nd lieutenant, Duke of Cornwall's Light Infantry, 5th February, 1887; lieutenant, 14th August, 1889. Served in Burmah campaign, 1891.

KENDALL, EDWARD C. Lieutenant, 3rd battalion Duke of Cornwall's Light Infantry, 30th June, 1877; captain, 12th March, 1881.

KENNEDY, JAMES MONTAGU BOWLE. Lieutenant, Duke of Cornwall's Light Infantry, 9th May, 1885.

KING, CHARLES THOMAS. Ensign, 32nd Regiment, 10th July, 1840; lieutenant, 27th May, 1842; captain, 25th February, 1848. Served at the first and second siege operations before

Mooltan, including the attack on the enemy's position in front of the advanced trenches on 12th September, 1848 (wounded), the action of Soorjkoond, 7th November, attack on the suburbs of Mooltan, 27th December, storm and capture of the city (wounded), and surrender of the fortress; also present at the surrender of the fort and garrison of Cheniote and battle of Goojerat.

KING, HENRY EDGERTON. Ensign, 32nd Regiment, 23rd November, 1849; lieutenant, 30th July, 1852.

KIRKWOOD, ADAM DUFF. Ensign, 32nd Regiment, 10th April, 1849.

KITCHENER, HENRY ELLIOTT CHEVALLIER. Ensign 46th Regiment, 10th July, 1866; lieutenant, 10th February, 1869; captain, 13th November, 1875; major, 26th July, 1885. Passed staff college. Served in Burmah campaign, 1891.

KNOLLYS, LOUIS FREDERIC. Ensign, 32nd Regiment, 17th April, 1866; lieutenant, 2nd September, 1868. Inspector-general of Police in Ceylon.

KNOX, ROBERT TROTTER. Ensign, 32nd Regiment, 15th May, 1855; lieutenant, 13th July, 1855; captain, 26th September, 1858.

LACON, ERNEST DE M. Captain, 3rd Battalion Duke of Cornwall's Light Infantry, 26th November, 1879.

LAKIN, EDMUND, Ensign, 32nd Regiment, 26th February, 1856; lieutenant, 5th February, 1858; captain, 12th June, 1869; major and lieutenant-colonel, 1st July, 1881. Died, 1892.

LAMBE, HUGH JOHN GIDDY. Lieutenant, Duke of Cornwall's Light Infantry, 6th May, 1885. Drowned, 27th April, 1892, off Perim, whilst *en route* to England on leave of absence.

LAWRENCE, SAMUEL HILL. Ensign, 32nd Regiment, 12th December, 1847; lieutenant, 22nd February, 1850; captain, 1st July, 1857; brevet major, 24th March, 1858. Served at

APPENDIX. 367

the second siege operations before Mooltan, including the storm and capture of the city and surrender of the fortress. Also at the surrender of the fort and garrison of Cheniote and battle of Goojerat (medal and clasps).

LAWRIE, JOHN P. Ensign, 2nd Regiment, 22nd March, 1864; lieutenant, 23rd October, 1867; captain, 24th November, 1877; hon. major, 22nd January, 1884; paymaster, 46th Regiment, 27th January, 1879.

LE QUESNE, CHARLES FRED. NICHOLAS. Ensign, 32nd Regiment, 16th October, 1866; lieutenant, 12th June, 1869; captain, 14th June, 1881; major, 29th June, 1886.

LEGH, PIERS RICHARD. Ensign, 32nd Regiment, 22nd January, 1879; lieutenant, 2nd October, 1880; captain, 22nd January, 1890. Now wing officer, 26th Bombay Native Infantry.

LENTHALL, ROWLAND J. Colonel, 3rd battalion the Prince of Wales' North Stafford Regiment, 5th October, 1887. Late lieutenant, 32nd Regiment.

LEWIN, ROBERT NICHOLAS SPENCER. Lieutenant, Duke of Cornwall's Light Infantry, 23rd August, 1884. Served in the Nile expedition in 1884-85 with the 2nd battalion of the Duke of Cornwall's Light Infantry (medal with clasp, and Khedive's star).

LEY, HUGH H. Major, 3rd battalion Duke of Cornwall's Light Infantry, 10th August, 1889.

LITTLETON, JOHN. Lieutenant, 3rd battalion Duke of Cornwall's Light Infantry, 21st May, 1891.

LISTER, MATTHEW WILLIAM. Ensign, 32nd Regiment, 22nd March, 1864; lieutenant, 2nd August, 1866.

LOFTHOUSE, RICHARD CHAPMAN, M.D., M.R.C.S., L.M., L.S.A. Assistant surgeon, 14th July, 1854; surgeon, 9th March, 1867; surgeon-major, 1st March, 1873; brigade-surgeon, 27th November, 1879; deputy surgeon-general, 6th August, 1884. Served with the 10th Hussars, in the Crimean campaign, from the 18th April, 1855, including the siege and fall of Sevastopol, battle of the Tchernaya, and affair of 21st September, near Kertch (medal with clasp, and Turkish medal). Served with the 14th Light Dragoons during the campaigns in central India, from 10th July, 1857, to April, 1859, under Hugh Rose and Sir R. Napier, including the siege of Rahutghur, action of Barodia, relief of Saugor, siege and capture of Garrakota, disarming the Bhopal contingent at Sehore, forcing the pass of Muddenpore, battle of the Betwa, siege and fall of Jhansi, action of Koonch, all the affairs during the advance on Calpee, including the battle of Golowlie, capture of the town and fort of Calpee, action of Morar, recapture of Gwalior, operations in Bundlecund, and affairs of Garotha and Jachlone, and pursuit of Tantia Topee. Was in medical charge of a wing of the regiment in India up to the capture of Gwalior (mentioned in despatches, and thanked by the director general, army medical department, medal with clasp for central India).

LLOYD, HENRY JOHN GREAME. Lieutenant, Duke of Cornwall's Light Infantry, 22nd October, 1881; captain, 22nd October, 1887. Served with the 2nd battalion Duke of Cornwall's Light Infantry throughout the Egyptian war of 1882, and was present at the reconnaissance in force from Alexandria on the 5th August, in the engagements at El Magfar and Tel-el-Mahuta, in the two actions at Kassasin, and at the battle of Tel-el-Kebir (medal with clasp, and Khedive's star). Served in the Nile expedition in 1884-85 with the 2nd battalion Duke of Cornwall's Light Infantry, and took part in the operations of the advance column under Major-General Earle (clasp).

LLOYD, THOS. EDWD. J. Major, 3rd battalion Duke of Cornwall's Light Infantry, 4th May, 1885.

LOW, JOHN MAXWELL. Ensign, 32nd Regiment, 19th December, 1862; lieutenant, 29th September, 1865; captain, 28th March, 1874; major, 10th January, 1883; transferred to West Riding regiment, 1883; lieutenant-colonel, 20th August, 1890; placed on half-pay, 20th August, 1890.

LOWE, EDWARD W. D., C.B. Ensign, 32nd Regiment, 20th May, 1837; lieutenant, 12th March, 1841; captain, 23rd May, 1845; major, 1st July, 1857; lieutenant-colonel, 24th March, 1858; colonel, 2nd June, 1863. Served at the first and second siege operations before Mooltan, including the attack on the enemy's position in front of the advanced trenches on 12th September, 1848, on which occasion he succeeded to the command of the companies of the 32nd Regiment that were engaged. He was also present at the action of Soorjkoond, storm and capture of the city and surrender of the fortress of Mooltan, surrender of the fort and garrison of Cheniote, and battle of Goojerat (medal and clasps). Commanded the regiment on the death of Sir J. Lawrence, at Lucknow, and through all the subsequent siege (brevet colonel, C.B., one year's service, mentioned in despatches.)

LUTTRELL, HUGH C. F. Hon. major, 3rd battalion Duke of Cornwall's Light Infantry, 6th July, 1887. Late Rifle Brigade, retired pay.

MABERLEY, EVAN FREDERICK. 2nd lieutenant, Duke of Cornwall's Light Infantry, 22nd October, 1881.

MACMULLEN, GEORGE READE. Lieutenant, 32nd Regiment, 11th September, 1876; captain, 11th September, 1887. Now wing officer, 6th Punjaub Infantry.

MAGENIS, RICHARD HENRY. Ensign, 32nd Regiment, 10th April, 1849; lieutenant, 5th May, 1854; captain, 25th February, 1855; brevet major, 20th July, 1858. Served with the 90th Light Infantry at the siege and fall of Sevastopol; commanded a party of the regiment at the taking of the Rifle Pits on the 19th April, 1855, and was of the storming party at the assault of the Redan on the 8th September (mentioned in despatches, medal and clasp, and 5th class of the Medjidie). Also, during the Indian campaign of 1857-58, present with Havelock's column at the actions of the 21st and 23rd September, relief and subsequent defence of Lucknow, defence of the Alumbagh under Outram, and fall of Lucknow (brevet of major, medal and clasp).

MAHONY, JOHN, C.M.G. Ensign and adjutant, 66th Regiment, 25th August, 1857 ; lieutenant, 5th May, 1861 ; captain, 3rd April, 1866 ; paymaster, 5th March, 1867 ; major, 5th March, 1877 ; staff-paymaster and honorary lieutenant-colonel, 1st July, 1879. Served as paymaster, 2nd battalion 24th Foot, during the Gaika rebellion in 1877-78. Served in Zulu war of 1879 as chief paymaster (promoted staff-paymaster, medal with clasp, and C.M.G.)

MANDER, JOHN HAROLD. 2nd lieutenant, Duke of Cornwall's Light Infantry, 16th July, 1890.

MANSFIELD, JAMES WILLIAM. Ensign, 32nd Regiment, 23rd June, 1843 ; lieutenant, 4th July, 1845 ; captain, 15th March, 1853.

MARK, EDGAR PENROSE. 2nd lieutenant, Duke of Cornwall's Light Infantry, 16th November, 1887 ; lieutenant, 23rd April, 1890.

MARLAND, W. M. Lieutenant, 3rd battalion Duke of Cornwall's Light Infantry, 17th November, 1880.

MARRIOTT, RICHARD CHARLES EDWARD. Lieutenant, Duke of Cornwall's Light Infantry, 28th February, 1885.

MARSHALL, FITZROY D. Lieutenant, 3rd battalion Duke of Cornwall's Light Infantry, 29th May, 1889.

MARTYR, CYRIL GODFREY. 2nd lieutenant, 46th Regiment, 23rd October, 1880 ; lieutenant, 1st July, 1881 ; captain, 14th August 1889. Served with the 2nd battalion Duke of Cornwall's Light Infantry throughout the Egyptian war of 1882, and was present at the reconnaissance in force from Alexandria on the 5th August, in the engagements at El Magfar and Tel-el-Mahuta, in the two actions at Kassasin, and at the battle of

Tel-el-Kebir (medal with clasp, and Khedive's star). Served in the Nile expedition in 1884-85 with the mounted infantry, and was present in the actions of Abu Klea and El Gubat, in the reconnaissance to Metammeh, and in the engagements at Abu Klea Wells on the 16th and 17th February (two clasps); also served in the operations in the Soudan, in 1888, including the engagement at Gemaizah (4th class of the Medjidie). Now serving with the Egyptian army.

MAYDWELL, RICHARD LAWRENCE WILLIAM MOORE. Ensign, 32nd Regiment, 13th November, 1860; lieutenant, 19th January, 1864; captain, 16th March, 1870; major, 27th July, 1881; hon. lieutenant-colonel, 27th July, 1881. Retired.

M'CABE, BERNARD. Ensign, 32nd Regiment, 8th May, 1846; lieutenant, 10th April, 1849. Served with the 31st Regiment throughout the campaign of 1842, in Afghanistan, under General Pullock, and was present in the actions of Mazeena, Tezeen, and Jugdulluck, and the occupation of Cabool and the different engagements leading to it (medal). Also the Sutlej campaign, in 1845-46, including the battles of Moodkee, Ferozesbah, Buddiwal, Aliwal, and Sobraon (wounded; medal and clasps). Served with the 18th Royal Irish at the operations in the Canton river, under General D'Aguilar, in April, 1847.

MICHELL, JOHN C. Lieutenant, 3rd battalion Duke of Cornwall's Light Infantry, 4th May, 1891.

MOLESWORTH, HONBLE. GEORGE BAGOT. 2nd lieutenant, Duke of Cornwall's Light Infantry, 8th December, 1888; lieutenant, 13th May, 1891.

MOLESWORTH ST. AUBYN, HUGH. Captain, 3rd battalion Duke of Cornwall's Light Infantry, 22nd June, 1889.

MONEY-KYRLE, J. E. Ensign, 32nd Regiment, 21st June, 1833; lieutenant, 5th October, 1838; captain, 22nd June, 1842: major, 29th January, 1847; lieutenant-colonel, 12th January, 1860.

MOORE, JOHN. Ensign, 32nd Regiment, 1st November, 1842; lieutenant, 3rd April, 1846; captain, 16th September, 1851. Was present at the surrender of the fortress of Mooltan, at the surrender of the fort and garrison of Cheniote, and at the battle of Goojerat (medal and clasps).

MORRIS, HENRY GAGE. Ensign, 46th Regiment, 30th January, 1878; lieutenant, 1st July, 1881; captain, 14th November, 1887. Served throughout the Egyptian war of 1882 with the 2nd battalion Duke of Cornwall's Light Infantry, and was present at the reconnaissance in force from Alexandria, on 5th August, in the engagements at El Magfar and Tel-el-Mahuta, in the two actions at Kassasin, and at the battle of Tel-el-Kebir (medal with clasp, and Khedive's star). Served in the Nile expedition in 1884-85, with the river column, as a staff captain under Major-General Earle and Brigadier-General Brackenbury (mentioned in despatches, clasp); also served with the Egyptian frontier field force, under Major-General Grenfell, in 1886, as senior water transport officer. Was adjutant, 2nd volunteer battalion Duke of Cornwall's Light Infantry, 1st January, 1891.

MORRIS, TIMOTHY. Ensign, 32nd Regiment, 18th November, 1857; lieutenant, 9th August, 1858.

MORRISON, ARTHUR. Lieutenant, Duke of Cornwall's Light Infantry, 1st July, 1881.

MURPHY, THOMAS. Lieutenant, 46th Regiment, 3rd July, 1856; captain, 5th August, 1870; major, Berkshire regiment, 1st July, 1881; lieutenant-colonel, 8th January, 1883. Adjutant, auxiliary forces, 20th September, 1875, to 19th September, 1880. Served in the Royal Artillery throughout the Eastern campaign, from June, 1854, to January, 1856; was present at Inkerman, and engaged in the six bombardments of Sevastopol, and not absent from regular trench duty for a single day from first breaking ground to the end of the siege (recommended for distinguished conduct). Served in the Turkish contingent at

APPENDIX. 373

Kertch, from January, 1856, to the end of the war (medal with two clasps, and Turkish medal).

NEWBURY, BERTRAM ARCHDALL. Lieutenant, Duke of Cornwall's Light Infantry, 23rd August, 1884. Served in the Nile expedition in 1884-85 with the 2nd battalion Duke of Cornwall's Light Infantry (medal with clasp, and Khedive's star).

NEWMAN, HENRY HORATIO. Ensign, 32nd Regiment, 23rd August, 1864; lieutenant, 16th October, 1867; captain, 5th June, 1875; transferred to North Staffordshire Regiment; major, 11th December, 1882.

NICHOLSON, SAMUEL. Lieutenant, Duke of Cornwall's Light Infantry, 14th May, 1884.

NOBLE, SAMUEL BLACK. Ensign, 32nd Regiment, 18th May, 1855; lieutenant, 23rd March, 1858. Served during the Indian mutiny, in 1858-59, and was present at the action of Doadpore and throughout the Oudh campaign (medal).

NORRIS, PAUL BUZZARD. 2nd lieutenant, Duke of Cornwall's Light Infantry, 23rd March, 1889; lieutenant, 23rd April, 1892.

O'CALLAGHAN, HENRY D. Ensign, 32nd Regiment, 19th December, 1845; lieutenant, 10th December, 1847.

OGILVY, HONBLE. JAMES BRUCE. Ensign, 32nd Regiment, 12th October, 1860; lieutenant, 11th April, 1865. Served through Franco-German war as aide-de-camp to General Bourbaki.

ONSLOW, SIR W. W. R. Captain, 3rd battalion Duke of Cornwall's Light Infantry, 5th January, 1875; late lieutenant, 12th Foot.

ORMAN, FRANK LESLIE. 2nd lieutenant, Duke of Cornwall's Light Infantry, 3rd May, 1890.

PATTERSON, WILLIAM. Ensign, 32nd Regiment, 17th April, 1842; lieutenant, 14th April, 1846. Served in the first and second siege operations before Mooltan, including the storm and capture of the city. Also present at the surrender of the fort and garrison of Cheniote, and at the battle of Goojerat (medal and clasps).

PELLY, SAVILLE HERBERT. Lieutenant, Duke of Cornwall's Light Infantry, 10th May, 1882; now wing officer, 24th Bombay Native Infantry.

PERKINS, HEWLETT CHARLES. Lieutenant, 46th Regiment, 29th November, 1876; captain, 29th June, 1886. Served with the 2nd battalion Duke of Cornwall's Light Infantry throughout the Egyptian war of 1882, and was present at the reconnaissance in force from Alexandria on the 5th August, in the engagements at El Magfar and Tel-el-Mahuta, in the two actions at Kassasin, and at the battle of Tel-el-Kebir (medal with clasp, and Khedive's star). Served in the Nile expedition in 1884-85 with the 2nd battalion Duke of Cornwall's Light Infantry, and took part in the operations of the advance column under Major-General Earle (clasp).

PETAVEL, PAUL G. 2nd lieutenant, Duke of Cornwall's Light Infantry, 13th August 1892.

PHILLIPPS, ROBERT. Ensign, 32nd Regiment, 20th September, 1864; lieutenant, 16th October, 1866; captain, 31st January, 1877; major, 14th November, 1885. Retired as lieutenant-colonel.

PONSONBY, FREDERICK EDWARD G. 2nd lieutenant, Duke of Cornwall's Light Infantry, 11th February, 1888; transferred to Grenadier Guards.

POWER, WILLIAM. Ensign, 32nd Regiment, 6th April, 1846; lieutenant, 25th February, 1848. Served at the first and second siege operations before Mooltan, including the attack on the enemy's position in front of the advanced trenches on 12th September, 1848, the action of Soorjkoond, attack on the suburbs, 27th December, storm and capture of the city, and surrender of the fortress. Present at the surrender of the fort and garrison of Cheniote and at the battle of Goojerat (medal and clasps).

PRIESTLY, HORATIO. Ensign, 32nd Regiment, 28th August, 1846; lieutenant, 19th June, 1848; captain, 3rd April, 1857; major, 12th June, 1869. Served during the Indian campaign of 1857-58, and was present with Colonel Maxwell's column in the operations before Calpee early in 1858, and proceeded with it to the Alumbagh during the taking of Lucknow, in March, 1858; capture of the intrenched position at Dehaign and fort of Tyrool, actions at Doadpore and Jugdespore, surrender of the forts at Ahmetie and Shunkerpore, and pursuit of Beni Madhoo across the river Gogra (medal).

PRIMROSE, PHILIP. Ensign, 32nd Regiment, 18th August, 1848; lieutenant, 4th August, 1851.

PROWSE, GEORGE WILLIAM THURSBY. Lieutenant, Duke of Cornwall's Light Infantry, 7th February, 1885.

RAWLINSON, GEORGE BROOKE MILLERS. Lieutenant, Duke of Cornwall's Light Infantry, 25th November, 1885.

REEVES, JOHN. Ensign, 32nd Regiment, 9th August, 1868; lieutenant, 5th March, 1870; captain, 26th September, 1877; hon. major, 26th January, 1884. Served in the Egyptian war of 1882 (medal, and Khedive's star).

RHODES, FRANCIS MARY JOHN DOMINIC. Ensign, 23rd October, 1880; lieutenant, 1st July, 1881; transferred to Royal Fusiliers.

RICHARDSON, WILLIAM STEWART, C.B. Ensign, 46th Regiment, 23rd November, 1852; lieutenant, 9th February, 1855; captain, 24th August, 1858; major, 5th July, 1872; lieutenant-colonel, 1st May, 1880; colonel, 1st May, 1884; major-general, 30th June, 1887. Served with the Saugor field force in the 43rd Light Infantry, during the Indian mutiny campaign in 1857-59; marched through central India, from Bangalore to Calpee, in 1858, a distance of one thousand three hundred miles, during the hottest season of the year; present at the surrender of Kirwee; commanded a detachment of the 43rd at the siege of Kirwee, when surrounded by five thousand rebels, on the 21st, 22nd, and 23rd December, 1858; also commanded a detachment of the 43rd when engaged against the rebels in the Balabet jungles, under Feroze Shah, on the 26th August, 1859 (mentioned in despatches by General Whitlock for both actions, medal with clasp). Commanded the 2nd battalion Duke of Cornwall's Light Infantry in the Egyptian war of 1882, and was present in the actions at Kassasin on the 28th August (mentioned in despatches) and the 9th September, and at the battle of Tel-el-Kebir—severely wounded (mentioned in despatches, C.B., medal with clasp, 3rd class of the Medjidie, and Khedive's star). Also served with the Nile expedition in 1884-85 (clasp).

RICKETTS, CHARLES RODICK. Ensign, 32nd Regiment, 8th October, 1850; lieutenant, 31st December, 1852; captain, 14th September, 1857. Served during the Indian mutiny in 1858-59, and was present at the action of Doadpore and throughout the Oudh campaign (medal).

ROBERTS, C. JOHN CRAMER. Ensign, 32nd Regiment, 21st January, 1853.

ROBERTS, WILLIAM EDWARD. Ensign, 7th Fusiliers, 11th March, 1862; lieutenant, 19th July, 1864; captain, 21st July, 1875; major, 1st July, 1881; lieutenant-colonel, 18th January, 1889. Commanding 2nd battalion Duke of Cornwall's Light Infantry, 31st July, 1889. Served in the campaign on the north-west frontier of India in 1863, with two companies of the 7th Fusiliers, comprising part of the Doaba field force, and was present at the action near Fort Shubkudder (medal and clasp).

RUDMAN, WILLIAM. Ensign, 32nd Regiment, 22nd December, 1845; lieutenant, 11th February, 1848; captain, 15th May, 1857; brevet major, 24th March, 1858. Served with the 62nd Regiment in the campaign on the Sutlej (medal and clasp), including the battles of Ferozesbah and Sobraon.

SALMON, ARTHUR F. Captain, 3rd battalion Duke of Cornwall's Light Infantry, 5th November, 1887.

APPENDIX. 377

SANDERSON, ARTHUR. Assistant surgeon, 12th January, 1859.

SEWARD, ELIOTT THOMAS. Ensign, 32nd Regiment, 9th December, 1836; lieutenant, 15th February, 1839; captain, 17th June, 1842.

SHAKERLEY, ERNEST ALFRED. 2nd lieutenant, Duke of Cornwall's Light Infantry, 30th November, 1887; lieutenant, 23rd May, 1890.

SHEWELL, EDWARD W. Lieutenant, 3rd battalion Duke of Cornwall's Light Infantry, 22nd June, 1889.

SHORTT, JOHN ALEXANDER. Ensign, 32nd Regiment, 20th October, 1848.

SIBLEY, HENRY WILLIAM. Ensign, 32nd Regiment, 17th October, 1845; lieutenant, 9th February, 1848.

SIDNEY, HENRY MARLOW. Lieutenant, Duke of Cornwall's Light Infantry, 25th August, 1883; captain, 14th August, 1889. Served in the Nile expedition in 1884-85 with the 2nd battalion Duke of Cornwall's Light Infantry, and took part in the operations of the advance column, under Major-General Earle (medal with clasp, and Khedive's star). Now serving with the Egyptian army.

SILLERY, ALFRED JOHN MOORE. Ensign, 32nd Regiment, 22nd February, 1868.

SMURTHWAITE, PHILIP ALAN. Lieutenant, Duke of Cornwall's Light Infantry, 9th September, 1882.

SOUTHEY, WILLIAM MELVILL. Lieutenant Duke of Cornwall's Light Infantry, 30th January, 1886.

ST. AUBYN, EDWARD. Hon. colonel, 3rd battalion Duke of Cornwall's Light Infantry, 16th February, 1884.

ST. AUBYN, GUY STEWART. Lieutenant, 3rd battalion Duke of Cornwall's Light Infantry, 22nd June, 1889; appointed to 60th Rifles, 17th January, 1891.

ST. LEVAN, LORD. Hon. colonel, 3rd battalion Duke of Cornwall's Light Infantry, 1st May, 1882.

STABB, HENRY SPARKE. Ensign, 32nd Regiment, 29th April, 1856; lieutenant, 1st August, 1856; captain, 5th November, 1861. Served as adjutant of the 32nd Regiment during the Indian campaign af 1857-58, and was present with Colonel Maxwell's column in the operations before Calpee early in 1858, and proceeded with it to the Alumbagh during the taking of Lucknow, in March, 1858. Capture of the intrenched position at Delhainn and fort at Tryhool, actions of Doadpore and Jugdespore, surrender of the forts at Ahmetie and Shunkerpore, and pursuit of Benhi Madho across the river Gogra (medal). Appointed colonel on staff in Natal; took part in the suppression of rising in 1889 (mentioned in despatches). Died from over-exertion.

STANDEN, ROBERT HARGRAVE FRASER. 2nd lieutenant, Duke of Cornwall's Light Infantry, 29th March, 1890.

STANLEY, CHAS. GEOFFREY. Ensign, 32nd Regiment, 5th February, 1858; lieutenant, 26th September, 1858.

STEELE, FREDERICK WILLIAM. Lieutenant, 46th Regiment, 11th November, 1876; captain, 29th June, 1886. Captain, Army Service Corps, 16th May, 1885. Served with the 2nd battalion Duke of Cornwall's Light Infantry throughout the Egyptian war of 1882, and was present at the reconnaissance in force from Alexandria on the 5th August; in the engagements at El Magfar and Tel-el-Mahuta, in the two actions at Kassasin, and at the battle of Tel-el-Kebir (medal with clasp, and Khedive's star). Served in the Nile expedition in 1884-85 with the 2nd battalion Duke of Cornwall's Light Infantry (clasp).

STEEVENS, CHARLES. Ensign, 32nd Regiment, 7th August, 1840; lieutenant, 28th December, 1841; captain, 18th January, 1850.

STEWART, RUPERT. Lieutenant, Duke of Cornwall's Light Infantry, 25th August, 1883; captain, 23rd April, 1890. Served in the

Nile expedition in 1884-85 with the 2nd battalion Duke of Cornwall's Light Infantry (medal with clasp, and Khedive's star).

STOPFORD, JOHN GEORGE BERESFORD. Cornet, 8th Hussars, 23rd August, 1859; lieutenant, 30th July, 1860; captain, 32nd Regiment, 2nd October, 1866; brevet major, 1st January, 1880; major, 29th June, 1881; lieutenant-colonel, 5th April, 1886; colonel, 5th April, 1890. Commanded 1st battalion 1st July, 1887. Was aide-de-camp and military secretary to Governor of Cape Colony, 1873-77.

STRACHAN, JAMES. Ensign, 32nd Regiment, 30th August, 1855; lieutenant, 1st July, 1857. Served during the Indian mutiny in 1857-59, and was present at the capture of the forts of Dehaign and Tyrhool, and the Oudh campaign (medal).

STRAUBENZEE, BOWEN VAN. Ensign, 32nd Regiment, 4th April, 1846; lieutenant, 25th February, 1848. Served at the first and second siege operations before Mooltan, including the action of Soorjkoond; was severely wounded on the 27th December, 1848 (medal and clasp).

STREETEN, BERNARD S. 2nd lieutenant, Duke of Cornwall's Light Infantry, 23rd May, 1891.

STRIBLING, FRANCIS. Quarter-master, 32nd Regiment, 28th November, 1856; hon. captain, 3rd April, 1867. Served during the Indian mutiny in 1857-59, and was engaged in the defence of the Residency of Lucknow from the 30th June until its final relief on 24th November by Lord Clyde (mentioned in despatches by Sir John Inglis); was subsequently engaged in the defeat of the Gwalior rebels at Cawnpore on 6th December, capture of the forts of Dehaign and Tyrhool, action of Doadpore, and throughout the Oudh campaign (medal and clasp).

STUDDY, ERNEST HOLDSWORTH. Lieutenant, 32nd Regiment, 10th January, 1872; captain, 7th February, 1883; transferred to Argyll and Sutherland Highlanders.

STYLES, GEO. Lieutenant and quarter-master, 46th Regiment, 11th July, 1874 ; quarter-master, 3rd battalion, Duke of Cornwall's Light Infantry, 1st April, 1882 ; hon. captain, 3rd battalion, 11th July, 1884.

SWINEY, GEORGE CLAYTON. Cornet, Bengal Cavalry, 20th October, 1857 ; lieutenant, 6th Dragoon Guards, 18th May, 1858 ; captain, 32nd Regiment, 15th May, 1866 ; brevet major, 31st December, 1878 ; major, 14th June, 1881 ; lieutenant-colonel, 1st July, 1881 ; colonel, 1st July, 1885. Commanded the 1st battalion Duke of Cornwall's Light Infantry, 29th June, 1886. Served in the Indian Mutiny campaign, in 1857-58, with the 7th Hussars, and was present in an engagement at Secundragunge, near Allahabad, in December, 1857 (medal). Was aide-de-camp and military secretary to Governor of Cape Colony, 1870-73.

TAWKE, ARTHUR CHRISTIAN. Ensign, 32nd Regiment, 25th January, 1865 ; lieutenant, 3rd April, 1867 ; captain, 29th January, 1879 ; major, 1st January, 1886. Retired.

TEALE, EDWARD JOHN JENKINS. Ensign, 32nd Regiment, 2nd July, 1879 ; lieutenant, 1st July, 1881 ; captain, 11th April, 1888. Served in the Nile expedition in 1885 with the commissariat and transport staff.

THISTLETHWAYTE, A. R. WM. Ensign, 32nd Regiment, 16th March, 1855 ; captain, 26th October, 1855.

THOMSON, JAMES DUGALD. Ensign, 32nd Regiment, 4th May, 1849 ; lieutenant, 17th January, 1851.

TREGEAR, VINCENT F. W. 2nd lieutenant, Duke of Cornwall's Light Infantry, 23rd May, 1891.

TRELAWNY, HENRY R. S. Lieutenant-colonel commandant, 3rd battalion Duke of Cornwall's Light Infantry, 4th May, 1872 ; late lieutenant, 6th Dragoons.

TRELAWNY, JAMES E. S. 2nd lieutenant, 3rd battalion Duke of Cornwall's Light Infantry, 30th December, 1891.

TREMAYNE, HENRY ARTHUR. 2nd lieutenant, Duke of Cornwall's Light Infantry, 16th November, 1887; lieutenant, 29th June, 1890.

TREMAYNE, JOHN CLAUDE L. Lieutenant, 3rd battalion Duke of Cornwall's Light Infantry, 6th November, 1886.

TRETHEWY, THOMAS LANGDON. 2nd lieutenant, Duke of Cornwall's Light Infantry, 23rd March, 1889; lieutenant, 16th December, 1891.

TREVELYAN, HERBERT. Ensign, 32nd Regiment, 21st August, 1867; captain, 28th October, 1871; captain, Bedford Regiment, 29th June, 1881; transferred to Inniskilling Fusiliers, 15th October, 1881. Now retired.

TRUEMAN, CHARLES HAMILTON. Ensign, 32nd Regiment, 29th October, 1858; lieutenant, 20th September, 1864; captain, 25th September, 1869. Hon. lieutenant-colonel, retired.

TULLOCH, J. G. M'DONALD. Ensign, 32nd Regiment, 26th December, 1851.

TURNBULL, CHARLES FRED. ALEX. Ensign, 32nd Regiment, 9th March, 1866; lieutenant, 22nd July, 1868; captain, 26th May, 1880; major, 5th April, 1886. Served as aide-de-camp to General Officer Commanding, Aldershot; to Brigadier-General, Aldershot; and to Governor and Commander-in-Chief, Malta, 1st July, 1887.

TURNER, MARTIN NEWMAN. 2nd lieutenant, Duke of Cornwall's Light Infantry, 23rd July, 1890.

UNIACKE, HENRY PERCY. Lieutenant, 3rd battalion Duke of Cornwall's Light Infantry, 19th November, 1881.

VALLETORT, VISCOUNT P. A. H. Captain, 3rd battalion Duke of Cornwall's Light Infantry, 23rd March, 1891. Appointed aide-de-camp to Governor-General of India.

VAUGHAN, EDWARD. Quarter-master, 32nd Regiment, 3rd April, 1867. Served with the 32nd Regiment during the Indian mutiny of 1857-59, including the defence of the Residency of Lucknow until its final relief by Lord Clyde on 24th November, 1857 (twice wounded), battle of Cawnpore, on 6th December, and subsequent operations in Oudh, including the capture of forts Dehaign and Tyrhool and actions of Doadpore and Jugdespore (medal with clasp, and grant of a year's service for Lucknow). Died at Aldershot, 1881.

VERSCHOYLE, JOHN HAMILTON. Lieutenant, 32nd Regiment, 13th June, 1875; captain, 29th December, 1883. Served with the 2nd battalion Duke of Cornwall's Light Infantry throughout the Egyptian war of 1882, and was present in the engagements at El Magfar and Tel-el-Mahuta, in the two actions at Kassasin, and at the battle of Tel-el-Kebir (medal with clasp, and Khedive's star).

VIGOR, FREDERICK GEORGE. Lieutenant, 32nd Regiment, 11th September, 1873; captain, 1st September, 1881; major, 1st July, 1891. Served in the Egyptian war of 1882 (medal and Khedive's star). Served in the Nile expedition in 1884-85 with the 2nd battalion Duke of Cornwall's Light Infantry, and took part in the operations of the advance column under Major-General Earle (clasp).

VYVYAN, HERBERT N. Lieutenant, 3rd battalion Duke of Cornwall's Light Infantry, 12th March, 1881; 32nd Regiment, 1881; Exchanged to Royal Welsh Fusiliers. Died in India.

VYVYAN, PERCY EDMUND. Lieutenant, Duke of Cornwall's Light Infantry, 30th January, 1886. Died at Burmah, 26th June, 1892.

VYVYAN, RICHARD T. 2nd lieutenant, 3rd battalion Duke of Cornwall's Light Infantry, 9th March, 1891.

WAINWRIGHT, FREDERICK. Ensign, 32nd Regiment, 23rd May, 1846; lieutenant, 12th September, 1848.

WALES, H.R.H. ALBERT EDWARD PRINCE OF, Field Marshall, K.G., K.T., K.P., G C.B., G.C.S.I., G.C.M.G., G.C.I.E., A.D C. Hon. Colonel, 3rd battalion Duke of Cornwall's Light Infantry, 28th April, 1875.

WALKER, GEORGE. Ensign, 32nd Regiment, 11th May, 1855; lieutenant, 27th November. 1857. Served with the 88th Regiment at the siege and fall of Sevastopol in 1855, was wounded in the trenches on the 8th August, and twice severely wounded at the final attack on the Redan (medal and clasp, and Turkish medal). Served in the Indian campaign in 1857-58, and was present at the repulse of the Gwalior contingent at Bogneepore and fall of Calpee, under Sir Hugh Rose (medal).

WALKER, HAROLD BRIDGEWOOD. Lieutenant, Duke of Cornwall's Light Infantry, 14th May, 1884; captain, 16th December, 1891. Served in the Nile expedition in 1884-85 with the 2nd battalion Duke of Cornwall's Light Infantry, and took part in the operations of the advance column under Major-General Earle (medal with clasp, and Khedive's star); also served with the Egyptian frontier field force under Brigadier-General Butler, in 1885-86, and was present at the engagement at Giniss.

WALKER, LAUNCELOT HENRY. Lieutenant, Duke of Cornwall's Light Infantry, 29th August, 1885.

WALSHE, WALTER PHILIP. Ensign, 32nd Regiment, 31st March, 1858.

WARD, HONBLE. BERNARD MATHEW. Ensign, 47th Regiment, 12th July, 1850; lieutenant, 10th February, 1854; captain, 14th March, 1856; major, 32nd Regiment, 1st October, 1862; lieutenant-colonel, 12th June, 1869; colonel, 12th June, 1874; major-general, 25th April, 1885; lieutenant-general, 2nd October, 1886. Served in the Eastern campaign of 1854, and up to the 3rd May, 1855, with the 47th Regiment, including the battle of Inkerman, siege of Sevastopol, and sortie of 26th October (medal with two clasps, Sardinian and Turkish medals).

WARE, FRANK COOKE WEBB. 2nd lieutenant, Duke of Cornwall's Light Infantry, 16th November, 1887; lieutenant, 28th February, 1889. Now officiating squad officer 7th Bombay Cavalry.

WARREN, ARTHUR FREDERICK, C.B. Ensign, Rifle Brigade, 23rd July, 1847; lieutenant, 11th October, 1853; captain, 29th December, 1854; major, 2nd November, 1855; lieutenant-colonel, 3rd August, 1866; colonel, 1st October, 1877; major-general, 30th September, 1887. Served with the Rifle Brigade in the Eastern campaign of 1854-55, including the battles of Alma, and Inkerman, and siege of Sevastopol (medal with three clasps, brevet of major, 5th class of the Medjidie, and Turkish medal). Served with the 2nd battalion during the whole of its service in the suppression of the Indian mutiny, including the actions at Cawnpore, and capture of Lucknow (medal with clasp). Embarked for the Gold Coast in command of the 2nd battalion Rifle Brigade, and served throughout the second phase of the Ashantee war in 1874, including the battle of Amoaful, battle of Ordahsu, and capture of Coomassie (several times mentioned in despatches, C.B., medal with clasp). Commanded 32nd Regimental District.

WASHBOURN, A. S. B. Lieutenant, 3rd battalion Duke of Cornwall's Light Infantry, 22nd December, 1880.

WEBB, PELHAM CARVER. Ensign, 32nd Regiment, 17th August, 1852.

WILBRAHAM, RALPH JAMES. Ensign, 32nd Regiment, 21st August, 1878; lieutenant, 1st July, 1881; captain, 14th December, 1887. Served with the Nile expedition in 1884-85 (medal and clasp, and Khedive's star). Adjutant, 3rd battalion, January, 1892.

WILLIAMS, EUSTACE SCOTT. Lieutenant, Duke of Cornwall's Light Infantry, 27th January, 1886. Served with the Bechuanaland expedition, under Sir Charles Warren, in 1884-85, with the Mounted Rifles.

WILLIAMS, R. EDW. L. H. Ensign, 32nd Regiment, 23rd May, 1845; lieutenant, 23rd September, 1847. Served at the first and second siege operations before Mooltan, including the attack on the enemy's position in front of the advanced trenches

APPENDIX.

on 12th September, 1848, the action of Soorjkoond, storm and capture of the city and surrender of the fortress. Also present at the surrender of the fort and garrison of Cheniote and at the battle of Goojerat (medal and clasps).

WOODS, ADRIAN SAMUEL. Ensign, 32nd Regiment, 2nd December, 1868; lieutenant, 28th October, 1871; captain, Leinster Regiment, 2nd February, 1881; major, 18th November, 1882; lieutenant-colonel commanding battalion, 12th August, 1891.

WYLD, CHARLES E. Lieutenant, 3rd battalion Duke of Cornwall's Light Infantry, 4th March, 1891.

YARD, FREDERICK. Ensign, 32nd Regiment, 12th March, 1841; lieutenant, 22nd July, 1842; captain, 25th February, 1848; major, 26th November, 1857. Served at the first and second siege operations before Mooltan, including the attack on the enemy's position in front of the advanced trenches on 12th September, 1848, the action of Soorjkoond, storm and capture of the city and surrender of the fortress. Also present at the surrender of the fort and garrison of Cheniote, and at the battle of Goojerat (medal and clasps).

YOUNG, KEITH HENRY ST. GEORGE. Lieutenant, 46th Regiment, 4th December, 1874; captain, 1st October, 1883. Served in the Nile expedition in 1884-85 with the 2nd battalion Duke of Cornwall's Light Infantry, and took part in the operations of the advance column under Major-General Earle (medal with clasp).

LIST OF WARRANT OFFICERS OF THE DUKE OF CORNWALL'S LIGHT INFANTRY SINCE 1881.

Sergeant-Major	J. Conway	- -	1st Batt. Duke of Cornwall's L.I.
,,	I. Johnstone	-	32nd Regimental District.
,,	C. Hale -	- -	2nd Batt. Duke of Cornwall's L.I.
,,	R. Pearce -	-	1st ,, ,, ,, ,,
,,	G. Carr -	- -	2nd ,, ,, ,, ,,
,,	H. Archer -	-	1st ,, ,, ,, ,,
,,	R. Peel -	- -	1st ,, ,, ,, ,,
,,	R. Best -	-	2nd ,, ,, ,, ,,
Bandmaster	M. Gould	- -	1st ,, ,, ,, ,,
,,	T. Campbell	-	2nd ,, ,, ,, ,,
,,	G. Halliwall -	-	1st ,, ,, ,, ,,
,,	T. Blench	-	1st ,, ,, ,, ,,

ORIGINAL SUBSCRIBERS

TO THESE RECORDS.

Anderson, Colonel W. J.
Ashby, Major G. A.

Ballard, Colonel J. F.
Beaumont, Captain L. B.
Bliss, Lieutenant L. P. H.
Bond, Colonel D.
Bowles, J. T., Esq.
Bradford, Lieutenant S. H.
Browne, Colonel H. G., V.C.
Browne, Major W. B.
Buck, 2nd Lieutenant W. K.

Cantan, 2nd Lieutenant H. T.
Canteen, Depôt, D.C.L.I.
Carden, Major H. P.
Carpenter, Major Wallace G. W.
Case, Mrs.
Chapman, Captain F. H.
Clapcott, Colonel Charles
Clarke, Major A.
Clery, General C. F.
Cochrane, Major W. F. D.
Collier, Mortimer, Esq.
Colls, Colonel R. S.
Conway, Captain J.
Cornish-Bowden, 2nd Lieutenant J. H. T.
Custance, Captain S.

deMontmorency, Lieutenant Hon. W. J. H.
Dillon, Mr. James M.
Dillon, Sir John F.
Disney-Roebuck, Lieutenant-Colonel
Drake, T. Hyde, Esq.
Ducat, 2nd Lieutenant R.

Edmondstoune, Miss
Edmondstoune, Mrs.
Edye, Major L.
Eliot, Colonel Hon. C.
Evelegh, Captain C. N.
Every, Rev. T.

Foll, R. N. C., Esq.
Ford, Mrs.
Foster, Major C. M.
Foster, Colonel L. C.
Francis, Captain Woltsan
Frankfort de Montmorency, Major-General Viscount

Garforth, Rev. J.
Garnett, Captain Percy
Glascott, Colonel J. J.
Glegg, E. M., Esq.
Grant, Major F. W. Seafield
Griffin, Captain F. G. G.

Hammans, Major A. W.
Hardinge, Colonel H. R.
Harris, Brigade-Surg.-Lt.-Col. W. H.
Hartley, Captain James
Harvey, Captain W. L.
Hatherell, Lieutenant W. G.
Havelock, Sir Arthur E., K.C.M.G.
Heath, Major C. E., D.A.A.G.
Hollway, Captain E. J.
Hill, Lieutenant B. U.
Hill, General J. T.

Iremonger, W. H., Esq.

Jervis-Edwards, Lieutenant C. B.
Johnston, Colonel Patrick
Jones-Parry, Lieutenant J. J. B.

Kennedy, Lieutenant J. M. B.
Kitchener, Major H. E. C.
Knight, Mr. Thomas

Lakin, Colonel Edmund (the late)
Lambe, Lieutenant H. J. G.
Legh, Captain Piers R.
Lenthal, Colonel R. J.
Le Quesne, Major C. F. N.
Lewin, F. T., Esq., D.L., J.P.

ORIGINAL SUBSCRIBERS—*continued*.

Lewin, Lieutenant R. N. S.
Lofthouse, Surgeon-General R. C., M.D.
Lowe, Dillon Ross-Lewin, Esq.
Lowe, Captain F. M., R.A.
Lowe, Wm. Ross-Lewin, Esq.

Mander, Lieutenant John H.
Mark, Lieutenant E. P.
Marriott, Lieutenant R. C. E.
Martin-Atkins, Mrs. F.
Maunsell, Major-General T., C.B.
M'Cormick, Rev. F. H. J., F.S.A. Scot.
Molesworth, Lieutenant Hon. G.
Money-Kyrle, Colonel J. E.
Moore-Stevens, Mrs. John
Morris, Captain H. G.
Milne, S. Milne, Esq.
Murphy, Colonel T.
Murphy, Mr. W. C.

Newbury, Lieutenant Bertram A.
Norris, Lieutenant P. B.

Officers' Mess, Depôt D.C.L.I.
Officers' Mess, 1st Bn. D.C.L.I.
Officers' Mess, 3rd Bn. D.C.L.I.
Officers of 1st Bn. D.C.L.I., for presentation to H.M. The Queen.
Officers of 1st Bn. D.C.L.I., for presentation to H.R.H. The Prince of Wales.
Orman, Lieutenant F. L.

Perkins, Captain H. C.
Petavel, 2nd Lieutenant P. G.
Phillipps, Major R.
Prowse, Captain G. J. W., J.P.
Prowse, Lieutenant G. T. W.

Rashleigh, Jonathan, Esq.
Rawlinson, Lieutenant G. B. M.

Recreation Room, 1st Bn. D.C.L.I.
Roberts, Colonel W. E.
Rose, W. M. Esq., J.P.
Ross-Lewin, Rev. G. H.
Ross-Lewin, Rev. R. O. D., R.N.

Sergeants' Mess, 1st Bn. D.C.L.I.
Shearman, Mrs.
Sidney, Captain H. M.
Stabb, Mrs. Sparke
Stewart, Captain Rupert
St. Levan, The Right Hon. Lord
Stopford, Colonel J. G. B.
Streeten, 2nd Lieutenant B. S.
Stribling, Captain Francis
Stuart, General Charles
Swiney, Colonel G. C.

Tawke, Major A. C.
Teale, Captain E. J. J.
Tragear, 2nd Lieutenant V. F. W.
Tremayne, Lieutenant H. A.
Trethewy, Lieutenant T. L.
Trevelyan, Colonel H. W.
Trueman, Colonel C. H.
Truro, Bishop of
Turnbull, Major Chas. F. A.
Turner, Lieutenant M. N.

Vigor, Major F. G.
Verschoyle, Captain L. H.
Vyvyan, Lieutenant P. E.

Walker, Captain H. B.
Ward, General Hon. B. M.
Westropp, Thos. Johnson, Esq.
Wilbraham, Captain Ralph J.
Williams, Mrs. Ellis
Williams, Lieutenant E. S.
Woods, Colonel A. S.

Yard, Major Frederick.